Away for the WEEKEND®

MIDWEST

Away for the WEEKEND®

MIDWEST

52 Great Getaways in
Illinois
Indiana
Michigan
Wisconsin

REVISED AND UPDATED EDITION

ELEANOR BERMAN

Three Rivers Press
New York

Three Rivers Press, 201 East 50th Street, New York, New York 10022. Member of the Crown Publishing Group.

Random House, Inc. New York, Toronto, London, Sydney, Auckland
www.randomhouse.com

Originally published by Crown Trade Paperbacks in 1996.

Printed in the United States of America.

Library of Congress Cataloging-in-Publication Data
Berman, Eleanor.
Away for the weekend, Midwest: 52 great getaways in Illinois, Indiana, Michigan, Wisconsin / Eleanor Berman.—2nd ed.
Includes index.
1. Middle West—Guidebooks. 2. Illinois—Guidebooks. 3. Indiana—Guidebooks. 4. Michigan—Guidebooks. 5. Wisconsin—Guidebooks. 6. Chicago Region (Ill.)—Guidebooks. I. Title.
F350.3.B47 1999
917.704'33—dc21 98-17595

ISBN 0-609-80401-1

10 9 8 7 6 5 4 3 2 1

Second Edition

Contents

FALL

WINTER

INDEX

Acknowledgments

My sincere appreciation to all the state and local tourist offices that supplied information and guidance for my travels through these four great Midwestern states.

Introduction

From the sandy shores of Michigan to the hills of southern Indiana, the green valleys of Wisconsin to the Great River Road in Illinois, the four states bordering Lake Michigan are filled with weekending treasures. This is a guide to the best of the getaways, places offering a change of pace and a recharge of spirits for every mood and season.

The 52 weekend trips that follow will take you from small-town charm to big-city sophistication; from art galleries to underground caverns, covered bridges, and cranberry bogs; from festive celebrations to relaxing resorts. Throughout, you will discover the rich history of the region where pioneers tamed the wilderness to develop farms, industries, and great American cities.

Most of the trips are within 300 miles of Chicago, and within easy reach of Milwaukee, Detroit, and Indianapolis. Since Chicago is at the heart of the region, driving directions and mileage are given from that city, but major routes are noted to make it easy to plan a trip from any direction.

It should be noted from the start that this is a personal and selective guide. Instead of trying to include all the myriad possibilities for travel in four great states, I've selected what I feel are the cream of the weekend destinations. Nor is every single sightseeing attraction, lodging, and restaurant included. I've limited my selection to places I've visited myself or to those that have been recommended by knowledgeable local sources or frequent visitors to these areas, people whose opinions I respect.

Since many Midwestern lodgings are very special places, the best are noted in each area; a few are even presented as tourist destinations in themselves. This is primarily a guide to destinations and events, however, not a guide to inns or resorts, so where motels are the only accommodations available, the listings reflect this. Bed-and-breakfasts are another popular option—these may be small inns or private homes that open a few rooms to guests and serve homemade breakfast. Statewide registries are given at the end of this section.

Since changing seasons may bring different events and attractions in the same area, you will find repeat mentions of some destinations. The trips themselves are arranged by season, not only because activities change with the calendar but also to allow you time to read ahead about upcoming events and reserve rooms early. Advance information enables you to plan a relaxing and leisurely weekend of sightseeing rather than a tiring day trip.

Don't feel bound by my calendar, however. Many of these destinations are equally appealing and less crowded when nothing special is going on. In fact resorts along the Lake Michigan shoreline, for example, can be special delights on "out-of-season" weekends when you have them almost to yourself. The information listings at the end of each chapter are appropriate to any season.

HOW TO USE THIS BOOK

Like its predecessors in the series, *Away for the Weekend®: Midwest* assumes you have a normal two-day weekend to spend, leaving on Friday night and returning late on Sunday. Each chapter suggests activities for a two-day stay, with added suggestions to accommodate varying tastes and time schedules. I've included what I hope is just enough history and background to make each area more interesting without bogging you down in detail. You can almost always get more detailed information on the spot, if you want it.

When there is enough to do to warrant a longer stay, a symbol at the start of each trip will tell you so. When you do have more than a weekend to spend, use these symbols and also check the map at the back to combine nearby weekends to fill out an extended stay. Michigan's shore towns, for example, might all be combined for a coastline tour. The same is true for destinations along the Mississippi, in central and southern Wisconsin, and in southern Indiana.

Symbols also indicate trips that seem appropriate for children, though you are the best judge of what your own family might enjoy.

The symbols for these various categories are as follows:

 = recommended for children

 = recommended for long weekends

Lodging prices are for a double room; dining listings indicate the cost of main courses only rather than a whole dinner, since not everyone chooses to order a three-course meal. When prices bridge two categories, a combination of letters is used.

For lodgings:

I (inexpensive) = under $80
M (medium) = $80 to $135
E (expensive) = $135 to $200
EE (extra expensive) = over $200

When meals are included in the rates, these letters are used:

CP = continental plan (breakfast only)
MAP = modified American plan (breakfast and dinner)
AP = American plan (all three meals)

For dining, the letters are as follows:

I = most entrées under $12 per person
M = most entrées between $12 and $20
E = most entrées between $20 and $30
EE = most entrées over $30 (often means a prix fixe menu)

Sightseeing attractions have the following price symbols:

$ = up to $2.50
$$ = $2.50 to $5
$$$ = $5.01 to $7.50
$$$$ = $7.51 to $10
$$$$$ = over $10

Rates frequently increase, often before a book makes it from author to publisher to bookstore. The same is true of admission prices. Rates and prices here are as accurate as could be determined at the time of publication, and are included as a *general indication* of what to expect. Please use them just that way, as a general guide *only*. *Always* use the telephone numbers included to check for current prices when you plan your trip. It's wise to verify current hours and holiday closings, too.

When it comes to restaurants and lodgings, remember that a new chef or new owner can make a big difference, and changes and closings cannot always be predicted. If you find that any information here has become seriously outdated, that a place has closed or gone downhill, I hope that you will let me know in care of Three Rivers Press, at Crown Publishers, Inc., 201 East 50th Street, New York, NY 10022, so that the entry can be corrected. If you discover new places, or some appealing ones that I have missed, I hope you will let me know about these as well.

The maps in this book are simplified to highlight locations of suggested destinations. They are not necessarily reliable as road maps. You can get excellent free maps by writing ahead to the individual state travel or tourist offices. These offices offer many excellent free guides as well. Names and addresses are included at the end of this section. Addresses of offices that can provide additional information on specific regions and destinations are provided at the end of each chapter.

One last tip: Reserve well ahead if you want to stay in country inns or visit beach resorts or fall-foliage meccas in high season. Most lodgings offer refunds on deposits if you cancel with reasonable notice, so write ahead and take your pick instead of settling for leftovers. Three or four months in advance is none too soon.

For this New Yorker, traveling through four great Midwestern states to research and update this book has been a wonderfully rewarding experience. Having spent two years at Northwestern University, I was familiar with some of northern Illinois, but my work on this guide took me into a lot of new territory, and each discovery was a treat. I savored the rich tastes of Wisconsin—freshly made cheese, fish boils, frozen custard, beer, and brats. I took in the cultural riches and chic shops of Chicago, and discovered unexpected treasures in small towns like Nauvoo, Illinois, and Madison, Indiana. I acquired Amish toys in Illinois, country crafts in Indiana, and a collection of miniature lighthouses on the Michigan shore. I was awed by the majestic wooded banks of the Ohio River, the eagle-dotted bluffs of the Mississippi, and the expanse and beauty of Lake Michigan. I also got a refresher course in pioneer history and Lincoln lore, made all the more meaningful by having the opportunity to walk the grounds where it all happened. And everywhere, I found genuine hospitality and warm and helpful friends to make my job easier and my travels more rewarding.

I hope that my very real enthusiasm for these Midwestern places and pleasures comes through and inspires you to share my discoveries and make some of your own.

STATE TOURIST OFFICES

All of the following offices provide maps as well as information on attractions throughout the respective states:

Illinois Bureau of Tourism
100 West Randolph Street
Suite 400
Chicago, IL 60601
(312) 814-4732
(800) 226-6632
www.enjoyillinois.com

Indiana Division of Tourism
One North Capitol, Suite 700
Indianapolis, IN 46204
(800) 289-6646
www.indianatourism.com

Travel Michigan
Victor Office Center, 2nd floor
201 North Washington Square
Lansing, MI 48913
(517) 373-0670
(800) 78-GREAT
www.michigan.org

Wisconsin Division of Tourism
201 West Washington Avenue
P.O. Box 7976
Madison, WI 53707
(608) 266-2161
WI and neighboring states:
(800) 372-2737
National (800) 432-TRIP
www.tourism.state.wi.us

BED-AND-BREAKFAST ASSOCIATIONS

The associations listed here offer statewide listings of bed-and-breakfast homes and small bed-and-breakfast inns. Members have been inspected and meet minimum standards. Where no telephone number is listed, there is no permanent office, so write for the local guide. In some cases, you can get a free directory from the state tourist office.

Illinois Bed-and-Breakfast Association
P.O. Box 82
Port Byron, IL 61275
(309) 523-2406
(888) 523-2406
www.bbonline.com/il

Indiana Bed-and-Breakfast Association
P.O. Box 1127
Goshen, IN 46526
c/o Larry Lakins, president
(219) 773-2223

Michigan Lake-to-Lake Bed-and-Breakfast Association
33143 Logan Valley Road
Traverse City, MI 49684
(616) 486-0484
www.laketolake.com

Wisconsin Bed-and-Breakfast Association
108 South Cleveland Street
Merrill, WI 54452
(715) 536-2507
(800) 432-TRIP
www.bbonline.com/wi/wbba

Spring

Overleaf: Door County, Wisconsin. *Photo courtesy of Eleanor Berman.*

Doorfadil Season in Door County

You say you've never heard of the "doorfadil"? Then you've never been to Door County, Wisconsin, in May. That is when this distinctive white-and-apricot variety of daffodil make its appearance as one of the stars of the annual Festival of Blossoms.

Not that Door County isn't beautiful year-round. The tiny villages, fishing boats, and lighthouses are so reminiscent of New England that some call this narrow peninsula the Cape Cod of the Midwest. And there's a pastoral quality to the area that has made it a haven for artists as well as a favorite Midwestern vacation getaway for more than a century. Even the growing number of condos can't spoil the serenity you'll find once you abandon the highway for the shoreline.

Extending 60 miles out to sea between the waters of Lake Michigan and Green Bay, this 72-mile thumb-shaped strip of land feels almost like an island. Some 250 miles of coastline offer a variety of vistas, from wave-battered bluffs to sheltered coves to sandy beaches. Inland are placid dairy farms, cherry and apple orchards, fields of wildflowers, and pristine woodland. In many areas, the forest rises up almost to the water's edge, making for very picturesque scenery.

The peninsula's widest point is just 15 miles across, so fishermen and sailors are never far from the water. Five state parks provide opportunities for swimming and hiking, and bikers have their own 110-mile Backroad Bicycle Route. Golfers can pick among five scenic courses, including one, in Peninsula State Park, with prize water views.

It's understandably crowded in summer, but many believe that spring is the loveliest season of all on the peninsula. That's when clouds of cherry and apple blossoms light up the landscape, blue iris and white trillium color the roadsides, and over a million daffodils—including that one-of-a-kind doorfadil—burst into bloom. In May, each town has its own festivities, so something is happening every weekend. Guided Wildflower Pilgrimages in Baileys Harbor take in the Ridges Sanctuary, one of America's largest wildflower preserves. Sister Bay has its annual Taste of Scandinavia food festival and maypole raising; Jacksonport's Mayfest features a Festival of Blossoms parade; Egg Harbor gives free 45-minute guided tours of the town's most beautiful flower gardens; and Fish Creek, the heart of cherry country, offers wagon rides through the orchards and a chance to tour a cherry-processing plant.

The Door County Lighthouse Walk, sponsored by the Door County Maritime Museum, leads visitors on a tour of seven lighthouses, including several not normally open to the public.

Door County begins northeast of the town of Green Bay. The county seat and biggest town (population 10,000), Sturgeon Bay, is a shipbuilding center for racing crafts and fine yachts. In addition to offering some very nice inns, the town is also the main headquarters of the Maritime Museum, which preserves the history and lore of shipbuilding in the region. Exhibits include classic boats, a restored pilot house, and ship models, including a series depicting famous Great Lakes shipwrecks. The museum maintains the Cana Island Lighthouse in Baileys Harbor and a second installation dedicated to the fishing industry in Gills Rock, where you can actually board a tug.

Beyond Sturgeon Bay are the quaint villages and quiet coves that people love most about the area. The most popular resort towns are on the upper side of the peninsula along State Highway 42, paralleling the warmer, calmer waters of Green Bay.

Egg Harbor is growing as a shopping center. Thanks to a town beautification project that is transforming roadsides into bountiful flower beds, it grows more attractive each year. The Bay Point Inn is a small, secluded complex with attractive quarters that include a full living room and kitchen and balconies perfect for watching the famous Door County sunsets. It is one of the best lodgings in Door County for those who want privacy and water views.

Fish Creek, which still has the look of a 19th-century village, is one of the most picturesque towns (and often the most crowded in summer). The Episcopal church, the town hall, and both grocery stores date back well over 100 years. Several early homes have been converted to shops, and two inns, the Whistling Swan and the White Gull, also remain from the town's early days. The cultural center of the county in summer, Fish Creek has been home to the Peninsula Players for the last 65 years, as well as host to the annual Peninsula Music Festival and the American Folklore Theater, which presents comedy, storytelling, and folk music under the stars at Peninsula State Park.

Choosing between Fish Creek's two historic inns is not easy. The Whistling Swan wins for decor with fresh print fabrics, fine antiques, and a pleasant wicker-filled porch where breakfast is served. The meticulously restored 1887 building includes a store. But the "competition," the old-fashioned White Gull, a simple white clapboard 1896 beauty, is the best known of all Door County's inns. Nestled at the end of town, a bit away from the browsers, the inn complex includes cottages that are ideal for families.

North of town is Peninsula State Park, where the wooden observation tower provides a fabulous vista of park, countryside, and the deep blue water beyond. Eagle Bluff Lighthouse within the park is a favorite with photographers.

Next comes Ephraim, a town beautifully situated along the edge of Eagle Harbor. The name, meaning "doubly fruitful," was bestowed in 1853 by Norwegian settlers, members of the Moravian Church. Many of the pristine white buildings from the town's early days have been preserved, including the original church, a white meetinghouse up the hill on Moravia Street. Turn right off the highway at Anderson Lane at the north end of town to find the Anderson Barn, headquarters for the Ephraim Foundation, where the old photos on display look amazingly like the present town. The 1870 barn features an unusual square silo.

Ellison Bay and Gills Rock at land's end are fondly known as the Top of the Thumb. This area is the favorite haunt of many of the artists and artisans of Door County. The sea vista from Garrett Bluff near Ellison Bay is not to be missed.

Ellison Bay is the home of The Clearing, a 128-acre retreat founded in 1935 by the great Danish-born Midwestern landscape architect Jens Jensen. Weeklong classes in nature, art, music, crafts, and the classics in literature are offered from mid-May to mid-October. A Wildflower Pilgrimage weekend is offered in mid-May, and other shorter programs are available in winter, spring, and fall. Situated on limestone cliffs above Green Bay, the buildings of logs and native stone are in perfect harmony with the setting. If you are willing to climb down to find it, Jensen's small shoreline studio in the shadow of the bluff is magical, almost part of the cliff itself. The complex is open for tours on weekend afternoons. If you love it so much you want to stay, two three-bedroom chalets are available for rent for periods from three to seven days.

Gills Rock offers another remarkable view, the overlook above the point where the cold Lake Michigan waters and the warmer waters of Green Bay meet. This especially turbulent passage is known among sailors as Death's Door because of the many shipwrecks that happened here. Ferries ply the channel from Gills Rock to Washington Island, a safe journey popular for its views of rocky bluffs and the chance it affords to explore the unspoiled island.

Closer to Ellison Bay is Newport State Park, a 2,200-acre semi-wilderness area with lots of prime hiking trails and a Lake Michigan beach. Europe Lake, adjacent to the park, is preferred by those who opt for warm, calm water rather than Lake Michigan surf.

Make your way back to the mainland along Highway 57, the Lake Michigan side of the peninsula. Sister Bay, where Highway 57 branches off from Highway 42, is the largest community at the northern end; total population: 715.

Sister Bay's best-known attraction is Al Johnson's restaurant, with live goats on the thatched roof. It's a bit of the old Swedish countryside brought to Wisconsin. The menu features Swedish specialties, from meatballs to pancakes with lingonberry sauce. An offbeat dining favorite is Sister Bay Bowl, known for its prime rib and Friday fish fry; you can work off dessert at the bowling lanes.

Farther along Highway 57, Baileys Harbor is an active fishing town right on Lake Michigan. Make a detour here to Ridges Sanctuary, a preserve noted for its wild orchid, the lady's slipper.

If you want to avoid crowds, consider two resort complexes away from it all on the lake, the rustic Gordon Lodge and the modern Baileys Harbor Yacht Club.

Take Cana Island Road and walk across a narrow strip (sometimes partially submerged but worth the wade) to the photogenic 1851 Cana Island Lighthouse.

Closer to the mainland near Valmy, Whitefish Dunes State Park and Cave Point County Park are good places to see the handiwork of Lake Michigan's angriest waves in the form of caves and other naturally sculptured forms along the shoreline.

Wherever you go, you'll find interesting galleries featuring art and crafts, many of them surrounded by lovely gardens. Fish Creek's Edgewood Orchard Galleries shows work in all media by national artists, artfully displayed in a restored fruit barn. Ephraim is home to the Hardy Gallery of the Peninsula Arts Association, and the Door County Art League Showcase Gallery is in Sister Bay, both galleries displaying art and photography inspired by the beauty of Door County. The Miller Art Center in Sturgeon Bay, another nonprofit community arts association, has changing exhibitions in its main-floor gallery as well as a permanent collection of work by 20th-century Wisconsin artists.

One of the pleasures of driving around Door County is making your own discoveries, exploring the many appealing shops. One worth special mention is the Blue Dolphin House, notable for its garden setting as well as its selection of home accessories.

Door County's best-known culinary treat is the traditional Scandinavian fish boil. The recipe calls for cooking the freshest Lake Michigan whitefish steaks with potatoes and onions over a blazing wood fire. The real fun comes with the final "boilover," when whooshing flames proclaim that the meal is done. It's all served up with lots of melted butter and sides of coleslaw and fresh-baked bread. Door County cherry pie is the customary dessert. The White Gull Inn is the best place to sample this specialty, but it is also a daily offering at the Viking Grill in Ellison Bay, where it's served in an informal picnic setting, as well as at many other local restaurants.

The C & C Supper Club in Fish Creek and Voight's Supper Club in Ellison Bay are good examples of another Wisconsin phenomenon, the "supper club," which isn't really a club at all but a place that you can count on to have steaks, fresh seafood, *and* a liquor license (not all restaurants in Door County have one). For dining with a view of the turbulent water, the hands-down winner is the informal Shoreline in Gills Rock, where the specialty is whitefish supplied by local fishermen.

<u>Area Code: 920</u>

DRIVING DIRECTIONS Door County begins east of Green Bay and north of Manitowoc. It can be reached via State Highway 57 from the east, State Highway 42 from the south. From Chicago, take I-94 to Milwaukee, then I-43 to Green Bay and Highway 57 on to Sturgeon Bay and Door County, about 230 miles. Sturgeon Bay is 150 miles from Milwaukee.

ACCOMMODATIONS Rates are lower before Memorial Day; expect minimum-stay restrictions in season. **Bay Point Inn,** 7933 Highway 42, P.O. Box 287, Egg Harbor 54209, 868-3297 or (800) 707-6660, romantic suites, prime private waterfront location, fireplaces, kitchens, small pool, E • **Egg Harbor Lodge,** 7965 Highway 42, P.O. Box 57, Egg Harbor 54209, 868-3115, pool, tennis, putting green, water views, M–EE • **Whistling Swan Inn,** 4192 Main Street, P.O. Box 193, Fish Creek, 54212, 868-3442, M–E, CP • **White Gull Inn,** 4225 Main Street, P.O. Box 160, Fish Creek 54212, 868-3517, M–E; cottages E–EE • **Thorp House Inn,** 4135 Bluff Road, Fish Creek 54212, 868-2444, country Victorian bed-and-breakfast home, plus cottages tucked into the trees, M–E, CP • **Eagle Harbor Inn,** 9914 Water Street, P.O. Box 588, Ephraim 54211, 854-2121, pleasant small private complex, nicely decorated rooms and suites, indoor pool and sauna, M–E, CP • **Ephraim Inn,** Highway 42, P.O. Box 247, Ephraim 54211, 854-4515, old-fashioned rambler in the heart of the village, M–E, CP • **Grand View Motel,** off Highway 42, P.O. Box 135, Ellison Bay 54210, 854-5150 or (800) 258-8208, the name says it, I, CP • **Griffin Inn,** 11976 Mink River Road, Ellison Bay 54210, 854-4306, comfortable country retreat, I, CP; cottages, M, CP • **Harbor House Inn,** 12666 Highway 42, Gills Rock 54210, 854-5196, quaint Victorian bed-and-breakfast at the tip of the peninsula, I–M, CP • **Baileys Harbor Yacht Club,** 8150 Ridges Road, Baileys Harbor 54202, 839-2336 or (800) 927-2492, modern complex and marina on the water, indoor pool, M–EE • **Gordon Lodge,** 1420 Pine Drive, Baileys Harbor 54202, 839-2331, ultimate seclusion on Lake Michigan, motel-style rooms, M–EE, CP • **White Lace Inn,** 16 North Fifth Avenue, Sturgeon Bay 54235, 743-1105, a complex of four in-town Victorian charmers, antiques, canopy beds, some fireplaces, M–E, CP • **Scofield House,** 908 Michigan Street, Sturgeon Bay 54235, 743-7727 or (888) 463-0204, elegant 15-room Victorian mansion, M–E, CP • **Inn at Cedar Crossing,** 336 Louisiana Street, Sturgeon Bay 54235, 743-4200, 100-year-old commercial building transformed into attractively furnished country inn, M–E, CP • **The Clearing,** 12183 Garrett Bay Road, P.O. Box 65, Ellison Bay 54210, 854-4088, three-bedroom chalets, three-day minimum, E; also Bed-and-Breakfast weekends, Wildflower Pilgrimage in May, special theme weekends, M.

DINING **White Gull Inn** (see above), longtime favorite, M • **Kortes' English Inn,** Highway 42, Fish Creek, 868-3076, formal menu amid beams, stained glass, artwork, for a special night out, M–E •

Casey's Inn, Highway 42, Egg Harbor, 868-3038, tavern atmosphere, tasty American menu, scenic views, M • **Paulson's Old Orchard Inn,** 10341 Highway 42, Ephraim, 854-5717, pleasant dining room overlooking gardens, entertainment on weekends, serves all three meals, I–M • **Al Johnson's Swedish Restaurant,** 702 Bayshore Drive, Sister Bay, 854-2626, Swedish specialties, M • **Hotel Du Nord,** Highway 42, Sister Bay, 854-4221, continental menu, M–E • **Sister Bay Bowl,** 504 North Bay Shore Drive, 854-2841, improbable location for prime prime ribs and Friday fish fry, M • **Inn at Cedar Crossing** (see above), varied menu in period setting, serves all three meals, I–E • **The Shoreline,** Highway 42, Gills Rock, 854-2950, varied menu, whitefish specialties, I–M • **Gordon Lodge** (see above), continental menu, lake views, M • **Common House,** 8041 Main Street, Baileys Harbor, 839-2708, regional cuisine, old-fashioned setting, I–E • **Village Cafe,** Highway 42, Egg Harbor, 868-3342, informal spot for breakfast and lunch, fish boils on weekends starting mid-June, I • ***Fish boils:*** **White Gull Inn** (see above), Wednesday and Saturday year-round, also Friday and Sunday in summer, M • **Viking Grill,** 12029 Highway 42, Ellison Bay, 854-2998, fish boils daily 4:30 P.M. to 8 P.M., mid-May to October, I • ***Supper clubs:*** **C & C Supper Club,** Highway 42, Fish Creek, 868-3412, I–E • **Voight's Supper Club,** 12010 Highway 42, Ellison Bay, 854-2250, I–M • **Florian II,** Baileys Harbor, 839-2361, overlooking Lake Michigan, I–M.

SIGHTSEEING **Door County Festival of Blossoms,** variety of events for three weeks beginning in early May, contact Chamber of Commerce for current dates and schedule • **Door County Lighthouse Walk,** usually third weekend in May, sponsored by Door County Maritime Museum–Shipbuilding, 120 North Madison Avenue, Sturgeon Bay, 743-5958. Hours: Memorial Day to Labor Day, daily 9 A.M. to 6 P.M., rest of year, to 5 P.M. $$ • **Maritime Museum–Fishing Industry,** 12724 Wisconsin Bay Road, Gills Rock, same phone. Hours: Memorial Day to Labor Day, Monday to Saturday 10 A.M. to 4 P.M., Sunday 1 P.M. to 4 P.M.; September to mid-October, Monday to Saturday, noon to 4 P.M., Sunday 1 P.M. to 4 P.M. Donation • **Ridges Sanctuary,** 8270 Highway 57, Baileys Harbor, 839-2802. Hours: Mid-May to mid-October, Monday to Saturday 9 A.M. to 4 P.M., Sunday 1 P.M. to 4 P.M. Guided tours offered in summer. $ • **The Clearing,** 12183 Garrett Bay Road, Ellison Bay, 854-4088. Hours: Mid-May to mid-October, Saturday and Sunday 1 P.M. to 4 P.M. Year-round classes, including weekends in winter, spring, and fall. Ask for current schedule • ***State parks:*** Wisconsin parks are usually open daily 6 A.M. to 11 P.M.; best to phone for off-season hours. Parking admission fee, $$$; Wisconsin cars, $$. **Peninsula State Park,** off Highway 42, Fish Creek, 868-3258, six miles of Green Bay shoreline, 18-hole golf course, hiking, biking, boat rentals, observation tower, lighthouse • **Newport**

State Park, 475 County Road NP, Ellison Bay, 854-2500, semiwilderness area, 28 miles of hiking trails, swimming, 11 miles of shoreline • **Potawatomi State Park,** 3740 Park Drive, Sturgeon Bay, 746-2890, two miles of Green Bay shoreline, hiking, biking trails, observation tower • **Whitefish Dunes State Park,** 3701 Clark Lake Road, Sturgeon Bay, 823-2400, rugged Lake Michigan shore, highest dunes in Wisconsin, 847 acres of forest, 11 miles of hiking trails • **Rock Island State Park,** Washington Island, 847-2235, remote 906-acre island, Wisconsin's oldest lighthouse, hiking, swimming • ***Summer entertainment:*** Phone for current schedules, locations. **Peninsula Music Festival,** ticket office at Ephraim Village Hall, Highway 42, Ephraim, 854-4060 • **Peninsula Players,** W4351 Peninsula Players Road, Fish Creek, 868-3287 • **American Folklore Theater,** Peninsula State Park Theatre, 868-9999 • **Birch Creek Music Center Concert Series,** Country Road E, Egg Harbor, 868-3763.

INFORMATION **Door County Chamber of Commerce,** Highway 42/57, P.O. Box 406, Sturgeon Bay, WI 54235, 743-4456 or (800) 52-RELAX; www. doorcountyvacations.com

Going Dutch in Holland

The Dutch immigrants who came to Holland, Michigan, back in 1847 would likely be pleased if they could see what has become of their settlement. It is a city where Dutch influence remains strong, and delft pottery, wooden-shoe factories, tulip gardens, and a working 1780s windmill continue to delight visitors.

They would no doubt have a good time along with everyone else in May, when Holland is abloom with millions of tulips. It is the occasion for one of the Midwest's most popular festivals, ten days of costumes and dancing, craft and quilt shows, storytelling and big-name entertainment that have been a local tradition for nearly 70 years.

The favorite attractions during Tulip Time are three big parades. They start with the Volksparade, set off when the town crier has announced that the streets don't live up to Dutch cleanliness standards. A brigade of costumed scrubbers with pails swinging from shoulder yokes steps in to remedy the situation, sweeping and scrubbing until the pavement shines.

Photographers love the Children's Costume Parade, when hundreds of schoolchildren dress up and carry signs and banners proclaiming the town's Dutch heritage.

The grand finale on the final Saturday features *klompen* dancers strutting their stuff in wooden shoes, a procession of flower-laden floats, and more than 50 marching bands. If you want to enjoy the parades to their fullest, a few extra dollars will buy you grandstand seats.

Eight miles of Tulip Lanes beckon in Holland in May with over 50 varieties of blooms. You can follow the arrows for a self-drive tour or take the Tulip Trolley guided rides, a popular festival pastime. A costumed guide is aboard to share information about Holland's history while you admire the flowers. The Tulip Time Market features crafts demonstrations, more klompen dancers, and traditional foods like *Saucijzenbroodjes,* pig-in-the-blanket treats.

Without question, Holland is at its most beautiful during Tulip Time, but whenever you come, you'll encounter the distinctive Dutch influence that makes this area so colorful. Pious early pioneers, resisting a movement to modernize the old state church, came here in large numbers beginning in 1847, searching for religious freedom and opportunity. They settled around Lake Michigan, establishing Holland and outlying villages like Zeeland, Groningen, and Drenthe, named for the towns they had left behind. These tight-knit communities remained primarily Dutch for almost a century. You can in fact still attend an authentic Dutch service in the historic Pillar Christian Reformed Church.

The church also spread its influence to education. Dutch Reverend Albertus C. Van Rallte founded Hope College in 1857; it was chartered as a four-year college affiliated with the Reformed Church in America in 1866. The early buildings of this respected small college clearly show their Dutch heritage, as do names such as Voorhees Hall, Van Wylen Library, the Van Rallte Commons, and the Nykerk Hall of Music. Van Vleck Hall, constructed in 1857, is a state historic site.

Many of the small businesses begun by industrious Dutchmen prospered; especially well known were the furniture makers who founded companies, like Herman Miller, a highly regarded manufacturer of office furniture in Zeeland. The success of Holland's industries and the resulting employment opportunities have attracted a more cosmopolitan mix of residents in recent years, including many Mexicans.

But the original Dutch flavor remains strong. Windmill Island, a park about two miles from the center of town, boasts DeZwaan, America's only 230-year-old working Dutch windmill, standing 12 stories high and with sails spanning 80 feet. Authentically costumed guides take visitors through the structure. The park is aglow with 100,000 tulips in spring. Other features include a replica of a 225-year-old Dutch country inn, a miniature Dutch town, and rides on a *draaimolen,* an authentic old carousel. The island's double drawbridge is a reproduction of a bridge over the Amstel River in the Netherlands—sections are raised and lowered by hand to allow boats to pass through. Klompen dancing demonstrations add to the fun.

The Dutch Village is a theme park re-creation of a Dutch town of

100 years ago. Granted, it is a bit touristy, but the Amsterdam street organs providing music for the klompen dancers are authentic, as are the wooden-shoe carving demonstrations and some of the foods at the Queen's Inn. There are rides for the kids and a petting zoo, along with the chance to get weighed on a 1708 witch's scale. And the shops are filled with delftware, carved ships, windmill lamps, hand-carved candles, and Dutch cheese and chocolate.

Some of the most handsome tulip displays are found at Veldheer Tulip Gardens, where the rainbow of brilliant colors is set off by windmills, drawbridges, and canals. You may well be inspired to buy some bulbs for your own garden.

Nearby is the DeKlomp Wooden Shoe Factory, one of two in town where you can see craftsmen transforming logs into pointy-toed wooden clogs. Adjoining is the only delftware factory in the U.S.; here you can watch costumed artisans handpaint the famous blue-and-white pottery.

If you want to see historic Dutch delftware and decorative arts, the Holland Museum in the old post office will oblige. The Volendam Room re-creates a fisherman's cottage as it might have looked in the old country. Among the other mementos are a dollhouse and an 11-foot bronze clock.

Today's Holland has a pleasantly refurbished downtown with half a dozen interesting art and craft galleries along River Avenue and on Eighth Street. Miller Creek Folk Art at 78 East Eighth is definitely worth a stop.

Antiquers will find a number of choices around town, including the Tulip City Antique Mall north of town at U.S. Highway 31 and Greenly, with 200 dealers. Nob-Hill Country Store, 1261 Graafschap Road, has 16 dealers in a century-old building, offering country accents and handmade baskets, as well as antiques.

On U.S. 31 at James Street, the Horizon Outlet Center beckons to bargain hunters, and Saugatuck's dozens of boutiques and galleries are just 12 miles to the south.

Or, if it's an especially fine spring day, you might prefer to forget about further sightseeing or shopping and simply go for a ride along South Shore Drive, past the fine lakeshore homes on Lake Macatawa, or for a walk along the shoreline of Holland State Park, where Lake Michigan and Lake Macatawa meet. Here you'll be able to admire one of the best-known landmarks on the Michigan shore—the little red lighthouse—and the surrounding natural beauty that attracted those first Dutch settlers.

Area Code: 616

DRIVING DIRECTIONS Holland can be reached via I-196 or U.S. Highway 31. From Chicago take I-94 northeast to I-196, about 160 miles. It is about 170 miles from Detroit, 30 miles from Grand Rapids.

ACCOMMODATIONS *Bed-and-Breakfasts:* **North Shore Inn,** 686 North Shore Drive, 49424, 394-9050, on the lake, quiet location, M, CP • **Dutch Colonial Inn,** 560 Central Avenue, 49424, 396-3664, pleasant home in town, M–E, CP • **The Parsonage,** 6 East 24th Street, 49423, 396-1316, 1908 former parsonage, M, CP • **Centennial Inn,** 8 East 12th Street, 49423, 355-0998, fine Elizabethan home, M, CP • *Motels:* **Lake Shore Resort Motel,** 1645 Lake Shore Drive, 49423, 335-5355, on Lake Macatawa, play area, many kitchenettes, I • **Country Inn by Carlson,** 12260 James Street, 49424, 396-6677 or (800) 456-4000, attractive furnishings, M, CP • **Holiday Inn,** 650 East 24th Street at U.S. 31, 49423, 394-0111 or (800) 279-5286, indoor pool, game room, M • **Comfort Inn,** 422 East 32nd Street, 49423, 392-1000, I–M • **Fairfield Inn,** 2854 West Shore Drive, 49424, 786-9700, indoor pool, I–M, CP.

DINING **The Piper,** 2225 South Shore Drive, Macatawa, 335-5866, lake view, best in town, M • **Queen's Inn,** Dutch Village, U.S. 31 and James Street, 393-0310, Dutch decor and specialties, I–M • **The Hatch,** upscale casual, I–M • **84 East,** 84 East Eighth Street, 396-8484, moderately priced pastas, I • **Alpenrose Restaurant,** 4 East Eighth Street, 393-2111, German/American food, delicious European pastries, M • **Till Midnight,** 208 College Avenue, 392-6883, eclectic menu, art on the walls, M–E • **Eighth Street Grill,** 20 West Eighth Street, 392-5888, downtown, good lunch choice for soup and salad bar, I.

SIGHTSEEING **Tulip Time Festival,** 171 Lincoln Avenue, Holland 49423, 396-4221 or (800) 822-2770. Annual 10-day celebration featuring parades, entertainment, many special events, and lavish floral displays. Call for current schedule and rates • **Windmill Island,** 7th and Lincoln, 355-1030. Hours: Open May through mid-October. May, July and August, Monday to Saturday 9 A.M. to 6 P.M., Sunday 11:30 A.M. to 6 P.M.; June and September, Monday to Saturday 10 A.M. to 5 P.M., Sunday 11:30 A.M. to 5 P.M.; October, Monday to Friday 10 A.M. to 4 P.M., Saturday 9 A.M. to 5 P.M., Sunday 1:30 P.M. to 5 P.M. $$$ • **Dutch Village,** U.S. 31 and James Street, 396-1475. Theme park and shopping. Hours: July and August, daily 9 A.M. to 6 P.M.; mid-April to June and September to October, 9 A.M. to 5 P.M. $$. Shops open all year, free admission • **Veldheer Tulip Gardens and DeKlomp Wooden Shoe and Delft Factory,** 12755 Quincy Street and U.S. 31, 399-1900. Hours: May, daily 8 A.M. to dusk; April and June to December, Monday to Friday 8 A.M. to 6 P.M., Saturday and Sunday 9 A.M. to 5 P.M.; January to March, Monday to Friday 9 A.M. to 5 P.M. $$ • **Holland Museum,** 31 West 10th Street, 392-9084. Hours: Monday, Wednesday to Saturday 10 A.M. to 5 P.M., Thursday 8 P.M., Sunday 2 P.M. to 5 P.M. $$ • **Holland State Park,** 2215 Ottawa Beach Road, 399-9390. Hours: Daily 8 A.M. to 10 P.M. Admission: $$.

INFORMATION **Holland Area Convention and Visitors Bureau,** 76 East Eighth Street, Holland, MI 49423, 394-0000 or (800) 506-1299; www.Holland.org

Breaking Away to Bloomington

With a fortunate location in the midst of hilly Indiana lake country, Bloomington, Indiana, would be a fine breakaway destination even if there were no university around. Lots of people come here for the resorts on Lake Monroe (the state's largest lake), for the scenic ridges and ravines of Lake Lemon or Griffy Lake, and for some magnificent biking territory.

Add one of the oldest and most beautiful campuses in the Midwest, and you have an unbeatable combination. Indiana University (IU) has first-class offerings for visitors beyond its lovely campus. The art museum, designed by I. M. Pei, would be the envy of many cities. The top-notch music department is widely known for its opera company as well as for its Musical Arts Center, considered to be second only to New York's Metropolitan Opera for its acoustics.

And IU is the home of one of the most famous bicycle races in the nation, the annual mid-April Little 500, which was immortalized some years back by the hit movie *Breaking Away.* The race was the brainchild of Howard S. Wilcox, then executive director of the IU Foundation. It all started back in 1950 when he saw students racing their bikes around a residence hall, with coeds leaning out the window and cheering them on. Wilcox patterned his bike race after the legendary Indy 500 car race, which his father once won in the 1930s. The hard-pedaling bikers now compete at IU's Bill Armstrong Stadium, and thousands of cheering spectators pay to watch (the admission proceeds go into a scholarship fund). Celebrities from Bob Hope to David Letterman have shown up for the fun, which includes not only serious men's and women's races but also a Mini 500 Trike Race. The weekend always includes special events like a Golf Jamboree and concerts, as well. It's an ideal time to visit the campus.

Founded in 1820 with an enrollment of 10 young men, IU now numbers nearly 35,000 students. After a fire in the original building in 1883, the school was moved to its current site, 1,860 acres of lovely rolling, wooded grounds. The campus was rated one of the five most beautiful in the U.S. in the book *The Campus as a Work of Art.*

The Old Crescent, with its Gothic and Romanesque buildings made of

Indiana limestone, makes for a splendid stroll. The ornamental facades and archways are the work of the many talented local stone carvers.

Many of the campus's buildings, including the Kirkwood Observatory, are nearly 100 years old; newer buildings, of similar stone, manage to blend in nicely. Part of the original tract known as Dunn's Woods has been retained, so you may find yourself detouring through woodland right in the heart of the campus. Two landmarks of particular merit are the Showalter Fountain in the Fine Arts Plaza on East Seventh Street, and the 91-foot Metz Carillon Tower, at the highest point on campus. The 61-bell carillon usually serenades on Saturday afternoon.

You can't miss the Indiana Memorial Union, the largest student-union building in the world. It takes 15 or 20 minutes just to walk around it and take in its Gothic arches and carved rosettes and details. Inside, the halls and rooms are a virtual museum, with more than 1,200 works of art. The Union includes the University Club (used by faculty and alumni), an art gallery, shops, dining areas ranging from a cafeteria to the formal Tudor Room, and a recreation center with 12 bowling lanes, eight pool tables, the latest video games, and interactive television. Part of the mix is the IMU Hotel, which offers 186 comfortable, recently renovated rooms, an ideal place to stay if you want to be right in the center of things.

The sleek white IU Art Museum presents one of the country's outstanding college art collections in a stunning airy setting around an asymmetric atrium. Represented in the 30,000 works are paintings by Matisse, Monet, Picasso, and Andy Warhol, and sculptures by Rodin. The third-floor gallery of Arts of Africa's Oceania and the Americas is a standout.

Other places to see on campus include the Mathers Museum, with exhibits on anthropology, history, and folklore; and the Jordan Hall Greenhouse, which is filled with tropical and desert plants from around the world. The Lilly Library has an extensive collection of rare books and manuscripts, including a set of John James Audubon's *Birds of America* plates and extensive works on Abraham Lincoln. On permanent display are a 1454 Gutenberg Bible and a copy of the Coverdale Bible of 1535, the first complete Bible in English.

Be sure to see the Thomas Hart Benton murals in the lobby of the Auditorium on Fine Arts Plaza, and if you are a fan of the late songwriter-singer Hoagy Carmichael, stop into Morrison Hall, where a room is filled with memorabilia from the IU grad's life. Carmichael wrote many of his songs, including "Stardust," in a hometown bar, Bloomington's Book Nook, now known as The Gables Restaurant.

For all its cultural riches, Bloomington remains a quintessential Midwestern town, centered around a fine old beaux-arts limestone courthouse. First look up at the fish weather vane, commissioned in 1826 for an earlier courthouse, and then step inside to see the handsome rotunda and stained-glass ceiling.

At one end of the courthouse square, a group of period buildings have been reconfigured into Fountain Square Mall, a particularly attractive shopping complex with a glass elevator in the atrium. Shops here specialize in books, games, art, jewelry, and music. Bobby's Pub and Grill is a good lunch stop, famous for its trademark barbecued-bison sandwich and a big selection of beer.

Walk around the square for a look at the many other interesting little shops and galleries. One of the best eating places in town is the Malibu Grill on North Walnut Street, a touch of California cuisine in Indiana. Like most major college towns, Bloomington has many interesting ethnic choices.

If you're after antiques, the Bloomington Antique Mall, 311 West Seventh Street, has more than 100 dealers.

Save plenty of time to appreciate the great countryside. Lake Monroe, a lovely sight surrounded by 78,000 acres of natural forestland, attracts eagles, wildlife, and fish as well as people. It was created by the damming of Salt Creek, a flood-control project back in 1963. Located about six miles southeast of town, this is a prime spot for fishermen after catfish, crappies, northern pike, and stripers.

The lake has several recreational areas and two resorts on its shores. The Eagle Pointe Golf and Tennis Resort offers comfortable condominium lodgings, a pool, tennis, and an 18-hole golf course. The recently renovated Fourwinds Resort has a large marina offering boat rides and boats for rent, as well as an indoor-outdoor pool.

Even closer to town is Griffy Lake, a 1,200-acre nature preserve five miles to the north, popular for canoeing, fishing, or strolling. Lake Lemon, about 10 miles northeast of Bloomington, is surrounded by the ravines and ridges that make this area so scenic. Riddle Point Park, a peninsula jutting into the lake, offers spectacular views. The lakeshore also features some attractive walking trails, notably the Little Africa Wildlife Area on the eastern end of the lake near the headwaters, which has a three-quarter-mile trail winding through grasslands; it's a favorite with bird-watchers.

Another popular stop north of town is the Oliver Winery, where you can tour the cellars, taste the wines, and picnic beside a small lake.

If you want to find the best biking routes in the area, maps are available at local bike stores and at the Visitors Center. The 33-acre Wapehani Bike Park in Bloomington was designed for mountain-bike use; there are trails for all levels.

Bloomington is also a perfect home base for some terrific excursions. Within half an hour to the east are Nashville and Columbus (see pages 145–150); to the west is McCormick's Creek State Park, known for its unique limestone formations and scenic waterfalls.

Drive south to Bedford to see where they got some of that limestone for the IU campus. Early in the century Bedford was the "Limestone Capital of the World." Structures ranging from the Empire State Building to Chicago's Tribune Tower to the Washington Cathedral were built with limestone quarried in this area, and the town was as famous for its stone carvers as it was for its stone. An interesting exhibit telling the story of this heritage can be seen in the Bedford College Center, a 1926 building made of Bedford limestone just north of the town's Courthouse Square Historic District.

There's another reason to come to Bedford. Limestone country is also the start of Indiana's cave country. Bluespring Caverns, the state's longest cave, offers one of the most unique underground experiences. You can take a one-hour ride on lighted electric boats along a subterranean river, where you can observe fish and crayfish pale in color and blind from living in passages that were begun eons ago and are still forming today. Bring along a jacket; the cave temperature stays at 52 degrees year-round.

Area Code: 812

DRIVING DIRECTIONS State Highways 446, 46, and 37 lead into Bloomington. From Chicago, take I-90 east to I-65 south to I-465 (skirting Indianapolis), then Highway 37 south. Bloomington is 227 miles from Chicago, 50 miles from Indianapolis.

ACCOMMODATIONS **IMU Hotel,** Indiana Memorial Union building, 900 East Seventh Street, Bloomington 47405, 856-6381 or (800) 209-8145, M • **Grant Street Inn,** 310 North Grant Street, Bloomington 47408, 334-2353 or (800) 328-4350, handsome 24-room inn near campus in a restored 1880s home; rooms, M, CP; suites (some with Jacuzzis and fireplaces), M–E, CP • **Scholars Inn,** 801 North College Avenue, 332-1892 or (800) 765-3466, turn-of-the-century mansion turned bed-and-breakfast, dessert cafe and wine bar in adjacent home, M–E, CP • **Century Suites,** 300 Highway 446, 47402, 336-7777 or (800) 766-5446, attractive Colonial-style all-suite motel around a green, M–E • **Holiday Inn,** 1710 Kinser Pike, 47404, 334-3252, indoor pool, M • **Courtyard by Marriot,** 310 South College Avenue, 47403, 335-8000, indoor pool, M • **Hampton Inn,** 2100 North Walnut, 47401, 334-2100, outdoor pool, reasonable rates, I, CP • ***Resorts on Lake Monroe:*** **Eagle Pointe Golf and Tennis Resort,** 2250 East Pointe Road, Bloomington 47401, 824-4040 or (800) 860-8604, one-bedroom condominiums, M, larger condos, E–EE • **Fourwinds Resort and Marina,** 9301 Fairfax Road, Bloomington 47402, 824-9904 or (800) 538-1187, M.

DINING **Malibu Grill,** 106 North Walnut Street, 332-4334, top choice, creative California cuisine, casual atmosphere, M • **Tudor Room,** IMU Hotel (see above), 855-1620, elegant atmosphere, popular Sunday brunch, huge array of desserts, M • **Le Petit Cafe,** 308 West

Sixth Street, 334-9747, French bistro menu, M • **Ristorante Puccini,** 420 East Fourth Street, 333-5522, romantic setting in a restored historic home, traditional Italian menu, I–M • **Chapman's,** at Century Suites (see above), 337-9999, varied menu in pleasant Colonial dining room, M–E • **Michael's Uptown Cafe,** 102 East Kirkwood Avenue, 339-0900, New American, casual ambience, M–E • **Brewpub at Lennie's,** 1795 East 10th Street, 323-2112, the local microbrewery; adjoining restaurant is a favorite for pizza, I • **Crazy Horse,** 214 West Kirkwood, 336-8877, fajitas, burgers, and 80 kinds of beer, I • ***Ethnic choices:*** **Janko's Little Zagreb,** 223 West Sixth Street, 332-0694, Yugoslavian specialties, plus steak and ribs, M • **Shanti,** 221 East Kirkwood Avenue, 333-0303, traditional Indian menu, I • **Snow Lion Tibetan and Oriental Cuisine,** 113 South Grant Street, 336-0835, unique Tibetan dishes, I–M • **Irish Lion Restaurant and Pub,** 212 West Fifth Street, 336-9076, Celtic stew and other Irish specialties in an 1882 building, I–M • **Siam House Thai Cuisine,** 430 East Fourth Street, 331-1233, near the university, I–M • **Trojan Horse,** 100 East Kirkwood Avenue, 332-1101, Greek, I–M.

SIGHTSEEING **Little 500 Bicycle Race,** held mid-to-late April, sponsored by Indiana University Student Foundation (IUSF), 855-9152; phone for current dates and information • **Indiana University: Indiana University Art Museum,** Fine Arts Plaza, East Seventh Street, 855-5445. Hours: Wednesday to Saturday 10 A.M. to 5 P.M., Sunday noon to 5 P.M., open to 8 P.M. first Friday each month. Free • **Mathers Museum,** 416 North Indiana Avenue, 855-MUSE. Hours: Tuesday to Friday 9 A.M. to 4:30 P.M., Saturday and Sunday 1 P.M. to 4:30 P.M. Free • **Jordan Hall Greenhouse,** 900 East Third Street, 855-7717. Hours: Monday to Friday 8 A.M. to 4 P.M., Saturday and Sunday 9 A.M. to 3 P.M. Free • **Lilly Library,** East Seventh Street, 855-2452. Hours: Monday to Friday 9 A.M. to 6 P.M., Saturday 9 A.M. to 1 P.M. Free • **Indiana University Opera Theater,** Musical Arts Center, Jordan Avenue, 855-7433; check for current schedules • ***Outside Bloomington:*** **Oliver Winery,** 8024 North Highway 37, Bloomington (seven miles north of town), 876-5800. Hours: Tastings Monday to Saturday 10 A.M. to 6 P.M., Sunday noon to 6 P.M. Cellar tours on weekends • **Land of Limestone Exhibition,** Bedford College Center, 405 I Street, Bedford, 275-7637. Hours: Monday to Friday 8 A.M. to 5 P.M., Saturday 9 A.M. to noon. Free • **Bluespring Caverns,** U.S. Highway 50, 3¼ miles southeast of Bedford, 279-9471. Hours: May to October, daily 9 A.M. to 6 P.M., weekends only in April. $$$$ • ***Bloomington's lakes:*** **Lake Monroe,** Take Highway 37 south to Harrodsburg exit, turn east at stop sign and continue to Strain Ridge Road, turn left and follow signs. Indiana Department of Natural Resources headquarters, Allen's Creek–Monroe Reservoir, 4850 South Highway 446, 837-9546. Park fees: April to September, $$ per vehicle, $ for Indiana residents • **Lake**

Lemon, Riddle Point Park, 334-0233. State Highway 45 east to Tunnel Road, turn north and continue to gatehouse. Parking area, $ • **Griffy Lake,** 349-3732. Follow the 45/46 bypass to Matlock Road, turn north and continue to lake.

INFORMATION Monroe County Convention and Visitors Bureau, 2855 North Walnut Street, Bloomington IN, 334-8900 or (800) 800-0037.

Blossom Time in Michigan

According to one story, the farmers in Michigan's southwestern "Fruit Belt" discovered their region's great potential in the mid-1800s by accident. It seems that a bitter winter killed peach trees almost everywhere in the state, except on this blessed land, where the cold was tempered by Lake Michigan's breezes.

There is no doubt that fruit trees thrive here, and the gentle hills rolling eastward from the shore near St. Joseph have been planted with thousands of them. Their blossoms put on one of spring's most dazzling pastel displays each year.

The show begins in late April, when delicate pink flowers adorn the apricot trees. They are soon joined by pink-and-white cherry blossoms, blooms on the plum and pear trees, and then, in a billowing crescendo, a fragrant early-May canopy of white, as countless apple blossoms light up the hillsides.

Driving through orchard country makes for a festive entrée into the season, especially when warm breezes swirl the delicate petals into the air like confetti at a celebration parade. The beauty has inspired Michigan's oldest festival, Blossomtime, an eight-day event from late April to early May celebrated by 30 communities, each of whom selects a queen who competes for the title of Miss Blossomtime. The lucky queen presides over the festival's main event, the annual Grand Floral Parade held on the last Saturday. This lavish affair features high-stepping high school bands, all the lovely local queens, and over a hundred flower-laden floats winding their way through St. Joseph to its twin city, Benton Harbor.

St. Joseph provides a perfect site for the festivities. The town is perched on a bluff on Lake Michigan and has a lakeside park that provides a scenic setting for festival booths and activities. As the region's largest metropolitan area, with a population of 10,000, St. Joseph also offers plenty to see and do between blossoms.

The idea of celebrating the blossom season dates back to 1906. It started with local ministers blessing the blooms to ensure a bountiful harvest. That ceremony grew into an indoor nondenominational service at which regional choirs sing and each community queen presents blossom-laden boughs for blessing. The festival now also includes a carnival with an old-time midway and rides, and arts-and-crafts displays. Events include a fashion show by the Blossomtime queens, wine tastings, and a winning youth parade of costumed family pets and decorated bikes and wagons. Each year brings special features like an air show or an antique car show.

Almost any back road offers a chance to admire the blossoms, but a free printed map, "Drive Among the Blossoms," available from the Southwestern Michigan Tourist Council, points the way to nine special driving tours.

The Orchard Crest Blossom Tour, which follows orchard-lined State Highway 140, allows for a detour at Eureka Road to the Tree-Mendus Fruit Farm, Michigan's best-known orchards. The farm does not open for business until fruit is ripe for picking, but the public is welcome to drive through the beautiful 500 acres of orchards and woodland, where hundreds of cherry trees and some 200 varieties of apple trees in bloom are a wondrous sight. The views from the meadow are so enchanting that many couples choose to get married here.

Golfers should note the Indian Lake Hills Golf Course nearby; the course includes blossoming orchards.

The driving tours also take you through old-fashioned country towns, many of which hold delightful small surprises. Dowagiac, for example, was once the home of the Round Oak Stove Company, which manufactured the country's most popular cast-iron stove. Now antique stoves adorn the restored storefronts along Main Street.

If you stop into the Caruso Candy Kitchen in Dowagiac, you can step into the past. Perch on a stool at the old-fashioned soda fountain for refreshments, or order a sample of the chocolate that Mary "Butch" Myers makes by hand, just as her father and grandfather did before her. The Peddler's Cart, in another historic building with tin ceiling and hardwood floors, offers two floors featuring 75 crafters, gourmet coffees, and interesting gifts.

St. Joseph has some handsome examples of early-20th-century architecture, one of its prominent landmarks being the People's State Bank. You can admire the buildings by following the self-guided walking tour available from the tourist bureau. The chief attraction in town for families is the imaginative Curious Kids' Museum, a hands-on chance to learn about machines, sound, and how the body works while having a lot of fun. Kids love this museum because it isn't so huge that it overwhelms. They can sail a kid-sized ship, observe a steamy rain forest complete with miniature waterfall and an iguana, and serve customers in a make-believe diner. After seeing the orchards, children can learn here about the seasons of the apple trees, pick apples from a pretend tree, weigh them, and tend to a fruit stand.

St. Joseph also has an attractive small art museum, the Krasl Art Center, with three changing galleries that are matched to the attention span of most children. Here you can also pick up a free self-guided walking tour of nearby sculptures, such as the monuments in Lake Bluff Park; these include a bronze firefighter carrying a child, commemorating 12 city firemen who died in a fire at the turn of the century.

If the weather is kind and you've got the kids in tow, drive south to Warren Dunes State Park and let them work off steam climbing up and sliding down Tower Hill, the tallest of the dunes at 240 feet. You can often watch hang gliders taking off from the top of the ridge. Warren Woods Nature Center, known for its tracts of virgin beech and maple trees, is also a wonderful place to see abundant spring wildflowers in bloom. There are over 100 species. Both the dunes and the woods were named for E. K. Warren, a local conservationist who used the fortune he made manufacturing corset stays to buy up these irreplaceable tracts and give them to the state.

Fernwood Botanical Gardens also has a spring wildflower nature preserve, wooded paths, and attractive gardens; it's a long drive from St. Joseph, but a worthwhile destination.

In Benton Harbor, the Herb Barn on Greenly Avenue is a pleasant stop even if it's too early to admire the herb gardens. There is a fine restaurant for lunch called the Farmhouse and a shop called Pleasantly Surprised, filled with gifts, herbal and otherwise. This shop is run by owners of another enchanting little stop, the Christmas Tree on Mitzpah Park Road, west off Highway 63, stocked with artfully designed holiday decorations for collectors. Benton Harbor's Days Inn, with an indoor pool, is an unusually nice member of the budget chain.

The best place to stay in St. Joseph is the Boulevard Inn, an all-suite hotel facing the lake. St. Joseph's shopping streets have been nicely restored to an old-fashioned look. Currie Beads at 317 State has an intriguing collection of beads, from African trading beads to Venetian glass. Another recommended stop is Gallery on the Alley, 611 Broad Street, filled with contemporary artwork including paintings, photographs, jewelry, pottery, glass, and floral designs.

You'll find a variety of eating places in and around St. Joseph. For fine dining, local residents recommend The Mansion Grille, which is located in an elegant old home, and Grand Mere Inn, in nearby Stevensville, where they serve sunset views over Lake Michigan with dessert.

Things are livelier and less formal right in town at places like H.I's, which is filled with Hollywood memorabilia, or Schu's Grill and Bar (an informal outpost of legendary Schuler's in Marshall), where they give you binoculars to make the most of the lake views. Like Schu's,

Caffe Tosi is the offspring of a well-known restaurant in Stevensville, in this case Tosi's, a local favorite for Northern Italian food for over 50 years.

Along with restaurants, Stevensville offers an interesting shop, Native Treasures, with handmade clothing, jewelry, and artwork from around the world. And the Bit of Swiss bakery is legendary for such desserts as apple triple mousse cake. Fresh fruit may not be in season yet, but this will definitely provide a sweet souvenir of the weekend.

Area Code: 616

DRIVING DIRECTIONS St. Joseph is along the Red Arrow Highway, reached via I-94. From Chicago, follow I-94 east to Exit 23 and follow Business 94 into town, about 100 miles. It is about 180 miles from Detroit.

ACCOMMODATIONS **Boulevard Inn,** 521 Lake Boulevard Street, St. Joseph 49085, 983-6600 or (800) 875-6600, all-suites hotel with spacious quarters, lake views, best in town, M • **Holiday Inn by the Lake,** 100 Main Street, St. Joseph 49085, 983-7341, M • **Days Inn,** 2699 Highway 139 South, Benton Harbor 49022, 925-7021, good bet for families, nice indoor pool, game room, under 18 free, I • **South Cliff Inn,** 1900 Lakeshore Drive, St. Joseph 49085, 983-4881, attractive in-town bed-and-breakfast, overlooking the lake, M, CP; suites, E, CP • **The Chestnut House,** 1911 Lakeshore Drive, St. Joseph 49085, 983-7413, bed-and-breakfast across the road from the lake, whirlpools, pool, M, CP.

DINING **The Mansion Grille,** 3029 Lakeshore Drive, St. Joseph, 982-1500, 1920s mansion, elegant dining, overlooks Lake Michigan, M–E • **H.I.'s,** 214 State Street, St. Joseph, 983-3607, fun spot with Hollywood memorabilia, I–M • **Schu's Grill and Bar,** Lake Boulevard, St. Joseph, 983-7248, casual, lake views, I–M • **Caffe Tosi,** 516 Pleasant Street, St. Joseph, 983-3354, informal outpost of the Stevensville restaurant of the same name, I–M • **Clementine's,** 1235 Broad Street, St. Joseph, 983-0990, varied menu, overlooks marina, M–E • **The Farmhouse,** 1955 Greenly Avenue, Benton Harbor, 927-9961, creative lunch menus, I • **Grand Mere Inn,** 5800 Red Arrow Highway, Stevensville, seafood with sunset views over Lake Michigan, M • **Tosi's,** 4337 Ridge Road, Stevensville, 429-3689, a longtime favorite for Northern Italian food, I–E • **Schuler's of Stevensville,** 5000 Red Arrow Highway, Stevensville, 429-3273, offspring of famous Schuler's in Marshall, MI; try the prime rib, M • **Tabor Hill Winery,** 185 Mt. Tabor Road, Buchanan, (800) 283-3363, wonderful setting overlooking vineyards; lunch, I; dinner, M.

SIGHTSEEING **Blossomtime Festival,** 8 days in late April–early May in St. Joseph; contact Southwestern Michigan Travel Council for current dates and information • **Krasl Art Center,** 707 Lake Boulevard, St. Joseph, 983-0271. Hours: Monday to Thursday and Saturday 10 A.M. to 4 P.M., Friday 10 A.M. to 1 P.M., Sunday 1 P.M. to 4 P.M. Free • **Curious Kids' Museum,** 415 Lake Boulevard, St. Joseph, 983-2543. Hours: Tuesday to Saturday 10 A.M. to 5 P.M., Sunday noon to 5 P.M. May be open Monday in July and August. $$ • **Warren Dunes State Park,** off Red Arrow Highway, Sawyer, 3 miles southeast of Bridgman, 426-4013. Hours: Daily 8 A.M. to 10 P.M., hours may be shorter in winter. Admission per car, $$ • **Warren Woods Nature Center,** Elm Valley Road (off Warren Woods Road), south of Bridgman, phone c/o state park. Hours: Daily dawn to dusk. Free • **Tree-Mendus Fruit Farm,** 9351 East Eureka Road, Eau Claire (off State Highway-140), 782-7101. Hours: Open for picking late June to Labor Day; phone for current hours and special tours. Admission free; varying fees for tours.

INFORMATION **Southwestern Michigan Travel Council,** 2300 Pipestone Road, Benton Harbor, MI 49022, 925-6301; www.swmichigan.org

Following Abe Lincoln in Illinois

Abraham Lincoln was 22 years old in 1831, the year he moved from Indiana to New Salem, Illinois. He came as a frontiersman with little education. Six years later, he packed all his belongings in a saddlebag and left on a borrowed horse for Springfield, a fledgling lawyer on a journey to immortality.

Lincoln never lost his fondness for the places where his future was cast. Following his footsteps in the places he loved best is an enlightening experience, highly recommended for families or anyone who wants to understand more about our country and one of its most remarkable leaders.

Since Springfield is the Illinois state capital, it has its own attractions, both stately official buildings and lovely parks that make for a nice break from sightseeing. Fans of Frank Lloyd Wright will find one of his most interesting Illinois homes here. You'll need a long weekend to take it all in. As a nice bonus, most of the state and national sites are free.

The logical place to begin is Lincoln's own first stop, New Salem.

According to some accounts, he landed here almost by accident, when the flatboat he had helped pilot to New Orleans got stuck in the mud on the return trip. It turns out Lincoln was wise to leave New Salem. The settlement on a rise above the Sangamon River never did prosper and had all but disappeared by 1840. Today's site is a reconstructed frontier village like the one that Lincoln knew.

Visitors enter a world of split-rail fences and ox-drawn farm carts. Among the authentically re-created and furnished buildings along dirt paths are 12 log houses, a tavern, 10 workshops, shops, mills, and a school that doubled as a church. Costumed interpreters demonstrate crafts and bring the village to life. On certain weekends frontier skills like quilting or surveying are showcased, and there are festivals for storytelling, harvesting, and early music. You can watch the blacksmith or the cooper at work, inspect a saw and grist mill like the one that went up in 1829, watch a homemaker performing magic with her spinning wheel, and see how bread was baked in the Rutledge Tavern, where stagecoach passengers often stopped overnight. The *Talisman,* a replica of a steamboat that traveled the Sangamon River in Lincoln's day, takes visitors on hourly trips on the river in season.

Lincoln made a living in New Salem any way he could. He clerked in a store, got work as a surveyor, led his town's troops in the Black Hawk War, served for a while as postmaster, and made two unsuccessful attempts to run a business. The Berry-Lincoln general store was the second store where the future president had tried his hand and failed, running up a debt that took 15 years to repay. All the while, cheered on by the town schoolmaster, he was reading law books by candlelight and running for the state legislature. He lost in 1832, but succeeded two years later.

New Salem's modern Visitors Center has a time-walk exhibit area that depicts events from 1809 to the present, as well as an 18-minute presentation on the years Lincoln spent here. The site includes the outdoor "Theater in the Park," which stages musicals, including *Abraham,* chronicling the time Lincoln spent in the town.

Having gained some knowledge of his early days, follow Lincoln's path to Springfield, which was his home for 24 years. Though he arrived without much money, the future was promising for the young lawyer and up-and-coming state legislator. Here he would meet politicians and leaders from all over the state and emerge as a national figure known for his eloquence. And it was here that he met and married Mary Todd. The house where they lived with their four children on Jackson Street is the only home Lincoln ever owned.

The one-room office where Lincoln practiced law, sharing space with William H. Herndon, his future biographer, has been restored, along with the Federal Court in the same building where he argued cases. You'll learn that he used to lie on the sofa reading the newspaper aloud, a practice that did not always delight his partner; Lincoln had formed this habit in his youth, when he taught himself to read. A doting father, Lincoln also brought his children to the office, much to Herndon's chagrin.

Also meticulously restored is the Old State Capitol. Built in 1837, it is considered to be a perfect example of Greek Revival architecture. The rooms are furnished in the period from 1840 to 1860, with many objects relating to famous people who used the building, such as Lincoln, Stephen A. Douglas, and Ulysses S. Grant. It was in this building that Lincoln delivered his "House Divided" speech; an original copy of his Gettysburg Address is on display in the rotunda. And it was here—in the House of Representatives—that Lincoln's body lay in state in 1865.

The Lincoln home has been restored as closely as possible to the way it was when Lincoln lived here. It is part of a four-block Historic Site administered by the National Park Service. The tour guides tell you much about Lincoln's life in Springfield, including the loss of a son and the emotional problems of his wife. Short of money at the start, Lincoln chopped his own wood, and milked the cow himself. To bring in income, he traveled the judicial circuit on horseback, at the same time making a name for himself and winning an election to the U.S. House of Representatives for a two-year term in 1847.

Happy to be home again after his term, he stayed out of politics until 1854, when he was spurred by his opposition to Stephen A. Douglas's Kansas-Nebraska Act, which repealed the Missouri Compromise prohibiting slavery north of Missouri's southern border. Lincoln lost an 1855 race for the Senate, lost again to Douglas in 1858, but the series of Lincoln-Douglas debates held that year brought Lincoln national prominence as a brilliant speaker and antislavery advocate who would eventually win the Republican nomination for president of the United States in 1860.

Another moving site is the depot where Lincoln left for his inauguration in 1862. A 20-minute multimedia presentation describes his trip across country. On the balcony is a replica of his famous farewell speech, a loving tribute to his friends and neighbors.

Though the present First Presbyterian Church has replaced the one Lincoln knew, the pew where his family worshiped has been preserved. The church also is notable for its fine Tiffany stained-glass windows.

Lincoln's body was brought back to be buried in the town he considered home. The 117-foot-tall marble tomb, dedicated in 1874, was built with public contributions. Three of Lincoln's sons and Mary Lincoln are also buried here. The tomb is enhanced by an impressive array of sculpture, including a bust of Lincoln by Gutzon Borglum and a replica by Daniel Chester French of the famous seated figure in the Lincoln Memorial in Washington, D.C.

The Lincoln Memorial Garden and Nature Center is a living memorial to the slain president. The 77 woodland acres along the shore of

Lake Springfield were designed by the great Midwestern landscape architect Jens Jensen; the entire complex is planted entirely with plants, trees, and flowers native to Illinois. The garden includes five miles of nature trails, a nature center, and a gift shop featuring items handcrafted from native materials.

When your Lincoln tour is complete, take time for the elegant state Capitol, which went into service in 1877. The building's vast 361-foot dome is topped with a spectacular stained-glass design with a rendering of the state seal in the skylight. The building is in the form of a Latin cross, impressively placed in the center of a nine-acre plot. The grounds are filled with fine sculptures, including a 10½-foot statue of Abraham Lincoln by Andrew O'Conner, and statues of Illinois statesmen from Stephen A. Douglas to Senator Everett McKinley Dirksen.

The Capitol Complex Visitors Center has more information about the Capitol and the state, and the Illinois Artisans Shop, located in the Illinois State Museum, is devoted to the finest crafts made by Illinois artisans.

The Illinois State Museum also offers three floors of exhibits on the state's natural history, including a mastodon skeleton, fine and decorative arts, a special hands-on exhibit area for children, as well as an interactive computer exhibit, "At Home in the Heartland."

Frank Lloyd Wright is another great man who got his start in Illinois. The Dana-Thomas House, which he designed in 1902–04 for Springfield socialite and women's activist Susan Lawrence Dana, has been called the best-preserved and most complete of Wright's early so-called Prairie Houses. One of his largest and most elaborate homes, this structure is unique among Wright's projects because he was required to incorporate the original Italianate brick home on the site. Inside are more than 100 pieces of original Wright-designed white-oak furniture, 200 original light fixtures and skylights, and 250 art-glass doors, windows, and light panels. The home was bought by Mr. and Mrs. Charles C. Thomas in 1944 and for 37 years was the executive office for their publishing firm. Few original features were removed. It was sold to the state of Illinois in 1981 and has been totally restored. It should not be missed by anyone who admires Wright's work.

If you'd rather spend time outdoors, head for the city's very handsome Washington Park, where the Botanical Gardens feature a formal rose garden, perennial, scent, and texture gardens, and changing floral displays. The domed conservatory holds six indoor flower shows each year. The Thomas Rees Memorial Carillon in the park, also surrounded by gardens, is said to be the third-largest set of bells in the world, and is one of the few open to the public. The guided tour incudes a video and a firsthand look at the keyboard pedals that control the bells.

A good option for kids is the Henson Robinson Zoo, situated in a picturesque locale near Lake Springfield.

Springfield has a variety of restaurants, with Maldaner's and Baur's among the perennial favorites. Many dining places offer a children's menu, another good reason why Springfield makes a great family getaway.

If time allows, you can add a bit of color to your trip with an hour's drive east to Arthur, the heart of Illinois Amish country. Browse the shops on the main street of the small town, and visit the information center at the end of Vine for a map of businesses in the countryside offering Amish-made quilts, crafts, and furniture. If you want to learn more about the lifestyles of the Amish, stop at Wood Loft Tours, 138 South Vine Street, to make arrangements for a local guide who will accompany you in your car for an hour or two, filling you in on local lore and pointing out many attractions you might otherwise miss.

Area Code: 217

DRIVING DIRECTIONS Springfield is at the intersection of I-55 and I-72. From Chicago follow I-55 south, 199 miles. It is 193 miles from Indianapolis, 97 miles from St. Louis.

ACCOMMODATIONS **Renaissance Springfield Hotel,** 701 Adams Street, 62701, 544-8800 or (800) 468-3571, best in town, indoor pool, M • **Springfield Hilton,** 700 East Adams Street, 62701, 789-1530, downtown high-rise, indoor pool, M–E • **Mansion View Inn and Suites,** 529 South Fourth Street, 62701, 544-7411 or (800) 252-1083, across from governor's mansion; rooms, I–M, CP; suites, M, CP • **Best Inns of America,** 500 North First Street, 62702, 522-1100, motel, I • **Best Western Lincoln Plaza,** 101 East Adams Street, 62701, 523-5661 or (800) 528-1234, motel, I; suites, M. There are also many motels just outside the city; write to the visitors bureau for a list.

DINING **Maldaner's,** 222 South Sixth Street, 522-4313, downtown landmark since 1884, traditional menu, prime-rib specials on weekends, I–M • **Norb Andy's,** 518 East Capitol Street, 523-7777, steak and seafood, legislators' favorite lunch hangout, known for the "horseshoe sandwich," I–M • **Baur's,** 620 South First Street, 789-4311, American menu, elegant, M • **Tokyo of Japan,** 2225 Stevenson Drive, 585-0088, dinner prepared at the table, M • **Sebastian's Hide-Out,** 221 South Fifth Street, 789-8988, creative menu, M • **Saputo's,** 801 East Monroe Street, 544-2523, tiny popular Italian, I–M • **Gumbo Ya Ya's,** Springfield Hilton (see above) 789-1530, Creole and Cajun, M • **Feed Store,** 516 East Adams Street, 528-3355, recommended lunch spot, soups and salads, I.

SIGHTSEEING **Lincoln's New Salem State Historic Site,** State Highway 97, Petersburg, 20 miles northwest of Springfield, 632-4000. Hours: March through October, daily 9 A.M. to 5 P.M.; rest of year, daily

8 A.M. to 4 P.M. $ • **Theater in the Park,** June through August, 632-5440, $$$; ***Talisman*** riverboat cruises, May to Labor Day, daily 10 A.M. to 4 P.M.; weekends only Labor Day to late October. $$ • **Lincoln Home National Historic Site,** 413 South Eighth Street, 492-4241. Hours: April through mid-August, daily 8 A.M. to 6 P.M.; late August and September, 8:30 A.M. to 6 P.M.; rest of year, 8:30 A.M. to 5 P.M. Free; tickets distributed on first-come first-served basis at visitors center, 426 South Seventh Street • **Lincoln-Herndon Law Offices State Historic Site,** Sixth and Adams Streets, 785-7960. Hours: March to October, daily 9 A.M. to 5 P.M.; rest of year, daily 9 A.M. to 4 P.M. Last tour 45 minutes before closing. $ • **Old State Capitol State Historic Site,** 785-7961. Hours: Daily 9 A.M. to 5 P.M.; last tour begins 4:15 P.M. Living History programs June 1 to mid-April, 10 A.M. to noon, 1 P.M. to 4 P.M. Donation • **Lincoln Depot,** Monroe Street between Ninth and Tenth Streets, 544-8695. Hours: April through August, daily 10 A.M. to 4 P.M. Free • **Lincoln Tomb State Historic Site,** Oak Ridge Cemetery, 1500 Monument Avenue, 782-2717. Hours: March through October, June through August 8 A.M. to dusk; rest of year to 5 P.M. Free • **Lincoln Memorial Garden and Nature Center,** 2301 East Lake Drive, 529-1111. Hours: Daily, sunrise to sunset; Nature Center, Tuesday to Saturday 10 A.M. to 4 P.M., Sunday 1 P.M. to 4 P.M. Free • **Capitol Complex Visitors Center,** 425 College Street, 524-6620. Hours: Monday to Friday 8 A.M. to 4:30 P.M., Saturday 9 A.M. to 4 P.M. **Illinois State Capitol,** Second and Capitol Streets, 782-2099. Hours: Weekdays 8 A.M. to 4 P.M., weekends 9 A.M. to 3 P.M. Tours on the hour and half hour. Free • **Illinois State Museum,** Spring and Edwards Streets, 782-7386. Hours: Monday to Saturday 8:30 A.M. to 5 P.M., Sunday noon to 5 P.M. Free • **Dana-Thomas House State Historic Site,** 301 East Lawrence Avenue, 782-6776. Hours: Wednesday to Sunday 9 A.M. to 4 P.M. $$ • **Henson Robinson Zoo,** 1100 East Lake Drive, 753-6217. Hours: Late March through mid-October, daily 10 A.M. to 5 P.M. $ • **Washington Park Botanical Gardens,** Washington Park, off Macarthur Boulevard, 753-6228. Hours: Monday to Friday noon to 4 P.M., weekends noon to 5 P.M. Free • **Thomas Rees Memorial Carillon,** Washington Park, 753-6219. Hours: June through August, Tuesday to Sunday noon to 8 P.M.; spring and fall, weekends only. Tours, $ • **Amish Visitors Center,** 106 East Progress Street, Arthur, (800) 72-AMISH.

INFORMATION Springfield Convention and Visitors Bureau, 109 North Seventh Street, Springfield, IL 62701, 789-2360 or (800) 545-7300; www.springfield.il.us/visit

Spring in Bloom in Indiana

It might be Maryland instead of the Midwest. The early settlers from the mid-Atlantic states who made their home beside the Ohio River in Madison, Indiana, brought with them the Federal and Greek Revival architecture they had left behind. The result is a remarkable little town, a community of 12,000 boasting no fewer than 133 blocks of early-19th-century buildings unmatched in this part of the country. Madison's heritage is significant enough to have earned the entire center of town a listing on the National Register of Historic Places.

The profusion of pre–Civil War structures is ample reason for a visit—especially since many fine homes are now receiving bed-and-breakfast guests and Main Street is lined with tempting antiques shops. But Madison has natural surroundings that are equally inviting. Clifty Falls State Park, on the western edge of town, offers soaring river views, canyons, and rushing waterfalls, and the hiking is superb.

The ideal time to enjoy Madison's double dose of pleasures is in the spring, when the cascades are at their splashiest and the woodlands are canopied with dogwood and redbud blossoms. Choose one of the two Madison in Bloom weekends in late April and early May and you can add exquisite private gardens in town to an already memorable agenda. Proceeds go to the Jefferson County Historical Society to help preserve more of that exceptional early architecture.

When it was settled nearly 175 years ago at a point advantageous for crossing the Ohio River, Madison quickly became the gateway to the Northwest Frontier. Settlers moved along the river in canoes, or on rafts and flatboats, then came ashore here, striking out northward on an old Indian trail into the wilderness. The pioneers needed horses, saddles, wagons, carts, and harnesses for their journeys, and Madison prospered by supplying them. As the settlers established farms, Madison became a thriving port, shipping produce on flatboats or rafts made of logs that traveled downstream as far as New Orleans. Later, the steamboats took over.

By midcentury, having grown into a busy port and shipbuilding center, Madison was the largest city in Indiana. Foundries grew up making fancy ironwork, much of it shipped to New Orleans, but some remaining to grace sidewalks and balconies in town.

Many early pioneers coming from the mid-Atlantic states to seek their fortunes on the frontier intended only to pass through Madison, but once they saw the prosperity and the incomparable setting above the Ohio, they decided to stay and build the Federal-style brick row houses that still grace the town.

One of those who came in 1837 was Francis Costigan, who arrived from Baltimore after training under Benjamin Henry Latrobe, the man who established Greek Revival architecture as a dominant style in this country. Costigan was responsible for designing some of Madison's most notable homes. His buildings include the Shrewsbury House, a splendid residence built for a riverboat entrepreneur in 1846, known for its freestanding spiral staircase rising three stories.

Costigan's masterpiece is the stately columned and porticoed Lanier mansion, constructed in 1844 for a wealthy financier who had come west from North Carolina at age 18 and struck it rich in banking. Lanier was instrumental in building Indiana's economy prior to the Civil War, and during the war, he personally saved the state twice from fiscal disaster by lending it over a million dollars to meet its obligations. Crowned with a 16-foot octagonal cupola, Lanier's home was considered the finest in what was then "the West," an example of the lifestyle the truly wealthy could achieve even on the frontier. The home is now a state historic site, restored and open for touring. About one-third of the furnishings actually belonged to the Laniers.

Costigan's own Federal town house has been restored, but is open only by appointment for group tours.

When railroads spelled the end to river traffic, Madison became a sleeping beauty, until the town was awakened by the kiss of tourists, who love strolling and admiring the period buildings. The best way to do that is with one of the printed walking tours available at the visitors bureau on Main Street.

Many of the most significant homes are on the west side of town between First and Third Streets, some of them adorned with lacy ironwork. A brick walkway lends itself to leisurely strolls on the banks of the Ohio, where the steamboats *Delta Queen* and *Mississippi Queen* sometimes come to call.

The handsome cast-iron fountain on Broadway, just off Main Street, was a gift from the Republic of France to the 1876 Philadelphia Centennial Exposition. It was bought and given to Madison 10 years later by the state Odd Fellows Lodge. The community raised the money to have it recast in bronze to mark the 1976 American bicentennial.

A number of notable buildings have been restored and are open for tours. These include the Dr. William D. Hutchings Office and Hospital and the 1818 Judge Jeremiah Sullivan House, the town's earliest mansion, said by experts to be one of the best examples of Federal architecture in the Midwest. The third-floor family schoolroom of the Sullivan house has been restored, and the smokehouse and bake oven have been reconstructed.

Main Street also has some notable public buildings, such as the Greek Revival Jefferson County Courthouse, constructed in 1854–55, the adjacent Old Jail—built in 1849, the oldest intact jail in the state—and the Fair Play Fire Company, built in 1875 as a trolley barn. When the fire company took over in 1888, the Italianate bell tower was added to support the large alarm bell; the bell was cast from silver coins donated by the community. Atop the tower is a fireman weather vane, fashioned by a local craftsman. It is a favorite landmark in town.

The Madison County Public Library, the first public library in the Northwest Territory, has extensive collections of local history, photographs, and genealogy. The octagonal building on First Street between Vine and Mill Streets was the third passenger-train station on the Pennsylvania Railroad. Today it is part of the headquarters of the Jefferson County Historical Society, whose exhibits focus on the Civil War, steamboating, and Victorian eras.

The Talbott Hyatt Pioneer Garden on a rise above the Ohio River has also been restored, showing the influence of English gardens on early-19th-century America.

The land for one of the town's great assets, Clifty Falls State Park, was saved from development by area residents who raised funds to buy it in 1920 and presented it to the state. It was doubled in size in 1965. A product of the southernmost glacier on the North American landmass, and subsequent erosion, the park offers rugged limestone bluffs above the Ohio River and three miles of canyons with plunging waterfalls where Clifty Creek winds its way down to the Ohio River below. The deteriorating cliffs are known for their abundant fossils.

Four major waterfalls from 60 to 83 feet in height, and many minor ones, can be seen from overlooks or on the park's many hiking trails parallel to the creek. Hiking trails vary from three-quarters to four and a half miles, and from easy to rugged. An observation tower near the Ohio yields lofty panoramas of the town and the river.

In spring the woods are a patchwork of pastel hues and the ground is carpeted with wildflowers. Special Wildflower Weekends of guided woodland hikes and slide programs are held in spring. The park has its own lodge, the modern motel-like Clifty Inn, as well as a swimming pool, picnic areas, and a nature center with many programs.

But it's hard to turn down the appealing bed-and-breakfast options in Madison. Autumnwood and Cliff House are two fine Victorian homes with canopy beds and period antiques, set high in the hills overlooking the town and the river. Downtown, within an easy walk of shops and dining, you can choose from the Schussler House, an 1849 Federal/Greek Revival home; Stonefield's Dream, an 1892 Victorian; or the delightfully restored and furnished 1850 Carriage House, a cozy story-and-a-half home occupied by just one set of lucky lodgers at a time.

Don't think that the Cinnamon Tearoom is just for tea; it actually serves the best dinners in town. The menu at Key West Shrimp House, located in an old building on Ferry Street, is not limited to seafood, and the restaurant has a generous salad bar.

There's plenty of scenic driving around Madison. Hanover College, seven miles west on State Highway 56/62, founded in 1827, has a picture-book campus of 30 red-brick Georgian buildings, set on 630 hilltop acres filled with spring blooms. Highway 56 East runs along the

Ohio River part of the way to Vevay, a tiny river town with a Swiss heritage where you can have lunch with a river view at the Ogle Haus Inn.

Bicyclists can stop at the visitors bureau for a map listing several routes for regular and mountain bikes, including one through Clifty Falls State Park and another that leads across the picturesque Ohio River bridge into the hills of Kentucky.

Back in town, antiques shops are easy to find; just take a stroll down Main Street. Other locations worth exploring include the Broadway Antique Mall, with over 60 dealers and a large stock of furniture, glassware, china, quilts, and all kinds of collectibles, and the Old Town Emporium on East Second Street, specializing in 18th- and 19th-century furniture, English china, and delftware. The Lumber Mill Antique Mall at 721 West First Street near the riverfront is one of the local mainstays.

If you can't make it in spring, consider a fall trip to Madison. Late September brings the annual Chautauqua, with an outstanding outdoor show and sale held on the banks of the Ohio and the lawn of the Lanier House, showcasing the work of over 200 artists and craftsmen. The annual Tri Kappa Tour of Homes in mid-October lets you into some fine residences not usually open to the public. Whenever you come, you'll be discovering a treasure, a small town with a large share of beauty, both natural and man-made.

Area Code: 812

DRIVING DIRECTIONS Madison is on State Highway 56, on the banks of the Ohio River. From Chicago, take I-80/90 east to I-65 south to Scottsburg, then Highway 56 east, about 300 miles. Madison is 95 miles from Indianapolis.

ACCOMMODATIONS All of the following listings have the Madison zip code, 47250. **Carriage House,** 308 West Second Street, 265-6892, M, CP • **Cliff House,** 122 Fairmount Drive, 265-5272, M, CP • **Autumnwood,** 165 Autumnwood Lane, 265-5262, M, CP • **Schussler House,** 514 Jefferson Street, 273-2068 or (800) 392-1931, M, CP • **Clifty Inn,** 1501 Green Road, Clifty Falls State Park, Highway 56/62 West, 265-4135, I–M.

DINING **The Cinnamon Tearoom,** Second and West Streets, 273-2367, I–M • **Key West Shrimp House,** 117 Ferry Street, 265-2831, seafood plus, salad bar, M • **Ogle Haus Inn Restaurant,** Highway 56 East, Vevay, 427-2020, European, I–M.

SIGHTSEEING **James F. D. Lanier State Historic Site,** 511 West First Street, 265-3526. Hours: Tuesday to Saturday 9 A.M. to 5 P.M., Sunday lp.m. to 5 P.M. Donation • **Shrewsbury House,** 301 West First

Street, 265-4481. Hours: April to December, daily 10 A.M. to 4:30 P.M. $ • **Dr. William D. Hutchings Office and Hospital,** 120 West Third Street, 265-2967. Hours: May to October, Monday to Saturday 10 A.M. to 4:30 P.M., Sunday 1:15 P.M. to 4:30 P.M. $; under 12, free • **Schofield House,** 217 West Second Street, 265-4759. Hours: Monday to Saturday 9:30 A.M. to 4:30 P.M., Sunday 12:30 P.M. to 4:30 P.M. $ • **Judge Jeremiah Sullivan House,** 304 West Second Street, 265-2967. Hours: May through October, Monday to Saturday 10 A.M. to 4:30 P.M., Sunday 1:15 P.M. to 4:30 P.M. $ • **Madison Railroad Station and Jefferson County Historical Society Museum,** 615 West First Street, 265-2335. Hours: April to October, Monday to Saturday 10 A.M. to 4:30 P.M., Sunday 1 P.M. to 4 P.M.; rest of year, weekdays only, $$; under 16, free • **Clifty Falls State Park,** 1501 Green Road, off Highway 56/62 West, Madison, 265-1331. Hours: Daily 8 A.M. to 11 P.M. Admission charged March to October, out-of-state cars, $$; Indiana cars, $ • ***Festivals:*** Double-check for current dates. **Madison in Bloom,** Jefferson County Historical Society, 265-2335, usually last weekend in April and first weekend in May • **Clifty Falls Wildflower Weekends,** Clifty Nature Center, 265-1331, dates vary with the weather each year, so check • **Madison Chautauqua,** last weekend in September, 559-2967 • **Historic Madison Tour of Homes,** c/o Tri Kappa Sorority, (800) 559-2956, usually three days in mid-October.

INFORMATION **Madison Area Convention and Visitors Bureau,** 301 East Main Street, Madison, IN 47250, 265-2956 or (800) 559-2956; www.seidata.com/~madison/

The Best of Both Worlds in Ann Arbor

A local historian once claimed that the pioneers who settled Ann Arbor, Michigan, were "people of a finer stock." While there is no proof of his boastful claim, it is certainly true that the town they began has grown into a sophisticated, arts-conscious community, a place that somehow manages to be a leafy small town and cosmopolitan center at the same time.

It is easy to see why many affluent folks find Ann Arbor to be a desirable place to live. Known as the City of Trees because of its shady neighborhoods and woodsy preserves, parks, and paths along the Huron River, Ann Arbor is also home to one of America's finest public universities, which makes for a cultural life far richer than what you'd expect to find in a city of 110,000. Many U of M alumni stay put after graduation, which means the city has an unusually well-educated population, as well. In addition to the many bookstores, music stores, and coffee shops you'd expect to find in a college town, Ann Arbor is filled with intriguing specialty shops, over 30 art galleries, and more than its share of creative restaurants. It all makes for a very desirable place to visit, as well as to live.

It was the region's profusion of trees (and a pair of wives named Ann and Mary Ann, respectively) that prompted the founders, John Allen and Elisha Walker Rumsey, to choose the name Ann Arbor in 1824. Ann Arbor became the county seat but lost its bid for state capital. As a consolation prize, it was given the state university, which was moved here from Detroit in 1837. The campus grew to become the first great educational institution in what was then "the West." Today the U of M is consistently rated among the top 10 universities in the country, is a leader in sponsored research funding, and has the largest pre-law and pre-med enrollment in the nation.

Michigan graduates include a U.S. president (Gerald Ford), three Supreme Court justices, eleven Pulitzer prize winners (including poet Robert Frost), six Nobel prize winners, and such well-known personalities as playwright Arthur Miller, cartoonist Cathy Guisewite, actor James Earle Jones, and soprano Jessye Norman. The entire crew of *Apollo 15* were U of M graduates; in fact, they established a Michigan Club chapter on the moon.

A look at the campus is usually the first order of business for visitors to Ann Arbor. Covering over 3,000 acres divided into four sections—some connected by shuttle bus—the campus is vast; it is the downtown section, however, that is of most interest to visitors. Burton Memorial Tower on South Thayer is the best-known landmark; it houses the 55-bell Baird Carillon, whose bells can usually be heard Monday to Friday from noon to 12:30 P.M.

The heart of campus life is the center of the "Diag," a long X-shaped walkway cutting across a square block of classroom buildings from North to South University Avenues between East University and State Streets. It is always abuzz with activity and filled with posters, from sign-ups for the Star Trek Fan Club to fervent warnings to "Repent—Believe the Gospel."

The students you see milling around are part of a student body of nearly 37,000, who among them represent all 50 states and nearly 100 foreign countries; 90 percent were in the top 20 percent of their high-school graduating classes.

The grounds here are flat, the buildings a mix of old and new in no particular style. If halls of ivy are what you're looking for, proceed to South University Avenue and the elegant Gothic-style Law Quadrangle. The long, vaulted, richly paneled reading room of the Law Library is not to be missed. The stained-glass windows represent colleges all over the world. An ingenious modern addition at the rear of the building unobtrusively leads to the underground stacks (in all, the library boasts 771,000 volumes).

The Michigan Union, with lavish facilities for students, is across the street on South University at State Street; walk upstairs to see the vast poolroom. A plaque on the front of the building marks the spot where John Fitzgerald Kennedy first announced the Peace Corps program.

A few blocks farther north on campus are the city's big performance venues—Hill Auditorium, the Power Center, Lydia Mendelssohn Theatre, and Rackham Auditorium.

To understand what the campus does for Ann Arbor's cultural life, just take a look at the season's offerings of the University Musical Society. In one recent year a partial list included the Boston, San Francisco, and St. Louis symphonies; the Israel Philharmonic; Russia's Bolshoi Symphony and St. Petersburg Philharmonic; the Tokyo String Quartet; the Juilliard String Quartet; the New York City Opera; the Guthrie Theatre of Minneapolis; Wynton Marsalis and the Lincoln Center Jazz Orchestra; and the Alvin Ailey American Dance Theatre—a lineup many a major city might envy.

The campus art museum is small, but has some interesting features, including a Japanese tearoom, one prize Monet, a wonderful Tiffany peacock mosaic, and small sculptures by Rodin and Lipschitz. The university's museums for natural history and archaeology are not musts, but are worth a look if you have the time. The natural history museum houses a planetarium.

You'll certainly want to take a look at State Street bordering the Diag. It's the center of campus shopping, where you'll find many of the city's book and music stores, as well as plenty of coffee bars, where you can replenish your energy between browsing (among the favorites are Cava Java and Espresso Royale). Nickels Arcade just off State Street has shops for antiques, pottery, and clothing. The arcade was built in the 1920s and retains its vintage charm. Turn down Liberty Street for more shops, including a big Borders Book Store (the chain was born right here in Ann Arbor). The Michigan Theatre, built in 1928, has been nicely restored and is still used for films and live entertainment.

Michigan has been fiercely proud of its football team ever since it defeated Stanford 49–0 in the first-ever Rose Bowl in 1902. It's fun to join the crowds roaring their support at home football games—if you can get a ticket, that is. The 107,000-seat stadium built in 1927 is America's largest, but is often sold out, so plan well ahead if you want to get to a game. They usually leave a gate open on Stadium Boulevard on days when there is no game, so visitors can walk in and gawk at the awesome size.

When you've had enough campus life, head for downtown and the low-rise Victorian buildings on Main and Washington Streets, where you'll find art galleries, more bookstores, and a lot of restaurants. You can combine lunch with browsing at Cafe Zola, 112 West Washington, then come back to 330 South Main for a dessert of homemade ice cream at Lovin' Spoonful.

If you want to see how art-conscious the community is, come back in mid-July, when the streets of downtown host the Midwest's biggest outdoor art show, a four-day extravaganza.

They start their art young here. If your children are along, head for ArtVentures, a unique supervised hands-on workshop upstairs at the Ann Arbor Art Center. You can drop the kids off or join them as they become familiar with other cultures by creating little works of art like Guatemalan worry dolls, Navajo sand paintings, Javanese shadow puppets, or Pueblo kachina dolls. The downstairs gallery has changing exhibits. There's more participatory fun at the Ann Arbor Hands-On Museum, where the emphasis is on science. The museum is undergoing a major expansion.

Ann Arbor's very best shopping awaits at the Kerrytown Shops, a trio of century-old warehouses nicely restored around a courtyard between Fourth and Fifth avenues, Catherine and Kingsley Streets.

A standout among the 30 shops in this area is ATYS, which offers an amazing array of "contemporary living accessories" by the best designers from around the world. You might find a German "origami" chair made of polymer sheets, a shaving set of chrome and marble made in Florence, or a bud vase from a glassworks in Santa Fe. When I visited, there were no fewer than 15 kinds of bottle openers on display in sleek and imaginative shapes. This is the kind of unique shop that makes Ann Arbor a treat for visitors; *Detroit* magazine called it "the best example that Ann Arbor really is different from other cities."

Another special stop for admirers of folk and fine art is the Bruise Gallery, which displays wares from African drums to "outsider art"; they have some terrific handpainted tables in whimsical designs. The Deboer Gallery has a nice array of fine contemporary crafts.

Kerrytown is also the site of an outdoor farmers' market on Saturdays year-round (also Wednesdays May to November) and an artisans' market on Sunday from May to November. The Kerrytown Concert House is home to many small theater productions, chamber-music concerts, and solo performances.

You'll probably want to spend a lot of time in Kerrytown, but when you need a break you can walk across to Detroit Street and one of Ann Arbor's most famous institutions, Zingerman's Delicatessen. It was one of only 24 restaurants in the state awarded four stars by the *Detroit Free Press* restaurant reviewer, and when you taste the sandwiches, you'll know why. Zingerman's has lots of gourmet foods also, and they run the market in Kerrytown, where, among other treats, you'll find a host of unusual salsas, from pineapple and mango to feta cheese.

Ann Arbor is also a choice destination for antiquers, with over a dozen shops and two malls, including the Antiques Marketplace, a former brewery on South First Street between Liberty and Washington housing 50 dealers. The Ann Arbor Antiques Market, with over 300 dealers on hand, is held periodically at indoor quarters at the Ann Arbor–Saline Fairgrounds.

Even when you are strolling on Main Street in Ann Arbor, you can see the trees beckoning in the distance. To get closer to nature, first follow the Huron River out of town along Geddes Road, where the thick trees between Observatory Street and Huron Parkway hide handsome homes of CEOs. On Geddes, east of Observatory, is the Nichols Arboretum, an unspoiled area maintained by the university, with scenic trails for walking, jogging, or bicycling among 600 species of trees and plants. Farther to the northeast is the university-owned Matthaei Botanical Gardens, where there are 150 acres of walking trails plus an indoor conservatory boasting 2,000 kinds of lush tropical plants and a whole room of cacti of every size and shape.

Nearby is the big, wooded U of M North Campus, with modern buildings for the schools of music, architecture, and engineering. The school of music was designed by Eero Saarinen. The Gerald R. Ford Presidential Library at 1000 Beal Avenue houses Ford's presidential, vice-presidential, and congressional papers.

Follow the Huron Parkway northwest of town and you'll come to the hiking and biking paths of Gallup Park. You can rent a bike and then follow the Geddes Bike Path along the river for about eight miles. Paddleboats and canoes are also for rent.

Golfers will be pleased to know that the city has more than 20 public courses; the Stonebridge Golf Club, designed by Arthur Hills, is nationally ranked. *Golf Digest* magazine named Ann Arbor among the nation's top midsized cities for golfers.

When it comes to dining, the choices are wide. Moveable Feast and The Earle are consistent favorites for continental fare, Gandy Dancer is recommended for seafood, and Palio for Italian. Many inexpensive ethnic cafes and new places are opening all the time, so ask your innkeeper about new favorites.

After-dinner entertainment? On the weekend I was in town, the choices ranged from Beethoven to Creole to bluegrass, heavy metal to funk rock, jazz to a German Oktoberfest. Theater offerings ranged from Sam Shepard's *True West* and Shakespeare's *As You Like It* to plays by Noel Coward and Agatha Christie. You can count on an equally stimulating selection; it's hard to be bored in Ann Arbor.

<u>Area Code: 734</u>

DRIVING DIRECTIONS Ann Arbor is off I-94 about 35 miles west of Detroit. From Chicago, follow I-94 east, just over 200 miles. Amtrak train service is available from Chicago.

ACCOMMODATIONS **Bell Tower Hotel,** 300 South Thayer Avenue, 48104, 769-3010, European-style decor, walking distance to campus and town, M–E, CP • **Campus Inn,** 615 East Huron Street, 48104, 769-2200, in-town hotel, pool, M • **Weber's,** 3050 Jackson Road, 48103, 769-2500 or (800) 443-3050, attractive complex with indoor pool just outside town, M, CP; poolside suites, EE, CP • **Courtyard by Marriott,** 3205 Boardwalk, 48108, south of town, 995-5900 or (800) 321-2211, indoor pool, M–E • **Comfort Inn,** 2455 Carpenter Road, 48108, 973-6100 or (800) 973-6101, indoor pool, I–M • **Best Western Wolverine Inn,** 3505 South State Street, 48108, 665-3500, budget choice, I • ***Bed-and-breakfast inns:*** **Old West Side,** 805 West Huron Street, 48103, 741-8794, I • **Artful Lodger,** 1547 Washtenaw Avenue, 48109, 769-0653, M, CP • **Woods Inn,** 2887 Newport Road, 48103, 665-8394, I, CP.

DINING **Moveable Feast,** 326 West Liberty Street, 663-3278, fine dining in a Victorian home, prix fixe, E–EE • **The Earle,** 121 West Washington Street, 994-0211, European country flavor, wine bar, jazz many evenings, M • **Bella Ciao Trattoria,** 118 West Liberty Street, 995-2107, casual regional Italian, I–M • **Gandy Dancer,** 401 Depot Street, 769-0592, restored century-old train station, seafood plus, M–EE • **Gratzi,** 326 South Main Street, 663-5555, attractive upscale Italian, music on weekends, M • **Metzger's,** 203 East Washington Street, 668-8987, cuckoo clocks and beer steins, German food, I–M • **Argiero's,** 300 Detroit Street, 665-0444, family-owned Italian, I–M • **Prickly Pear,** 328 South Main Street, 930-0047, cheery southwestern cafe, I • **Real Seafood Company,** 341 South Main Street, 769-5960, very attractive, wide seafood menu, M • **Sweet Lorraine's Cafe,** 303 Detroit Street, 665-0700, in Kerrytown, eclectic menu, I–M • **Weber's** (see above), longtime standby for American fare, M • **Cafe Zola,** 112 West Washington Street, 769-2020, convenient spot for lunch, I • **Conor O'Neill's,** 318 South Main Street, 665-2968, authentic Irish pub, I–M • **Zanzibar,** 216 South State Street, 994-7777, bright decor, eclectic dishes, Asian noodles to spicy salsa, unique sandwiches, I–M • **Zingerman's Delicatessen,** 422 Detroit Street, 663-DELI, tops for deli food, I • **Fleetwood Diner,** 300 South Ashley, 995-5502, old-time diner, open 24 hours, I • ***Inexpensive ethnic:*** **Blue Nile,** 221 East Washington Street, 998-4746, Ethiopian, communal dining sans cutlery, I • **China Gate,** 1201 South University Avenue, 665-8767, Chinese, I • **Kana Family Restaurant,** 114 West Liberty Street, 662-9303, Korean, I • **The Old Siam,** 2509 Jackson Road, 665-2571, Thai, I–M • **Mongolian Barbeque,** 200 South Main Street, 913-0999, choose your own ingredients for stir-fry, all you can eat, I • ***Brewpubs:*** **Grizzly Peak Brewing Co.,** 120 West Washington Street, 741-7325, bistro menu, I • **Arbor Brewing Company,** 114 East Washington Street, 213-1393, dartboards, brewery tours, I.

SIGHTSEEING **University of Michigan**. Free one-hour campus tours leave from the visitors center, Student Activities Building, 31 East Jefferson, 763-4654. Monday to Thursday 11 A.M., Friday 10 A.M. and 11 A.M., Saturday 10 A.M. and 11 A.M. Phone to verify tour times. Maps and information are also available at the Michigan Union Campus Information Center, State Street and South University Avenue, 763-4636 • ***University museums:*** **Museum of Art,** 525 South State Street, 764-0395. Hours: September to May, Tuesday to Saturday 10 A.M. to 5 P.M., Sunday noon to 5 P.M.; June to August, Tuesday to Saturday 11 A.M. to 5 P.M., Sunday noon to 5 P.M. Free • **Kelsey Museum of Archaeology,** 434 South State Street, 764-9304. Hours: Tuesday to Friday 9 A.M. to 4 P.M., Saturday and Sunday 1 P.M. to 4 P.M. Free • **Museum of Natural History,** Geddes Road and North University Avenue, 763-6085. Hours: Monday to Saturday 9 A.M. to 5 P.M., Sunday 1 P.M. to 5 P.M. Free. Planetarium shows, Saturday, hourly 10:30 A.M. to 3:30 P.M., Sunday 10:30 A.M. to 1:30 P.M. $$ • **Nichols Arboretum,** 2400 Geddes Road, 998-7175. Daily dawn to dusk. Free • **Matthaei Botanical Gardens,** 1800 North Dixboro Road, 998-7061. Hours: Daily 10 A.M. to 4:30 P.M.; guided tours Sunday, 2 P.M. $; free on Saturday and Monday from 10 A.M. to 1 P.M. • **Ann Arbor Art Center,** 117 West Liberty Street, 994-8004. Gallery hours: Monday to Thursday 10 A.M. to 6 P.M., Friday and Saturday 10 A.M. to 9 P.M., Sunday noon to 5 P.M. Free • **ArtVentures,** Art Center (see above), Tuesday to Thursday, 1 P.M. to 6 P.M., Friday 1 P.M. to 9 P.M., Saturday 10 A.M. to 6 P.M., Sunday noon to 5 P.M. $$ • **Ann Arbor Hands-On Museum,** 219 East Huron Street, 995-5439. Hours: Tuesday to Friday 10 A.M. to 5:30 P.M., Saturday 10 A.M. to 5 P.M., Sunday 1 P.M. to 5 P.M. $$.

INFORMATION **Ann Arbor Area Convention and Visitors Bureau,** 120 West Huron, Ann Arbor MI 48104, 995-7281 or (800) 888-9487; www.annarbor.org

Doing the Dunes in Indiana

The land of dunes and singing sands is calling. When the first warm days make you long to escape to the great outdoors, make haste to the Indiana Dunes National Lakeshore, the most accessible of Lake Michigan's towering dunes. Take a walk by the water or atop the dunes, breathe the sweet air, and listen for the musical tones as your footsteps resonate on the quartz-rich sand. There's no better tonic for spring fever.

It's almost a miracle that this world of open beaches, bird-filled marshes, oak and maple forests, prairie, ponds, and dunes as high as 180 feet exists in the very shadow of Gary's smokestacks and just an hour from Chicago. Only the intervention of determined conservationists preserved this precious asset from industrial development. A 2,182-acre state park was established in 1923, and the creation of the National Seashore in 1966 enlarged the preserved area to over 15,000 acres. The visitors center is named for one of the early conservationists, Dorothy Buell, and the Center for Environmental Education bears the name of former Illinois Senator Paul H. Douglas, who worked tirelessly for a decade to convince Congress to save the dunes.

For those who want to understand the forces of nature, the lakeshore is a magnificent classroom, and spring is the ideal time for hiking, before the hot summer sun slows the pace. Stop at the visitors center for maps. Guided walks of both inland and shore areas are available year-round; check the current schedules. Heed the advice of the printed park guide to bring along a camera—or a sketchbook.

In 1892, Henry Cowles, a young botanist at the University of Chicago, became intrigued with the diverse plant life of the area and published an important paper in 1899 describing how one form of plant life prepares the soil for the development of new species. A pioneer in the study of plant succession, Cowles helped establish a new science, ecology.

The changing landscape Cowles discovered—first formed 14,000 years ago by the receding Wisconsin glaciers—is still here to be explored. Ponds are scattered among younger dunes closer to the lake. Marshes are found on old lake bottoms between long dune ridges. Bogs are tucked in glacial moraines. The bogs and marshes are gradually filling with vegetation and will eventually become new meadows, then forests. The Hoosier Prairie, a 335-acre state nature preserve, is the largest tract of ancient prairie in Indiana and a favorite place for bird-watchers in the spring.

The shoreline dunes show the might of the wind blowing off Lake Michigan. The open expanse of the lake allows the prevailing south-westerly winds to pick up speed without hindrance, lifting grains of sand and transporting them inland until plants or hills slow the force and the wind deposits its cargo. On windy days, you can actually place an obstacle on the beach and watch a mini-dune form.

The dunes are constantly shifting because of the power of the wind. Mount Baldy, one of the "climbing dunes" that visitors are permitted to scale, is the ultimate example. A 40-acre, 123-foot living dune that is retreating at the rate of four to five feet a year, Mount Baldy is relentlessly burying all the forest in its path.

The highest dunes are in the Indiana Dunes State Park to the west—Mount Tom (192 feet), Mount Holden (184 feet), and Mount Jackson

(176 feet). There are 10 trails in the state park, one running along the summits of all three of these elevations. Other trails take you through wind-hollowed dune canyons and inland forests and bogs. West Beach to the east is squeezed between industrial areas. You can climb some of the dunes here via boardwalks built along their slopes and get a good view of the Chicago skyline.

Those who prefer biking to hiking can take advantage of the 9.2-mile Calumet Trail, which runs adjacent to the national lakeshore and connects several points of interest in the park.

Part of the fascination of the lakeshore is its human history. The dunes were visited first by the Miami and Potawatomi Indians, who came to hunt and collect medicinal plants. A French-Canadian fur trader named Joseph Bailly built the first homestead and established a trading post in 1822 on the trail that ran between Fort Dearborn and Fort Wayne, the sites, respectively, of today's Chicago and Detroit. Fifty years later Swedish immigrants, Anders and Johanna Chellberg, carved a farm out of the prairie and their family remained there for nearly a century.

The Bailly/Chellberg Trail traces these settlements, offering the chance to visit the restored main house of the Bailly farm and many of its outbuildings and the farmhouse, barn, and other structures where three generations of Chellbergs lived and worked. Every Sunday there are guided tours of the Bailly homestead and grounds, and a "Life on the Farm" program at the Chellberg farm that lets you peek into the corncrib, explore the wood-pegged barn, and enjoy the aromas from the dishes being concocted on an old-fashioned stove fired with wood. On Friday, Saturday, and Sunday at 3 P.M., feeding time on the Chellberg farm, children are invited to help the ranger slop the pigs and haul feed for the horses, chicks, cow, and goat.

Chesterton, just five minutes from the state park, is a convenient place to stay, and one of the nicest lodgings there is the Gray Goose Inn. Though just off the main road, this elegant clapboard home with English country decor is set completely apart, on a 100-acre tract overlooking a small lake. Nearby is Indian Oak Resort, an attractive resort-motel on a lake with an indoor pool and health club.

From the highway, Chesterton looks like a string of fast-food outlets, but drive farther and you'll find yourself in a pleasant small town that will definitely appeal to antiquers. Yesterday's Treasures (700 West Broadway), with its 120 dealers, is the largest of several shops on the same street.

More pleasant browsing can be found. A cooperative gallery shows the work of regional artists at 540 Indian Boundary Road, as does the Chesterton Art Gallery at 115 South Fourth Street. Antiques, art, and all kinds of gifts can be found at the Schoolhouse Shop, a restored 1886 brick schoolhouse turned emporium, not far away in Furnessville, north of Highway 20.

An unexpected Chesterton find is the Oz Fantasy Museum and Yellowbrick Road Gift Shop, which features dolls and dollhouse accessories and memorabilia from the MGM classic *The Wizard of Oz*. The town actually stages a Wizard of Oz festival each September, with an Oz parade complete with original Munchkin costumes from the movie and look-alike contests.

Another lodging favorite in the area is the Spring House Inn in Porter, a larger inn in a wooded setting with an indoor pool that is an especially welcome amenity in the off-season.

Michigan City, near the northernmost end of the lakeshore, seems almost citified in this area, but its Prime Outlets Mall, with over 100 outlet stores, may appeal to the bargain hunter in you. The Creekwood Inn, set on 33 acres of woods and creeks outside Michigan City, is another good place to stay, with spacious rooms, hotel comforts, and a convenient location for motorists arriving via I-94. Michigan City also has some of the best restaurants in the area.

Most of the towns in Indiana's dune country are small and more laid-back than those across the Michigan line—which is just right when you want to unwind and concentrate on enjoying spring and nature at its spectacular best.

Area Code: 219

DRIVING DIRECTIONS From Chicago, take I-90 east, connect with I-94 at Exit 21 and continue east to exit 26, Route 49 north to Route 12, which parallels the National Lakeshore, about 50 miles. From the east, drive west on I-80/90, take Exit 31 and follow Route 49 north, past I-94, to Route 12 and the shore.

ACCOMMODATIONS **Gray Goose Inn,** 350 Indian Boundary Road, Chesterton 46304, 926-5781, M, CP; suites, M–E, CP • **Indian Oak Resort,** I-94, Chesterton 46304, 926-2200 or (800) 552-4232, M–E • **Dunes Shore Inn,** 33 Lakeshore County Road, Beverly Shores 46301, 879-9029, casual inn, one block from Lake Michigan, I, CP • **Spring House Inn,** 303 North Mineral Springs Road, Porter 46304, 929-4600 or (800) 366-4661, M, CP • **Creekwood Inn,** U.S. 20/35 at I-94, Michigan City 46350, 872-8357, M–E, CP • **Duneland Beach Inn,** 3311 Potawatami Trail, Michigan City 46360, one block from private beach, tennis, some whirlpools, balconies, M.

DINING **Duneland Pizza,** 520 Broadway, Chesterton, 926-1163, Italian dishes and thick cornmeal-crust pizza, I • **The Spa,** 333 North Mineral Springs Road, Porter, 926-1654, popular, creative dishes and sauces, M–E • **The Ferns,** Creekwood Inn (see above), continental dishes, open weekends only, M–E • **Basil's,** 521 Franklin Square, Michigan City, 872-4500, American menu, paintings by local artists on the walls, M • **Pumps on 12,** 3085 West Dunes Highway (U.S. 12), Michigan City, 874-6201, burgers to formal dining, prime rib special on Saturday, I–M • **Sole,** 3300 North Calumet Avenue, Valparaiso, 462-0992, Mediterranean, I–E • **Clayton's,** 66 West Lincoln Way, Valparaiso, 531-0612, excellent reviews, eclectic menu, M.

SIGHTSEEING **Indiana Dunes National Lakeshore,** Visitor Center at U.S. 12 and Kemil Road, Beverly Shores, 926-7561. Hours: Daily, 9 A.M. to sunset. Free except for parking fee at West Beach, $$. Lakeshore also includes **Indiana Dunes State Park,** 1600 North 25E, Chesterton, 926-1952. Hours: Daily 8 A.M. to 4 P.M. Out-of-state cars, $$; Indiana cars, $.

INFORMATION **Porter County Visitor Center,** 800 Indian Boundary Road, Chesterton, IN 46304, 926-2255 or (800) 283-TOUR; www.casualcoast.com

Rendezvous in Prairie du Chien

Three hundred years ago, a prime location near the beautiful spot where the Wisconsin and Mississippi Rivers meet made Prairie du Chien, Wisconsin, a favorite gathering spot, a place where Indians, fur traders, and river travelers could conveniently rendezvous to barter goods—and to party.

A lot may have changed in three centuries, but the trading and the partying live on. For more than 20 years now, the Prairie Villa Rendezvous in June has attracted ever-increasing numbers of revelers who want to keep the days of explorers and fur traders alive. There are many rendezvous events around the Midwest, but none more colorful than this one, sponsored by the Prairie du Chien Jaycees and the Big River Long Rifles. One of the organizers calls it "the state fair of rendezvous." A sea of hundreds of white tents spreading across an open field serves as home base for over 600 latter-day traders, who come from as far away as Florida and Canada. They dress like mountain men, pioneer women, or buckskin-clad Indian braves and cook over open fires, using authentic early utensils and ingredients.

Why do they do it? Said one longtime participant, "Because we care for the time period. It seems so peaceful. Many of us feel misplaced in this hectic world and think it would be great to live like this." These would-be time travelers not only dress like traders and Indians, but work on mastering their frontier skills as well. Competitions give participants a chance to test their mettle at throwing knives and tomahawks, starting fires using flint and steel, or black-powder rifle shooting. The ladies take part in these events, but also indulge in such domestic arts as pancake flipping, rolling-pin throwing, and cooking over a campfire. And the kids can have a go at hoop toss or a yarn hunt.

Many participants come to sell and swap frontier-era wares such as knives, furs, pipes, powder horns, leather pouches, tin lanterns, handmade moccasins, wood carvings, and Indian jewelry. Throughout the three-day event there are demonstrations of old-time crafts, from basketmaking to beadwork to wood carving. There's a blacksmith at work, creating useful things such as tripods for cooking over the campfire. Entertainment includes storytellers and Indian dancers, a drum-and-fife corp, and a mock buckskinner wedding. Refreshment stands offer Indian fry bread and buffalo burgers. The crowds of 30,000 to 40,000 spectators who come to see the rendezvous also have the option of visiting a more conventional flea market; more than 200 vendors now set up their booths on the edge of the campgrounds.

Those coming to Prairie du Chien for the first time may be pleasantly surprised to discover that it's situated at one of the most scenic spots along the Mississippi. Some of the best views are from Wyalusing State Park about ten miles south of town, at the historic junction of the Wisconsin and Mississippi Rivers. Marquette and Jolliet were the first to land here, in 1673. The 22 miles of hiking trails in the park include the Sentinel Ridge Trail to the boat landing, which turns the corner from the Wisconsin to the Mississippi. Park naturalists regularly offer combination canoe/hikes, a great way to explore the Mississippi and its backwaters.

Prime views can also be had just across the river from Prairie du Chien in Iowa. From the 500-foot bluffs at Pikes Peak State Park in McGregor, you can see the confluence of the two rivers to the south and twin suspension bridges across the river to the north. *Midwest Living* magazine chose this as the most scenic view in a ten-state survey.

The park was named for explorer Zebulon Pike, the same Pike who later made his way southwest to Pikes Peak in Colorado. It offers picnic areas and hiking trails through beautiful wooded bluffs and valleys. The Pictured Rocks Trail goes along sheer walls of limestone rich with fossil remains and past Bridal Veil Falls, a refreshing natural spring. A paved bike trail runs from Pikes Peak to Guttenberg, Iowa, along the Great River Road.

McGregor's picturesque Main Street, lined with brick buildings dating back over a century, offers enticing antique and specialty shops. Check out the River Junction Trade Company, a clothing store right out of the nineteenth century.

As you cross the bridge into Iowa, you'll also note the area's newest attraction, the Port of Marquette and the *Miss Marquette* Riverboat

Casino, with three floors of gambling space and weekend entertainment in the Pink Elephant Showroom.

If you turn north in Marquette and proceed for three miles on State Highway 76, you'll come to Effigy Mounds National Monument, home to 191 prehistoric Indian burial mounds estimated to be 2,500 years old. Most are in the conical or elongated shapes common to such mounds, but 29 of these structures are built in shapes of animals and birds, making them unique in North America. The term *effigy* refers to the appearance of these unusual mounds, created to resemble eagles, falcons, bears, bison, deer, turtles, and other animals. Some are monumental in size; the Great Bear Mound, for example, measures 70 feet across the shoulders and forelegs, is 137 feet long, and three and a half feet high.

An audiovisual presentation in the visitors center explains the history of the mounds. A one-hour walk along the self-guided Fire Point Trail takes in the Little Bear Mound, Hopewellian mounds, and scenic viewpoints along 300-foot bluffs. Rangers lead walks from Memorial Day to Labor Day—including occasional romantic moonlight hikes—and in summer there are river tours along the Mississippi from Effigy Mounds to Wyalusing State Park.

Back in Prairie du Chien, the rendezvous grounds are near the town's most visited attraction, the Villa Louis Historic Site. Operated by the State Historical Society, this landmark is Wisconsin's most celebrated Victorian restoration. A film at the visitors center and a tour led by a costumed guide explain the history of Wisconsin's second-oldest town and its most illustrious citizen, an enterprising young frontiersman named Hercules Dousman.

Dousman came to Prairie du Chien in 1826 as an agent for the American Fur Company and proceeded to amass a fortune from fur trading, railroads, and steamboating. The elegant cream-colored brick mansion built by Dousman's widow and son in 1870 re-creates the lifestyle of one of the state's leading early families; demonstrations in the kitchen include the preparation of meals according to actual family recipes.

Also on the 13-acre grounds are the 1843 Dousman office building and game room, an icehouse, and a preserve house that served as a summer kitchen. The carriage house is now a museum of early town history, and a circa-1850 general store holds exhibits documenting the Upper Mississippi Valley fur trade.

A quite different but nonetheless fascinating bit of history is found at the town's other historic landmark. The Prairie du Chien Museum at Fort Crawford gives insight into the eventful military history of the town, from Indian days to the Civil War.

The museum is located on the site of a former fort, whose military hospital is where medical pioneer Dr. William Beaumont practiced in the 1830s, performing surgery and experiments that form the basis of present-day knowledge of the digestive system. Exhibits in the restored hospital include many relics of 19th-century medicine and trace the progress of surgery during the past century. There is also a reconstructed pharmacy of the 1890s.

Since Prairie du Chien is not a tourist town most of the year, lodgings and dining are somewhat limited, but there is bountiful history and beauty to be found—not to mention the rare chance to relive the past at the annual rendezvous.

Area Code: 608

DRIVING DIRECTIONS Prairie du Chien is on the Great River Road, State Highway 35, at the intersection with U.S. Highway 18. From Chicago, take I-90 north to Madison, then Highway 18 west, about 240 miles. It is 180 miles from Milwaukee, 100 miles from Madison, 210 miles from Minneapolis.

ACCOMMODATIONS The first five listings have the zip code 53821. **Best Western Quiet House Suites,** Highways 18/35 South, 326-4777, indoor/outdoor pool, M • **Bridgeport Inn,** Highways 18/35 South, 326-6082 or (800) 234-6082, motel, indoor pool, M • **Brisbois Motor Inn,** Highway 35 North, 326-8404 or (800) 356-5850, pool, I–M • **Delta Motel,** Highways 18/35 South, 326-4951, budget choice, I • **Newmann House,** 121 North Michigan Street, 326-8104 or (800) 290-0566, modest in-town bed-and-breakfast home, I, CP • **Eagles Landing Bed-and-Breakfast,** 82 North Street, Marquette IA 52158, I, CP (319) 873-2509, contemporary home with river views, I, CP

DINING **Jeffers Black Angus,** Highway 18/35 South, Prairie du Chien, 326-2222, best in town, M • **Kaber's Supper Club,** Blackhawk and Main Streets, Prairie du Chien, 326-6216, M • **Captain's Reef Restaurant,** *Miss Marquette* Riverboat Casino, Port of Marquette, Marquette, IA, (800) 4-YOU-BET, all-you-can-eat buffets all three meals, I • **Coaches Family Restaurant,** 634 South Marquette Road, Prairie du Chien, 326-8115, I • **The Barn,** Main Street and French Town Road, 326-4941, rustic ambience for Sunday brunch, I • **Pete's Hamburger Stand,** local landmark, Blackhawk Avenue, Friday, Saturday, and Sunday, May to October only, I.

SIGHTSEEING **Prairie Villa Rendezvous,** three-day event mid-June in Prairie du Chien; contact Chamber of Commerce for current information • **Villa Louis,** 521 North Villa Louis Road, Prairie du Chien, 326-2721. Hours: May through October, daily 9 A.M. to 5 P.M. $$ • **Prairie du Chien Museum at Fort Crawford,** 717 South Beaumont Road, Prairie du Chien, 326-6960. Hours: May through October, daily 10 A.M. to 5 P.M. $ • ***Miss Marquette* Riverboat Casino,** Port of Marquette, Marquette IA, (800) 4-YOU-BET. Hours: Open daily 24 hours • **Pikes Peak State Park,** McGregor, IA, (319) 873-2341. Hours: Daily 4 A.M. to 10:30 P.M. Free • **Effigy Mounds National Monument,** 151 Highway 76 North, Harpers Ferry, IA (three miles north of Marquette), (319) 873-3491. Hours: Daily 8 A.M. to 5 P.M., to 7 P.M. in summer. $ • **Wyalusing State Park,** County Road C, Bagley, WI (ten miles south of Prairie du Chien), 996-2261. Hours: June to August, daily 6 A.M. to 11 P.M. Wisconsin cars, $$; out-of-state cars, $$$ • **Blue Heron Boat Tours, Ltd.,** 805 South Wacouta Avenue, Prairie du Chien, 326-2930, sighteeing and bird-watching boat rides on the Mississippi; phone for current offerings.

INFORMATION **Prairie du Chien Area Chamber of Commerce,** P.O. Box 326, Prairie du Chien, WI 53821, 326-8555 or (800) PDC-1673; www.prairieduchien.org

Racing Around in Indianapolis

Where would you go to find the world's largest children's museum? What about the largest museum of Western art east of the Mississippi? If you know that the answer is Indianapolis, you know that Indiana's state capital is an unheralded gem. It is recognized mainly on just one day, the date of the legendary Indianapolis 500 auto race. But racing is only a small part of this booming city's lures.

Now the 12th-largest metropolitan area in the country, Indianapolis is a great destination for families and for anyone who enjoys sightseeing. In fact, you'll have to do some racing around just to fit in all of the attractions.

A $3-billion revitalization program has brought new life to downtown. The changes include an expanded convention center, a domed stadium, and a new baseball park. Just three blocks away, in 1999, the state-of-the-art Conseco Fieldhouse replaced the old Market Square Arena as home for the Indiana Pacers NBA basketball team.

Across the street from the convention center and the RCA Dome is the growing White River State Park, a 250-acre oasis in the center of the city, which includes the adobe-style Eiteljorg Museum, a first-class zoo, an IMAX 3-D theater, playing fields, greenspace for picnics and concerts, and a River Promenade along the White River. The Indiana State Museum is slated to open in the park in grand new quarters in 2001.

The city's Central Canal was extended into the heart of the park recently. The extension is part of a $20-million project that also includes renovation of the Old Washington Street Bridge into a pedestrian crossing that links the Indianapolis Zoo and River Promenade with the rest of the park, and the creation of Celebration Plaza. The plaza's focal point is McCormick's Rock, which commemorates the founding of the city in 1822. At this point, there is a 17-foot waterfall just before the canal empties into the White River. Flood walls were reconstructed along the river, creating a small amphitheater with terraced seating built into the side of the hill. It is used for both public and private events.

The spiffy Circle Centre is another downtown innovation, an imaginative urban shopping complex blending new construction with eight restored facades from downtown buildings dating as far back as 1867. It brings to the heart of downtown a hundred specialty stores anchored by a Nordstrom's department store and a striking glass-walled Artsgarden that serves as a performance and exhibit space.

The city has come a long way, and like the Circle Centre, it has maintained much of its early architecture, as well. After being selected as state capital in 1820 because of its central location, Indianapolis was laid out by Alexander Ralston, an architect who had worked with Pierre L'Enfant on Washington, D.C. Ralston planned a mile-square grid with Monument Circle as a starting point for four diagonal spoke streets. The circle and its tall Soldiers and Sailors Monument remain the city's best-known feature, the reason Indianapolis is sometimes referred to as Circle City.

The stately Renaissance Revival statehouse was built in 1888 of Indiana limestone. Restoration has returned the stained-glass rotunda to its original beauty. The State Museum is housed in the building that was the original City Hall. The terra-cotta auditorium and Spanish facade of the Indiana Theater Building, a luxurious 1927 movie palace, have also been saved; the theater is now home to the Indiana Repertory Theatre.

If you check into a downtown hotel, you will be within walking distance of all of these sites. You can get your bearings at the Indianapolis City Center, the visitors-information center at the Pan American Plaza downtown.

Make your first stop at one of the Midwest's most unique museums, the Eiteljorg Museum of American Indians and Western Art. Built in 1989 in a style to evoke the spirit of the Southwest, the exhibits here highlight America's frontier experience. The collection originated with an Indianapolis businessman, Harrison Eiteljorg, who ventured west 45 years ago looking for coal deposits and fell in love with the land and its people.

In the Western galleries are works by Charles Russell, Frederic Remington, Georgia O'Keeffe, and other members of the original Taos, New Mexico, artists' colony. The Native American gallery shows off 10 regions of North America with items such as pottery, basketry, clothing, and kachina dolls. The museum's spring Indian Market is a great place to buy Indian crafts.

The museum is on the edge of the White River State Park, where the Indianapolis Zoo can continue your Southwestern experience with a trip to the Desert Biome, which re-creates the Arizona desert, complete with canyon and rocks, inhabited by birds, iguanas, and tortoises. An 80-foot transparent dome allows the animals to bask in natural sunlight year-round. On cloudy days, heated rocks and mats simulate the warmth of sunlight.

The rest of this modern, virtually cageless 64-acre zoo is arranged in other biomes, or habitats, that re-create the plains, forests, and waters of the world. An Encounters Biome highlights domestic animals and includes a goat yard where children can pet the animals. Animal demonstrations take place in the arena, and little ones can enjoy pony and camel rides here.

The World of Waters building is the state's largest aquarium, and its whale and dolphin pavilion is the zoo's most popular feature, especially during the daily dolphin shows.

Along the northern boundary of the zoo is the half-mile River Promenade, built of 1,271 huge blocks of local limestone. Along the path are 14 stone tablets with carved renderings of famous buildings constructed of Indiana limestone, such as New York's Empire State Building.

You'll need the car to visit more of the city's top attractions. The Children's Museum of Indianapolis can easily take up a day. This five-story wonderland was a pioneer when it opened in 1926, and is still a trendsetter, with features such as the SpaceQuest Planetarium, which turns the usual planetarium experience into a flight through space. This is a museum you can appreciate and enjoy even without kids.

Visitors to the welcome center are greeted by the largest water clock in the world, a 30-foot timepiece whose tubes and spirals delight everyone. The museum's 10 major galleries cover a wide range, and provide sections for preschoolers as well as for children ages 10 to 18, an audience forgotten in many children's museums.

Starting at the top, Level 5 could well be called Toyland. It offers 7,500 toys, dolls, and trains reflecting the past 150 years, plus a ride on an antique carousel. The science section is filled with entertaining hands-on lessons about change, motion, structure, and function.

"Mysteries of History" on Level 4 lets children learn about the past by visiting a reconstruction of a French trading post or a 19th-century Indiana log cabin, strolling a turn-of-the-century street, and using the computer to pick the supplies a pioneer family would need to cross the country.

Teens will be intrigued by a host of classes and programs specially designed for them, teaching everything from jewelry making to how to create their own videos. They also enjoy the Fantasy laser concerts held on Friday and Saturday nights in the museum's SpaceQuest Planetarium.

On Level 3, "Passport to the World" presents the cultures of nearly 75 countries via displays, videos, tapes, stories, and music. This area also includes part of the fabulous Caplan collection of 50,000 folk-art objects, including a delightful array of miniature costumed bands from different parts of the world. The Spurlock Gallery and the Johnson Weaver Pavilion on this level showcase special temporary exhibits.

Level 1 features "What If," a gallery where children can study fossils and participate in a mock archaeological dig, learn about mummification in a re-created mummy's tomb, and observe live sea creatures in a coral reef in a 500-gallon aquarium tank. The "All Aboard" gallery, a favorite with train enthusiasts, houses a 19th-century locomotive and historic miniature toy trains.

The museum's Ruth Lilly Theater offers live productions for children, and the IWERKS CineDome was Indiana's first large-format movie theater.

Another major family attraction awaits about 30 minutes from the city center at Conner Prairie, where you step back in time to a frontier village of 1836, sharing the lives of the first generation of settlers to the Midwest. In this living museum with 39 vintage buildings, you may attend a town meeting or a wedding celebration, or observe frontier methods of farming or food preparation. The authentically costumed "residents" have been carefully rehearsed to play characters who live in the town. They're happy to talk about their lives, share town gossip, and answer your questions about current events—but be sure "current" means 1836 or earlier or they will not know what you're talking about!

To join in the spirit of the past, visitors can stop at the Pioneer Adventure Area, where they are invited to try their hands at such skills as soap making, butter churning, candle dipping, or weaving.

Conner Prairie also includes a modern museum building, which has changing exhibits, an introductory film, an excellent shop, and a restaurant, as well as the restored William Conner home or the grounds built on this site in 1823 by fur trader, Indian scout, and Indiana statesman William Conner. Many special events take place on the 250-acre grounds.

Back in the city, the Indianapolis Museum of Art is among the 10 largest in the country and one of the oldest. Among the prize exhibits are the exceptional Eli Lilly Collection of Chinese art, the Eiteljorg Collection of African art, and the largest group of watercolors and drawings by British artist J. M. W. Turner found outside of Great Britain. This is also where you will find the famous *Love* sculpture by Robert Indiana. A recent bequest presented the museum with a unique treasure, a collection of 17 paintings and 84 prints by Paul Gauguin.

The museum setting, 152 magnificent acres including the former Eli Lilly estate, is as impressive as the art. Oldfields, the former Lilly mansion, is now the Lilly Pavilion of Decorative Arts, with landscaping by the noted Olmsted brothers. Besides four art pavilions, the grounds include gardens, a botanical garden, a greenhouse, nature trails, restaurants, and a theater.

The Indianapolis 500 weekend in late May packs the city, but if you don't want to fight the crowds, you can see qualifying races on the weekend preceding the big event. Practice days are also open to the public. According to race aficionados, the two or three days before the first day of qualifications are a good time to see the faster competitors working out to boost their speeds. Whenever you visit, you can see the Hall of Fame Museum at the Speedway. It is a small museum, but does display many previous race winners, and the kids get a chance to sit in a race car and take a bus ride around the famous track.

Sports, both professional and amateur, are a big part of Indianapolis. Depending on the season, you can also see two major-league teams in action, the Pacers basketball team at their new arena, Conseco Fieldhouse, and the Colts football team in the RCA Dome. The city's AAA baseball team, the Indians, are at home downtown at Victory Field in White River State Park. The Indianapolis Tennis Center hosts one of the top professional tournaments, the RCA Championships, each year in August.

If you want to participate in sports, stay at the University Place Hotel on the Indiana University–Purdue University at Indianapolis (IUPUI) campus. The hotel is connected by covered skywalk with the IUPUI Sport Complex. An inexpensive guest card gives free or reduced rates for use of facilities such as the Tennis Center; the Natatorium, a world-class swimming facility with three indoor pools; and the Track and Field stadium, an all-weather track that has hosted NCAA championships.

The Major Taylor Velodrome, the site of many national bicycle competitions, is also open to the public; bicycles and helmets are available for rent. And ice skating goes on year-round at the Indiana/World Ice Skating Academy downtown, which has two indoor rinks for hockey and figure skating. Olympic stars have trained here.

If shopping is your favorite sport, Circle Centre will certainly tempt, and even more unusual shops are found in Broad Ripple Village, about 20 minutes northeast of downtown, a charming neighborhood of eclectic boutiques, galleries, cafes, pubs, and nightlife. Many of the shops are housed in renovated clapboard houses.

By the time you're done, you may well be planning a second circle, having learned firsthand that Indianapolis is a winner every day of the year.

Area Code: 317

DRIVING DIRECTIONS Indianapolis can be reached via I-65 or I-70. From Chicago, take I-90 to I-65 south, about 182 miles. It is 283 miles from Detroit, 277 miles from Milwaukee.

ACCOMMODATIONS ***Within walking distance of downtown attractions:*** **Canterbury Hotel,** 123 South Illinois Street, 46225, 634-3000, elegantly restored small hotel, best in town, EE • **Omni Severin,** 40 West Jackson Place, 46225, 634-6664 or (800) 843-6664, top choice among larger hotels, prime location, indoor pool, M–E • **Crowne Plaza at Union Station,** 123 West Louisiana Street, 46206, 631-2221, part of old railroad station, suites in Pullman sleepers are fun, M–E • **Embassy Suites Downtown,** 110 West Washington Street, 46204, 236-1800, spacious quarters, small indoor pool, E–EE • **Hyatt Regency Indianapolis,** 1 South Capitol Avenue, 46204, 632-1234, indoor pool, E–EE • **Westin Indianapolis,** 50 South Capitol Avenue, 46204, 262-8100, indoor pool, EE • **Courtyard by Marriott Downtown,** 501 West Washington Street, 46204, 236-1800, pool, M • ***Other locations:*** **Doubletree-University Place Hotel,** 850 West Michigan Street, IUPUI campus, 46206, 269-9000 or (800) 627-2700, great for sports enthusiasts, E • **Boone Docks on the River,** 7159 Edgewater Place, Indianapolis 46240, 257-3671, quaint Tudor home, riverside deck, about 20 minutes from downtown, I, CP • **Frederick-Talbott Inn,** 13805 Allisonville Road, Fishers 46038, 578-3600 or (800) 566-BEDS, pleasant 11-room inn near Conner Prairie, M–E, CP. Check chamber of commerce for current list of in-town bed-and-breakfast homes.

DINING **The Restaurant at the Canterbury,** Canterbury Hotel (see above), elegant atmosphere, imaginative menu, M–EE • **Benvenuti,** 36 South Pennsylvania Street, 633-4915, sophisticated Northern Italian in elegant setting, E–EE • **The Majestic,** 47 South Pennsylvania Street, 636-5418, 1895 building, seafood and steak, M–EE • **St. Elmo Steak House,** 127 South Illinois Street, 635-0636, favorite for steak since 1902, building is on the National Register, M–EE • **Ruth's Chris Steak House,** Circle Centre, 45 West Maryland Street, 633-1313, reliable upscale chain, M–E • **Palomino Euro Bistro,** Circle Centre, 49 West Maryland Street, 974-0400, trendy pizza, wood-grilled seafood, rotisserie, current favorite, M • **Milano Inn,** 231 South College Avenue, 264-3585, long-established downtown favorite for traditional Italian, I–M • **Old Spaghetti Factory,** 210 South Meridian Street, 635-6325, budget standby in a picturesque old warehouse, I • **Shapiro's Delicatessen and Cafeteria,** 808 South Meridian Street, 631-4041, a local landmark for mile-high sandwiches, I • **Hollyhock Hill,** 8110 North College Avenue, 251-2294, longtime favorite for fried chicken, shrimp, steak served family style, M • ***In Broad Ripple area:*** **Renee's,** 839 Westfield Boulevard, 251-4142, French-American, informal, reasonable, I–M • **Aristocrat Pub,** 5212 North College Avenue, 283-7388, pasta specialties, I–M • **Henry Grattan Pub,** 745 Broad Ripple Avenue, 257-6030, traditional Irish pub, I • **Union Jack Pub,** 924 Broad Ripple Avenue, 257-4343, British-style pub, I–M • ***Best breakfast:*** **Le Peep,** 301 North Illinois Street, 237-3447, also good for lunch, I.

SIGHTSEEING **Children's Museum of Indianapolis,** 3000 North Meridian Street, 924-5431. Hours: March through Labor Day, daily 10 A.M. to 5 P.M., closed Monday rest of year. $$$; combination tickets with CineDome Theater, $$$$$ • **Indianapolis Museum of Art,** 1200 West 38th Street, 923-1331. Hours: Tuesday to Saturday 10 A.M. to 5 P.M., Thursday to 8:30 P.M.; Sunday noon to 5 P.M. Free, except fees for special exhibitions • **Eiteljorg Museum of American Indians and Western Art,** 500 West Washington Street, 636-9378. Hours: Tuesday to Saturday 10 A.M. to 5 P.M., Sunday noon to 5 P.M. June through August, also open Monday. Guided tour daily at 2 P.M. $$ • **Indianapolis Zoo,** 1200 West Washington Street, 630-2010. Hours: June through August, daily 9 A.M. to 5 P.M.; April, May, September, October, weekdays 9 A.M. to 4 P.M., Saturday, Sunday 9 A.M. to 5 P.M.; November through March, daily to 4 P.M. $$$$ • **Indianapolis Motor Speedway Hall of Fame Museum,** 4790 West 16th Street, 484-6747. Hours: Daily 9 A.M. to 5 P.M. $$ • **Conner Prairie,** 13400 Allisonville Road, Fishers, 776-6000. Hours: April to October, Tuesday to Saturday 9:30 A.M. to 5 P.M., Sunday 11 A.M. to 5 P.M.; November, Wednesday to Saturday 9:30 A.M. to 5 P.M., Sunday 11 A.M. to 5 P.M. $$$$

SPORTS Call for current hours and schedules. Professional events: **Indianapolis Motor Speedway,** information from Hall of Fame Museum listed above • **Indianapolis Raceway Park,** 10267 U.S. Highway 136, 291-4090, another major motor-racing venue • **Indiana Pacers,** Conseco Fieldhouse opens 1999, check Visitor Center for address and phone of new arena • **Indianapolis Colts,** RCA Dome, 297-7000 • **Indianapolis Indians,** 501 Maryland Street, 269-3545 • ***Sports facilities:*** **Indiana University Natatorium,** 901 West New York Street, 274-3518 • **Indiana University Track and Field Stadium,** 1001 West New York Street, 274-3518 • **Indiana/World Ice Skating Academy,** 201 South Capitol Avenue, Pan American Plaza, 237-5565 • **Indianapolis Tennis Center,** 755 University Boulevard, 278-2100 • **Major Taylor Velodrome,** 3649 Cold Spring Road, 327-8356.

INFORMATION **Indianapolis Convention and Visitors Association,** One RCA Dome, Suite 110, Indianapolis, IN 46225, 639-4773; www.indianapolis.org • **Visitors Center,** 201 South Capitol Avenue, Pan American Plaza, 237-5206 or (800) 468-INDY.

An Inventive Visit to Dearborn

Henry Ford was a man who admired innovation. Having changed the world with his own invention of the automobile, Ford was drawn to others who shared his genius for turning dreams into reality. In 1929, when he came up with the idea of relocating historic buildings at Greenfield Village and creating the Henry Ford Museum in Dearborn, Michigan, Ford was once again proving his own astuteness. His tributes to the creative mind are like no other places in America, and definitely succeed in his stated goal, "to show how far and fast we have come." With over a million visitors each year, these attractions dedicated to American ingenuity have become the most visited indoor/outdoor historical complex in North America.

Add the Automotive Hall of Fame, which opened in 1997 right next door, and the Spirit of Ford, an interactive auto exhibit created by the Ford Motor Company, due for a 1999 opening, and you have many good reasons to plan a visit to Dearborn.

Better plan a long weekend. The town dominated by Ford headquarters is also an ideal home base for seeing the mansions of the Fords and other auto barons, and to discover one of America's most interesting and beautiful art-education centers. While you are in the neighborhood, you can sample the cuisine and culture of America's largest Middle Eastern community, and take in some of the top museums and new attractions in nearby Detroit.

The best plan for seeing Ford's tribute to American know-how is with the two-day combination ticket, for it is difficult to do justice to both attractions in one day. The Henry Ford Museum houses 12 acres of exhibits spanning the eras from Colonial times to the present; the 81-acre Greenfield Village highlights some 80 historic structures that have been relocated from across America, places like Thomas Edison's workshop, brought from Menlo Park, New Jersey, and Orville and Wilbur Wright's bicycle shop, moved from Dayton, Ohio.

The complex was dedicated on October 21, 1929, the 50th anniversary of Thomas Edison's invention of the incandescent lamp. The museum was originally called the Edison Institute Museum as a tribute to Ford's hero and friend; the name was changed to honor Ford when he died in 1947.

It has been said that Henry Ford attempted to collect at least one example of everything ever made in America; in fact, some people referred to the early museum as "Mr. Ford's attic." Now the exhibits have been organized to explore the impact of various technologies on American life, but there are still an amazing number of things to see.

Audiovisual presentations, hands-on activities, and operating machines help to keep things interesting.

Among the highlights are "Made in America," an enormous display of American industrial achievement, from the world's oldest steam engine to the first industrial robot. "The Automobile in American Life" shows more than a hundred significant vehicles, including the only existing 1896 Duryea Motor Wagon (the first American-production vehicle), plus roadside landmarks such as a 1946 diner, a 1950s drive-in movie, and a 1960s-era drive-through McDonald's.

Henry Ford's first automobile, the 1896 Quadricycle, is displayed beside a Lunar Rover Vehicle built in the 1960s for exploration of the moon, proof of how far technology advanced in less than 100 years. "Henry's Story: The Making of an Innovator" details Ford's life, the trials and failures as well as the successes.

One of the newest exhibits, "The Story of a Champion: Locomobile's Old 16," highlights a car that was pivotal in American automobile history, winning the Vanderbilt Cup in 1908.

The Home Arts area includes historic kitchens, demonstrating how homemaking was drastically changed by electricity, running water, and a continuing stream of new products and materials.

Visitors are invited to try their own creativity at the Innovation Station, a hands-on encounter with problem solving.

At Greenfield Village, Ford has created a unique village landscape filled with some of the most important landmarks in American innovation, picked up and transplanted to this site. Besides Edison's laboratory and the shop where the Wright brothers worked on the first successful airplane, you can see the home of Henry J. Heinz, an innovator in food production and packaging, who produced his first vinegar, pickles, and other products in his own basement, and the home of Noah Webster, who compiled America's first dictionary. Ford's own birthplace and the garage where he tinkered with his invention are also here. The farm where automotive pioneer Harvey Firestone grew up is still a working farm, a "living history" re-creation of life on an 1880s farm in eastern Ohio.

In the Daggett House, built in Connecticut in the mid-1700s, staff members in period clothing re-create the activities of a resourceful rural household of the time, spinning their own wool, cooking at an open hearth, and tending the garden. Artisans also demonstrate such skills as glassblowing, blacksmithing, printing, cider pressing, and pottery making.

Some of the exhibits are just for fun. Visitors can still climb aboard the hand-carved wooden tigers and horses for a nostalgic ride on a 1913 carousel, or get a taste of river travel on the lagoon aboard the paddle steamboat *Suwanee,* a replica of one Thomas Edison rode during his winters in Florida. On a more modern note, the newest facility, an IMAX theater, is due to open in 1999.

Besides all of these attractions, special events are scheduled all year long, from garden tours to antiques shows to Civil War reenactments.

Next door, the sleek, modern Automotive Hall of Fame beckons. This is not a car museum, but another testament to innovation, inventiveness, and determination. The interactive displays feature not only Fords, but also cars from makers such as Benz, Chevrolet, Chrysler, Ford, Honda, and Mack, and the people who created them. Hall of Fame inductees are honored in a circular dedication gallery featuring a 65-foot mural by artist John Gable depicting nearly 100 landmarks in automotive history. A video theater and demonstrations add to the experience, and a "Personality Profile" in the lobby allows you to identify your own character traits so you can find the innovators in the museum you most resemble.

All of this will probably leave you curious to know more about one of the greatest automotive pioneers, Henry Ford. You'll see more of the personal side of this remarkable man at Fair Lane, the nearby estate on the Rouge River where Ford and his wife, Clara, entertained some of the most influential people in the world. The main floor of the 31,000-square-foot mansion includes a ballroom that can hold hundreds.

The tour begins with the six-level powerhouse, where Thomas Edison combined his know-how with Ford's to make Fair Lane self-sufficient in the production of power, heat, and light. From here, a walk through a 300-foot underground tunnel leads to the baronial mansion. On the lower floor is a one-lane bowling alley and a recreation room where the Fords hosted folk-dancing sessions. Upstairs, you can admire the eight different intricately designed fireplaces and reflect on some of Ford's philosophies carved into the wood, such as "Chop your own wood and it will warm you twice," and "Gather ye rosebuds while ye may."

A handsome space with a skylit vaulted ceiling that once soared over an actual swimming pool is now the Pool Restaurant, a delightful place for lunch. Soybeans and Poland Spring water, mainstays of Mr. Ford's diet, are always on the menu.

One of the family secrets shared by the guide is that Clara Ford, tired of the priceless but gloomy dark-wood paneling in her living room, decided to paint the room white while Henry was away. Imagine his face when he returned home.

The Fords apparently agreed on the importance of the grounds surrounding their home. The meadow landscape and river cascade designed by Jens Jensen are considered among the greatest examples of landscape art in America. You can still walk the terraced paths along the river where Ford once strolled with his friends, Thomas Edison and Harvey Firestone. Hike the paths in the area where Ford and his companion, naturalist John Burroughs, once stalked wildlife with binoculars and sketch pads, and discover the gardens and grottoes where Clara Ford guided hundreds of the nation's garden clubs when she was president of the Women's National Farm and Garden Association.

By most accounts, Henry Ford and his wife got along well, and Ford was reportedly fond of his grandchildren. He was nonetheless a stern taskmaster, said to have made life miserable for his only child, Edsel, who succeeded him as head of Ford Motors. Some speculate this abuse may have contributed to Edsel's untimely death at age 49 from cancer.

Edsel and his wife, Eleanor, chose not to remain in Dearborn, but in 1926 built their home some miles away on 90 acres along Lake St. Clair in Grosse Pointe Shores. Forty-three acres were later sold to provide a park for the community.

This is the most beautiful and gracious of the four "auto barons' mansions" open for touring. Built in the style of the Cotswolds in England, the 60-room sandstone residence by Albert Kahn has leaded-glass windows and a stone shingled roof imported from Great Britain. The magnificent naturalistic landscaping was another Jens Jensen design.

Inside are fine examples of 16th-, 17th-, and 18th-century English paneling and hand-plastered ceilings, each room displaying a different motif. A surprise amid all the period furnishings is one modern room known as the Art Deco room, designed by Walter Dorwin Teague, one of the country's top industrial designers. It was one of the first in the Detroit area done in this style, evidence of Edsel's appreciation of contemporary design. One of the upstairs bedrooms was also done in Art Deco style by Teague; it was occupied at various times by each of the Ford sons.

Edsel and Eleanor Ford loved the arts, and their house is filled with fine furnishings and paintings gathered from around the world. Original works by Cézanne, Matisse, and Diego Rivera remain, but much of their excellent art collection was given to the Detroit Institute of Arts and is represented here by specially commissioned reproductions. A lifelong supporter of the museum, Edsel Ford was responsible for the museum's most famous work, the impressive frescoes by Diego Rivera known as Detroit Industry.

Each of the other auto baron mansions is unique in its way. The most lavish of the four, Meadow Brook Hall, is an ornate Tudor-style 100-room showplace that cost a cool $4 million in 1926, when that was a vast sum, indeed. The huge house has 39 brick chimneys and 24 fireplaces. Automaker John Dodge began building the residence, but he did not live to occupy it. After Dodge's death, it was his widow, Matilda Dodge Wilson, who completed and furnished the home and subsequently lived there with her second husband, Alfred Wilson. Her furnishings, art treasures, and personal items remain. One of the unusual features on the grounds is Knole Cottage, a home built on two-thirds scale for 12-year-old Frances Dodge. It was the first all-electric home in the Detroit area.

Lawrence Fisher, the founder of the Fisher Body Company and Cadillac Motors, brought in 200 craftsmen from all over the world in

1927 to work on his showy Mediterranean-style mansion on the Detroit riverfront. It is a blend of Italian Renaissance and vintage Hollywood, with ornate stone and marble work, doors and arches carved from woods imported from India and Africa, rosewood parquet floors, and pure gold and silver leaf adorning the ceilings and moldings.

The house was purchased in 1975 by Alfred Brush Ford, a great-grandson of Henry Ford, and Elisabeth Reuther Dickmeyer, daughter of UAW president Walter Reuther. While still open for touring, part of the home now houses the Bhaktivedanta Cultural Center and Govinda's, a vegetarian restaurant.

Anyone interested in design will want to visit two other homes that have no connection with the auto industry. Eliel Saarinen, the noted Finnish architect, designed a modernist home for himself and his family while he was resident architect at the Cranbrook Academy of Art in Bloomfield Hills from 1925 to 1950. His wife, Loja, created carpets, curtains, and upholstery fabrics; his daughter, Pipsan, painted designs on doors; and his son, Eero, who would became a master architect himself, turned out master-bedroom furniture and tubular metal chairs for the studio. After careful restoration, the house was opened for public tours in 1994. It is now part of one of the Midwest's most interesting educational complexes—an undergraduate private school and a noted graduate school of art, design, and architecture.

The Cranbrook story began in 1904 when George Gough Booth, publisher of the Detroit *Evening News,* and Ellen Scripps Booth, daughter of the owner of the paper, purchased a neglected farm in the rolling countryside of Bloomfield Hills. The Booths were noted patrons of the arts-and-crafts movement and encouraged its full expression at Cranbrook, creating on its 325 acres a progressive school and a community dedicated to art and education. They named it Cranbrook after the village in Kent, England, from which George's grandfather had emigrated in 1844.

Noted architect Albert Kahn was commissioned to design a family home on 40 acres of the complex; it's now the community's administrative offices. The formal gardens and terraces were enhanced by sculptures, fountains, and features such as a Greek theater and a man-made lake with an Italian-style boathouse. Beautiful any time of year, it is glorious in spring when the "Gold Glade" blooms with thousands of daffodils, native Michigan wildflowers, masses of tulips, and blossoming redbud and dogwood trees.

Visitors can tour the Saarinen home, the gardens, and two museums on the magnificent Cranbrook campus, the Academy of Art and the recently expanded Institute of Science, whose spectacular entry is a three-story tower of specially coated glass prisms and lenses creating a natural light show. Cranbrook can easily fill a rewarding afternoon.

Other sights beckon, as well. On the way from Dearborn to Bloomfield Hills, you will drive through Royal Oak, which is becoming the liveliest of Detroit's outlying communities. A detour will take you to a lineup of funky and original shops on Main and Third Streets.

In the city, the Detroit Institute of Arts awaits with its many treasures, including the murals of the Rivera Court. Detroit's Motown Historical Museum is a priceless bit of nostalgia, housed in the modest wooden house where Michael Jackson, Diana Ross, Stevie Wonder, the Temptations, and other megastars got their starts, recording hit tunes from 1959 to 1972.

One of Detroit's newest prides is the Museum of African American History, the largest black historical and cultural museum in the world. The core exhibition covers more than 600 years of history.

More improvements are planned for Detroit, including new baseball and football stadiums, gambling casinos, and new hotels. The recently renovated Detroit Opera House is part of the renaissance of the city's Harmonie Park downtown neighborhood, where several new restaurants have opened.

Back in Dearborn, you are in America's largest Arab community. The first settlers came to work in the auto plants, and the neighborhoods continue to grow. Head over to West Warren Street between Schaefer and Miller to see the many markets and shops with signs in Arabic. If you stop at the New Yasmeen Bakery, at 13900 West Warren, three blocks west of Schaefer, you can lunch on a delicious spinach pie for under a dollar, and take home a big bag of freshly baked pita bread for an equally small tab. It's a tasty memento of the weekend.

Area Code: 313 (except where noted as 248)

DRIVING DIRECTIONS Dearborn can be reached via I-94; Oakwood Boulevard Exit 206A is closest to Greenfield Village. It is about 20 miles west of Detroit, 280 miles from Chicago.

ACCOMMODATIONS **Dearborn Inn,** a Marriott hotel, 20301 Oakwood Boulevard, 48124, 271-2700, built by Henry Ford in 1931, recently refurbished, garden grounds, pool, health club, M–E • **Ritz-Carlton Dearborn,** 300 Town Center Drive, Fairlane Plaza, 48126, 441-2000, elegant lodgings near the town's posh shopping center, indoor pool, health club, E • **Hampton Inn–Dearborn,** 20061 Michigan Avenue, 48124, 436-9600, indoor pool, M • **Holiday Inn–Fairlane/Dearborn,** 5801 Southfield Service Drive, 48228, 336-3340 or (800) 465-4329, indoor and outdoor pools, free shuttle to Greenfield Village and Fairlane Town Center, M • **Residence Inn by Marriott Dearborn,** 5777 Southfield Service Drive, 48228, 441-1700, all suites, fireplaces, kitchens, pool, E, CP • **Courtyard by Marriott–Dearborn,** 5200 Mercury Drive, 48126, 271-1400, indoor pool, I–M.

DINING **The Grill,** Ritz-Carlton Dearborn (see above), elegant, E–EE • **La Shish,** 12918 Michigan Avenue, Dearborn, 584-4477, the local favorite for Middle Eastern food, big and busy, I–M • **La Shish West,** 22039 Michigan Avenue, Dearborn, 562-7200, same as the above with fancier decor, I–M • **Talal's,** adjoining La Shish West, more elaborate menu plus seafood, M • **Eagle Tavern,** Greenfield Village, lunch and dinner served in 1831 stagecoach tavern, American menu, I • **Big Fish,** 700 Town Center Drive, Dearborn, 336-6350, popular seafood, piano bar, M–E • **Kiernan's Steak House,** 21931 Michigan Avenue, Dearborn, 565-4260, longtime local favorite for steak, M • **The Pool Restaurant,** Henry Ford Estate–Fair Lane, 4901 Evergreen, 593-5590, great spot for lunch Monday to Friday, I • ***Detroit picks:*** **Rattlesnake Club,** 300 Stroh River Place, 567-4400, creative menu from Detroit's best-known chef, Jimmy Schmidt, E • **Cyprus Taverna,** 579 Monroe Street, 961-1550, one of the best of the lineup in Detroit's popular Greek Town, I–M.

SIGHTSEEING **Greenfield Village and Henry Ford Museum,** 20900 Oakwood Boulevard, Dearborn, 271-1620. Hours: Daily 9 A.M. to 5 P.M. each, $$$$$. The best deal is the combination ticket, good for both properties for two days • **Automotive Hall of Fame,** 21400 Oakwood Boulevard, 240-4000. Hours: Memorial Day through October, daily 10 A.M. to 7 P.M.; rest of year, Tuesday to Sunday 10 A.M. to 5 P.M. $$$ • **Fair Lane,** the Henry Ford estate, 4901 Evergreen Road, Dearborn, 593-5590. Hours: April to December, tours Monday to Saturday hourly 10 A.M. to 3 P.M. except at noon, and Sunday on the half hour 1 P.M. to 4:30 P.M.; January to March, Monday to Friday only, daily tour at 1:30 P.M. $$$ • **Edsel and Eleanor Ford Home,** 1100 Lakeshore Road, Grosse Pointe Shores, 884-4222. Hours: Tours April through December, Tuesday to Saturday 10 A.M. to 4 P.M., Sunday noon to 4 P.M.; rest of year, Tuesday to Sunday 1 P.M. to 4 P.M. $$ • **Meadow Brook Hall,** Adams Road, Oakland University, 3 miles northeast of Pontiac, (248) 370-3140. Hours: Daily tours at 1:30 P.M.; additional tours available in July and August; phone for schedule. $$$ • **Fisher Mansion,** 383 Lenox, Detroit, 331-6740. Hours: Guided tours Friday, Saturday, Sunday 12:30 P.M., 2 P.M., 3:30 P.M., 6 P.M. Walk-in tours Monday to Friday 9 A.M. to 5 P.M. $$$ • **Cranbrook Educational Community,** 1221 North Woodward Avenue, Bloomfield Hills, (248) 645-3323. Includes **Cranbrook Art Museum,** Academy Way, 500 Lone Pine Road, (248) 645-3312. Hours: Wednesday to Saturday, 10 A.M. to 5 P.M., also Thursday to 9 P.M.; Sunday 1 P.M. to 5 P.M. $$ • **Cranbrook Institute of Science,** Academy Way, 500 Lone Pine Road, (248) 645-3000. Hours: Monday to Thursday noon to 5 P.M., Friday and Saturday 10 A.M. to 10 P.M., Sunday noon to 5 P.M. $$$ • **Cranbrook House and Gardens,** 380 Lone Pine Road, (248) 645-3149. Hours:

mid-June to late September, guided tours of house and garden, Thursday 11 A.M. and 1:15 P.M., Sunday 1:30 P.M. and 3 P.M. $$$ • Saarinen House, (248) 645-3323. House: May to October, tours Thursday, Saturday, and Sunday at 1:30 P.M., 2 P.M., 3 P.M., 3:30 P.M. $$ (fee includes admission to art museum) • **Detroit Institute of Arts,** 5200 Woodward Avenue, Detroit, 833-7900. Hours: Wednesday to Friday 11 A.M. to 4 P.M., Saturday and Sunday 11 A.M. to 5 P.M. $$ • **Motown Historical Museum,** 2648 West Grand Boulevard, Detroit, 875-2264. Hours: Tuesday to Saturday 10 A.M. to 5 P.M., Sunday and Monday noon to 5 P.M. $$$ • **Museum of African American History,** 315 East Warren Street, Detroit, 494-5800. Hours: Tuesday to Sunday, 9:30 A.M. to 5 P.M. $$.

INFORMATION **Metropolitan Detroit Convention and Visitors Bureau,** 211 West Fort Street, Suite 1000, Detroit, MI 48226, 202-1800, (800) DETROIT; www.visitdetroit.com

Looking for Utopia in New Harmony

New Harmony, Indiana, is a place that attracts dreamers. From 1814 to 1827, this village in the southwest corner of the state was the site of two quite different utopian living experiments, making it one of the unique settlements in the Midwest. Since 1960 it has been the center of a rather utopian restoration, one that has not only preserved buildings from the past but also has brought in some revolutionary new architecture.

Two other welcome additions are an exceptional inn and restaurant, which make it possible to explore the restored village and ponder the failures and successes of New Harmony's visionaries while living in modern comfort. There is an inviting real town, as well, where you can stroll an old-fashioned Main Street, poke around in antiques shops, or visit a weaving workshop.

June is a prime time for a visit. That's when New Harmony's unique tree, the golden raintree, bursts into peak bloom, turning the town into a vision of yellow blossoms. New Harmony celebrates the beauty with a festival each year in mid-June.

New Harmony's first settlers were immigrants from Germany, Lutheran Separatists who called themselves the Harmonie Society. They followed their leader, Father George Rapp, to the New World in search of freedom to practice their beliefs. After settling briefly in a place they called Harmony, Pennsylvania, in 1814 the group purchased

30,000 acres of heavily forested land on the Wabash River in the Indiana Territory. It was to be their home as they prepared a place for the second coming of Christ and the establishment of the kingdom of God on earth, events they believed were imminent. The entire community of 800 traveled down the Ohio River to their new home to await the millennium.

Within a year, a town, "a new harmonie," was created in the wilderness. Its citizens practiced communal living and celibacy. For 10 years the Harmonists prospered, building homes, mills, and churches and planting gardens and vineyards. They studied music, organized orchestras, and sang hymns. They designed state-of-the-art machinery and bought equipment from the industrious Shakers, who shared the Harmonist work ethic as well as their belief in a second coming of Christ.

The hardworking Harmonists brewed and sold highly regarded beer, manufactured cloth that rivaled the finest woolens from Scotland, and turned out 6,000 pounds of hemp rope every year. By 1824, New Harmony was selling more than a dozen products in 22 states and 10 countries. The incomes and cultural amenities of its residents rivaled those of large Eastern cities.

But for various reasons (perhaps because he thought life had become too easy), Father Rapp decided to take his flock back to Pennsylvania. Their prosperous village, vineyards, and fields were purchased by another utopian, Welsh-born industrialist Robert Owen, a social reformer who owned cotton mills in Scotland. Owen had been looking for a place in America to put into practice his own dream of communal living and a better life for the working class. His utopia would be based on social equality and education rather than religion.

With a partner, geologist and philanthropist William Maclure of Philadelphia, Owen brought a boatload of idealistic intellectuals, teachers, and scientists down the Ohio River into the Indiana wilderness in 1826. The new residents were thinkers rather than doers, and the town's economy began to flounder. Soon there were quarrels and the experiment in communal living failed.

Robert Owen went back to Scotland, but he left a valuable legacy. Many of the residents, including Owen's sons and daughter, stayed in New Harmony, and they made lasting contributions to the development of American science and education.

From 1830 to 1860 New Harmony bloomed as an intellectual center. Its residents helped revise the Indiana state constitution, published major scientific works, pioneered new methods of education, encouraged the founding of libraries, and worked for property rights for women.

The town became one of the most important training and research centers for the study of geology in America. David Dale Owen became chief geologist for the U.S. government and completed surveys of 12 states, helping to open the Midwest. Robert Dale Owen was elected to

Congress, where he sponsored legislation establishing the Smithsonian Institution. Both brothers were involved in the design and construction of the Smithsonian.

The character of the town changed after the Civil War, but descendants of Owen and Maclure worked to preserve its unique heritage. In the 1930s the state of Indiana began to reclaim some of the historic buildings. Things really got moving in the early 1940s when Jane Blaffer, a Texas oil heiress, married a young geologist, Kenneth Dale Owen, a great-great-grandson of Robert Owen. Owen took his bride to New Harmony, where she developed a dream of her own—a place where people would be spiritually, creatively, and intellectually nourished.

With funds from the Blaffer Trust, Indiana's Lilly Endowment, the state of Indiana, and other contributors, many old buildings have been rescued and new ones commissioned. In 1974, Historic New Harmony, Inc., was created to carry out a comprehensive plan of restoration. In 1985 it became a division of the University of Southern Indiana. The arts flourish in some of these restorations.

One former dormitory was returned to its 1888 appearance as Thrall's Opera House and became a performing-arts center once again. The New Harmony Theatre presents classic plays here and in the town's Murphy Auditorium.

Some of the modernistic new buildings are a startling contrast to the old. The first was Philip Johnson's roofless church, completed in 1960, a striking open-air pavilion with a Jacques Lipschitz sculpture, *The Descent of the Holy Spirit,* beneath a shingled dome. The church reflects the idea that only the sky is large enough to embrace all of worshiping humanity.

A contemporary ceramic studio was designed by architect Richard Meier in 1978, and the following year Meier's Atheneum was dedicated as a visitor center and learning center. The stark white curving structure, winner of several architectural awards, rises improbably at the corner of the town's historic district. A visit begins here with a 17-minute film and a look at a 7-by-14-foot model of New Harmony in 1824. Guided walking tours are conducted from the center by Historic New Harmony. They concentrate first on the Rappite structures, then move to the Owen period.

The tour includes the Eigner Cabin, furnished as an early Harmonist home, and other replica cabins. Salomon Wolf House, once a Harmonist residence, features an automated model presentation, "Panorama of New Harmony in 1824."

The David Lenz House, a typical Harmonist period home, has been restored and nicely furnished by the Colonial Dames of America. The garden includes dwarf fruit trees, a Harmonist specialty.

The intersection of Tavern and Brewer Streets is the only one where the houses on all four corners remain on their original sites. The Schoolle House, which housed the village shoemaker, has been remodeled and shows changing exhibits of regional art and history. The 1830 Owen House, a brick duplex, was built as a model dwelling for two families, possibly by two of Owen's sons. The George Keppler House, another Harmonist home, has exhibits on the life and work of geologist David Dale Owen.

Tours also visit the Fauntleroy House, a Harmonist dwelling that was bought and remodeled in 1840 by Robert Owen's daughter, Jane, and her husband, Robert Henry Fauntleroy.

New features are regularly added to the historic tours. Among these are the Maximilian-Bodmer Collection, which commemorates one of the most important explorations of the upper Missouri River region.

There are interesting sites off the tour, as well. One of the most intriguing is a restored maze of hedges near the site of the original Harmonist labyrinth, designed to symbolize the difficult journey to perfection.

Tillich Park is the burial place of German theologian Paul Johannes Tillich; stones in the park are engraved with selections from his writings. The Harmonist Cemetery off West Street holds 230 members of the Harmonie Society buried in unmarked graves, as well as woodland Native American mounds dating back to A.D. 800. New Harmony's Workingmen's Institute was built in 1838 by William Maclure as a library for craftsmen and mechanics. It's now the oldest continuously operating pubic library in the state.

The red-brick New Harmony Inn was constructed in the 1970s in the spirit of the early Harmonist architecture. Though furnishings are understated and almost spartan, the rooms are quite comfortable. Many have fireplaces and balconies overlooking the peaceful landscape and gardens. The inn offers a heated swimming pool, tennis courts, and a health spa with a sauna and Jacuzzi. The Red Geranium, the gracious restaurant adjoining the inn, has become widely known for its fine cuisine. For a change of pace, there is the less formal Bayou Grill, which serves all three meals. The Red Geranium Bookstore is the place to find good reading about New Harmony.

The present town of New Harmony, a pleasant, unpretentious village of about 1,000 residents, offers several antique shops, galleries, and gift shops on Main and Church Streets. The Antique Showrooms in the Mews, 531 Church Street, tempts browsers with nine shops.

If you want a change of pace, a 3,823-acre state park south of town on the Wabash River beckons with an Olympic-size pool and 110-foot water slide, plus six scenic hiking trails. It's a chance to wander down to the river and do some dreaming of your own.

Area Code: 812

DRIVING DIRECTIONS New Harmony is on the southwestern Indiana border at the intersection of State Highways 66 and 68, seven miles south of I-64. From Chicago, take I-57 south to I-64 east and follow State Highway 14 south, about 275 miles. It is about 165 miles from Indianapolis.

ACCOMMODATIONS **New Harmony Inn,** 506 North Street, P.O. Box 581, New Harmony 47631, 682-4491, M • **Raintree Inn,** 503 West Street, New Harmony 47631, 682-5625 or (888) 656-0123, fine 1899 home turned bed-and-breakfast, M, CP • **Harmonie State Park,** off State Highway 69, four miles south of New Harmony 47631, 682-4821, two-bedroom housekeeping cabins, I.

DINING **The Red Geranium,** 504 North Street, New Harmony, 682-4431, M–E • **Bayou Grill,** New Harmony Inn (see above), 682-4491, airy, modern surroundings, serves all three meals, dinner, M.

SIGHTSEEING **Historic New Harmony Visitors Center,** North and Arthur Streets, 682-4474. Hours: April through October, daily 9 A.M. to 5 P.M.; phone for winter hours. Walking tours daily April to October, weekends November, December, March. Two-hour tours, $$; three-hour tours, $$$ • **Harmonie State Park,** 682-4821. Hours: Daily 7 A.M. to 11 P.M. Parking fee, $$; Indiana cars, $ • **New Harmony Theatre,** c/o Murphy Auditorium, 419 Tavern Street, 682-3115. Four productions, mid-June through August. Check current offerings.

INFORMATION **New Harmony Business Associates,** P.O. Box 45, New Harmony, IN 47631, no phone • **Historic New Harmony,** P.O. Box 579, New Harmony, IN 47631, 682-4488.

Keeping Time in Rockford

The 139,000 citizens of Rockford, Illinois—the state's second-largest city—refuse to be overshadowed by Chicago. Rather than accept the label of "second city," Rockville proudly promotes itself as "Illinois' Number-One Family Destination." And the town backs up that claim with a host of first-rate attractions that visitors of all ages can enjoy—at rates that are a lot more reasonable than big-city prices.

Rockford's most unique enticement is the Time Museum, which has been featured in dozens of international publications and on NBC's *Today* show. One of the most impressive collections of timepieces in the world, the museum's 1,500 items span the development of timekeeping from the ancient to the atomic. It is a fascinating place for young and old—and only one of many good reasons to get acquainted with this agreeable small city along the Rock River, a place that is sometimes known as the Forest City because of its many tree-lined streets. You can step back to the turn of the century at Midway Village, stroll or ride a bicycle through lovely riverside gardens, take a ride on a riverboat or an old-fashioned trolley, cool off at a year-round skating rink or an action-packed water park, take a horseback or hay-wagon ride, or visit the Discovery Center, a wonderfully creative hands-on museum for kids. Nearby Rock Cut State Park adds even more recreation to the mix.

When Rockford was founded in 1834, it was called Midway because of its central location between Chicago and Galena. The name that prevailed came three years later, inspired by the shallow ford where the Chicago-Galena stagecoach used to cross the Rock River. Early settlers used the river's water power to build mills and manufacturing plants, and Rockford quickly grew into a major supplier of farm implements and furniture. It remains a manufacturing center, producing tools, hardware, and paints, among many other products.

Immigrants played an important part in Rockford's development, particularly the large population from Sweden, whose skills helped secure the city's reputation for furniture making. The Swedish community still accounts for some of the city's color and cuisine.

The recommended lodging in town is the Clock Tower Resort, since it includes the Time Museum and provides guests with unlimited free visits to take in its many treasures. This all came about because the timepieces are the personal collection of Seth Atwood, chairman of the Atwood Company, manufacturers of auto-body hardware. About the time his collection began to outgrow his home, Seth Atwood found himself the owner of a motel, due to a default on a loan. Reasoning that a resort and conference center would provide needed traffic, he decided to expand the facilities and include the museum, which opened in 1970 and was expanded in 1981.

A visit to the Time Museum begins with a 20-minute introductory video (which runs on the hour), then proceeds through galleries that trace the evolution of timekeeping, from early sundials and water clocks through the perfection of mechanical clocks and watches, and on to modern precision devices. Included is the most complicated astronomical clock in the world, a model built in Norway between 1958 and 1964 that shows not only time and astronomical and calendrical measures but also the motions of the planets and the procession of Earth's axis, a cycle of about 24,800 years.

Many of the pieces are beautiful to behold, both the decorative tall clocks and such smaller timepieces as a 20-inch English clock made in 1865 in the shape of the Royal Pavilion at Brighton. A whole section is devoted to American styles from the 18th to 20th centuries.

Most fascinating are the clocks that "perform." One of the earliest is a gilded German clock circa 1600 depicting Gambrinus, the legendary inventor of beer, in a large chariot pulled by animated elephants. A singing-bird clock dated 1834 contains a music box as well as eight birds who sing on the hour. There's even an enamel pocket watch hiding a small bird that springs up warbling from the back of the case.

Other memorable exhibits include a clock commissioned by Napoleon in 1810 that features two ships doing battle to the accompaniment of booming cannon and music from a 72-pipe organ hidden inside, and a magnificent German astronomical and automaton clock that stages a procession of disciples before Christ each day at noon.

The museum's gift shop has a terrific selection of books on clocks, watches, and astronomy.

Allow plenty of time for the Time Museum, and when you are ready to explore the rest of the city, be sure to pick up a map, since Rockford meanders on either side of the river. It's a short, easy drive from the Time Museum to another main attraction, Midway Village and Museum Center, a replica of a rural Illinois settlement of 100 years ago combined with an interesting complex of museums. Once again, there's an audiovisual presentation to give you an overview.

Most of the 20-plus buildings are authentic structures that were moved to this site and restored; these include a one-room school, fire station, bank, church, barbershop, law office, town hall, shops, and many Victorian homes. A water-powered machine shop and a 19th-century hospital and print shop have been re-created on the site. Costumed guides are on hand to take visitors on a tour.

The museum buildings on the site trace Rockford's history. Exhibits portray the city as a manufacturing center, tracking the history of 30 industries, with examples of early Rockford-made furniture and the city's contributions to the aviation and auto industries, including the Ceres, a three-wheeled vehicle designed by Seth Atwood.

Other exhibit areas include the Swedish Singer Gallery, featuring recordings of the Svea Soner Swedish Chorus; "The First Nations," depicting the Native Americans of northern Illinois; and "Play Ball," with memorabilia from the All American Girls' Baseball League and the Rockford Peaches, who were brought to life in the film *A League of Their Own.*

The Mill House, located on a lake, features a functioning water wheel. A delightful finale is a visit to the Old Dolls' House Museum, which has dozens of dollhouses depicting lifestyles and furnishings of countries around the world.

Midway Village sponsors many special events, from Wild West Days to a Scarecrow Festival. The best known is the annual summer Civil War Days reenactment, the largest such event in Illinois.

Riverfront Museum Park, in a space that once held only a Sears department store, is a highly recommended stop. It includes the Discovery Center, a children's museum, as well as the Rockford Art Museum, the Storefront Cinema (which shows independent and foreign films), and offices for the local dance company, symphony, and radio station.

The Discovery Center is a standout, a place as entertaining as it is educational. It isn't just the kids who will have fun here—everyone gets involved experimenting with electricity and magnetism (including a hair-raising experience with an electrostatic generator); working with pulleys, gears, and other simple machines; learning how the body works; walking through an infinity tunnel; standing inside a bubble; and matching wits with computers and puzzles. "Tot Spot" offers children five and under a ball ramp, telephones, electronic finger painting, and an irresistible waterworks exhibit. Outdoors is an imaginative Science Park, a two-story maze for climbing and crawling and learning about weather, water, caves, structures, bridges, and how sound travels down long tunnels.

The nearby Burpee Museum of Natural History is housed in two historic mansions, plus a new addition connected to the Riverfront Museum through a 4,000-square-foot tunnel. The museum features displays on fossils, dinosaurs, rocks, and minerals and the story of the Indians of the Rock River Valley told with a life-size wigwam and participatory exhibits.

You can learn something about the city's rich ethnic heritage by visiting two house museums. The Erlander Home, a showcase of Swedish decor, is located in Haight Village, a National Historic District that was once one of the largest Swedish centers in the Midwest. It is the setting for two traditional Swedish celebrations, Midsummer's Day in mid-June, when Swedish dancers perform in the street, and the Saint Lucia Fest in early December, the colorful beginning of the Swedish Christmas season. The Tinker Swiss Cottage, famed for its stunning walnut spiral staircase, is filled with fine art and furnishings.

When you've had your fill of museums, head for one of Rockford's loveliest areas, Riverview Park, and the Sinnissippi Park Gardens, known for colorful seasonal displays and 73 varieties of roses. Stroll the gardens, admire the floral clock, feed the swans on the lagoon, and visit the greenhouse and its aviary.

Riverview Park is also the place to board Trolley Car 36 for a 45-minute nostalgia ride beside the river, or to get out on the water aboard the riverboat *Forest City Queen.* If you are ready for some exercise, you can take the city's 5.05-mile paved Recreation Path, popular with walkers, bicyclers, and skaters, or visit the Riverview Ice House, where there is indoor skating year-round.

There's pleasant strolling also at the Klehm Arboretum, a project being developed by the North Illinois Botanical Society. The Trailside Centre Stables in Lockwood Park offers horseback or hay-wagon rides and a petting corral. The Guilford Tennis Center provides 14 lighted courts for some friendly family competition, or you might want to check what is happening at the Sportscore, a huge athletic facility with eight lighted baseball diamonds and eight soccer fields that often hosts major Midwest tournaments. Two miles of paved walking and bike paths also wind through the 105-acre site.

If the weather is warm, splash over to the Magic Waters Waterpark, where a big wave pool and all manner of water slides await. Or take a drive northeast of the city to Rock Cut State Park, where you can sail, boat, and fish on 162-acre Pierce Lake, or swim in a separate 50-acre lake. The park's 3,000 acres include 10 miles of hiking trails as well as playgrounds and picnic areas; it's a fine place for a final family outing.

Area Code: 815

DRIVING DIRECTIONS Rockford is reached via I-90, U.S. Highway 20 Business exit. It is 90 miles west of Chicago, 90 miles from Milwaukee, 70 miles from Madison.

ACCOMMODATIONS **Best Western Clock Tower Resort and Conference Center,** 7801 East State Street, 61108, 398-6000, 3 pools (1 indoor), tennis, exercise room, M–E • **Courtyard by Marriott,** 7676 East State Street, 61108, 397-6222, small indoor pool, M • **Fairfield Inn by Marriott,** 7712 Potawatomi Trail, 61107, 397-8000, pool, I • **Hampton Inn,** 615 Clark Drive, 61107, 229-0404, small indoor pool, M • **Victoria's Bed-and-Breakfast,** 201 North Sixth Street, 61107, 963-3232, handsome Victorian home, M–E, CP. Ask about family packages available at most Rockford lodgings.

DINING **Cliffbreakers,** 700 West Riverside Boulevard, 282-3033, on the cliffs above the Rock River, filled with rare antiques, special, M–E • **Cafe Patou,** 3029 Broadway East, 227-4100, country French, M–EE • **St. James Envoy,** Greater Rockford Airport, 965-5577, fine dining with airport view, M • **Bellamy's,** Clock Tower Resort (see above), fine dining, E–EE • **Giovanni's,** 610 North Bell School Road, 398-6411, steak and seafood, M–E • **Lucerne's Fondue and Spirits,** 845 North Church Street, 968-2665, fondue in a restored Victorian home, M • **Stockholm Inn,** Rockford Plaza, 397-3534, Swedish specialties including pancakes with lingonberries, I–M.

SIGHTSEEING **Time Museum,** Clock Tower Resort, 7801 East State Street, 398-6000. Hours: Tuesday to Sunday 10 A.M. to 5 P.M. $$; free to guests of the resort • **Midway Village and Museum Center,** 6799 Guilford Road, 397-9112. Hours: Memorial Day to Labor Day, Monday to Friday 10 A.M. to 5 P.M., Saturday and Sunday noon to 5 P.M.; April, May, September, October, Thursday to Sunday noon to 4 P.M.; special December hours. $$ • **Riverfront Museum Park,** 711 North Main Street, 962-0105. Hours: Tuesday to Saturday 11 A.M. to 5 P.M., Sunday 1 P.M. to 4 P.M., includes **Discovery Center and Out-**

door Science Park, $$; **Rockford Art Museum,** same hours as above, except open 10 A.M. to 5 P.M. on Saturday. Free • **Burpee Museum of Natural History,** 737 North Main Street, 965-3433. Hours: Tuesday to Saturday 10 A.M. to 5 P.M., Sunday noon to 5 P.M. $$ • **Erlander Home Museum,** 404 South Third Street, 963-5559. Hours: Sunday 2 P.M. to 4 P.M. $ • **Tinker Swiss Cottage Museum,** 411 Kent Street, 964-2424. Hours: Tours Tuesday to Sunday 1 P.M., 2 P.M., 3 P.M. $$ • **Riverview Park,** 324 North Madison Street, 963-7408; includes **Riverview Ice House,** 963-7408, indoor skating, rentals, seasonal hours, check for current hours and fees; ***Forest City Queen,*** 987-8893, riverboat rides June to late September, check current hours, $; **Trolley Car 36,** 987-8894, 45-minute excursion rides, June to late September, Tuesday, Thursday, Saturday, Sunday, on the hour noon to 5 P.M. $ • **Klehm Arboretum and Botanic Garden,** 2701 Clifton Avenue, 965-8146. Hours: Daily 9 A.M. to 4 P.M.; many varying programs; phone for current information • **Magic Waters Waterpark,** 7820 Cherryvale Boulevard North, 332-3260. Hours: Memorial Day to Labor Day, daily 10 A.M. to 6 P.M. $$$$$ • **Trailside Centre Stables,** 5209 Safford Road, 987-8809. Hours: April to October; check current schedules and rates • **Rock Cut State Park,** 7318 Harlem Road, Loves Park (10 miles northeast of Rockford), 885-3311. (I-90 north to North Riverside Boulevard exit, turn left on Riverside to Alpine Road, right on Alpine to Highway 173, right to park.) Hours: Summer, daily 6 A.M. to 10 P.M.; rest of year 8 A.M. to 5 P.M. Free • **Guilford Tennis Center,** 5702 Spring Creek Road, 987-8807. Hours: May to October; check for hours and rates • **Sportscore,** 100 Elmwood Road, 654-7452. Check for current activities.

INFORMATION Rockford Area Convention and Visitors Bureau, Memorial Hall, 211 North Main Street, Rockford, IL 61101, 963-8111 or (800) 521-9849.

Summer

Overleaf: A boat tour beneath the magnificent sandstone cliffs in the Wisconsin Dells. *Photo courtesy of the Wisconsin Dells Visitor & Convention Bureau.*

Meeting Mr. Wright in Spring Green

> *"I scanned the hills of the region where the rock came cropping out in strata to suggest buildings. How quiet and strong the rock-ledge masses looked with the dark red cedars and white birches, there, above the green slopes. They were all part of the countenance of southern Wisconsin. I wished to be part of my beloved southern Wisconsin, too."*
>
> —Frank Lloyd Wright, *My Autobiography*

Taliesin is Welsh for "shining brow," and the house bearing this name sits very much like a brow, wrapped on the edge of a great hill overlooking the river near Spring Green, Wisconsin. It is partially hidden among the trees, hard to discern as the tour van winds its way up, for the rooflines blend into the hillside as gracefully as the natural rock layers.

Frank Lloyd Wright's own home, and his most personal creation, Taliesin (pronounced "tally-*ess*-en"), was begun in 1911 and continually revised and rebuilt for nearly 48 years, until the architect's death at age 91. With its many levels following the contour of the land, the exterior design of Taliesin is part Japanese, part Tuscan hill town, part American Arts and Crafts movement, fused together into Wright's own distinctive signature. The interior reveals his genius for spatial drama. One architecture critic, Robert Campbell of the *Boston Globe,* called the house the "greatest single building in America."

Wright's home has been fully open to public tours only since 1993, so it is not as well known as some of his creations; the proceeds are being used for much-needed restoration. Funds are needed even more since a falling oak tree crushed the roof of Wright's office in one wing.

Beautifully embodying all the features that make Wright unique, it is a must for anyone who admires the work of America's greatest architect, a place that has been rightfully called his self-portrait.

A few miles south of Taliesin lies a more curious and far more publicized attraction. The House on the Rock is known for its Infinity Room, a slim 218-foot glass-walled structure projecting above the valley like a missile, and a dizzy wonderland of museums. This vast and almost inconceivable collection of collections covers almost everything, from suits of armor to carousels.

These two quite opposite main attractions bring many visitors to tiny Spring Green, a town also blessed with magnificent natural surroundings.

A restaurant that Frank Lloyd Wright designed overlooking the river in 1953 has been converted to a visitors center with a small cafe. It is the departure point for tours of Taliesin and other buildings on the 600-acre property. A guided tour is essential because the house complex is enormous—37,000 square feet.

Wright envisioned Taliesin as a self-sustaining community, a working farm with chicken coops and pigpens, housing for farm help, and a workshop where his many apprentices could live and study. It was to be his refuge after he abandoned his first wife, Catherine, and their six children and ran off with the wife of a client. The scandal ostracized him from society in Oak Park, Illinois, where he had started his career.

His retreat was the family farm, which had been settled by his mother's family in the 1850s, a place that he had loved as a boy and where, in 1901, he had designed the Hillside Home School, an experimental school run by two of his aunts. Across the valley is Tan-y-deri House, created for his sister in 1907. "I turned to the hill in the Valley as my Grandfather before had turned to America," he wrote, "as a hope and haven."

But like Wright's life, the house was to experience periods of great upheaval. Just three years after Taliesin was built, a disgruntled workman went berserk, burned the house, and killed Wright's companion and two of her children. Wright rebuilt the house then, and yet again following an electrical fire in 1924.

A sense of anticipation builds as you wind your way into a semi-hidden courtyard, step through a low, dim entry hall, and finally emerge into a soaring living space that is the most breathtaking interior this writer has ever seen. The room is a work of art made to live in, to sit and gaze at the view, to gather around the fireplace or the piano, to dine at the table, then perhaps step outside to the 40-foot tree-level "bird walk," a walkway designed for enjoying the commanding view.

Wright is unique among architects in that most of his greatest creations were homes rather than public monuments, and in these houses as much attention was given to function as to form. Like most of his buildings, Taliesin is built of natural materials, in this case native sandstone and cypress.

The same pattern is repeated throughout the house—low, narrow spaces build a sense of drama as they inevitably open to dazzling space and light. Every detail, every view, seems to have been carefully planned. Light filters in from unexpected angles, every room has built-in nooks for conversation, and the walls have built-in shelves to show off Wright's favorite pieces of Japanese art. From his massive desk, you can look one way to the living room, another to the valley, yet another way toward the garden.

Even after age 70, when he built Taliesin West and spent his winters in Arizona, Wright returned each spring, always changing and fine-tuning the home. "When I am away from it," he said, "like some rubber band stretched out but ready to snap back immediately the pull is relaxed . . . I get back to it happy to be there again."

Several tours are offered in addition to Taliesin. One of these takes in the Hillside Studio, with the magnificent timbered drafting room where Wright once worked with his apprentices and where his disciples still work and study. This is the school building that Wright designed for his aunts and where he first broke the mold of the boxlike rooms popular at the turn of the century. The two-story living room with walls that seem to vanish was astoundingly modern for a time when buildings were lit by gas lamps and students traveled on horseback. In the 1930s, the building became the center for the Taliesin Fellowship, a program that included not only study in architecture, but also in all the arts, as well as construction, farming, gardening, and cooking. Wright added the drafting room and converted other spaces into a theater, galleries, and dormitories still used by the Frank Lloyd Wright School of Architecture.

Adding greatly to a visit is the dramatic setting of the house. Taliesin overlooks the steeply carved Wyoming Valley and the Wisconsin River. It is part of Wisconsin's "Driftless Area," land protected by hills to the north from being flattened or filled by the "drift," accumulated rock and soil left by retreating glaciers.

The beauty that had attracted Frank Lloyd Wright drew another innovator, Alex Jordan, a sculptor who built his home in the 1940s atop a 60-foot column of rock, not far from Taliesen. Jordan was a showman, and his real showstopper is a 14th room added in 1985, known as the Infinity Room. Suspended 156 feet above the valley, it was constructed piece by piece, each section built inside the last and then extended outward and secured.

From the start people wanted to see the house, and Jordan began charging admission, using the proceeds to further his mania for collecting. Approached by a 375-foot ramp through the treetops, the house is filled to overflowing with Asian art, stained-glass lamps, bronze statuary, waterfalls, massive fireplaces, and a three-story bookcase filled with rare books.

But this is now just a small part of a 40-acre complex of buildings and gardens on the grounds surrounding the rock, all of it connected by walkways and dim tunnels. It takes at least two hours just to walk through all the amazing displays. The effect is so overwhelming that some visitors can't take it all in, and they turn back halfway through.

The Mill House, for example, holds hundreds of antique guns, dolls, mechanical banks, and paperweights. Streets of Yesterday re-creates a 19th-century brick street complete with a sheriff's office, carriage house, wood-carver's shop, and Grandma's House. The Armor Collection was made for Jordan by the staff of the Tower of London, and the Crown Jewel Collection has replicas of the Tower's jewels and the

Royal Tiara Collection. The organ room features three of the greatest theater-organ consoles ever built. The dollhouse building shows a collection of over 250 houses.

One of the most wonderful displays is Music of Yesterday, perhaps the world's greatest collection of automated music machines, most of them designed by Alex Jordan. Among the wonders are an entire mechanical symphony orchestra and a baroque music chamber whose mirrors and chandeliers are backdrop for the instruments. Bring plenty of coins; it's well worth investing in tokens to hear these ensembles in action.

Equally dazzling is the circus building, with the world's largest carousel, a million-piece miniature circus, and more mechanical musical wonders, like a circus band playing in concert with an 80-piece orchestra.

The year before his death in 1988, Jordan sold the House on the Rock to Arthur Donaldson, another fanatic collector and showman who has continued expanding the displays and collections. Under Donaldson, the complex gained the Heritage of the Sea Building, which features a 200-foot sea creature battling an enormous octopus. His Transportation Building, opened in 1995, has replicas of all kinds of vehicles from the past, from open stagecoaches to hearses, popcorn wagons to balloons, and trains to planes and cars.

When you've overdosed on sightseeing, you can relax amid the ancient sandstone bluffs and lakes at Governor Dodge State Park, a few miles south between Spring Green and Dodgeville. The park offers hiking and biking trails, boating, fishing, swimming, and picnicking.

At Tower Hill State Park in Spring Green, you can visit a relic of the past. The shot tower in the heart of the park is the last remnant of a settlement where lead was made. To make lead shot, molten lead was dropped from the tower to the level of the river below, where it was finished and loaded on boats. A film shows the process.

You can also detour north to the town of Plain to see how Wisconsin cheese is made at Cedar Grove Cheese Factory.

In Spring Green itself, Taliesin architects have left their mark all around, in structures like a round barn converted to a restaurant on State Highway 23, the bank on Jefferson Street, and St. John's Catholic Church on Daley Street.

One of the most interesting shops in town is the Jura Silverman Studio and Gallery at 143 West Washington Street, a showcase for some 125 talented Wisconsin artists in an early-1900s cheese warehouse. Not to be missed are Silverman's own handmade paper art works, from sculptures to gift cards.

Many local artists open their studios for tours and sales during the annual Fall Art Tour in mid-October. Another excellent time to see the work of local and national artists is the Spring Green Arts and Crafts Fair, held the last weekend in June, with more than 200 participants.

Lexington Station Shops is several stylish shops in one, with a variety of offerings, including Amish furniture, baskets, quilts, art, jewelry, country gifts, and all kinds of collectibles. The Spring Green Cafe and General Store on Albany Street offers both lunch and an interesting array of clothing, jewelry, and specialty foods, housed in another former cheese warehouse.

The happiest gift shop in town is part of the American Calliope Center on U.S. Highway 14, where priceless antique circus calliopes can be seen and heard. The collection, one of the best in the world, includes the largest air calliope ever built, the oldest 43-whistle calliope in the world, built in 1914. The gift shop offers everything from teddy bears to cookie jars to mechanical banks.

The favorite evening entertainment in Spring Green from mid-June through September is the American Players Theater, where Shakespeare and other classics are presented in a lovely hilltop outdoor amphitheater.

Adjacent to the theater is The Springs, a resort set amid the rocky bluffs and rolling hills, with Frank Lloyd Wright–inspired architecture, an indoor pool and spa, and a scenic Robert Trent Jones Sr. golf course. It's a relaxing refuge when sightseeing is done.

Area Code: 608

DRIVING DIRECTIONS Spring Green is at the intersection of U.S. Highway 14 and State Highway 23. From Chicago, take I-90 north to U.S. Highways 12/18, exit at Madison, follow the Madison Belt line to Highway 14 exit (La Crosse, Spring Green) at Middleton, and follow Highway 14 west to Spring Green, about 190 miles. Spring Green is 38 miles from Madison, 120 from Milwaukee, 250 from Minneapolis.

ACCOMMODATIONS The zip code for all of the following listings is 53588. **The Round Barn Lodge,** Highway 14, 588-2568, motel with interesting barn architecture, indoor pool, M • **The Prairie House Motel,** Highway 14, 588-2088, I • **The Springs Resort,** 857 Golf Course Road, 588-7000 or (800) 822-7774, all-suite full resort in sylvan setting, E • **Hill Street Bed-and-Breakfast,** 353 West Hill Street, Spring Green, 588-7751, modest in-town Victorian home, I–M, CP • *Farther afield:* **Deer Acres,** S11569 Highway 23 North, Spring Green, new timber frame home on 52 wooded acres, I, CP • **Silver Star,** 3852 Limmex Hill Road, Spring Green, 935-7297, log inn with artistic decor, way out in the country on 340 acres, M–E, CP.

DINING **The Springs Resort** (see above), most elegant setting around, M–E • **The Post House–Dutch Kitchen,** 127 East Jefferson Street, 588-2595, excellent food in the town's oldest building, outdoor garden and Flying Dutchman bar designed by Taliesin architect, I–M • **The Round Barn** (see above), fried chicken, ribs, salad bar, seafood buffet Friday, roast beef on Saturday, I–M • **Arthur's,** U.S. 14 at Highway 23 North, Spring Green, 588-2521, steak, seafood, salad bar, M–E • **Spring Green Cafe and General Store,** 137 South Albany, 588-7070, good stop for lunch, I.

SIGHTSEEING **Taliesin,** Highway 23, 3 miles south of Spring Green, 588-7900. Hours: **Frank Lloyd Wright Visitors Center,** May 1 to October 31, daily 8:30 A.M. to 5:30 P.M. Several tours are offered; check current hours for each: **Taliesin House Tours,** reservations required, $$$$$ (children under 12 discouraged); **Hillside Studio and Theater,** one-hour tours, $$$; **Walking Tour,** two-hour walk, $$$$$ • **House on the Rock,** 5754 Highway 23, south of Spring Green, 935-3639. Hours: Memorial Day to Labor Day 9 A.M. to 8 P.M.; mid-March through May, September, October daily 9 A.M. to 7 P. M., $$$$$; holiday season, early November to early January daily 10 A.M. to 6 P.M. last ticket sold 5 P.M. $$$$ • **American Players Theater,** Box 819, Spring Green, 588-2361, four classic plays; performances mid-June through September. Tuesday through Sunday. Check current schedules • **Governor Dodge State Park,** 4175 Highway 23, Dodgeville (about 15 miles south of Spring Green), 935-2315. Hours: Daily 8 A.M. to 11 P.M. in summer, shorter hours rest of year. Hiking, lake beach, boating, guided nature programs, horseback trails. Wisconsin residents, $$; nonresidents, $$$ • **Tower Hill State Park,** off County Road C, Spring Lake, 588-2591. Hiking, video on shot tower. Hours: Late April to October, daily 7:30 A.M. to dusk. Wisconsin residents, $$; nonresidents, $$$ • **Cedar Grove Cheese Factory,** Mill Road off County Road B, Plain (seven miles west of Spring Green), 546-5284. Hours: Tours Monday to Saturday 9 A.M., 10 A.M., and 11 A.M. Free.

INFORMATION Spring Green Area Chamber of Commerce, P.O. Box 3, Spring Green, WI 53588, 588-2042 or (800) 588-2042.

Reliving the Past in Nauvoo

When Joseph Smith Jr. led his Mormon followers to this scenic bend on the Illinois side of the Mississippi River in 1839, he called it Nauvoo, Old Hebrew for "beautiful place." The tiny hamlet has waxed and waned over the years, but the name still applies. Today's Nauvoo is one of the most interesting restorations in the Midwest, with a fascinating history to share with visitors.

Banished from Missouri, Joseph Smith and his flock, the Church of Jesus Christ of Latter-day Saints (LDS), had fled across the Mississippi to Illinois to find freedom to worship. They flourished during their early years in Nauvoo, a period when the town became the 10th-largest community in America. Then jealousy and religious bigotry reared their heads once again. Smith was killed, and in 1846, faced with forced expulsion, most of the Mormons left on a long march to safety in the West under the leadership of Brigham Young.

The ghost town of fine homes they left behind was soon occupied by another group seeking political asylum. Etienne Cabet was a Frenchman who dreamed of a utopian society that would bring peace, justice, and equality to its members. Forced to leave France, he and his followers came to the United States and learned of Nauvoo, purchasing Temple Square and homes around it from the Mormons and settling here in 1849.

Their communal colony survived only until 1856, but the Icarians, as they were called, made a lasting contribution to Nauvoo. Finding climate and soil similar to their native land, the Icarians began cultivating grapes and making wine, activities that continue in this area to the present day. Some of the original wine cellars were converted to caves for aging the town's best-known product, Nauvoo blue cheese.

Nauvoo presently has only 1,100 residents, so it's a bit of a surprise to find three visitors centers. One is a modest storefront run by the town; the others are under the auspices of two different factions of the Mormon Church. The family of Joseph Smith remained in Nauvoo when most of the residents fled, and Smith's son grew up to become head of a group known as the Reorganized Church of Jesus Christ of Latter-Day Saints. Both branches of the church maintain headquarters in Nauvoo to tell their own version of history and to show guests around. Visiting both paints an illuminating picture.

The most elaborate center by far is the grand red-brick building belonging to the LDS church headquartered in Utah. Inside is a scale model of Nauvoo as it was in 1846, and behind the building is a quiet park, the Monument to Women, a tribute to early Mormon pioneer women with 12 life-size figures expressing the varied roles women play in home and society.

Restoration of its Nauvoo roots has been a major church project, and over 20 of the town's old brick and clapboard homes and shops in the historic district have been restored and opened for tours; volunteer staffs at each building demonstrate crafts of the period. Included is the restored home of Brigham Young, and the jail in Carthage where Smith was killed.

Among the properties that can be visited in Nauvoo are the drugstore, tin shop, post office, and printing office, as well as a number of early homes. All are free, as are horse-drawn wagon rides leaving from the visitors center.

Volunteers make the various sites lively—you can watch a potter, barrel maker, and gunsmith in action—and many places yield souvenirs: candles from the candlemaker, bricks from the brickworks, cookies from the bakery.

Several lavish live musical entertainments are offered in the evening, including an outdoor musical production in early August called *City of Joseph.* The cast of 600 tells the story of Nauvoo—and a gentle message from the church is the only price of admission. So talented are these amateur performers, you might wonder whether a good singing voice is a prerequisite for church membership.

Other evening activities include "Sunset by the Mississippi," an evening campfire by the river with stories, songs, dancing, and fun for all ages. "Pioneer Pastimes" re-creates activities and games that the early pioneers enjoyed.

At the Joseph Smith Historic Center, a video tells the tale of those who stayed behind in Nauvoo, and also more about why the original settlers were forced to leave. The new city was a victim of its own success. Prosperity and a strong missionary effort brought large numbers of new members. In the spring of 1841, a grand temple of gray limestone, the House of the Lord, was begun on high ground overlooking the river. It was to be four stories high, the finest building in the West, with an estimated cost of $1 million.

Such visible signs of size and wealth made neighbors in Hancock County wary. When some opponents published a newspaper in 1844, the Nauvoo council feared it would promote anti-Mormon prejudice, and the press was destroyed. The publishers filed a complaint against Joseph Smith, his brother, and other members of the city council. When they went to Carthage, the county seat, for a hearing, the two Smith brothers were arrested and placed in jail. On the afternoon of June 27, 1844, a mob stormed the jail and killed both leaders. Afterward, the Nauvoo town charter was revoked by the state and its militia disbanded. Church members fled, most of them following Brigham Young to the Great Salt Lake valley in Utah. The unfinished temple was burned by an arsonist; several buildings and cellars in Nauvoo were later built of stone from the destroyed edifice.

Smith's mother was too old to undertake the trip, and his widow and children stayed with her. When Joseph Smith III grew up, he returned to Nauvoo to lead a remnant of the church and was ordained president in 1860. His Reorganized Church today has its headquarters in Independence, Missouri. Church leaders established the Joseph Smith center in 1918 to restore the Smith Homestead as well as the Mansion House that had served as a hotel for visitors to early Nauvoo. There is a guided tour of these properties and the restored 1841 general store where Joseph Smith had his office and council room.

When you've had enough history, you can take a break for a picnic at shady Nauvoo State Park and visit the Nauvoo Historic Society Rhineberger Museum, which has a room for each period in Nauvoo history: Native American, Mormon, Icarian, and pioneer. The park also includes grape vineyards, a tribute to the Icarians, who have their own small museum in town, as well.

Or perhaps you'd rather head for the Baxter Vineyards, the state's oldest, for a short tour on wine making and a tasting. You'll probably be convinced to buy a bottle to go with your Nauvoo blue cheese. The winery complex also includes Baxter's Village, with artists', crafts, and gift shops.

Nauvoo cheese can be found at many shops on Mulholland Street, the main street of the area known as Uptown, where you'll also find a few antique shops.

The Hotel Nauvoo is a restored 1840s Mormon residence with plain but comfortable guest rooms and a legendary buffet dinner. Come with a hearty appetite for all-you-can-eat fried chicken, roast turkey, roast beef, fish, plenty of vegetables and salads, and yummy desserts.

The other nearby eateries are basic—Nauvoo is not a town for frills. In addition to the hotel, there are a few bed-and-breakfast homes in town. Mississippi Memories south of town is the choice location—it's on a bluff with a fine lookout on the river.

Don't miss the drive of about 15 miles along the Great River Road south of Nauvoo to the Keokuk Bridge, with its view of high wooded bluffs on one side, wide blue water on the other. It is one of the loveliest, least spoiled sections along the Illinois side of the Mississippi River.

Cross the bridge into Keokuk, Iowa, to visit the Museum of River History in a historic steamboat and to observe the action at Lock and Dam No. 19, where you can watch the water being raised or lowered. An old swing-span bridge has been converted into a wood-planked observation deck, from which you can get a bird's-eye view of the river and the lock. The museum is to the left as you enter town, the lock and dam and observation deck to the right.

If you want nighttime excitement, your best bet is to drive north of Nauvoo about eight miles and across the river to the Catfish Bend Riverboat Casino in Fort Madison, Iowa. In town, evening choices are limited to LDS entertainment or a good book—perhaps a saga about the dreams and intrigues, passions, and murder that once took place in tiny, peaceful Nauvoo.

Area Code: 217

DRIVING DIRECTIONS Nauvoo is on State Highway 96, the Great River Road. It is 245 miles from Chicago, 125 miles from Springfield, 185 miles from St. Louis.

ACCOMMODATIONS **Hotel Nauvoo,** 1290 Mulholland Street, Nauvoo 62354, 453-2211, I • **Mississippi Memories Bed-and-Breakfast,** Highway 96, Box 291, Riverview Heights, Nauvoo 62354, 453-2771, river views, I–M, CP • **Ancient Pines Bed-and-Breakfast,** 2015 Parley Street, Nauvoo 62354, 453-2767, modest, homey, shared baths, I, CP • **Motel Nauvoo,** 1610 Mulholland Street (Highway 96), Nauvoo 62354, 453-2219, I • **Nauvoo Family Motel,** 1875 Mulholland Street (Highway 96), Nauvoo 62354, (800) 416-4470, indoor pool, I.

DINING **Hotel Nauvoo** (see above), bountiful buffet, I–M • **Grandpa John's Cafe,** 1255 Mulholland Street, 453-2211, 1840 structure, lunch only, I • **Dottie's Red Front,** 1305 Mulholland Street, 453-2284, all three meals, tavern with billiards, I.

SIGHTSEEING **LDS Visitor Center,** Main and Young Streets, 453-2237 or (800) 453-0022, movies, entertainment, maps. Hours: Memorial Day to Labor Day, daily 9 A.M. to 9 P.M.; rest of year to 5 P.M. Free. *City of Joseph* performances, one week, late July and early August; check current dates. Free • **Joseph Smith Historic Center,** Water Street, 453-2246. Hours: Daily 9 A.M. to 5 P.M. Free • **Nauvoo Historic Society Museum,** Nauvoo State Park, 453-6648. Hours: May to mid-October, daily 1 P.M. to 5 P.M. Free • **Catfish Bend Riverboat Casino,** Riverview Park, Fort Madison, IA, (319) 372-1000. May through October, 24-hour action. Free parking and boarding.

INFORMATION **Nauvoo Tourism,** P.O. Box 41, Nauvoo, IL 62354, 453-6648.

Clowning Around in Baraboo

The smiles begin as soon as you leave your car and hear the music of the calliope. It is the siren song of the circus beckoning, causing you to dance along a little faster in anticipation of the show that has never ceased to delight "ladies and gentlemen and children of all ages."

The Circus World Museum, the largest circus museum in the world, is located along the banks of the Baraboo River, the site of the original winter quarters for the Ringling Brothers Circus for 34 years. Under the auspices of the State Historical Society of Wisconsin, the museum brings to life the history of the circus with showmanship that the Ringlings would surely applaud.

To make things all the merrier, recognizing that museums are no substitute for the real thing, the museum stages its own one-ring circus two or three times daily under a little "big top," and offers nonstop entertainment in other venues around the park. Events include demonstrations of train loading and making up the clowns, circus music, clown shows, and guided tours through the world's greatest collection of colossal, colorful antique circus parade wagons, some of which appear in the circus parade staged each day at 1 P.M.

With cotton candy, pony and elephant rides, and even a miniature circus (where you can push buttons to see the high-wire walker practice, and help the animal trainers with their tasks), it's hard to imagine a better family outing.

What's more, Baraboo is located near some of Wisconsin's best scenery at Devil's Lake State Park and is within an easy ride of the restored steam trains of the Mid-Continent Railway in North Freedom. This seven-mile, 50-minute nostalgia trip into the Baraboo River Valley takes you past cornfields and silos and forests to Quartzite Lake.

The Ringling brothers went from rags to riches in Baraboo, and put their hometown on the map while they were at it. It was 1884 when Al, Charles, Alf T., Otto, and John Ringling published an item in the *Baraboo Republic* heralding the organization of the circus that would become "the greatest show on earth." With an investment of under $1,000, the Ringlings made their own tent poles, bleacher seats, and costumes. They staged their first show in Baraboo on May 19 of that year, with 23 performers, including themselves.

The circus began to travel in wagons pulled by horses rented from local farmers. At the end of the season each year until 1918, they returned home to Baraboo to prepare for the next season. Only after the circus merged with Barnum and Bailey and outgrew its quarters did they move on.

As soon as you step onto the grounds, you are immersed in the world of the circus. The first building you come to is the Irvin Feld Exhibit Hall and Visitor Center, filled with old posters and paraphernalia, exhibits on the five Ringlings, and reminiscences of the old days when humans were shot from cannons and teams of acrobats somersaulted over elephants. Among the displays are the rhinestone tuxedo and wedding dress worn by Mr. and Mrs. Michu, 33-inch midgets, who went through a mock wedding ceremony twice daily.

Step into the old Elephant House to see souvenirs of the Wild West shows, a Buffalo Bill statue, a tepee, and a stagecoach among them. Don't miss the daily Elephant Encounter, where you can learn fun facts about elephants and the caring relationship between these intelligent animals and their owners and handlers.

If weather permits, the encounter is followed by the Elephant Splash-Around, as they frolic in the normally tranquil Baraboo River.

Two popular features are the Kids' Clown Show, where children (and their adult friends) can learn a circus skill or two, and the Circus Music Demonstration, featuring rare musical instruments once used at the circus.

At the sideshow exhibit, you can see replicas of the attractions that Ringling made famous at the turn of the century: the Snake Lady; the Fat Lady; Jo Jo, the Dog-Faced Boy; Chang and Eng, the Siamese twins; and Gargantua, the world's most terrifying creature, housed in a 26-foot wagon.

The most spectacular displays at Circus World are the dozens of circus wagons, a dazzling array of color and glitter. There are English models dating from 1864, a giant Mother Goose, and a Wild West Wagon big enough to hold an 18-piece band. At the C. P. Fox Wagon Restoration Center you can watch the intricate process of restoring the old wagons.

The wagons leave Baraboo once a year for a journey to Milwaukee and the Great Circus Parade, one of the nation's most colorful events (see pages 107–108).

But there's plenty of excitement right here when you take your seat in the tent and the ringmaster signals the start of a small and quite wonderful parade around the big top. A miniwagon pulled by tiny horses, along with clowns, camels and elephants, and hoop twirlers, absolutely delights the audience. Some of the performers are pros, others are young and they may not be quite ready for the big time, but by the time the trapeze artists and bareback riders have thrilled, the acrobats have turned impossible somersaults, and the clowns have proven themselves to be among the most talented acrobats of all, everyone in the audience is ready to heed the invitation of the music to "Join the Circus."

If you want a break, you can board a trolley for a tour of downtown Baraboo, population 10,000, and check out the town square and the houses once owned by the Ringling family.

Baraboo's other main attraction may seem tame after the circus, but it is interesting nonetheless. The International Crane Foundation is dedicated to protecting the graceful crane and its wetland homes all around the globe. You can begin by viewing a film about the tallest flying birds in the world, and then go outside to see more kinds of cranes than you probably knew existed. There are 15 varieties, including wattled, black-necked, hooded, whitehead, bonny gill, Siberian, demoiselle, red-crowned, and Eurasian, along with the sandhill, the only crane found in Wisconsin. A separate exhibit is devoted to the rare whooping crane, North America's largest bird. The foundation has 29 members of this once-endangered species, and uses them for research and for breeding.

June is the big hatching month, when you may find chicks in the breeder or see a mother feeding, exercising, and protecting her chicks. Over the summer, the chicks progress from their first steps to flights over the Chick Yard fence. In the Schroeder Exhibit Room you can learn about crane development and about how quickly they grow up—they gain 10 percent of their body weight each day. You can see how you measure up against a six-foot sarus crane or try your hand at feeding a crane chick.

The grounds of the foundation offer walking trails through a variety of terrains, over a restored prairie filled with flowers, around a wetland, and through groves of oak and cherry trees. All are designed to inspire visitors to help save these natural habitats.

The area's most magnificent hiking areas are to the south. Follow Highway 123 south (or U.S. Highway 12 south to Highway 159 and east onto Highway 123) into Devil's Lake State Park, where the blue waters of the spring-fed lake are surrounded by sheer ancient bluffs of quartzite as high as 500 feet. Sandy beaches at either end of the lake attract swimmers.

Climb the West Bluff to find the Great Stone Face that gazes down on the valley. If you want to know how the glacier formed this fabulous scene, take in one of the naturalist talks.

One of the most beautiful walks nearby is in Parfrey's Glen, a quarter-mile-long rocky gorge four miles due east of Devil's Lake on County Road DL. Follow the cool stone walls to the end and you'll find a waterfall.

Not far away, hidden off a narrow country road, is the low-key Devil's Head Resort, where the rooms are motel-style but the grounds and 18-hole golf course are lovely. The resort offers indoor and outdoor pools, tennis, and a ski hill in winter.

Another recommended lodging three miles east of Baraboo is Pinehaven, a small, modern, air-conditioned bed-and-breakfast retreat on 80 acres, with shady decks and a small swimmable lake with rowboats and paddleboats available. Visit the farm across the highway if you want to go on a wagon ride pulled by a team of sturdy Belgian draft horses.

There are a few modest bed-and-breakfast inns in town, and a scattering of shops for browsing around the old Courthouse Square. Many of the motels are a few miles north of town, near the Ho Chunk Casino on U.S. Highway 12. And Wisconsin Dells, with its lineup of water slides, wax museums, and go-cart tracks, is just 17 miles up the road (see pages 170–174).

<u>Area Code: 608</u>

DRIVING DIRECTIONS Baraboo can be reached via I-90/I-94 (exit State Highway 33 west) or via U.S. Highway 12. It is about 175 miles from Chicago, 100 miles from Milwaukee.

ACCOMMODATIONS **Devil's Head Resort,** S6330 Bluff Road, Merrimac 53561 (near Devil's Lake), 493-2251 or (800) DEVILSX, motel-style rooms, resort facilities, lovely setting, M • **Pinehaven,** 13083 Highway 33, Baraboo 53913, 356-3489, 80-acre bed-and-breakfast retreat on a pond, M, CP • **Quality Inn,** U.S. 12, Baraboo 53913, 356-6422 or (800) 355-6422, indoor pool, M–E • **Best Western Baraboo Inn,** 725 West Pine Street (U.S. 12), Baraboo 53913, 356-1100, I–M • **Baraboo's Gollmar Guest House,** 422 Third Street, Baraboo 53913, 356-9432, modest in-town bed-and-breakfast home, M, CP.

DINING **Sandhill Inn,** 170 Main Street, Merrimac (south of Devil's Lake), 493-2203, excellent creative menu, Victorian home setting, M–EE • **Little Village Cafe,** 146 Fourth Street, Baraboo, 356-2800, in-town cafe with above-average cuisine, I–M • **The Farm Kitchen,** S5718 Highway 123, Baraboo (at the entrance to Devil's Lake State Park), 356-5246, basic American fare, I–M

SIGHTSEEING **Circus World Museum,** 426 Water Street (State Highway 113), Baraboo, 356-8341. Hours: Early May to early September, daily 9 A.M. to 6 P.M., circus performances at 11 A.M. and 3 P.M.; late July to mid-August, open to 9 P.M., additional circus performance at 7:30 P.M. $$$$$ • **International Crane Foundation,** E11376 Shady Lane Road (off U.S. 12 north of Baraboo), Baraboo, 356-9462. Hours: May 1 to October 31, 9 A.M. to 5 P.M. Flight demonstrations, 11:45 A.M.; guided tours 10 A.M., 1 P.M., and 3 P.M. $$$ • **Mid-Continent Railway,** County Road PF (off State Highway 136), North Freedom, 522-4261. Museum hours: Daily 9:30 A.M. to 5 P.M. Free. Train departures: late May to Labor Day through August, daily 10:30 A.M., 12:30 P.M., 2 P.M., and 3:30 P.M.; early May, September to mid-October, weekends only. $$$$ • **Devil's Lake State Park,** S5975 Park Road (off Highway 123), Baraboo, 356-8301. Hours: Daily 6 A.M. to 11 P.M. Wisconsin residents, $$; nonresidents, $$$.

INFORMATION **Baraboo Area Chamber of Commerce,** 124 Second Street, Baraboo, WI 53913, 356-8333 or (800) BARABOO.

A Sunny Forecast in Grand Haven

Sometimes all it takes for a great summer weekend is a great beach—and they don't come much better than the long, wide, dazzling white stretch of sand in Grand Haven, Michigan.

Most of the year Grand Haven is a fine example of small-town America, with a well-tended main street, neat lawns and houses, and lots of local festivals. There's a scenic bonus with the pretty Grand River running through town to join Lake Michigan. A riverside boardwalk makes for pleasant strolls.

But come warm weather, all eyes and bodies turn to the beach. Basking in the sun and kite-flying vie for favorite sport, and the annual sand-sculpture contest and beach-volleyball competitions held the last weekend in June are major events. The sand sculptures are truly something to behold, representing everything from fantasy castles to banana splits.

This lively beach lover's mecca has other major assets, as well. You can take a scenic walk from downtown along the two-and-a-half-mile boardwalk. Nicely landscaped, the boardwalk (which is actually cement) offers pleasant places to sit and watch the action on the water, where you can see everything from freighters to sailboats to million-dollar yachts.

At its end, the boardwalk connects to Grand Haven's landmark South Pier, which extends well out into Lake Michigan. The pier is popular with perch fishermen as well as strollers. At the end of it is one of Michigan's classic lighthouses, painted a memorable bright red.

Kids especially seem to love the drama of walking right out over the lake on the pier. And it's guaranteed they'll enjoy the nightly entertainment on the waterfront even if some of the grown-ups find it hokey. When it gets dark (around 9:30 P.M. in summer), crowds gather at a viewing stand by the boardwalk for Grand Haven's claim to fame, the world's largest musical fountain, located on Dewey Hill across the river. Each night the fountain spouts as high as 125 feet in synchronized precision patterns, all framed in a rainbow of colored lights. The recorded music changes nightly, from popular tunes to Broadway favorites to rock (Tuesday) to hymns (Sunday).

You'll also find big-band dancing and country line dancing on the waterfront on selected summer evenings, and a bang-up Fourth of July fireworks display.

Also sure to please young visitors is the Imagination Station, 10,000 square feet of playground fun designed by the children of the town in Mulligan's Hollow, a park on Harbor Drive behind the local YMCA.

Grand Haven State Park, offering one of Michigan's most popular beaches, is next to the pier. You won't find solitude here, but you will find fun, especially if they happen to be demonstrating stunt kites from the local Mackinaw Kite Company. The official Great Lakes Stunt Kite Competition takes place in May. The park offers a food stand and playground. You'll save if you choose lodging close enough to walk into the park; walk-ins are free but they charge drivers the usual state-park parking fee. If you are early, you may be able to snag one of the few parking spots on the street.

The long expanse of sand continues south to City Beach, where parking is free. Geologists have called this pure white sand singing sand, because you can hear a kind of whistle when you walk on it.

If you want to get away from the crowds, North Beach on the far side of the river is less populated. Better yet, drive seven miles north to Hoffmaster State Park, where a fabulous beach runs for two and a half miles with splendid dunes as a backdrop. Most beachgoers cluster near the concession stand and bathhouse; walk a little farther and you can have a patch of sand all to yourself.

The park's excellent Gillette Nature Center provides one of the best views of Lake Michigan's dunes and tells the story of how they were formed with such vivid displays as an interactive Spinning Cube. There's also an informative slide show about the dunes. On rainy days, the hands-on classroom at the center is a lifesaver for families.

Outdoors, a boardwalk and 200-step dune stairway lead through dense maples and a beech forest and to a spectacular 180-foot overlook. On the walk you'll see clearly how the terrain varies from Sahara-like sands on the west to virtual jungles on the eastern slopes, where winds from the lake drop their moisture as they hit land.

Back in Grand Haven, there's plenty to do when you've had enough sunbathing. This is great bicycling terrain, with paths circling Spring Lake, running beside the Grand River, and paralleling the Lake Michigan shoreline from Grand Haven all the way to Holland. Bike rentals are available and you can pick up route maps at the visitors bureau. For the less energetic, half-hour Harbor Trolley rides provide colorful tours of the area.

You can spend time on the lake as well as along its shores. Grand Haven prospered in its early days as a shipping port when the many nearby mills provided lumber for early settlers. These days the harbor is better known as a sport-fishing center and home of one of the lake's largest salmon-fishing charter fleets. The season runs from spring through late fall. Charter operators at Chinook Pier, two blocks north of Washington Street, will supply license, equipment, and lunch, and they'll clean and ice your catch when you're back on land.

Local sailing and boating charters and one-and-a-half-hour harbor and river tours aboard a riverboat, the *Harbor Steamer,* are other ways to go to sea.

Golfers will be happy to know that Grand Haven Golf Club's course, nestled among the dunes and the pines, has been named one of America's 75 best public courses by *Golf Digest.*

As for shopping, you'll find some tempting stops along Washington Street, the town's main street. The Michigan Rag Company (121 Washington) hand-prints its own cotton beach and boating wear with colorful designs, including Michigan lighthouses; you can often see the printers in action. You might recognize the designs, since they are found in many fine shops throughout the country. The seconds for sale here are excellent buys.

The selection at the Mackinaw Kite Company (106 Washington) is hard to beat and Whims & Wishes (216 Washington) has a fine selection of crystal, silver, linens, unusual gifts, and antiques. The Bookman (715 Washington) has both new and used books, and above it, The Gallery Upstairs is a cooperative showing the work of 30 regional artists.

More touristy shopping is found along the waterfront. Harbourfront Place is a century-old piano factory renovated into a shopping/dining complex, and Chinook Pier has a lineup of shops selling fudge, T-shirts, swimwear, hammocks, and other beachy things. On Wednesday and Saturday mornings, the nearby farmers market offers garden-fresh produce, flowers, and a few crafts.

The miniature golf course at the pier is a popular family spot. Craig's Cruisers on U.S. Highway 31 provides more family amusements, including minigolf, batting cages, and bumper boats.

You might also want to step into the old train station, which has been converted into the Tri-Cities Historical Museum.

If you love inns, Grand Haven is your kind of place. The Harbor House Inn, a new property built to look old, has a perfect location, within walking distance of town shops and the beach. The Boyden House, a grand 1874 Victorian, is furnished with lots of antiques and interesting handmade furnishings. Seascape is a cottage on Lake Michigan with a private beach.

While rooms are modest at the Looking Glass Inn, they put you directly above the beach in the midst of the most picturesque section of Grand Harbor; there are wonderful views from the porch. A century-old colony of cottages in the steep, heavily wooded dunes above the lake, Highland Park, has long been a summer vacation retreat for wealthy families who come from as far away as St. Louis. Most of the quaint cottages have been in the same family for years, and when they do go on the market, they fetch high prices. Some of the homes can only be reached via the boardwalk that rambles up and down the hill. Wherever you stay in Grand Haven, this picturesque, shady walk should not be missed.

Area Code: 616

DRIVING DIRECTIONS Grand Haven is off U.S. Highway 31, 35 miles west of Grand Rapids. From Chicago, take I-80/90 west to U.S. 31 north, 165 miles. It is 157 miles from Detroit, 250 miles from Indianapolis.

ACCOMMODATIONS **Harbor House Inn,** 114 South Harbor, Grand Haven 49417, 846-0610 or (800) 841-0616, luxury hotel/inn with fireplaces, balconies, whirlpools, convenient, lake views but busy location, M–E, CP • **Boyden House,** 31 South Fifth Street, Grand Haven 49417, 846-3538, grand Victorian, personal decor, painted screens, handmade furniture, M, CP • **Looking Glass Inn,** 1100 South Harbor Avenue, Grand Haven 49417, 842-7150 or (800) 951-6427, modest rooms, unbeatable location overlooking the lake, M, CP • ***Outside town:*** **Lakeshore Bed-and-Breakfast,** 1100 Lakeshore Drive, Grand Haven Township, 49460, 844-2697 or (800) 342-6736, directly on the beach, Jacuzzis, fireplaces, E–EE, CP • **Seascape,** 20009 Breton Street, Spring Lake, 49456, 842-8409, on the lake with small private beach, M–E, CP • **Village Park Bed-and-Breakfast,** 60 West Park Street, Fruitport 49415, 865-6289 or (800) 469-1118, I–M, CP • ***Local motels:*** **Best Western Beacon,** 1525 South Beacon Boulevard (U.S. 31), Grand Haven 49417, 842-4720, M • **Days Inn,** 1500 South Beacon Boulevard (U.S. 31), Grand Haven 49417, 842-1999 or (800) 547-1855, indoor pool, I–M.

DINING **Bil-Mar,** 1223 Harbor Drive, 842-5920, fabulous waterside location, the place to eat fresh perch and watch the sunset, M–E • **22 Harbor,** 22 Harbor Drive, 842-5555, top dining in town, I–M • **Porto Bello,** 41 Washington Street, 846-1221, Italian, I–M • **Trumpets,** 1506 Beacon Street, 846-8802, ribs and fish, M • **Morning Star Cafe,** 711 Washington Street, 844-1131, good bet for lunch, Southwestern cuisine, special coffees and desserts, I • **Arboreal Inn,** 18191 174th Street, Spring Lake (adjoining Grand Haven), 842-3800, excellent food in attractive rustic setting, extensive wine selection, M–E.

SIGHTSEEING **P. J. Hoffmaster State Park,** 3 miles west of U.S. 31, Pontaluna Road exit, between Grand Haven and Muskegon, 798-3711. Hours: Daily 8 A.M. to 10 P.M. Autos, $$. Includes **Gillette Nature Center,** 798-3573. Hours: Memorial Day to Labor Day, daily 10 A.M. to 5 P.M.; rest of year, Tuesday to Friday 1 P.M. to 5 P.M., Saturday and Sunday 10 A.M. to 5 P.M. Free • **Musical Fountain,** Waterfront Stadium, Washington Street at Harbor Drive, 842-2550. Hours: Shows at dusk (about 9:30 P.M.) daily, Memorial Day to Labor Day, weekends May and September. Special nativity scene tableau in December. Donation • **Tri-Cities Historical Museum,** 1 North Harbor Drive, 842-0700.

Hours: Memorial Day to Labor Day, Tuesday to Saturday 10 A.M. to 9:30 P.M., Sunday noon to 9:30 P.M.; rest of year, Tuesday to Saturday 10 A.M. to 5 P.M., Sunday noon to 5 P.M. $ • ***Harbor Steamer* Excursion Boat,** Chinook Pier, 301 North Harbor Drive, 842-8950. Hours: Memorial Day to Labor Day, 1½-hour riverboat cruises daily. Check current schedules and rates • **Harbor Trolley,** Chinook Pier, 842-3200. Hours: Memorial Day to Labor Day, narrated ½-hour tours, 11 A.M. to dusk, $ • **Bike rentals: Rock 'n Road,** 300 North 7th Street, 846-2800 • **Golf**: **Grand Haven Golf Club,** 1700 Lincoln Street, 3 miles south of Grand Haven and ½ mile west of U.S. 31, 842-4040. Phone for tee times and fees.

INFORMATION Grand Haven/Spring Lake Area Visitors Bureau, One South Harbor Drive, Grand Haven MI 49417, 842-4910 or (800) 303-4096; www.grandhavenchamber.org

A Four-Star Stay in Kohler

Go ahead, you deserve it. Once in a while everyone ought to have a taste of the very best—and when it comes to Midwest resorts, that means the American Club in Kohler, Wisconsin. Nothing else comes close to the class and the warmth of this unique property, the only one in the region to be awarded a four-star rating by the *Mobil Guide* and five diamonds from AAA.

You'll live luxuriously here, right down to the bathroom whirlpool, the last word from the company that is the world's largest manufacturer of bathroom fixtures. Rooms are furnished with fine traditional pieces from Baker, the quality furniture manufacturer owned by Kohler, and rich burnished woods are in evidence everywhere, including the wooden shutters that are a signature of this inn. Choose one of the upper-category rooms and you'll have a complete climate chamber in the bathroom, where you can switch from sun to sauna to cooling spray.

The American Club has a different aura from most resorts, a residential feel and a rich history reflected in old photographs hung throughout the complex. While luxuriating in the spa, strolling the gardens, taking advantage of the lavish sports facilities, or challenging the legendary golf courses, you'll also be living part of a fascinating legacy in one of America's most unusual towns.

The facility was built originally to house male immigrant workers for the Kohler factory, located directly across the street. The whole town, in fact, was built to create a pleasant environment for workers.

The company began in nearby Sheboygan in 1873 when John

Michael Kohler, an Austrian immigrant, bought out his father-in-law's foundry, which made plows and horse troughs. Kohler had a newfangled idea he would add an enamel coating to the troughs and sell them to farmers as bathtubs. When things went well, Kohler decided to open a new plant on farmland four miles west in an area then called Riverside and created a model community for workers while he was at it. The idea was looked on with skepticism—the local newspaper even referred to it as Kohler's Folly.

John Michael died in 1900 before his vision could be realized. It was his son, Walter Kohler Sr., who built the red-brick, Tudor-style American Club in 1918, complete with an attractive dining room and a bowling alley. It was to be a place where employees—"single men of modest means"—could enjoy life while they learned English in order to become American citizens. Residents paid a monthly fee of $27.50 for room, board, and "plain washing."

Walter senior, one of two Kohlers who served as governor of Wisconsin, shared his father's belief that workers deserved an environment of beauty. He hired the nation's best landscape architectural firm, the Olmsted brothers, to lay out the village. Richard Phillips, a Milwaukee architect, was brought in to plan livable, attractive homes. The charm of their original designs remains more than 75 years later. Walter's younger brother, Herbert V. Kohler, and his son, Herbert junior, furthered the development of the village.

In 1975 Herbert Kohler Jr., grandson of the founder and the present head of the company, commissioned the Frank Lloyd Wright Foundation to come up with a plan to monitor the growth of the village over another 50 years. As a result, new construction is carefully regulated, and no electric or telephone wires are allowed above ground lest they spoil the look of things.

Like his grandfather, Herbert Kohler was greeted with doubts when in the 1970s he came up with the surprising notion of converting the American Club into a luxury hotel. But he went ahead anyway, taking care to preserve details of wood moldings and antiques and to create duplicates of missing original chandeliers. The top-rated dining room, the Immigrant Room, has a series of six areas dedicated to the Dutch, French, German, Norman, Scandinavian, and English origins of Wisconsin's early immigrants. The original dining hall, the Wisconsin Room, has period oak paneling, leaded-glass windows, and tapestries. Pen-and-ink portraits of famous Wisconsinites line the entry hallway. A 1993 expansion to mark the hotel's 75th birthday was done so skillfully that you can hardly tell where the old wing ends and the new one begins.

In keeping with its emphasis on tradition, each of the 184 rooms in the main hotel is dedicated to a famous American. Personalities ranging from Daniel Boone to Andrew Carnegie to John Philip Sousa (who twice performed in Kohler village) are commemorated with portraits, memorabilia, and biographical narratives. An additional 52 rooms are in the restored carriage house adjacent to the main building, which features a large collection of original horse and carriage artwork, including Currier & Ives prints.

Take a stroll or sign up for a tour of the lovely courtyard gardens, and don't miss a stop for dessert or coffee in the Greenhouse, a charming old-fashioned ice-cream parlor.

Other outstanding features of the hotel include its world-class recreational facilities, a posh shopping center on a man-made lake, and a multimillion-dollar Kohler showroom, the town's chief sightseeing attraction.

Golfers can play three world-class 18-hole Pete Dye courses, with a fourth due to open in 2000. Blackwolf Run, host site for the 1998 U.S. Women's Open, has two PGA championship courses. The River Course is rated one of the nation's top three public courses by *Golf* magazine. Even nongolfers may want to visit the restaurant in the clubhouse, a handsome rustic building with gigantic lodgepole-pine beams and views of the action on the greens.

In 1998, the Straits Course opened at Whistling Straits, a short drive northeast of Kohler. Designed in the style of the great seaside courses of the British Isles, it is built along two miles of Lake Michigan shore, with lake views from every hole.

Golfers and nongolfers alike will enjoy the Sports Core, a comprehensive spa offering fitness classes, an indoor lap pool, indoor and outdoor tennis courts, racquetball, and a small beach on Wood Lake. Massages and other services are available to ease the pain brought on by any unaccustomed exercise.

River Wildlife is a private game preserve, available to American Club visitors with the purchase of a guest pass from the concierge. It encompasses areas for fishing, canoeing, horseback riding, hiking, and hunting. The log-cabin lodge serves lunch daily and dinner on the weekend in rustic environs.

Prepare for temptation when you head for the Shops at Wood Lake, where more than 30 stores lure you with wares "from the essential to the exceptional." Two stops not to be missed are the Baker outlet, where beautiful furniture is found at excellent prices, and Artspace, a gallery outpost of the John Michael Kohler Art Center in Sheboygan.

The Kohler Design Center will likely send you home wanting to redecorate, after viewing two dozen dream bathrooms created by some of the nation's leading interior designers. You can also learn how enameled cast-iron fixtures are made, and see a film on the history of the Kohler company.

You may also want to tour Waelderhaus, a replica of an Austrian homestead, a gift to the village from Marie Christine Kohler, daughter of the company's founder.

Complimentary transportation takes you around to all of these attractions, and when your energy flags, you can come back to the hotel for tea, which is served in the library every afternoon. If you can't quite manage the tab at the American Club, you can still enjoy most of the amenities, including the Sports Core and golf courses, if you book a room at the moderately priced contemporary Inn on Woodlake (added in 1994). While you won't have a whirlpool, even these less expensive rooms come with unique stall showers, some featuring multiple showerheads, body sprays, foot whirlpools, and steam enclosures.

If you come to Kohler for the Fourth of July, you'll enjoy the annual Sousa Concert, an old-fashioned social recalling the concerts that John Philip Sousa himself gave in the village in 1919 and 1925.

While it is glorious in summer, this is truly a resort for all seasons. The American Club is a fairy-tale scene at Christmas, complete with twinkling lights, horse-drawn carriage rides, and Santa. All winter, you can enjoy cross-country skiing, tobogganing, or a hike through the snow on pristine wilderness trails, as well as all the indoor activities at the Sports Core. You can get an early start on Christmas shopping at the November holiday market, revitalize at the Women's Wellness Retreat in January, find cuddly companions at the Teddy Bear Classic in February, shop for choice pieces at the Antiquer's Weekend in March, or pick up unusual plants at the Spring Garden Market in April.

You could settle in happily and never leave Kohler at all, but if you do want to go exploring a bit, take the short trip into Sheboygan for a drive or a walk along the nicely landscaped Lake Michigan shoreline and a visit to the John Michael Kohler Art Center, which has five galleries of contemporary American art. Sheboygan is Wisconsin's bratwurst capital, and you can sample the traditional "brat and a brew" at the Hoffbrau.

For fine seafood dining try City Streets Riverside, a century-old building overlooking the town's historic Fish Shanty Village. If steak is on your mind, head for Rupp's Lodge, a supper club where you can watch your meal being prepared in the glass-walled kitchen.

Another area attraction is the Wade House in Greenbush to the west. An 1851 stagecoach inn and other buildings of old Greenbush have been accurately restored by the Kohler Foundation and donated to the state. The inn is furnished with many original early-American furnishings and hosted by costumed interpreters who perform such traditional tasks as fireplace cooking, gardening, blacksmithing, soap making, candlemaking, and horse grooming. The adjoining Jung Carriage Museum has a collection of more than 100 vehicles.

The Wade House is near the northern tip of the beautiful Kettle Moraine Scenic Forest, along the 25-mile Kettle Moraine Driving Tour through southwestern Sheboygan County, which is lovely in summer and a prime leaf-watching route in fall. The route is marked with acorn signs. Not far south of Greenbush is the 60-foot Parnell Tower, offering a panoramic view of the forest and surrounding farmlands. Driving through the forest is free, but you must buy a state-park sticker if you want to stop.

A worthwhile detour north from State Highway 23 on State Highway 67 leads to Elkhart Lake and the Osthoff Resort overlooking the 300-acre lake, a nice stop for lunch. Accommodations are all suites with fully equipped kitchens, gas fireplaces, and balconies; luxury suites include whirlpools. This new hotel built in an old-fashioned style may well inspire a return visit.

Area Code: 920

DRIVING DIRECTIONS Take I-43 north to State Highway 23 west and proceed ⅔ mile to the Kohler exit. From Chicago, take I-94 north into I-43, about 156 miles. Kohler is 56 miles from Milwaukee.

ACCOMMODATIONS **American Club,** County Road Y and Highland Drive, Kohler 53044, 457-8000 or (800) 344-2838, EE (ask about weekend packages) • **Inn on Woodlake,** 705 Woodlake Road, Kohler 53044, 452-7800 or (800) 919-3600, M–EE, CP • **Osthoff Resort,** 101 Osthoff Avenue, Elkhart Lake 53020, 876-3366 or (800) 876-3399, E.

DINING *At the American Club:* (All reached at 457-8888) **The Immigrant Room,** elegant dining, jackets required, E–EE • **The Wisconsin Room,** handsome main dining room, breakfast, I; Sunday brunch, M, three-course dinner, E–EE • **The Horse and Plow,** casual, pub ambience, I–M • **Cucina,** Shops at Woodlake, 452-3888, pasta, gourmet pizza, lake view, outdoor terrace, lunch and dinner, M • **Woodlake Market Cafe,** Woodlake Market, 457-6235, sandwiches, salads, deli, I • **Jumpin' Jacks Restaurant,** Sports Core, 457-4445, all three meals, I; **Blackwolf Run Restaurant,** Blackwolf Run, 457-4448, M–E • *Sheboygan dining:* **City Streets Riverside,** 712 Riverfront Drive, 457-9050, I–M • **Rupp's Lodge,** 925 North Eighth Street, 459-8155, I–M • **Hoffbrau,** 1132 North Eighth Street, 920-4153, I–M.

SIGHTSEEING **Kohler Design Center,** 101 Upper Road, Kohler, 457-3699. Hours: Monday to Friday 9 A.M. to 5 P.M., Saturday, Sunday, holidays 10 A.M. to 4 P.M. Free • **Waelderhaus,** Riverside Drive West, Kohler, 452-4079. Hours: Tours daily except holidays, 2 P.M., 3 P.M., and 4 P.M. Free • **John Michael Kohler Art Center,** 608 New York Avenue, Sheboygan, 458-6144. Hours: Monday to Friday 10 A.M. to 5 P.M., Saturday and Sunday noon to 5 P.M. Free • **Wade House and Wesley Jung Carriage Museum,** Highway 23, Greenbush, 526-3271. Hours: May to October, daily 9 A.M. to 5 P.M. $$$

INFORMATION **Kohler Visitors Information,** Kohler, WI 53044, 458-3450; **Sheboygan County Convention and Visitors Bureau,** 712 Riverfront Drive, Suite 101, Sheboygan, WI 53081, 457-9495 or (800) 457-9497.

Going Underground in Indiana

The thermometer read 92°, but we were happily donning sweaters. We were on our way underground where the temperature is always a coolish 50 degrees. Caving is the perfect activity for a hot summer day, and southern Indiana is superb cave country, with five notable underground caverns found within a 100-mile radius. One of these, Big Wyandotte Cave, boasts a massive 135-foot-high pile of rock known as Monument Mountain, which is billed as "the largest underground mountain in the world." All offer eerie formations and dim, spooky tunnels to explore, which combine majesty and mystery and are fascinating to adults and children alike.

Luckily for visitors, some of the most beautiful caves are found near Corydon, a charmer of a town with an impressive history. This was Indiana's first state capital and the site of one of the few Civil War battles fought on Union soil.

Equally important to today's travelers, Corydon boasts a showplace inn right on the town square, some excellent shops, and a number of unexpected pleasures, ranging from watching glass sculptors at work to visiting a buffalo farm to taking a scenic train ride through rolling hills. All this plus acres of forest make this a fine destination for summertime activities and family outings.

Start by reserving early for a room at the Kintner House Inn, an 1873 Victorian beauty that is on the National Register and has been featured on two Hallmark Christmas cards. It is elegantly restored with Victorian pieces, brass beds, claw-foot tubs, and country antiques. The gleaming wood floors and balusters supporting the handrail of the sweeping staircase have the same pattern of intricately carved light chestnut and dark walnut woods. Modern amenities include air-conditioning, private baths, TVs, and VCRs. For winter romantics, five rooms have gas log fireplaces.

Breakfast around the big dining room table is where guests meet and mingle while enjoying goodies like sausage-cheese grits, soufflés, and homemade coffee cake. You can watch the world go by while rocking on the front porch, or you can stroll over to the square, where band concerts are held at the gazebo on summer Friday evenings.

Before going underground, you might want to spend some time exploring Corydon, the seat of the territorial government in 1813 and the state's first capital from 1816 to 1825. The visitors center at the corner of Elm and Walnut will supply a town map.

The sights begin right on the square. You can visit the square limestone building that was built as the Harrison County Courthouse in 1816 and became the first Indiana state capitol. The original flagstone floor and fireplaces remain, and the House of Representatives and Senate chambers have been restored to the way they were in the 1800s. Not far away is the first state office building. Now a private residence, it was built in 1817 and used by the treasurer and auditor. State funds were stored in the cellar.

Other houses open to visitors are the 1817 Governor Hendricks House, home of the state's second governor, and the 1817 Thomas Posey House, now a museum, built by the son of the last governor of the Indiana Territory.

Indianans may also want to pay their respects to the Constitution Elm Memorial, which commemorates what is left of the huge elm whose branches sheltered the drafters of the first state constitution. The statehouse wasn't finished, so the legislators retired to the shade of the elm.

Also of interest is the Branham Tavern, a two-story log structure built in 1800 by territorial governor William Henry Harrison, for whom the county was named. Some say that Corydon was chosen as the capital because the influential Harrison owned property here. The former tavern has been restored and operates as a private business.

The Battle of Corydon Memorial Park, located south of town on Route 135, marks the battle fought on July 9, 1863, when 450 members of the Harrison County Home Guard attempted to delay General John Hunt Morgan's 2,400 Confederate soldiers, hoping that reinforcements would arrive and stop Morgan's march through southern Indiana. Morgan prevailed, four Indiana soldiers died, and 355 members of the guard were captured. The prisoners were released, but the Rebels looted the town before marching northward. Replicas of a Civil War cannon and the World War I German cannon that guarded the Harrison County Courthouse for 60 years stand in the park, and a small log cabin gives visitors an idea of what rural homes were like during this period.

When you are ready for caving, there are three choices within a 20-minute drive of Corydon, each different and each worth seeing.

If you will only have time for one site, make it Wyandotte Caves, which is under the auspices of the state of Indiana and the least commercial. The drive west from Corydon on State Road 62 takes you high into the wooded hills that make southern Indiana so scenic, with rugged limestone cliffs emerging to remind you of the stone that is responsible for the caves. Caverns are formed when rain and snow combine with carbon dioxide in the atmosphere to form an acid that seeps into the ground, slowly eating away over the centuries at the underlying limestone.

Make the trip at mealtime and you can stop at the region's best-known restaurant, the Overlook, perched on a high bluff in Leavenworth above a big, wide horseshoe bend in the Ohio River. The restaurant has two stories, each with picture-window views, and serves from breakfast through dinner. House specialties are country fare like chicken and biscuits and baked ham, and the coconut cream pie is legendary.

Wyandotte offers two caves and a choice of five tours, depending on your interest and stamina. The shortest and easiest trip is the 45-minute walk through Little Wyandotte, where you'll dip and wind through a host of stalactites and stalagmites, the strange formations formed by dripping water. Part of the fun of caving is seeing these shapes, which resemble ice-cream cones, animal heads, slices of bacon, or the skyscrapers of New York City in miniature. The shapes are all the more intriguing when reflected in an underground lake. Kids will no doubt be enthralled to learn there are bats, crickets, and salamanders living in the cave; they are sometimes spotlighted by the guides.

Even more of a showplace is Big Wyandotte Cave, with its vast caverns that once served as shelter for Indian tribes. Big Wyandotte's shortest tour—the Historical Tour—lasts about 90 minutes, but if you have the energy for a more strenuous outing, you shouldn't miss the two-hour Monument Mountain Tour through the deep recesses of the cave, where you can see rare grotesquely shaped formations called helictites and layered pillars known as speleotherms, as well as gypsum and prehistoric flint quarries.

Real spelunkers can sign up for the Pillar of the Constitution tour, a steep half-day trek, crawl, and climb via a wooden pole that takes you to the old upper-cave passages, to see the largest formation of its kind in the world. There's also an all-day trip for die-hard cavers who don't want to miss a thing.

A self-guided nature trail winds through the wooded terrain around the cave. Ask for the pamphlet that helps identify the trees of the forest. There's more hiking, from easy to rugged, not far away in Wyandotte Woods State Recreation Area off Highway 462. Part of the 24,000-acre Harrison-Crawford State Forest, this area also includes an Olympic-size swimming pool, picnic areas, a nature center, and access to the Ohio and Blue Rivers for boating and fishing.

If you head south from Corydon you can explore Squire Boone Caverns and Village. The cave here was discovered by Daniel Boone and his brother, Squire Boone, in 1790. Squire once escaped from a band of

Indians by hiding in the cave. Considering it good luck, he later moved here with his family, and is buried nearby. This cave is known for its rushing waters and underground waterfalls, as well as for its passageways filled with fantastic shapes. Note that the one-hour tour requires climbing a 73-step spiral stair.

On the grounds, the mill built by Squire Boone in the early 1800s has been restored and is again grinding grain, powered by the waters flowing from the cavern. The village also offers demonstrations of old-fashioned crafts in authentic log cabins, where you can watch candles being dipped and lye soap in the making. A petting zoo and a variety of shops and the chance to pan for gold and gems at the sluice are part of the fun.

The third choice, Marengo Cave, discovered accidentally by two schoolchildren in 1883, is a National Historic Landmark with many impressive formations aptly described by names like Pipe Organ, Lion's Cage, White Splendor, and Prison Bars. The most famous formation is the Crystal Palace, which is dramatically highlighted by a sound and light presentation, the high point of an easy 40-minute tour. The more detailed Dripstone Trail tour takes 70 minutes. Spelunkers can also opt for trips into sections of the great cavern that are not yet developed for tours.

In addition to the cavern, Marengo Cave Park offers horseback riding and canoe trips on the Blue River, Indiana's first designated scenic river.

Back in Corydon, there's still more to keep you busy. Shoppers will find some interesting wares around the square, including silk and dried flowers, gifts, art, crafts, and Christmas collectibles. The Griffin Building Antique Mall has over 40 dealers, and the Emporium offers eight interconnected shops in restored buildings listed on the National Register. Antiquers will also want to look into the Red Barn Antique Mall on State Highway 62 West, three floors overflowing with finds from old tools to chests to quilts. Save time for the Zimmerman Art Glass Company, where visitors are welcome to watch the third generation of one artistic family creating handblown paperweights, vases, and other beautiful items.

For a change of pace, visit the Needmore Buffalo Farm 11 miles east of Corydon, where you can see a herd of over 100 bison, sample a buffalo burger, and shop for bison leather, hides, and other buffalo-related crafts.

When your energy flags, why not sit back and enjoy the countryside from the windows of an old Louisville, New Albany & Corydon train. The 16-mile, 90-minute journey on the 1883 Corydon Scenic Railroad will give you a chance to admire the top side of the rolling hills of southern Indiana after you've explored what's underneath. The depot is at the corner of Walnut and Water Streets.

And if you want to try your luck, Caesars *Glory of Rome* riverboat, billed as "the world's largest gaming vessel," is slated to open not far away in Elizabeth, on the Ohio River.

Area Code: 812

DRIVING DIRECTIONS Corydon is reached via I-64, Exit 105. From Chicago, take I-90 east to Gary, then I-65 south through Indiana to I-64 east, about 315 miles. It is 140 miles from Indianapolis, 20 miles west of Louisville, Kentucky.

ACCOMMODATIONS The zip code for all listings is 47712. **Kintner House Inn,** Capitol and Chestnut Streets, 738-2020, I–M, CP (children under 18 free in parents' room) • **Best Western Old Capitol,** I-64 and State Highway 135, 738-4192, I • **Budgetel Inn,** 2495 Landmark Avenue NE (Highway 135 at I-64), 738-1500, I.

DINING **Magdalena's,** 102 East Chestnut Street, 738-8075, salads to full dinners, I–M • **Granny's Home Cookin',** 426 North Capitol Street, 738-1644, cafeteria, lunch and dinner until 9 P.M., I • **Overlook Restaurant,** State Highway 62, Leavenworth (about 15 minutes west of Corydon), 739-4264, country cooking, great river views, serves all three meals, dinner reservations recommended, I.

SIGHTSEEING **Corydon Capitol State Historic Site,** 202 East Walnut Street, Corydon, 738-4890. Hours: Tuesday to Saturday 9 A.M. to 5 P.M., Sunday 1 P.M. to 5 P.M. Free. Site includes **Governor Hendricks House,** 220 East Walnut Street • **Posey House Museum,** 225 Oak Street, 738-6921. Hours: May to October, Thursday to Sunday 10 A.M. to 4 P.M. Donation • **Battle of Corydon Memorial Park,** Old State Road 135, south of Corydon, c/o Harrison County Parks and Recreation Department, 738-8236. Hours: Daily 8 A.M. until dark. Free • **1883 Corydon Scenic Railroad,** Water and Walnut Streets, 738-8000. Hours: 90-minute rides late May through early November, Friday, Saturday, and Sunday afternoons; also Wednesday and Thursday afternoons in July and August. Schedules change, so it's best to call. $$$$ • **Needmore Buffalo Farm,** 4100 Buffalo Road SE (off Highway 11), Elizabeth, 11 miles east of Corydon, 968-3473. Hours: Monday, Wednesday, Thursday 9 A.M. to 6 P.M., Friday to Sunday 9 A.M. to 8 P.M. Free except Saturday and Sunday, guided tours, $$ • **Zimmerman Art Glass Company,** 395 Valley Road, 738-2206. Hours: Tuesday to Saturday 9 A.M. to 3 P.M. Free • **Wyandotte Caves,** Highway 62, Wyandotte, 10 miles west of Corydon, 738-2782. Hours: Visitors center open Memorial Day to Labor Day, daily 9 A.M. to 5 P.M.; rest of year, Tuesday to Sunday 9 A.M. to 5 P.M. **Little Wyandotte Cave tours,** $$; **Big Wyandotte Cave tours,** $$ • **Squire Boone Cave,** Highway 135, five miles south of Corydon, 732-4281. Hours: One-hour tours daily from 10 A.M. to 6 P.M. $$$$ • **Marengo Cave National Landmark,** State Highway 64, 10 miles north of I-64 Exit 92, via State Highway 66, Marengo, 365-2705. Hours: Memorial Day to Labor Day, daily 9 A.M. to 6 P.M.; rest of year 9 A.M. to 5 P.M.; Crystal Palace 40-minute tour, $$$$ or Dripstone Trail 70-minute tour, $$$. Combination tickets available • **Cave Country Canoes,** Milltown, c/o Marengo Cave. Hours: April to October, daily varied trips from 7 miles to 58-mile overnight camping. Call for details and reservations.

INFORMATION **Harrison County Chamber of Commerce,** 310 North Elm Street, Corydon, IN 47112, 738-2137 or (888) 738-2137.

Cruising Across Lake Michigan

There are many vantage points from which the wave-crested expanse of Lake Michigan seems as wide as an ocean, but nowhere is this impression stronger than from the decks of the S.S. *Badger.* Standing at the rail, sniffing the maritime breeze during the four-hour car ferry crossing from Ludington, Michigan, to Manitowoc, Wisconsin, there is water, water everywhere. There's no better way to appreciate why these are called the Great Lakes.

The trip has all the trappings of a mini–sea voyage—the crowd waving good-bye, a bountiful buffet on deck, lots of room for sunning, bingo in the lounge, video games, a small museum, and a movie theater. There's nothing fancy about the *Badger,* but it is comfortably fitted out, and there's never a problem snagging a chair or a chaise on deck.

The refurbished 410-foot *Badger,* some 4,000 tons of nostalgia, is the last passenger steamship making the crossing and one of the last coal-burning steamers. It continues a tradition that dates back to 1875. A dozen ferries used to carry railroad cars, freight, passengers, and cars, but they were done in by diesel locomotives that could pull more train cars and move faster. The last ferry stopped service in 1990, and the *Badger* was slated for the scrap heap until it was rescued by Ludington-born self-made millionaire Charles Conrad, who had loved the ferries in his youth and was determined that they should not die.

After a $500,000 refurbishing, the *Badger* went back into service in May 1992, with accommodations for 620 passengers, 180 automobiles, tour buses, or RVs. In its banner first season, the ship carried 115,000 passengers and 34,000 vehicles. The voyage can cut several hours off a drive around the lake between these two towns, but the sail is fun for its own sake. A visit in each port city combined with the crossing makes for a delightful weekend.

The *Badger* leaves Ludington for the four-hour trip early in the morning, and sails back from Manitowoc in the afternoon. Some added late-evening departures from Ludington give the opportunity for bed and breakfast on board. Which direction you choose to cross depends a lot on where you live, and whether you want to spend more time basking on the Michigan beach or sightseeing in Wisconsin.

My vote goes to spending extra time in Ludington, a cheerful town of 8,500 with a wide main street lined with old Victorian homes and flowers everywhere. The town's "Petunia Parade," which moves along Ludington Street and the marina, is the work of nearly 800 volunteers, who put in some 50,000 colorful blooms each year on a community-wide planting day, then tend to their two-and-a-half-mile flower trail throughout the season. The flowers are funded by area merchants.

Ludington's major asset is its fine beaches and one of the state's very best shoreline parks. If you have small children, you can stay in a motel right across from Stearns Park and the 2,500-foot town beach. The park includes a pleasant playground, minigolf, and volleyball and shuffleboard courts. Follow the little blue footprints down the walkway for a tour of the waterfront and the Coast Guard station.

An even more beautiful area awaits eight miles north of town in Ludington State Park. With 4,575 acres of enormous, ever-changing sand dunes, sugary beaches, hardwood forests, virgin conifers, and the Big Sable River running through, this is one of the prime spots along the Michigan shoreline.

Start at the Great Lakes Visitors Center, where there are displays and information about the park's trails, beaches, and wildlife; you can also pick up schedules for guided walks and talks. Well-marked foot and bicycle trails lead from the center through ever-changing wilderness. Hikers can choose from half-hour jaunts to four-hour excursions.

No one should miss the Skyline Trail Boardwalk, an exceptional wooden walkway through the treetops that gives a peerless view of river, dunes, and forest as well as a chance to spot the park's rich birdlife up close.

Another favorite walk is the mile-and-a-half stroll up the beach to Big Sable Point Lighthouse, a 112-foot landmark built in 1867. Lighthouse keepers kept lanterns burning here for 100 years, until the Coast Guard automated the station in 1968. Tours scheduled on three Saturdays during the summer take visitors through the tower and keeper's home; check with the visitors center for dates.

Big Sable Point is one of three much-photographed landmark lighthouses around Ludington. Little Sable Point Lighthouse, a red-brick structure dating from 1874, is a half-hour drive south near Silver Lake. The most active light is the Ludington North Breakwater Light downtown, which guides vessels through the channel connecting the harbor, the Pere Marquette River, and Lake Michigan. The first beacon went up here in 1871. The present pyramid was built in 1924.

Besides seven miles of sand along Lake Michigan, Ludington Beach State Park offers swimming in the warm waters of lower Hamlin Lake, a favorite with families. The 12-mile lake was formed over 100 years ago during logging days when lumbermen dammed the Big Sable River to make a holding pond for trees felled upstream. In 1888, the Mill Dam burst, completely flooding the hamlet of Hamlin. A new dam regulates the water level on Michigan's largest artificial lake.

Lake Hamlin's shallow bayous provide a prize canoe route—a marked trail past old logging camps and through tall reeds and cattails, where you may spot blue herons, otter, and all manner of wetlands wildlife. Canoes can be rented at the lake's concession building, and the loop takes one to three hours, depending on the skill of the paddlers.

When you've had enough beaching, you can explore the small cache of shops on Ludington Avenue and James Street, a mix of antiques, gifts, jewelry, and clothing. The Harbor Front Plaza, a condominium/office complex going up at the marina, plans more shops as well as restaurants.

Ludington's land-based sightseeing attraction is the pleasant restored community of White Pine Village, made up of some 20 buildings from the late 1800s set along picturesque walkways. The structures restored and moved to this site range from general store to trapper's cabin, blacksmith's shop to ice-cream parlor. One of the loveliest is a replica of a small, steepled rural church, a favorite of local brides.

The village has many special events, horseshoe tournaments to Civil War musters, as well as its own "Field of Dreams," where the Ludington Mariners play in authentic 1860s uniforms by the old rules: no gloves and you're out on the first bounce.

To complete your trio of lighthouse snapshots, drive south to Silver Lake. Much of this town has become go-cart and water-slide territory, but there is a nice state park where you can climb the dunes and take a slide down again, or go for a roller-coaster dune-buggy ride through the towering dunes. The Scenic Drive along the south shore of the lake will take you to Little Sable Point Lighthouse for that final photo.

Across Lake Michigan, Manitowoc, Wisconsin (population 32,500), is an industrial town and port, once a major shipbuilding center and still one of the nation's largest manufacturers of aluminum ware. It lacks the beach, the calm, and the blossoms of Ludington, but it does have its share of attractions.

Chief among them is the Wisconsin Maritime Museum, one of the best places to learn about the history of shipping on the Great Lakes. Two floors of exhibits allow you to walk the streets of a historical Great Lakes port and relive its story from sail to steam to diesel. You'll also learn something about how ships were and are constructed. A wonderful gallery of models traces the advances in ship design from 1847 three-masted schooners to today's speedy freighters. Displays tell the story of the Manitowoc Shipbuilding Company, where many Michigan car ferries and 28 World War II submarines were built. Right next door is the Submariners Memorial, which offers tours of the U.S.S. *Cobia,* a World War II submarine.

There's more to see in town, as well. It's worth the trip to the Rahr-West Art Museum just to see its quarters, a handsome 1891 mansion with a conservatory and many period furnishings. It contains a mix of 19th-century paintings, porcelains, fabulous Chinese ivory carvings, and a room full of antique dolls. A modern exhibition wing has changing art exhibits.

Antique-car buffs will find a display of 40 classics at Zunker's Antique Car Museum. And Manitowoc has its own collection of restored turn-of-the-century buildings in Pinecrest Village. Like its counterpart across the lake, this village has many special events all summer.

A very popular stop in town is Natural Ovens, where you can watch the mixing and baking and get free samples of warm, delicious whole-grain preservative-free breads. The bakery turns out 20,000 loaves every day. The Farm and Food Museum on the grounds, also open to visitors, has displays of John Deere tractors from 1920 to 1960 and a petting area with friendly sheep, goats, chickens, and rabbits.

Top off your stay with a delightful, time-honored Manitowoc tradition, a visit to Beerntsen's Candy Store at 108 North Eighth Street. This classic candy shop with arched doorways, Tiffany-style lighting fixtures, and black-walnut booths serves up hand-dipped chocolates, homemade candies, and ice-cream treats.

Area Codes: Ludington—616, Manitowoc—920

DRIVING DIRECTIONS Ludington is on U.S. Highway 31 and U.S. 10, 145 miles north of St. Joseph. From Chicago, take I-80/90 east to I-94 north, merging into U.S. 31/I-196 and continuing north on U.S. 31 at Holland, 240 miles from Chicago. It is 230 miles from Detroit. Manitowoc is on I-43 and U.S. 10. From Chicago, follow I-94 north until it merges with I-43 north in Milwaukee, 172 miles. It is 79 miles from Milwaukee.

ACCOMMODATIONS ***Ludington, MI:*** All of the following listings have the Ludington zip code, 49431. **Pier House,** 805 West Ludington Avenue, 845-7346 or (800) 968-3677, motel, walking distance to beach, car ferry, indoor pool, I • **Snyder's Shoreline Inn,** 903 West Ludington Avenue, 845-1261, 44-room lodging with lake views, walking distance to ferry, pool, some whirlpools, M–EE, CP • **Schoen-**

berger House, 409 East Ludington Avenue, 843-4435, grand, neoclassical lumber baron's mansion, M–E, CP • ***Victorian homes turned bed-and-breakfast inns:*** **Daniel Godenough House,** 706 East Ludington Avenue, 843-3197, M, CP • **The Inn at Ludington,** 701 East Ludington Avenue, 845-7055 or (800) 845-9170, I–M, CP • **The Ludington House,** 501 East Ludington Avenue, 845-7769 or (800) 827-7869, M, CP • **The Lamplighter,** 602 East Ludington Avenue, 843-9792 or (800) 301-9792, I–E, CP • ***Manitowoc, WI:*** The following listings have the Manitowoc zip code, 54220 • **Inn on Maritime Bay,** 101 Maritime Drive, 682-7000, attractive hotel on the lake, pool, special rates for ferry passengers, M • **Holiday Inn,** 4601 Calumet Avenue at I-43 and U.S. Highway 151, 682-6000, indoor pool, M.

DINING ***Ludington, MI:*** **Scotty's,** 5910 West Ludington Avenue, 843-4033, casual, prime rib the specialty, I–M • **P. M. Steamers,** 502 West Loomis Street, 843-9555, casual, seafood, I–M • **Gibbs Country House Restaurant,** 3951 West U.S. 10, 845-0311, casual family dining, all three meals, varied menu, huge soup/salad/dessert bar, I–M • ***Manitowoc, WI:*** **Inn on Maritime Bay** (see above), lake views, M • **Colonial Inn,** 1001 South Eighth Street, 684-6495, 1860s building, varied American menu, all three meals, I–M • **Kasper's Supper Club,** 1228 Memorial Drive, 684-7188, across from the lake, American fare, I–M.

SIGHTSEEING **S.S. *Badger* Lake Michigan Car Ferry,** 900 South Lakeview Drive, Manitowoc; 701 Marine Drive, Ludington, (800) 841-4243. Four-hour crossings between Manitowoc, WI, and Ludington, MI. Departures mid-May to early October. Call for current schedule and rates • ***Ludington, MI:*** **Ludington State Park,** 843-8671. Great Lakes Visitors Center hours: May to September, daily 10 A.M. to 4 P.M. Admission per car, $$ • **White Pine Village,** 1687 South Lakeshore Drive, 843-4808. Hours: Mid-June to Labor Day, Tuesday to Sunday 11 A.M. to 4:30 P.M.; early May to mid-June and Labor Day to mid-October, to 4 P.M. $$ • **Mac Wood's Dune Scooter Rides,** Scenic Drive and 16th Avenue just south of Silver Lake, Mears, 873-2817. Hours: Daily mid-May to mid-October, 9:30 A.M. to sundown. $$$$$ • ***Manitowoc:*** **Wisconsin Maritime Museum,** 75 Maritime Drive, 684-0218. Hours: Memorial Day to Labor Day, daily 9 A.M. to 6 P.M.; rest of year, Monday to Saturday 9 A.M. to 5 P.M., Sunday 11 A.M. to 5 P.M. $$ Combination tickets with Submariners Memorial, $$$ • **Rahr-West Museum,** 610 North Eighth Street at Park Street, 683-4501. Hours: Monday to Friday 10 A.M. to 4 P.M., Saturday and Sunday 11 A.M. to 4 P.M. Free • **Pinecrest Historical Village,** Pinecrest Lane off County Road JJ. Hours: July 1 to Labor Day, daily 9:30 A.M. to 5 P.M.; May, June, September to mid-October, Wednesday to Sunday, 10 A.M. to 4 P.M. $$ • **Zunker's Antique Car Museum,** 3722

MacArthur Drive, 684-4005. Hours: May to September, daily 10 A.M. to 5 P.M. $$ • **Natural Ovens,** 4300 County Trunk CR (off U.S. Highway 151), 758-2500. Hours: Monday to Friday 8 A.M. to 5 P.M., Saturday 8 A.M. to 3 P.M. Free.

INFORMATION Ludington Area Convention and Visitors Bureau, 5827 West U.S. Highway 10, Ludington, MI 49431, 845-0324 or (800) 542-4600; www.ludington.org • **Manitowoc Visitors and Convention Bureau,** P.O. Box 966, Manitowoc, WI 54221, 683-4388 or (800) 627-4896; www.manitowoc.org

A Visit to Old World Wisconsin

The European pioneers who made their way from Eastern ports to America's heartland faced daunting challenges as they fought to make new lives in a foreign land. You can see a bit of their lives at Old World Wisconsin in the town of Eagle, a visit guaranteed to give children (and their parents) a vivid new sense of the past.

Owned and operated by the State Historical Society of Wisconsin, this pine-studded complex of nearly 600 acres in the southern Wisconsin countryside is in the tradition of the great outdoor museums of Europe. It offers a tour of the 19th-century frontier through visits to 10 farmsteads where authentically costumed interpreters with charming ethnic dialects portray the varying lifestyles of immigrants in the 1800s.

They'll gladly tell you about the trip from the Old Country, and the travails as well as the pleasures of their new lives.

The farmhouses and their barns, bakehouses, stables, corncribs, and outhouses were actually built by Wisconsin pioneers, re-creating the farm architecture they knew in Europe. Some 65 structures were sought out by historians, moved to this site, and carefully restored.

Each farm is in a separate wooded location, as far from neighbors as pioneer families would have lived, and each reflects the origins of its inhabitants. An open-air tram transports visitors from site to site. The hardy can walk it, a two-and-a-half-mile tour.

You can drop in on a Norwegian log cabin, circa 1845, built by Knudt Fossebrekke and his wife, Gertrude, and learn about how Knudt trapped and sold pelts to augment their income. The 1860 Schulz Farm was home to a family from German Pomerania; the thatched roof and central chimney kitchen on their house were inspired by farms in their homeland.

Other sites include a seven-structure Finnish farm, three German farms from the 1860s, '70s, and '80s, and homesteads built by Danish settlers. At each, you'll find costumed interpreters planting crops, tending the animals, or occupied with such household chores as spinning, baking, candle dipping, doing laundry with boiling water and lye soap, or shearing sheep. Even the animals, like rare merino and Cotswold sheep, are appropriate for the period.

The 1870s Crossroads Village re-creates the kind of settlements early farmers traveled to when they needed to shop at the general store or visit the wagon maker, cobbler, or blacksmith. The village comprises typical town houses, a wooden church, as well as a three-story stagecoach inn that once provided meals and lodgings for travelers. A 15-minute slide program is offered on the lower level of the Ramsey Barn Visitors Center.

Almost every weekend brings special events at Old World Wisconsin, from a Scandinavian Midsummer Celebration with dancers around the maypole to Autumn on the Farm. Children's Day, repeated monthly in summer, invites kids to play traditional 19th-century games like sack races or hoop and stick, and to help with household tasks like quilting, gardening, and cloth making.

Lunch and dinner for visitors are served at the Causing Barn Restaurant, an octagonal barn built in 1897; ethnic favorites and a Friday fish fry are among the choices on the reasonably priced menu.

With a break for a meal, Old World Wisconsin can easily take up most of one day. Two appealing alternatives nearby can nicely fill out a family weekend: summer fun in Milwaukee or resort relaxation near Lake Geneva.

Time your visit right and you can take in one of the greatest shows on earth, the Sunday afternoon Great Circus Parade held in mid-July in Milwaukee, less than an hour's drive from Old World Wisconsin. This one-of-a-kind event, with its ferocious beasts, strutting bands, and glorious wagons, is in fact another facet of old Wisconsin, since it is a historic re-creation of the kind of parades once staged by the Ringling brothers, who established their circus in Baraboo, Wisconsin, over 100 years ago.

The fabulous wagons used in the parade are part of the collection of the Circus World Museum, located at the original Ringling winter quarters in Baraboo (see pages 82–85). They are transported to Milwaukee by train and are on display along the lakefront for three days before the parade. All kinds of special events take place during those days, varying each year, from a petting menagerie and clown shows to a Wild West encampment and circus performances.

The parade begins at 2 P.M. from the Lincoln Memorial Bridge and proceeds west along Wisconsin Avenue, detouring north on North Water Street and Old World Third Street, down Fifth Street and back east on Michigan Street. Pick a spot along the route and get there early for the best view. You'll have an excellent panoramic view of the parade if you camp out near its starting point at the south end of Juneau Park; if you want to hear the bands, place yourself near the review stand, which is usually on Wisconsin Avenue between Jackson and Jefferson Streets.

If you can't make the circus parade, think about visiting during the Wisconsin State Fair, held for 10 days starting the first Thursday in August. Known for its cream puffs filled with mounds of the Dairy State's finest whipped cream, the fair offers plenty of traditional fun to delight all ages, from prize animals to pig races, thrill rides to name entertainers to nightly fireworks.

Since summer is a continual series of music and ethnic festivals along the Milwaukee waterfront at the 85-acre Henry Maier Festival Park, you can count on something special happening whenever you come, with food, entertainment, and games for all. The festival lineup includes Italian, German, and Mexican celebrations, as well as Bastille Days.

Milwaukee also offers a number of places that are ideal for families. Across the street from the central waterfront is the Betty Brinn Children's Museum, where fun and learning combine with participatory exhibits like "My Body Works" and "A Trading Place."

Milwaukee's Museum Center offers three major family attractions. The creative Milwaukee Public Museum is known for its walk-through exhibits that let you visit a replica of a turn-of-the-century city, explore the award-winning Rain Forest of Costa Rica exhibit, and experience the Third Planet.

Discovery World, the James Lovell Museum of Science, Economics and Technology, features over 140 interactive exhibits, live theater shows, and workshops planned to allow kids to explore the future now. The third component is the Humphrey IMAX Dome Theater, the only one in Wisconsin.

For outdoor fun, the Milwaukee County Zoo is consistently ranked among the country's best, and it is easy to see why: A specially designed moat system allows visitors to view predator and prey in settings that are very much like their natural habitats. In the African Waterhole exhibit, for example, antelope, zebra, ostrich, and stork live in close but safe proximity to the African lions, and in the Savannah area, the cheetah overlook the Thompson's gazelles, impalas, and crowned cranes. The 30-minute Zoomobile ride is an excellent way to get an overview of the zoo, which has some 2,500 inhabitants representing five continents.

Favorite indoor exhibits include the popular Apes of Africa area in the primate building and the entire small-mammal building, home to a group of little furry survivors from all regions of the world. Hundreds of colorful birds move freely in the aviary's naturalistic tropical surroundings, and the aquarium has a splendid 25,000-gallon Pacific Coast display.

Popular summertime activities include the Raptory Theater, where the stars are magnificent birds of prey in flight; camel, elephant, and pony rides; and a miniature train traversing the zoo's attractive grounds.

At the three-acre Stackner Heritage Farm young children can hold and pet zoo babies such as lambs and birds. The Dairy Complex, an appropriate addition in the state that calls itself America's Dairyland, shows six varieties of dairy cattle and explains the production of milk. An actual milking demonstration is part of the fun.

If the summer day is warm, head for one of the nine beaches along Milwaukee's 60-mile lakeshore. But for a really novel way to cool off, take the family to the Pettit National Ice Center, the official Olympic training facility for speed skating, the best facility of its kind in the country. This huge complex houses a 400-meter speed-skating oval and two full-size rinks for hockey, figure skating, and short-track speed skating. There are spectator hours, and the ice is available for public skating several times daily; phone ahead for current schedules.

While you are in the city, with or without children, forget about cholesterol for a while and sample the local treat, frozen custard, a rich cream-and-egg concoction that makes regular ice cream seem positively wimpy. You'll find it at classic drive-ins that are throwbacks to the '50s. One of these, Leon's, at 3131 South 27th Street, is said to have been the model for Arnold's Drive-In on the TV show *Happy Days.*

It's hard to imagine a more family-friendly city than Milwaukee, but if you'd rather relax outdoors on a warm summer weekend, Lake Geneva area resorts, less than half an hour away from Old World Wisconsin, beckon with swimming, tennis, and special programs for children. And the fun is weatherproof, since each resort has indoor pools and game rooms.

The handsomely renovated Grand Geneva Resort and Spa, set on 1,300 acres just outside the town, is the most elegant choice. It will definitely attract golfers in the family with its highly rated Brute and Briar Patch golf courses. The spa treatments are another lure for grown-ups. For the kids, the resort offers horseback riding, minigolf, hayrides, and a "Grand Adventure Camp." The resort has its own year-round theater presenting musicals and, in winter, its own ski slope.

The Abbey, on the western end of Lake Geneva in Fontana, has attractive modern architecture and water views. Interlaken, on smaller Lake Como, is on the modest side, but still has plenty to offer families, including slightly lower rates. Lake Lawn Resort in Delavan has a long list of activities, too, including minigolf, ice skating, a petting zoo, and a children's program.

Railroad fans of all ages might also like an overnight stay in the nicely renovated railroad cabooses and Pullman cars at the End of the Line Vacation Station in Lake Geneva. The cars come with air-conditioning and television. Some of the suites of connected cars are perfect for families, and the complex includes a pool and a playground.

Lake Geneva itself has summer pleasures such as a swimming beach, lake cruises, miniature golf, and Uncle John's Fun Park, with go-carts and batting cages. On Wednesday and Sunday nights in the summer, Aquanut Water Shows go on in Lance Park, a few miles to the south in Twin Lakes.

Kids love the Ice Cream Social cruise from Lake Geneva, a 90-minute outing on the lake that includes a sundae with your choice of topping. Another unique and entertaining option is a ride on the *Walworth II,* one of the only remaining marine delivery vessels of the U.S. Postal Service. The boat slows down but does not stop for its deliveries, so the postlady on duty must be young and agile enough to be able to repeatedly jump onto the pier and back again. You can buy a postcard, write your message on board, and mail it right from the boat with a special "U.S. Mailboat" cancellation stamp.

If you want to show the kids another piece of the past, take a drive west on State Highway 36 to County Road G north through East Troy for a ride on Wisconsin's last interurban electric trolley. The East Troy Electric Railroad lets you examine these colorful former mainstays of transportation, and then board for a run to Troy Center. Kids love the *click*ety-*clack* of the train and sound of the bell warning pedestrians to get out of the way. At Troy Center you can stop for treats like "mudd-berries"—chocolate-dipped homegrown strawberries—at the Elegant Farmer. You can also make your own caramel apple, rolling it in any or all of five toppings.

A drive to Green Meadows Farm is another fun outing for families (follow U.S. Highway 12 north to I-43, then State Highway 20 east toward Waterford, about 20 miles in all). Hands-on two-hour tours provide young visitors with a close-up view of cows, sheep, goats, chickens, and other farm animals and allow them to help with milking and feeding. A petting zoo, horse-drawn hayrides, and pony rides are part of the fun.

Whether you choose city or resort to round out your stay, you'll be combining a visit to the Old World with some winning pleasures of today.

Area Code: 414

DRIVING DIRECTIONS Old World Wisconsin is just off State Highway 67, south of Eagle. From Chicago, take I-94 north to State Highway 50 west; at Lake Geneva, connect with U.S. 12 northwest into

Highway 67 north, about 91 miles. From Milwaukee, take I-94 west to Highway 67 south, 32 miles.

ACCOMMODATIONS ***Milwaukee:*** For midtown Milwaukee, see page 253. Motels near the zoo, convenient to state fairgrounds and Pettit Ice Center and on the way to Eagle, include: **Ramada Inn West,** 201 North Mayfair Road, just north of I-94 at State Highway 100 exit, Wauwatosa 53226, 771-4400, indoor pool, M • **Exel Inn of Milwaukee West,** 115 North Mayfair Road, also north of I-94 at Highway 100 exit, Wauwatosa 53226, 257-0140, I • **Best Western Midway Hotel–Highway 100,** 251 North Mayfair Road, 774-3600, indoor pool, M • ***Lake Geneva region resorts:*** **Grand Geneva Resort and Spa,** 7036 Grand Way at Highway 50 East and Highway 12, Lake Geneva 53147, 248-8811 or (800) 558-3417, E–EE • **The Abbey,** Highway 67, Fontana 53125, 275-6811 or (800) 558-2405, M–EE • **Interlaken Resort,** 4240 Highway 50, Lake Geneva 53147, 248-9121 or (800) 225-5558, M–E • **Lake Lawn Resort,** 2400 East Geneva Street (Highway 50 East), Delavan 53115, 728-7950 or (800) 338-5253, E • **End of the Line Vacation Station,** 301 East Town Line Road, Lake Geneva 53147, 248-RAIL or (800) 747-RAIL, real train cars, pool, open mid-April to mid-October, M, CP; family villas, E. For Lake Geneva inns, see page 163.

DINING For Milwaukee, see pages 253–254; for Lake Geneva, see pages 163–164.

SIGHTSEEING **Old World Wisconsin,** Highway 67, Eagle, 594-6300. Hours: July and August, daily 10 A.M. to 5 P.M.; May, June, September, and October, Monday to Friday 10 A.M. to 4 P.M., Saturday and Sunday to 5 P.M. $$$$; Shuttle tram, $ • ***Milwaukee special events:*** **Great Circus Parade,** (608) 356-8341. Hours: Showgrounds on the Milwaukee lakefront, mid-July, events, Wednesday to Saturday; parade Sunday afternoon, 2 P.M. • **Wisconsin State Fair,** Wisconsin State Fair Park, off I-94 west of the city, 266-7000 or (800) 884-FAIR, 10 days in early August • **Summer festivals:** Current roster and dates available from the Milwaukee Visitors Bureau • ***Milwaukee family attractions:*** **Betty Brinn Children's Museum,** Miller Pavilion, O'Donnell Park, 929 East Wisconsin Avenue, second floor, opposite the lakefront, 291-0888. Hours: Tuesday to Saturday 9 A.M. to 5 P.M., Sunday noon to 5 P.M. $$ • **Milwaukee County Zoo,** 10001 West Bluemound Road, 771-3040. Hours: May through September, Monday to Saturday 9 A.M. to 5 P.M., Sunday and holidays to 6 P.M.; rest of year, daily 9 A.M. to 4:30 P.M. $$$; parking, $$ • **Museum Center,** 710 West Wells, includes: **Milwaukee Public Museum,** 278-2700. Hours: Daily 9 A.M. to 5 P.M. $$$; **Discovery World, the James Lovell Museum of Science, Eco-**

nomics and Technology, 765-0777. Hours: Daily 9 A.M. to 5 P.M. $$; **Humphrey IMAX Dome Theater,** 319-IMAX. Hours: Daily 9 A.M. to 4:30 P.M. Phone for showtimes. • **Pettit National Ice Center,** 500 South 84th Street off I-94, a few minutes west of Milwaukee, across from the state fairgrounds, 266-0100. Hours: Daily 8 A.M. to 9 P.M. Admission free, except for special events. Skating, $$; skate rentals, $. Check for current public skating hours. For more Milwaukee sightseeing, see pages 254–255 • ***Lake Geneva:*** **Geneva Lake Cruise Line,** Riviera Docks, 812 Wrigley Drive, Lake Geneva, 248-6206 or (800) 558-5911. Hours: May through October; full schedule mid-June to late August; limited service spring and fall. Geneva Bay one-hour tour several times daily 10 A.M. to 4:15 P.M. $$$$$; check current schedules for Ice Cream Social and Mailboat tours • **Green Meadows Farm,** 33604 High Drive, off State Highway 20, Waterford, 534-2891. Hours: July 5 to Labor Day, Tuesday to Sunday 10 A.M. to 2 P.M.; early May to late June, Tuesday to Friday 10 A.M. to noon, Saturday and Sunday 10 A.M. to 2 P.M.; October 1–30, Monday to Friday 10 A.M. to noon, Saturday, Sunday 10 A.M. to 3 P.M. $$$$ • **East Troy Electric Railroad,** County Road G, 2 blocks north of Village Square, East Troy, 642-3263. Hours: Memorial Day through October, Saturday and Sunday 11:30 A.M. to 4:30 P.M.; mid-June to mid-August, also Wednesday to Friday 11:30 A.M. to 2 P.M. Departures usually four times daily; phone for exact times. $$$.

INFORMATION **Greater Milwaukee Convention and Visitors Bureau,** 510 West Kilbourn Avenue, Milwaukee, WI 53203, 273-7222 or (800) 554-1448 • **Lake Geneva Area Chamber of Commerce,** 201 Wrigley Drive, Lake Geneva, WI 53147, 248-4416 or (800) 345-1020; www.lakegenevawi.com

Breezing Around at Sleeping Bear

Of all the beautiful spots on the eastern shore of Lake Michigan, the most dramatic is the Sleeping Bear Dunes National Lakeshore. Here, the lake can resemble a mighty ocean with whitecapped waves, and the dunes stand as high as 460 feet, taller than many office buildings. The 70,000-acre preserve includes over 37 miles of sugar-soft sand, but it also extends far beyond the shoreline. The diverse landscape holds dense beech-maple forests and clear inland rivers and lakes.

More than a million people arrive each year to take the scenic drive through the dunes, walk the forest trails, swim, boat, and fish. They scale the dunes and laugh as they slither back down along the famous Dune Climb. Offshore, surrounded by the unpredictable waters of Lake Michigan, the Manitou Islands beckon, secluded and serene, a haven for hikers and picnickers who take the ferryboat from the town of Leland, Michigan.

Adding to the pleasures of the journey is the chance to explore the breezy Leelanau Peninsula, Michigan's "little finger," which starts at the national lakeshore and extends for 30 miles north between Lake Michigan and Grand Traverse Bay. Leelanau is a Chippewa Indian name meaning "delight of life," and for many visitors today the description still applies.

The continental glacier moved through this region like a giant bulldozer, scooping out the basins for Lake Michigan and its bays, and forming tall bluffs from deposits of soft sand and gravel. Prevailing westerly winds from across the lake continue to pick up sand and deposit it here, forming two kinds of dunes: beach dunes on the low-lying shores, and "perched dunes" such as the Sleeping Bear, high above. These higher dunes are actually a relatively thin blanket of windblown sand covering a thick deposit of glacial debris. On the beach on a windy day you can sometimes actually see a hazy zone of sand moving a foot or two above the ground.

One of the most curious phenomena occurs when dunes, pushed by the strong winds, actually begin moving, migrating inland to bury trees in their path. When the dunes are pushed on once again, dead trees are exposed, creating "ghost forests" that attest to the power of the wind.

To make the most of the area, first stop at the park headquarters in Empire, where you can pick up maps, a printed guide to the Pierce Stocking Scenic Drive, excellent reading material, and a program listing ranger-led talks and walks.

One of the best short hikes, and a perfect introduction to the scenery, is the mile-and-a-half Empire Bluffs Trail, which starts from the parking area off Wilco Road, a mile south of Empire off State Highway 22. After a gentle uphill walk through deep forest, the trail opens out to a sandy hill hundreds of feet above the deep blue expanse of Lake Michigan, and then rims the hilltop. A boardwalk eases your progress much of the way, and conveniently placed benches encourage you to stop and contemplate the view.

The 7.6-mile Pierce Stocking Scenic Drive takes you across the dunes and through some of the region's most dramatic stretches of dense forest. The dozen pull-off points afford marvelous vistas of glimmering lakes and towering hills of sand. Hiking trails wind among the dunes to even better vantage points.

Sleeping Bear got its name from an old Chippewa Indian legend of a mother bear and her two cubs, who were driven by fire from the land that is now Wisconsin to seek refuge across Lake Michigan. Mother Bear reached the Michigan shore and climbed to the top of a bluff to watch and wait for her babies. The exhausted cubs couldn't manage the long swim, however, and drowned. A solitary dune overlooking the lake marks the spot where Mother Bear rested and waited for her children. Her hapless cubs are the Manitou Islands.

You'll have to look hard to discern the sleeping-bear outline today, for the wind is a restless sculptor, continually reshaping the ridges, and the bear has lost much of its original 200-foot height.

The climb to the top of the dunes is strenuous, but it rewards the hale and hearty with wonderful views of Glen Lake and a desert of dunes. Other popular hikes are the 3.5-mile Dunes Trail and the 2.8-mile loop to Sleeping Bear Point. You may very well want to join the crowds at the Dune Climb happily sliding down the banks of sand.

Awaiting you as you exit the park is the rest of the Leelanau Peninsula, rimmed with 100 miles of shoreline. Highway 22 circles the peninsula. The temperature in towns like Glen Arbor and Leland is often 20 degrees cooler than it is in neighboring Traverse City, which makes them wonderful destinations for a summer getaway.

When Lake Michigan's logging boom bottomed out, vacationers began heading north on the same lake steamers that had once hauled logs south. As a result of the increasing demand, resorts, inns, and cottage colonies began springing up along the shore. Some resent the gentrification represented by the upscale shops appearing in Leelanau's towns, but compared to many resort areas, these oases remain small, quaint, and welcoming.

Glen Arbor, a dot of a village, and the town closest to the national lakeshore, has long been a favorite of artists. Several galleries specializing in regional art are found along the town's few blocks. Other stops include a general store called the Totem Shop, and Becky Thatcher Designs, the studio/shop of a popular jewelry designer who specializes in pieces using polished local beach stones.

Everything in town is informal, including dining in places like Art's Tavern, a local hangout for over 50 years, or Le Bear, which has an outside deck on Sleeping Bear Bay.

About a mile north of Glen Arbor is one of Michigan's finest resorts, The Homestead, proving that a resort can develop without destroying the landscape. Guests are housed in attractive contemporary condominiums or more economical lodge rooms in various locations on deeply wooded grounds. They can enjoy walks in the woods as well as a mile of Lake Michigan beachfront and a mile-and-a-half on the Crystal River. A host of facilities include swimming, tennis, a nine-hole golf course with breathtaking lake views, a small harbor with sailing, paddleboats, and canoes, and a choice of restaurants. Winter sports include a small ski slope and cross-country trails.

To the north is Leland, a delightful old fishing village. The Carp River runs right through town into the narrow harbor. The gray weathered shanties on the water, collectively known as Fishtown, are filled with new shops, but the ambience of old times remains. It's a pleasure to sit on the deck of The Cove restaurant and contemplate the action around the harbor as you feast on fresh-caught whitefish or perch.

You can still buy fish in Fishtown, but you'll also find leather goods or pottery. You can board a ferry to the Manitou Islands, watch the fishing boats come in, or charter a boat to try for your own catch of the day. The Carlson family in Fishtown, now in its fourth and fifth generations in business, still provides smoked fish and their famous whitefish sausage for the area.

The newer boutiques along Leland's Main Street are on the sophisticated side, which makes for agreeable browsing. Some of northern Michigan's finest artists display their work at the Main Street Gallery, and there's another location of Becky Thatcher Designs. Michigan Peddler has over 150 kinds of products made in the state, from wine and food to jewelry and artwork. Manitou Outfitters is the place to look for outdoor clothing, as well as their own exclusive "J. J. Skivvee" boxer shorts and "Saturday Pant" (they also have an outlet in Glen Arbor).

If you drive north to Northport, you'll find streets lined with tidy homes, and 1860s-era buildings near the marina now full of antiques and clothing shops. There are gifts galore at the Courtyard Shops, a nicely restored corner building in town, and more arts-and-crafts galleries on Nagonaba, the town's main street.

Keep going five miles north to the very tip of the peninsula and you'll reach Leelanau State Park and the nicely preserved Grand Traverse Lighthouse. A climb to the top yields heavenly water views. The park's trails lead to Cathead Bay and uncrowded beaches.

It's worth noting that the tall ship *Manitou* sails out of Northport harbor weekly on three- and six-day windjammer cruises in northern Lake Michigan and Lake Huron. The owners also offer a shorter sampling of life at sea on the tall ship *Malabar,* a floating bed-and-breakfast moored to the south in Traverse City, where it offers cruises by day.

If you complete your swing around the peninsula on Highway 22, you'll pass through Omena, where the Tamarack Craftsmen Gallery displays high-quality work by contemporary artisans. A detour inland brings you to the Leelanau Winery with its free tours and tastings. The drive continues past the Leelanau Sands Casino, and into Suttons Bay, which is rapidly becoming a suburb of Traverse City. It has retained its red antique telephone booths, as well as several good antiques stores and places to eat. Hattie's in Suttons Bay is often named as one of the best restaurants in northern Michigan.

From Suttons Bay, you can cut back across the peninsula toward Lake Michigan on State Highway 204 or continue to parallel the west side of the bay into Traverse City, the busy, rapidly growing hub at the bottom of the bay.

One good reason to extend your drive is to dine at Windows, an excellent restaurant with a wonderful lake view on Highway 22 before you get into town. Another is the 36-mile detour north on State Highway 37 from Traverse City onto the Old Mission Peninsula, a narrow spit projecting into Grand Traverse Bay. The drive hugging the shoreline leads past grand houses with manicured lawns and private beaches, through groves of cherry trees, and out to Old Mission Point and its 1870s lighthouse.

Along the way, you can have a tour and sample the vintages at two well-regarded wineries, Chateau Grand Traverse and Chateau Chantal, and then cap it all off with a fine dinner at Bowers Harbor Inn on the water.

One other highly recommended detour will take you 20 miles southwest of Traverse City on U.S. Highway 31 to the Interlochen Center for the Arts, site of a famous summer Arts Camp, a tradition dating back to 1928. A residential fine-arts high school during the year, Interlochen is a summer haven for over 2,100 young people in grades three through 12 who come to study music, visual arts, dance, and theater arts. It's a treat to wander the wooded grounds listening to the sounds of talented young musicians in the practice studios, or to have a seat in Interlochen Bowl, the amphitheater where full-scale rehearsals are often in progress. You may hear a chamber quartet, a concert choir, a jazz band, or the entire cast of an operetta.

The 1,200-acre grounds bordering two lakes also includes the free Walter E. N. Hastings Nature Museum. Free tours of the campus are offered morning and afternoon.

The Interlochen Arts Festival brings big-name performers into the area. Entertainers as diverse as Ray Charles, Bill Cosby, Yo Yo Ma, Itzhak Perlman, the rock group Chicago, and the Detroit Symphony have appeared at northern Michigan's most prestigious cultural event. Check the program while you are there; Interlochen is worth a trip.

Area Code: 616

DRIVING DIRECTIONS The headquarters of Sleeping Bear National Lakeshore is in Empire, reached via State Highway 72 from the east or State Highway 22 from the south. From Chicago, take I-90 into I-94, merging into I-196 north at Benton Harbor, into I-31 above Saugatuck, and picking up State Highway 22 above Manistee, about 311 miles. Empire is about 271 miles from Detroit.

ACCOMMODATIONS **The Homestead,** Highway 22, Glen Arbor 49636, 334-5000, lodge rooms, M–E; suites, EE; condominiums, M–EE • **Glen Arbor Bed-and-Breakfast,** 6548 Western Avenue, Glen Arbor 49636, 334-6789, 19th-century farmhouse near national lakeshore, I–M, CP • **Sylvan Inn,** 6680 Western Avenue, Glen Arbor 49636, 334-4333, restored 1885 inn, I–M, CP • **Manitou Manor Bed-and-Breakfast,** 147 North Manitou Trail West, Leland 49654, 256-

7712, M, CP • **Aspen House Bed-and-Breakfast,** Leland 49654, 256-9724, turn-of-the-century farmhouse overlooking the lake, M, CP • **Snowbird Inn,** P.O. Box 1124, Leland 49654, 256-9773, restored farmhouse on 18 wooded acres, M, CP • **Centennial Inn,** 7251 East Alpers Road, Lake Leelanau 49653 (4 miles east of Leland), 271-6460, restored 1865 farm, I, CP • **Leland Lodge,** 565 East Pearl Street, Leland 49654, 256-9848, lodge and cottages overlooking country club and Lake Leelanau, M–E • **Whaleback Inn,** 1757 Manitou Trail, Leland 49654, 256-9090 or (900) WHALEBACK, motel on the lake, I–E, CP • **Tall Ship *Malabar,*** 13390 South West Bay Shore Drive, Traverse City 49684, 941-2000, bed-and-breakfast accommodations, E, CP; rates include a sunset cruise.

DINING **Le Bear Waterfront Restaurant,** Lake Street, Glen Arbor, 334-4640, views of Sleeping Bear Bay, outdoor deck, varied menu, I–M • **Art's Tavern,** Highway 22, Glen Arbor, 334-3754, hamburgers to steak, I–M • **Leelanau Country Inn,** Highway 22, 8 miles south of Leland, 228-5060, old-fashioned country inn, M • **Jack's Glen Lake Inn,** County Roads 675 and 616, Burdickville (south of Glen Arbor), 334-3587, I–M • **The Bluebird,** River Street, Leland, 256-9081, river views, known for whitefish, cinnamon rolls, I–M • **The Cove,** 111 River Street, Leland, 256-9834, prime harbor views, tops for whitefish, perch, or prime rib, I–M • **Woody's,** 116 Waukazoo Street, Northport, 386-9933, known for cherrywood-smoked chicken and ribs, I–M • **Bowers Harbor Inn,** 13512 Peninsula Drive, Old Mission Peninsula, 223-4222, regional cuisine in a bayside mansion, outdoor cocktail deck, M–EE • **Windows,** 7677 West Bay Shore Drive (Highway 22), 7 miles north of Traverse City, 941-0100, heavenly views, extensive menu, M–E • **Early Bird,** Main Street, Leland, 256-9656, breakfast served all day, I • ***Gourmet choices:*** **La Becasse,** County Roads 675 and 616, Burdickville (south of Glen Arbor), 334-3944, French cuisine in a country-crossroads setting, M–E • **Hattie's,** 111 St. Joseph Street, Suttons Bay, 271-6222, elegant fare in an in-town cafe, M–E • Two restaurants in tiny Ellsworth, an hour's drive away north of Traverse City, are rated by many as the best in northern Michigan: **Rowe Inn,** 6303 County Road 48, Ellsworth, 588-7351, E–EE • **Tapawingo,** 9502 Lake Street, Ellsworth, 588-7971, prix fixe, EE.

SIGHTSEEING **Sleeping Bear Dunes National Lakeshore,** visitors center, Highway 72, Empire, 326-5134. Hours: Daily 9 A.M. to 5 P.M. in summer, to 4 P.M. the rest of year. Pierce Stocking Scenic Drive open April through November, 9 A.M. to sunset. Free • **Interlochen Center for the Arts,** off U.S. 31, P.O. Box 199, Interlochen, 276-7200. Hours: Visitors are welcome on campus anytime; check current hours for guided tours, and for current concert schedule • **Leelanau Sands Casino,** 2521 North West Bay Shore Drive (Highway 22),

Suttons Bay, 271-4104 or (800) 922-2WIN. Hours: Daily 24 hours • **Leelanau State Park,** County Road 629, Northport, 386-5422. Hours: Office open Monday to Friday 8 A.M. to 11 P.M., weekends 9 A.M. to 5 P.M. Parking fee, $$. Park includes **Grand Traverse Lighthouse,** 386-7553. Hours: July to Labor Day, daily 11 A.M. to 7 P.M.; May, June, September, and October, weekends only, noon to 5 P.M. Free with park admission • ***Cruises:*** Phone for current schedules and rates • **Manitou Island Transit,** Leland, 256-9061 • **Tall ship *Malabar* and schooner *Manitou,*** Traverse Tall Ship Company, 13390 West Bay Shore Drive, Traverse City, 941-2000 • ***Canoeing:*** **Crystal River Canoe Livery,** 6052 Western Street, Glen Arbor, 334-3090 • ***Bike rentals:*** **Geo Bikes,** River and Grand Streets, Leland, 256-9696 • ***Wineries:*** Usually open daily 11 A.M. to 5 P.M., sometimes later in summer, but hours vary, so it's best to check. Tours are free. • **Leelanau Wine Cellars,** 12683 East Tatch Road, Omena, 386-5201 • **Chateau Grand Traverse,** off Highway 37, Old Mission Peninsula, 223-7355 • **Chateau Chantal,** off Highway 37, Old Mission Peninsula, 223-4110.

INFORMATION **Glen Lake/Sleeping Bear Chamber of Commerce,** P.O. Box 217, Glen Arbor, MI 49636, 394-3238; **Leelanau Peninsula Chamber of Commerce,** 105 Phillips Street, P.O. Box 336, Lake Leelanau, MI 49653, 256-9895; www.Leelanau.com

Mr. Claus and Mr. Lincoln in Indiana

They couldn't be more opposite, the short, chubby fellow in red and the tall, lanky man in black. Yet both of those popular heroes, Santa Claus and Abraham Lincoln, are celebrated in southern Indiana in towns about 10 minutes apart, a disparate duo that make for an ideal family holiday.

Lincoln City is easy to explain. Abraham Lincoln and his family came here in 1816 when little Abe was seven, and this is where he grew up and lived until he left for Illinois at age 21. It was here that the nine-year-old boy lost his mother, Nancy Hanks Lincoln. The Lincoln Boyhood National Memorial re-creates the life of a wilderness family. Lincoln's own story is told in a museum, in a reconstructed farm with costumed interpreters, and in a musical drama presented on summer evenings at the outdoor theater in nearby Lincoln State Park.

The story of Santa Claus, home of the nation's first theme park, is a little less well-documented and a lot more romantic. It seems that in the early 1850s the few dozen inhabitants of this settlement just couldn't agree on a name for their town. After Christmas Eve services in 1852, everyone gathered around a potbellied wood-burning stove in the log church to try once again to settle on a name. The children, who had come along for services, were still present, and according to the legend, a gust of wind blew open the doors and the sound of sleigh bells came from the darkness. "Who could it be?" The little ones ran to the door, excitedly shouting "Santa Claus!"—and the little nameless town had its name.

The post office was soon drawing visitors who wanted to mail their Christmas cards from Santa Claus; today more than a million pieces of mail arrive during the holiday season from all over the country to be remailed with the Santa Claus postmark. But in the early years, kids who came to visit were disappointed to find there was no Santa in residence. In 1946, an Evansville industrialist and father of nine, Louis J. Koch, came up with a remedy, creating Santa Claus Land, the nation's first theme park. Santa's summer home for over 50 years, the park has grown into Holiday World and Splashin' Safari, two parks for the price of one and a bonanza of family entertainment.

In Lincoln City, the Lincoln Boyhood National Memorial surprises first-timers by its grandeur in rural surroundings. Erected by the state of Indiana in 1942, the memorial is an impressive building of Indiana limestone with two formal halls, one for Abe Lincoln and one for Nancy Hanks Lincoln, connected by a graceful cloister. Sculptured panels on the facade depict significant periods in the Lincolns' lives.

The fine interior is a salute to the skills of the early frontier families. The Abraham Lincoln Hall has walls of sandstone with cherry wainscoting, the kind of wood often used by Thomas Lincoln, Abraham's father, in his carpentry work. The ceiling is supported by thick handhewn trusses of yellow poplar, testimony to the pioneers' skill in cabin construction. The pew-type seats are typical of early meetinghouses.

The Nancy Hanks Lincoln Hall has similar yellow-poplar beams and columns, walnut wainscoting, pegged oak floors, a huge sandstone fireplace, and cherry-wood tables, benches, and chairs. The large handbraided rug and the window bench coverings, based on patterns Nancy Lincoln might have known, are made of wool, one of the most common materials of the frontier. The painting over the fireplace depicts the spot where the Lincolns crossed the Ohio River in 1816 on the way to their new home.

A formal landscape leads to Nancy Lincoln's grave. Her death in 1818 was caused by "milksickness," poisoning caused by the white snakeroot, a malady common in pioneer times. She was buried on a wooded knoll south of the family cabin in a rough wooden coffin made by her husband. In 1962 the National Park Service took over administration of the memorial site from the state, adding a museum exhibit and a film to help tell the story of Lincoln's youth.

Six years later, an 1820s-era working farm was re-created complete with log buildings, animals, and crops. This is the most meaningful part of the visit for youngsters. Park rangers in period clothing take the part of family members, acting out the kind of everyday life a frontier child like Lincoln would have known.

It was here that young Abe worked with his father, mourned the deaths of his mother and sister, and learned to conquer the hardships of life on the frontier. His stepmother, Sarah, encouraged the young boy's love of books and helped to develop the mind and forge the values that would make him a leader. Lincoln also sporadically attended a log-cabin school here, dressed in buckskin clothes and a raccoon cap.

Visitors can see how self-sufficient families like the Lincolns carved a life and made a living from the land and the forest around them. Cooking, sewing, quilting, and working the gardens and fields are some of the tasks demonstrated, along with chores that young Abe might have done, such as chopping wood, feeding the animals, milking the cows, and splitting rails.

The demonstrations change with the seasons. The making of linen, for example, goes from "seed to shirt," beginning with the sowing of flax, and ending with spinning the yarn. The fields are plowed and planted in spring, tended in summer, and harvested in the fall.

Across the road from the memorial is Lincoln State Park. Within its boundaries are the grave of Abraham Lincoln's only sister, Sarah Lincoln Grigsby, and the Noah Gorden Mill site, where young Abe used to read while waiting his turn to mill grain.

A 1,500-seat covered amphitheater is home to the *Young Abe Lincoln* musical outdoor drama.

The wooded park is a lovely place to take a break and relax. It includes a 58-acre lake, boat rentals, a swimming beach, a nature center, and more than 10 miles of hiking trails. The family housekeeping cabins in the park are favorite places to stay. The other choices are motels, the best being the recently built Santa's Lodge in nearby Santa Claus, where a mechanical Santa welcomes guests in the lobby. There are a few bed-and-breakfast options in surrounding towns also, most notably the River Belle, a Victorian charmer with steamboat-style gingerbread wraparound porches overlooking the Ohio River. It is in Grandview, about 20 miles south of Lincoln City.

Having spent one day learning about Lincoln, you can devote the next to visiting with Santa Claus in his home at Holiday World. This has grown into a major theme park, with more than 60 rides, games, and shows, though it will still seem low-key if you have been to giant parks in places like Wisconsin Dells. There's plenty for older children, but this remains a park that delights little ones with its holiday themes.

The original Santa Claus Land flourished as children came to sit on Santa's knee each summer and place an early order for Christmas. One of the original rides, the Fairyland Railroad, remains, though the name has been changed to the Freedom Train. The gentle rides in the Christmas section are reserved for kids under 54 inches.

In 1984 the park was expanded to include sections with Halloween and Fourth of July themes, and the name was changed to Holiday World. Bigger rides were added, including a popular Raging Rapids Raft Ride.

In 1993 a whole new park, Splashin' Safari Water Park, opened, with a wave pool and rides like the Congo River and the Bamboo Chute, a 350-foot water slide; Otorongo, three in-the-dark water slides; and Monsoon Lagoon, a family treehouse with lots of tricky ways to get wet. The little ones will love Crocodile Isle, a children's activity area with two pools and five smaller water slides.

To celebrate its 50th season in 1996, Holiday World introduced the Raven, a $2-million wooden roller coaster, the biggest in Indiana. This thrill ride includes 85-foot and 61-foot drops, a sharp turn over Lake Rudolph, and a run through a 120-foot tunnel. Santa Claus was aboard for the inaugural ride.

The park theaters now include the Holiday Theater and Santa's Storytime in the Christmas section, Hoosier Celebration Theater in the Fourth of July area, and an Aqua Stadium in the Halloween section.

In the shops in the park and in the town of Santa Claus you'll find plenty of ornaments for your Christmas tree. Antique collectors will want to note Holly Antiques and Quilts on Highway 245 in Santa Claus, Lincoln Homestead Antiques on the road to the Lincoln memorial in Lincoln City, and Lincoln Heritage Antiques in Dale. Golfers can spend a pleasant afternoon at the Christmas Lake Golf Course in Santa Claus.

Dr. Ted's Musical Marvels in Dale, a delightful collection of mechanical music machines, includes street organs, nickelodeons, player pianos, gramophones, and the prize exhibit, a Wurlitzer carousel organ. It should intrigue the kids—not to mention the grown-ups.

Between Santa Claus, Dale, and Lincoln City, you may have quite a full weekend, but many visitors enjoy taking the short drive to St. Meinrad to visit the St. Meinrad Archabbey and its beautiful turn-of-the-century Romanesque-style stone church. This community of Benedictine monks, founded by Swiss settlers in 1854, includes two schools, an undergraduate liberal-arts college for Catholic men, and a graduate-level school of theology offering training for the priesthood. The Guest House on the grounds is also open to the public for rooms and meals. A pamphlet or an audio-cassette available at the Guest House allows for self-guided tours anytime, and there is a guided tour on Saturday afternoons. The complex includes lovely statuary, murals, and other artwork. The Memorial Library and Chapter Room are special stops.

St. Meinrad also operates Abbey Press, a publisher of religious and inspirational gifts, cards, and books, and the gift shop offers a sampling of their products as well as a dining area featuring sandwiches and homemade soup and pies.

If you happen to be in the area in late summer you can add a German festival to your itinerary in the nearby towns of Jasper or Huntingburg. Both communities were settled by Germans and are proud of their heritage. If you have extra time, you might want to see two exceptional German-inspired churches, the St. Joseph Church in Jasper, and the Church of the Immaculate Conception, known as the Castle on the Hill, in Ferdinand (see page 239 for more about the churches).

Area Code: 812

DRIVING DIRECTIONS From Chicago take I-57 south to I-64 east, get off at Exit 57, and proceed south on U.S. 231, following signs to Lincoln Boyhood National Memorial; it is on State Highway 162. Total distance, about 300 miles. Santa Claus is 7 miles east of Lincoln City, via Highway 162 and State Highway 245 south. A more direct route is I-80/90 east to U.S. 41 south to I-64 east, but U.S. 41 can be slow. From Indianapolis, take I-65 south to I-64 west and follow directions above, about 170 miles.

ACCOMMODATIONS **Lincoln State Park,** Box 216, Lincoln City 47552, 937-4710, 10 housekeeping cabins accommodating up to six, I • **Santa's Lodge,** Highway 162, Santa Claus 47579, (800) 640-7895, indoor pool, I–M • **Baymont Inn and Suites,** 20857 North U.S. Highway 231, Dale, 47523, 937-7000, I–M • **Stones Budget Host Hotel,** 410 South Washington Street (U.S. 231), Dale 47523, 937-4448, I • **Scottish Inn,** U.S. 231 and I-64, Dale 47523, (800) 251-1962, I • **Best Western Dutchman Inn,** 406 East 22nd Street (U.S. 231), Huntingburg 47542, 683-2334, pool, I–M • **St. Meinrad Guest House,** State Highway 62, St. Meinrad 47577, 357-6585 or (800) 581-6905, I • ***Bed-and-breakfast homes:*** **River Belle,** State Highway 66, Grandview 47615, 649-2500 or (800) 877-5165, on the Ohio River, I, CP • **Rockport Inn,** Third and Walnut Streets, Rockport 47635, 649-2664, I–M.

DINING **St. Nick's Restaurant,** Santa's Lodge (see above), basic menu, I–M • **Country Dutchman Restaurant,** Best Western Dutchman Inn (see above), basic fare once again, I • **Schnitzelbank,** 393 Third Avenue, Highway 162, Jasper, 481-1466, German menu and ambience, M–E • **St. Meinrad Guest House** (see above), by reservation only, I.

SIGHTSEEING **Lincoln Boyhood National Memorial,** Highway 162, Lincoln City, 937-4541; www.nps.gov/libo. Hours: Daily 8 A.M. to 5 P.M., $; maximum family rate, $$ • **Lincoln State Park,** Highway

162, Lincoln City, 937-4710. Hours: Daily 7 A.M. to 11 P.M., office open 8:30 A.M. to 4 P.M. Parking fee, $$; Indiana cars, $ • ***Young Abe Lincoln Drama,*** Lincoln Amphitheatre, Lincoln State Park, (800) 264-4ABE. Hours: Mid-June to mid-August, Tuesday through Sunday 8 P.M. $$$$ • **Holiday World and Splashin' Safari Theme Park,** 7 miles south of I-64, Exit 63 or 57, Santa Claus, 937-4401 or (800) GO-SANTA. Hours: Daily mid-May to late August, weekends early May to October, opens 10 A.M. Closing varies with the season, so best to check. $$$$$ • **St. Meinrad Archabbey,** Highway 62, St. Meinrad, 357-6585. Hours: Daily 8:30 A.M. to 4 P.M. Guided tours March through November, Saturdays at 1:30 P.M. Donation • **Dr. Ted's Musical Marvels,** U.S. 231, Dale, 937-4250. Hours: Memorial Day to Labor Day, Monday to Saturday 10 A.M. to 6 P.M., Sunday 1 P.M. to 6 P.M.; weekends only rest of May and September. $$$

INFORMATION **Spencer County Visitors Bureau,** P.O. Box 202, Santa Claus, IN 47579, (888) 444-9252.

The Bears and the Bard in Platteville

Fans of the Chicago Bears need no introduction to Platteville, Wisconsin, because that's where their favorite football team goes for training camp each summer. The Bears are part of the "Cheese League," a quintet of teams who get into shape and play scrimmage games amid Wisconsin's lakes and hills, delighting football fanatics in the Midwest with an early sampling of the season.

The New Orleans Saints train in La Crosse, the Kansas City Chiefs in River Falls, the Jacksonville Jaguars in Stevens Point, and the Green Bay Packers at home in Green Bay.

In these informal settings, fans can see their favorite players close-up, talk to them, maybe even find them at the next table in a local watering hole or restaurant. Most players are good-natured about signing autographs and posing for pictures with admirers who have traveled so far just to cheer them.

Watching the workouts close-up may be nirvana for gridiron devotees, but partners of the Bear watchers may be less enthusiastic. Fortunately for them, Platteville offers other pleasures. Visitors can amuse themselves by exploring the town's early mining history or by going on any of several colorful nearby excursions, including a ferryboat ride across the Mississippi River.

Scrimmages and Shakespeare may seem like an unusual combination, but they coexist happily here each summer from mid-July to mid-August, when the Bears' camp schedule overlaps with the season of the Wisconsin Shakespeare Festival.

Platteville welcomes the Bears with open arms. Merchants like to "adopt" an individual player and decorate their windows with his photos. An excellent way to meet the players is to buy tickets for the annual Bears/Platteville Chamber of Commerce Hog Roast, held the first week of August at Legion Field, when the team comes out to mingle with the locals.

Practices are usually held at 9 A.M. and 4 P.M., so you can catch one session and still have plenty of time for other things. A few night practices are scheduled as well. Often another major team comes to town for a Saturday scrimmage game. If you can swing a long weekend, you can see both squads working out on the preceding Thursday and Friday. Sunday is typically the lightest day, and no practices are scheduled for the Sunday after a Saturday game. Exact schedules are available far in advance from the Platteville Chamber of Commerce or by calling the Bears Hot Line.

If you take time out to go exploring, you'll find that Platteville is an attractive small town with an interesting history. Like many settlements in this region, it grew up quickly in the 1820s as a mining boomtown, following the discovery of lead in 1827. It was the same man who found the first minerals in the area, John Rountree, who was also responsible for Platteville's original design and layout. Rountree commissioned an English architect, who incorporated many features of his native village of Yorkshire into the town plan. The nicely restored Main Street maintains that Old World look.

Dairy cattle now graze on the hillsides where miners once burrowed for lead, but you can relive the past vividly at the Mining Museum. Dioramas, artifacts, and photos tell about the old days, but the real fun involves donning a hard hat and descending the steps 50 feet underground into the Bevans Lead Mine. This is an especially welcome tour on a hot summer day, as the mine temperature remains at a constant 52 degrees year-round.

The story goes that Lorenzo Bevans was broke on the day that changed his fate back in 1845. He had used all of his resources searching in vain for ore, and had only enough money left to pay his helper until noon. The workman agreed to stay on until the end of the day, and was amply rewarded for his loyalty. At 2 P.M., the two men struck one of the richest veins of lead ever discovered in the state; the mine produced over two million pounds of lead ore in just one year.

In the underground mine shaft, you can see the hard conditions the early miners faced, digging out lead in cramped spaces with only the light of candles either fastened to their hats or stuck into the clay seams of the mine wall. A visit to a head frame shows how zinc ore was hoisted from the mine and hand-sorted. The tour ends with a bumpy train ride around the grounds in authentic ore cars pulled by a 1931 mine locomotive.

Next door in a former schoolhouse is the Rollo Jamison Museum, which holds the collections of a local resident who seemed to want to accumulate just about everything that had to do with everyday living. The assemblage that the city took over when Jamison died in 1981 at age 93 includes carriages, farm tools, a fully stocked tavern/general store, a kitchen and parlor, musical instruments, and mechanical music boxes. On the second floor of the Mine Museum building, the Rountree Gallery displays work by area artists.

The University of Wisconsin's Platteville campus was founded in Rountree Hall, which was built by the Platteville Academy in 1853. It later became the Wisconsin School of Mines, the first mining school in the nation. UW–Platteville is a merger of the School of Mines and the Platteville State Teachers College.

The original School of Mines left a large legacy in the form of the world's largest *M,* a giant limestone letter weighing 400 tons and measuring 214 by 241 feet. Located on the side of the Platteville Mound east of the city, the M is a loved local landmark that is whitewashed twice a year by volunteers from UW–Platteville. You can see it by taking U.S. Highway 151 east toward Belmont and turning on West Mound Road. If you tackle the steep steps to the top, you'll be rewarded with a spectacular view of rolling farmland and the town, a sight that is especially lovely at sunset.

If you want nourishment along the way, you'll find a fine assortment of Wisconsin's finest at Mound View Cheese House on Highway 151 East. The shop carries 50 varieties of cheese, fresh curds, brats, sausages, mustards, honeys, jams, and jellies—most of it produced in southwest Wisconsin—as well as a variety of Wisconsin wines and microbrewery beers. The Cheese House also organizes caravan tours of area sights and airplane tours over the area and the nearby Mississippi River.

Platteville is the starting point for several colorful excursions. Take State Highway 80-81 south for nine miles to reach Cuba City, known as the City of Presidents because its Main Street is lined with tributes to all of the nation's chief executives. Even the water tower is patriotic, painted red, white, and blue.

Following Highway 151 south for about 11 miles leads to Dickeyville, home of the famous glittering grotto built by Father Matthias Werneus, a Catholic priest. Made of stone and mortar, the grotto is adorned with two-foot-tall words of counsel: *faith, peace, chastity, mildness.* The structure is embedded everywhere with a remarkable assortment of brightly colored objects, including colored glass, gems, petrified wood and moss, pottery and porcelain, stalagmites, seashells, fossils, as well as chunks of iron, copper, lead, agate, quartz, rock crystals, onyx, amethyst, coal, and geodes. Not to mention thousands of gearshift knobs. Some Wisconsin Indians even donated arrowheads and axes. On the rear wall, petrified wood and broken pottery form a tree of life. You'll find the grotto on the east and south sides of Holy Cross Church at 305 Main Street.

The most scenic excursion from Platteville is to the west: take Highway 81 for about 27 miles to reach Cassville and the Mississippi River. If you arrive on the third weekend in July, you may think you're seeing double. The town's annual Twin-O-Rama attracts hundreds of sets of twins and triplets and thousands of spectators.

Two miles north of town is Nelson Dewey State Park, named for the state's first governor, whose estate once stood on this site. The park offers a driving loop and walking trails along bluffs with fine overlooks to the Mississippi.

Adjacent to the park and sharing its visitors center is the Stonefield Historic Site, a museum of agricultural history and village life operated by the State Historical Society of Wisconsin. It includes a turn-of-the-century village with 30 reconstructed buildings and the State Agricultural Museum with its rich collection of antique farm implements and tools. You can take a horse-drawn wagon ride through a covered wooden bridge past a turn-of-the-century farmstead to get to the agricultural museum. Special activities such as blacksmithing, broom-making, and cooking are demonstrated throughout the village area. At the farmstead, a costumed guide will take you through the re-creation of a progressive farmhouse of a century ago.

The Dewey Homesite is also open for tours. The house here occupies the site where Dewey's original mansion stood watch over a sprawling 2,000-acre farm that he called Stonefield. Several original outbuildings from the estate still stand.

If you want to get out on the river, there's no more picturesque way to do so than aboard the little Cassville Ferry, which first went into service in 1836, powered by horses working on a treadmill. In recent years, the car ferry had gone in and out of business several times; in 1988 the village purchased it and stabilized service.

If you take the 20-minute ride across the river, more sightseeing awaits in Iowa. Follow U.S. Highway 52 north for six miles to Guttenberg, and you can watch Lock and Dam No. 10 in action, raising and lowering the water level for passing boats. You can also visit a two-story art gallery in an 1858 brewery and an aquarium and fish hatchery, where you can get a close-up view of the walleyes, catfish, sturgeon, trout, and other fish that swim in the Mississippi.

You can also drive about 16 miles south on State Highway 136 to Dyersville, the town made famous as the home of *Field of Dreams.* Besides visiting the famous movie site, a baseball diamond carved from a cornfield, you can look in on the National Farm Toy Museum, where the toys—farm equipment in miniature—provide a lesson in the history of agricultural technology. The museum includes a theater with a multimedia show on the transformation of farm families from the post–Civil War era to the present, and a replica of a farmhouse porch, where you can peek into the window to see a tableau of family life.

Back in Platteville, you won't have to look far for evening entertainment. The Wisconsin Shakespeare Festival offers fine renditions of classics in the pleasant air-conditioned surroundings of the Center for the Arts on the UW campus. The festival celebrates its 25th season in 2001, performing a rotating repertory of three plays. The Renaissance stage is modeled after the bard's original Globe theater, while the theater itself is an exact duplicate of London's Cottesloe Theatre. Free tours of the theater, including the costume and scene shops, are offered on Saturday mornings.

Shakespeare, who liked conjuring up the unexpected, would no doubt have enjoyed sharing billing with those other Plattesville entertainers, the Chicago Bears.

Area Code: 608

DRIVING DIRECTIONS From Chicago, take I-90 west to U.S. 20, turning north past Galena to State Highway 80 to Platteville, about 190 miles. It is 151 miles from Milwaukee, 74 miles from Madison.

ACCOMMODATIONS **Best Western Governor Dodge Motor Inn,** U.S. Highway 151, Platteville 53818, 348-2301, I • **Mound View Inn,** 1755 East U.S. 151, Platteville 53818, 348-9518, motel, I • **Super 8 Motel,** 100 Highway 80/81 South, Platteville 53818, 348-8800, I • **Walnut Ridge Bed-and-Breakfast,** 2238 County Trunk Highway A, Platteville 53818, 348-9359, 1800s log house in the country 15 minutes north of Platteville, I, CP; Log Guest House, private cottage with fireplace, whirlpool, kitchenette, M, CP • **Cunningham House,** 110 Market Street, Platteville 53818, 348-5532, turn-of-the-century home in a park, shared baths, I, CP • **Gribble House Bed-and-Breakfast,** 260 West Cedar Street, 53818, 348-7282, in-town Victorian, I, CP • **Wisconsin House,** 2105 Main Street, Hazel Green 53811 (20 minutes south of Platteville), 854-2233, former stagecoach inn, I–M, CP.

DINING **The Timbers,** 670 Ellen Street, U.S. 151 and Highway 80/81 intersection, Platteville, 348-2406, Frank Lloyd Wright–style building, good steaks, known for their organ concerts, I–M • **Gadzooks,** 300 McGregor Plaza, Platteville, 348-7700, wide-ranging menu, informal, I–M • **Wisconsin House** (see above), multicourse dinners on Saturday by reservation only, E • **Ed's Cafe,** U.S. 151, Platteville, 348-8194, just a truck stop, but the place to sample Cornish pasties, I. You can also get pasties, soups, and salads and other treats to go at the **Hometowne Bakery,** 615 South Chestnut Street, Platteville, 348-6655.

SIGHTSEEING **Chicago Bears Summer Training Camp,** Ralph E. Davis Pioneer Stadium, Southwest Road, University of Wisconsin–Platteville, 34-BEARS. Hours: Mid-July to mid-August. Phone for current dates and practice schedules • **Wisconsin Shakespeare Festival,** Center for the Arts, University of Wisconsin–Platteville, 1 University Plaza, Platteville, 342-1298. Three plays, early July to mid-August. Phone for current offerings and prices • **Mining Museum/Rollo Jamison Museum,** 385–405 East Main Street, Platteville, 348-3301. Hours: May to October, daily guided tours 9 A.M. to 5 P.M.; rest of year, self-guided tours, Monday to Friday 9 A.M. to 4 P.M. $$ • **Nelson Dewey State Park,** County Road VV, two miles west of Cassville, 725-5374. Hours: In season, 8 A.M. to 11 P.M., hours vary rest of year. Wisconsin cars, $$; out-of-state, $$$; drive-through only, $ • **Stonefield Historic Site,** Nelson Dewey State Park, Cassville, 725-5210. Hours: July and August, daily 10 A.M. to 5 P.M.; May, June, September, early October to 4 P.M. $$$ • **Cassville Car Ferry,** Prime Street landing, operating between Wisconsin Highway 133/81, Cassville, and U.S. Highway 52 at Millville, Iowa. Check current schedules c/o Cassville Department of Tourism, 100 West Amelia Street, 725-5180. Hours: May through October.

INFORMATION **Platteville Chamber of Commerce,** 275 U.S. Highway 151 West, P.O. Box 16, Platteville, WI 53818, 348-8888; www.platteville.com

Storybook Scenes in Saugatuck

There's a fairy-tale feel to Saugatuck, Michigan. With quaint cottages and shops along the narrow streets, a forest of tall sailboat masts in the harbor, and a tiny gingerbread hand-cranked ferry floating visitors across the meandering Kalamazoo River, the town quickly casts its magical spell.

A host of inns and some of the most picturesque beaches and dunes on the Michigan shore add to the enchantment. Masses of strollers along the shopping streets may dilute the serenity, but if you walk just a few blocks away into the shady residential streets, you'll be back in a storybook small town.

With its river running directly into Lake Michigan, Saugatuck in its early days seemed a good bet to emerge as a major port. It thrived from the 1840s to the 1870s, as sawmills grew up and the harbor was busy dispatching shiploads of lumber to help build Chicago and Milwaukee. Then the forests were depleted and the boom went bust—just about the time that the first city dwellers began renting rooms in area farmhouses to take advantage of the beach and the breezes.

The town's future was settled in 1910, when the School of the Art Institute of Chicago opened an artists' camp at Ox-Bow Lagoon, in the shadow of Mount Baldhead, the tallest of the area's massive dunes. Saugatuck became an art center, and where artists congregate, tourists are sure to follow.

Today this town of 1,000 has scads of shops for those tourists—some 50 at last count—and more than two dozen art galleries. Many of the wonderful old homes have become bed-and-breakfast inns. The prize lodging is the Wickwood Country Inn, filled with French and English antiques and original art. The Kemah Guest House is a turn-of-the-century hilltop mansion with a blend of Old World and Art Deco decor. Fairchild House will please fans of Victoriana, and the Bayside Inn, a converted boathouse, offers casual accommodations and private decks on the river.

The Twin Oaks Inn gets this visitor's vote as the best buy in town. A former lumbermen's boardinghouse that has been transformed with pretty country decor, it offers in-room VCRs with a library of 700 complimentary movies, a screened porch, bicycles, and an outdoor hot tub. The attractive little Maplewood Hotel will please those who want the added privacy a hotel can offer.

Shopping is a major pastime in Saugatuck, and finding things is easy. Old-timers remember when the most common wares were T-shirts, but the town is now decidedly upscale. Most of the shops are clustered right on Butler Street. You'll find clothing both funky and chic, posters, fine art, crafts, art glass and antiques, a shop full of angels, and gourmet cookware alongside an occasional leftover T-shirt store. The Saugatuck Drug Store, at 201 Butler Street, is a must stop for its soda fountain and the famous "slow sodas" that have been a specialty for over 80 years.

Palazzolo's Gelateria, at 220 Culver Street, with its homemade sorbets, gelatos, and cappuccino, is a sign of Saugatuck's growing sophistication.

Saugatuck's adjoining sister town of Douglas has less charm but it does have a growing share of shops, including a number with home-decorating themes, and the Joyce Petter Gallery at 161 Blue Star Highway, the outstanding art showcase in the region since 1973.

Walk over to Saugatuck's Water Street for river views; the Dockside Marketplace, with everything from Latin American art to eastern European antiques; and the Discovery Art Center, featuring local artists. At the Water Street dock, you can board the gingerbread-trimmed ferry that goes across the river to the wooded peninsula and the dunes. The first ferry began service in 1838; this "new" boat went into service in 1965, with the same traditional mechanism. The captain hand-cranks a big, noisy winch that pulls the ferry along a 380-foot chain resting in the bed of the river.

It's a hilly but pleasant walk from the ferry landing to the beach and the tallest of the dunes, Mount Baldhead, or you can do a round-trip ferryboat ride just for fun and go beaching by car.

However you arrive, dune-backed Oval Beach is not to be missed. It was selected by one travel magazine as among the 25 best in the world.

Mount Baldhead got its name before the top of the mountain was covered with trees. Climbing the 279 steps to Mount Baldhead's peak is fun, even though some of the anticipated view is blocked by the trees. Above the beach, signs point out other walks along the dunes; the trail heading north along the ridge yields nice views of the lake. Tucked away in those dunes is a beach for those who like to do their sunbathing in the nude.

An easier and more exciting way to get dune-top vistas is to take a 35-minute dune-schooner ride, a rollicking romp up and down the hills of a moonlike landscape. The narration is corny, but some of the overlooks afford fabulous views, and you do learn about how the dunes were formed.

Dune-ride headquarters are on the way to Saugatuck Dunes State Park. The park's two miles of Lake Michigan beachfront are far less crowded than the beach closer to town, partly because there's a one-mile walk from the parking lot to the shore. It's worth it, however, if you want solitude.

Saugatuck's exceptional setting can also be appreciated from the decks of the *Star of Saugatuck,* an old-fashioned riverboat that cruises down the river past the 900 or so yachts and sailboats that populate the harbor, and then out into Lake Michigan, where you can look back to admire the dunes rimming the shore and the crest of Mount Baldhead.

Whether you tour by boat or dune buggy, the narration will include the story of Singapore, the lumber town right next to Saugatuck whose population departed when the trees were gone, leaving the buildings to be completely buried in sand by the shifting winds. All that remains is a giant mound of sand. Residents say that when the wind is right, you can sometimes see a roof corner peeking out.

Another highly recommended local sight is the S.S. *Keewatin,* the last intact passenger steamer from the era of ship travel on the Great Lakes, now a floating museum moored in the Kalamazoo. The curved mahogany stair rails, wooden-bunked staterooms, stately dining room, and rear deck where passengers once danced the night away are reminders of a vanished era of elegance.

When dinnertime comes, many say the best food in town is found at the Clearbrook Golf Club, though some do favor the French country cuisine at Restaurant Toulouse. Be prepared for lines at popular spots like Billie's Boat House or Coral Gables, where there is dancing and live music. The Global Bar and Grill is a favorite hangout; Southwestern dishes spice up the basic menu. The Red Barn Playhouse offers a changing roster of lighthearted summer theater. Lovers of classical music may want to take in the summer Chamber Music Festival at the Saugatuck Womens Club.

Just a few miles inland from Saugatuck is Michigan's fertile orchard country. Take a drive to Crane Orchards in Fennville to the southeast, where you can pick your own cherries, raspberries, or peaches in summer, or pears and apples in fall. At any time of year you can sample their legendary homemade fruit pies or cherry or apple strudels.

Mid-August also brings the annual Blueberry Festival in South Haven, a pretty shore town that is the heart of blueberry-growing country, 20 miles to the south. The Expo Tent displays the best locally grown products and teaches how they are grown and harvested. You can pick your own beauties at nearby farms from mid-July through Labor Day.

Area Code: 616

DRIVING DIRECTIONS Saugatuck is reached via I-196 or U.S. Highway 31. From Chicago, follow I-94 northeast into I-196, about 170 miles. It is 180 miles from Detroit.

ACCOMMODATIONS The zip code for all listings is 49453. **Wickwood Country Inn,** 510 Butler Street, 857-1465, E–EE, CP • **Bayside Inn,** 618 Water Street, 857-4321, M–EE • **Kemah Guest House,** 633 Allegan Street, 857-2919, M–E, CP • **Twin Oaks Inn,** 227 Griffith Street, 857-1600, I–M, CP • **Fairchild House,** 606 Butler Street, 857-5985, Victoriana and sumptuous breakfasts, M–E, CP • **Maplewood Hotel,** 428 Butler Street, 857-1771 or (800) 650-9790, M–E, CP • **Lake Shore Resort,** 2885 Lake Shore Drive, 857-7121, motel/resort, pool, M–E, CP in summer.

DINING **Clearbrook Restaurant,** Clearbrook Golf Club, 65th Street at 135th Avenue, 857-2000, fine dining, M–E • **Restaurant Toulouse,** 248 Culver Street, 857-1561, French country cuisine, lunch, I; dinner, M–E • **Billie's Boat House,** 449 Water Street, 857-1188, lively, informal, live music, M • **Chequers,** 220 Culver Street, 857-1868, pub menu and ambience, I–M • **Global Bar and Grill,** 215 Butler Street, 857-1555, M–E • **Loaf and Mug,** 236 Culver Street, 857-2974, favorite for breakfast treats, lunch, and informal dinners, I.

SIGHTSEEING ***Star of Saugatuck*** **Boat Cruises,** 716 Water Street, 857-4216. Hours: Early May through October, times vary with seasons, so best to check. $$$$ • **Saugatuck Dune Rides,** 6495 Washington Road, just north of Saugatuck, 857-2253. Hours: July and August, Monday to Saturday 10 A.M. to 7:30 P.M., Sunday noon to 7:30 P.M.; May and June, to 5:30 P.M.; September, weekdays 11 A.M. to 3:30 P.M., Saturday, Sunday 10 A.M. to 5:30 P.M. $$$$$ • **S.S. *Keewatin* Maritime Museum,** Blue Star Highway and Union Street, Douglas, 857-2464. Hours: Memorial Day to Labor Day, daily 10:30 A.M. to 4:30 P.M. $$ • **Saugatuck Chamber Music Festival,** Saugatuck Womens Club, Butler and Hoffman Streets, 857-2336. Hours: Mid-July to mid-August, usually Thursday and Saturday, events at 8 P.M. Phone for current schedule and prices • ***Beaches:*** **Saugatuck Oval Beach,** Blue Star Highway to traffic light in Douglas, right on Center Street, then right on Ferry Street to Oval Beach Road. Parking sticker, $$ • **Saugatuck Dunes State Park,** Blue Star Highway, A-2, north, turn left on 64th Street, then left on 138th Avenue to park signs. Parking sticker, $$ • ***Pick your own fruit:*** **Crane's Orchard,** four miles east of I-196, Fennville, 561-2297 • **DeGrandchamps Blueberry Farm,** 15575 77th Street, 637-3915; **Krupka's Blueberry Plantation,** 2647 68th Street, Douglas, 857-4279.

INFORMATION **Saugatuck/Douglas Convention and Visitors Bureau,** P.O. Box 28, Saugatuck, MI 49453, 857-1701; www.saugatuck.com

Taking Flight in Oshkosh

Most of the year Oshkosh, Wisconsin, is a quiet place, best known to most people for the overalls manufactured here. But come late July, Oshkosh soars into the spotlight as the aviation capital of the world. The Experimental Aircraft Association (EAA) AirVenture is the reason, an annual event now in its fourth decade that attracts more than 12,000 planes to the city's small Wittman Field, a regional airport—and over 800,000 people to admire them.

The EAA AirVenture is a wonderful opportunity to see a huge variety of planes close-up as well as in the air. Show or no, the EAA's showstopper Air Adventure Museum is worth a trip anytime for anyone with the slightest interest in flight. Happily, you can combine the trip with a resort stay, in Oshkosh or in nearby Green Lake.

The real crowd pleaser is the rip-roaring air show that takes off every afternoon during the Fly-In. Crowds seated on blankets or in lawn chairs have their eyes glued to the skies, where flying aces show off their stuff piloting everything from World War II bombers to sleek jets to barnstormers, not to mention home-built planes of all kinds. There are heart-stopping stunts like wing walking and loop-the-loops, dazzling races, precision formations, and mock military dogfights. Name any air maneuver and you'll likely see it in action at Oshkosh, in what has been called aviation's most diversified air show.

Showplanes that can be inspected on the ground include classics, warbirds, antiques, seaplanes, and many custom-built models. British Airways' Concorde, the world's only supersonic passenger jet, has also made several appearances in Oshkosh. Many of the small planes have been hand-built or lovingly restored by individual aviation buffs.

The AirVenture has its serious side for those who own or build private planes. There's an enormous Fly Market with everything from engines to wind socks, and plenty of souvenirs, from hats with whirling propellers to T-shirts. The weeklong event also includes dozens of seminars and workshops open to all, even a hands-on session on how to build your own small plane.

During the Fly-In, shuttle buses cover the half-mile ride from Wittman Field to the excellent EAA Air Adventure Museum. Exhibits in this 100,000-square-foot, multilevel modernistic masterpiece of a building show off 90 planes that were significant in the history of flight. The displays begin with a replica of Orville and Wilbur Wright's 1903 *Flyer,* move on through World War I into the 1920s and Charles Lindbergh's *Spirit of St. Louis,* and through the years to the Flying Fortresses of the 1940s, and the 1960 *Voyager II,* the ship that circled the world on a nonstop nine-day flight covering 24,896 miles. The Eagle Hangar is filled with classic planes from World War II.

The EAA was started to encourage amateur aircraft building, and the museum is unique for its emphasis on home-built aircraft. There are many small, sleek models that were constructed in someone's basement or garage. More than the giants, these are the planes that make you want to know how it feels to get behind the wheel and take to the sky.

Buses take museum-goers out to the museum's Pioneer Airport, where old flying machines can be seen in their appropriate surroundings. The airport's tower once stood in Chicago, where it was known as the Lindbergh Beacon. Barnstorming air shows take place during the summer, and rides in a 1929 Ford trimotor, a helicopter, and a biplane are available for a fee.

The museum complex also houses five theaters, two restoration workshops, a photo and art gallery, many hands-on exhibits, and two gift shops. You can easily spend an entire afternoon.

When you've had your fill of flight, head for Oshkosh's two other excellent museums, located catty-corner from each other on Algoma Boulevard. They are reached by taking State Highway 21 (exit east from U.S. Highway 41).

The Paine Art Center and Arboretum, built by lumber baron Nathan Paine in 1927, was modeled after the great timbered English Tudor country manors. Having derived their fortune from lumber, the Paines made their home a showcase for fine woods. There is exquisite detailing in the hand-carved paneling of oak and walnut as well as in the molded plaster ceilings. All of this is a splendid backdrop for antique furnishings, magnificent Oriental rugs, decorative arts and glassware, and a collection of paintings and sculpture by French and American artists of the 19th century. The five-acre arboretum, with rose and formal gardens, makes for a pleasant stroll.

The Oshkosh Public Museum across the way is another mansion that attests to the town's early wealth from lumber. The 1907 Tudor-style Edgar Sawyer home has interiors and iridescent stained-glass windows designed by the Tiffany studio. The most famous exhibit here is the Apostles Clock, with 12 figures that parade every hour on the hour. Recently rebuilt following a fire, the museum exhibits explore the natural history and heritage of the Lake Winnebago region.

More fine homes can be seen in the Washington Avenue Historic District on the east side of Oshkosh, some 130 in all, built between 1880 and 1920 for the city's leading families. Pick up a driving map at the EAA museum.

The 1883 Grand Opera House on High Street, which hosted touring artists from Jenny Lind to Enrico Caruso during its glory days, has been restored and continues to offer dance and musical productions.

Downtown Oshkosh is not a shopper's mecca, but there's plenty of opportunity for bargains at the 60-plus shops of the Horizon Outlet Center at U.S. 41 and State Highway 44 across from the EAA museum. Among the outlets promising savings are Oshkosh and Wisconsin-based Land's End.

If you're traveling with kids, you may want to visit the small Menominee Park Zoo on Lake Winnebago, where there's plenty to interest little ones, from wallabies to llamas to monkeys. Admission is free. There are amusements here, as well: bumper boats, paddle canoes, pedal boats, and a miniature train.

"Little Oshkosh," a community playground built by 6,000 volunteers, is unique, featuring a lighthouse, castle, airplane, tunnels, and many other play options that delight children.

Motels will accommodate those who want to be near to the EAA Museum, but to turn the trip into a resort vacation, head for the Pioneer Inn, a miniresort a few minutes from town on Lake Winnebago. On the handsome grounds are tennis, miniature golf, a putting green, and indoor and outdoor pools. Boats of all kinds can be rented, and the resort has its own excursion yacht, the *Pioneer Princess.* Reserve far ahead if you plan to come during the AirVenture; the inn is extremely popular.

An alternative is to drive half an hour west on State Highway 23 to Green Lake, a classic old-fashioned small resort town. The deepest inland lake in the state, Green Lake became the first summer resort west of Niagara Falls when the Oakwood Hotel was built in 1867. The old hotels are gone, but the seven-and-a-half-mile lake is as crystal clear as ever, still hooking fishing enthusiasts, particularly in summer when lake trout is the specialty.

The little town is gracious and quiet, and you can take your pick of resort accommodations at the Heidel House or at various smaller inns, all on or near the lake. The Heidel House offers a choice of two large lodges or individual guest houses, and activities include water sports, tennis, nature trails, and three golf courses. It's a fine place to escape the crowds of the Fly-In—or to escape anytime at all.

On the way to Green Lake, loyal Republicans can stop in Ripon, the birthplace of the party. It was formed on March 20, 1854, in the famed Little White School House by a group opposed to the spread of slavery caused by the Kansas/Nebraska Act. The schoolhouse is now a national monument open to the public.

Area Code: 920

DRIVING DIRECTIONS Oshkosh is on U.S. Highway 41. From Chicago, follow I-94 north to Milwaukee, then west on I-94 to U.S. Highway 45, which merges with U.S. 41, about 166 miles. It is 80 miles northwest of Milwaukee.

ACCOMMODATIONS ***Oshkosh:*** **Pioneer Inn and Marina,** 1000 Pioneer Drive, Oshkosh 54901, 233-1980 or (800) 683-1980, M–EE • **Oshkosh Hilton,** 1 North Main Street, Oshkosh 54901, 231-5000, I–M • **Ramada Inn,** 500 South Koeller Street, Oshkosh 54901, 233-1511, I–E • **Fairfield Inn by Marriott,** 1800 South Koeller Road, Oshkosh 54901, 233-8504, I • Motels closest to EAA Museum: **AmericInn of Oshkosh,** 1495 South Park Avenue, Oshkosh 54901, 232-0300, I • **Super 8,** 1581 South Park Avenue, Oshkosh 54903, 426-2885, I • ***Green Lake:*** **Heidel House Resort,** 643 Illinois Avenue, Green Lake 54941, 294-3344 or (800) 444-2812, E–EE • **Carvers on the Lake,** N5529 County Road A, Green Lake 54941, 294-6931, old country home, antiques, M–E • **Oakwood Lodge,** 365 Lake Street, Green Lake 54941, 294-6580, M, CP • **McConnell Inn,** 497 South Lawson, Green Lake 54941, 294-6430, pleasant bed-and-breakfast in a fine 1900 home, M, CP master suite, E, CP.

DINING *Oshkosh:* **The Granary,** 50 West Sixth Avenue, 233-3929, restored 1883 stone mill, prime rib is the specialty, M • **Fox River Brewing Company and Fratello's Italian Cafe,** 1501 Arboretum Drive, State Highway 21 at the Fox River, 232-BEER, • **Roxy Supper Club,** 571 Main Street, 231-1980, I–E • *Green Lake:* **Carvers on the Lake** (see above), M–EE • **Norton's Marine Dining Room,** 380 South Lawson Drive, 294-6577, overlooking the lake, outdoor dining, steak and seafood, I–E.

SIGHTSEEING **EAA Air Adventure Museum,** 3000 Poberezny Drive, off U.S. 41 at State Highway 44 exit, Oshkosh, 426-4800. Hours: Monday to Saturday 8:30 A.M. to 5 P.M., Sunday 11 A.M. to 5 P.M. $$$ • **EAA AirVenture,** convention and sports aviation exhibition, Wittman Field. Usually held last week of July; check museum for current dates • **Paine Art Center and Arboretum,** 1410 Algoma Boulevard, Oshkosh, 235-6903. Hours: Tuesday to Sunday 11 A.M. to 4 P.M., also to 7 P.M. on Friday. $$; under 12, free • **Oshkosh Public Museum,** 1331 Algoma Boulevard, Oshkosh, 424-4731. Hours: Tuesday to Saturday 9 A.M. to 5 P.M., Sunday 1 P.M. to 5 P.M. Donation • **Menominee Park Zoo,** Hazel Street and Merritt Avenue, 236-5082. Hours: May through September, 8 A.M. to 7:30 P.M., weather permitting. Free • **Little White School House,** Blackburn Street, Ripon, (920) 748-6764. Hours: May to September, daily 10 A.M. to 4 P.M., weekends in October. Donation.

INFORMATION **Oshkosh Convention and Visitors Bureau,** 525 West 20th Street, Oshkosh, WI 54901, 236-5250; www.oshkoshcvb.org • **Green Lake Chamber of Commerce,** P.O. Box 386, Green Lake, WI 54971, 294-3231.

Collecting Cars in Auburn

"I've got 53, 53, 53. Do I hear 54? 54? 54? 54? This one is a beauty folks, a prize. You won't see another one like it. A 1959 Aston-Martin DB Mark III Coupe, perfectly restored. Where are you going to find another one like it? Do I hear 54? 54? I've got $53,500, $53,500—going, going—sold for $53,500."

And so it goes, as the auctioneer's patter continues day and night for five days, as magnificent classic cars, one after another, go on the block at the annual Kruse International Collector Car Auction, an event held each Labor Day Weekend in Auburn, Indiana.

This Super Bowl of auto auctions, billed as the world's first and largest collector-car event, is the highlight of the annual Auburn-Cord-Duesenberg Festival, which draws some 300,000 people to a small, otherwise little-known town in northeast Indiana. Buyers and sellers, collectors, admirers, movie stars, models, Indy race drivers, sports stars, and just about anyone who likes to look at beautiful classic automobiles can be found in Auburn during the auction. The gala weekend also includes a colorful Parade of Classics (on Saturday afternoon), and just in case you weary of watching cars go by, top-notch antique, craft, and quilt shows are also on the agenda.

As a change-of-pace bonus, one of the nation's best museums devoted to Abraham Lincoln is not far away in Fort Wayne.

Auburn may be known mainly to auto aficionados, but it is an appropriate place to pay homage to the early carmakers, for this is where Auburn, Cord, and Duesenberg cars were manufactured in the 1920s and 1930s. Original, bold in styling, and advanced in engineering, the cars created a mystique that lives on to this day. Owners are a unique and proud group.

The first festival was held in 1956 when collectors of these classics gathered to swap car stories, salute the birthplace of their automobiles, and participate in a regal parade down Auburn's shady streets. Today celebrities and astronauts serve as marshal of the parade, and many owners arrive in Auburn after driving their babies in the annual Hoosier Tour of the state.

It was in 1971 that the inspiration arose to invite Kruse Auctions, which is based in Auburn, to hold a Collector Car Consignment Auction during the festival. That first year fewer than 100 vehicles were parked in a vacant lot in Auburn—and they drew an unheard-of crowd of 7,000. The numbers have mushroomed right along with the prices of the cars. By the mid-1990s, the festival grounds were expanded to 380 acres, and 5,000 collector cars were up for bids on the auction block and adjacent car corral.

Classics, sports cars, race cars, antique trucks, motorcycles, celebrity cars—you'll see almost every kind of auto, from a 1928 Stutz Blackhawk to a 1947 Tucker "Tin Goose" to a 1991 Lamborghini. The 1940 Mercedes-Benz grand touring car owned by German foreign minister Von Ribbentrop and a hand-built Cord circa 1935 were among the prizes in one recent year.

Some recent bids give an idea of the value of these collectors' gems: \$157,500 for a 1972 Mercedes-Benz 600, \$91,875 for a 1964 Ford Thunderbird, and \$52,000 for a 1929 Chrysler Imperial convertible with a rumble seat. A 1971 Mercedes 280 SE brought a cool \$74,555, and a 1954 Chevrolet Corvette Roadster netted \$52,500. Models less prized may go for a mere \$10,000 to \$15,000.

Serious collectors remain glued to the bidding, but most visitors vary their activities, spending some time watching the auction, more time roaming the grounds to admire the cars or to patronize the many food and souvenir stands.

On Saturday at noon the Auburn Community Band gets the downbeat and everyone in town rushes to find a curbside spot from which to view the big parade. Auburn and Cord owners love to show off their classics, and many dress in costumes to match the car's vintage. Afterwards, participants park around Auburn's splendid courthouse to give visitors a chance to inspect their shiny automobiles.

Since 1974 Auburn has also boasted a year-round attraction, the Auburn-Cord-Duesenberg Museum. It is housed in a prize Art Deco setting, the former headquarters and original showroom of the Auburn Automobile Company. The museum offers a look back at the golden age of motoring, displaying dozens of examples of the innovative cars once made here, along with classics. Over 100 vehicles trace the history of automobiles from the horseless carriages of the 1890s to current sports models.

Auburn's second museum, the National Automotive and Truck Model Museum, occupies the restored service and experimental buildings of the Auburn Automobile Company, adding still more classic cars plus trucks and antique automotive toys to the town's attractions. Again, more than 100 vehicles are on exhibit.

The Antique Show and Market sponsored by the Tri Kappa sorority at a local school, a tradition past its 30th anniversary, has been called one of the finest in the Midwest, with over 75 top-quality arts-and-crafts dealers representing 10 states. On Sunday, the courthouse square is filled with a giant arts-and-crafts show featuring over 200 artisans from across the region. Senior quilters show off their handiwork at the annual festival sponsored by the Retired Senior Volunteer Program of DeKalb, Noble, and Steuben counties, where the auctioning of an automotive quilt is a big event each year.

Free shuttle buses make the rounds from the auction grounds to all of these attractions. The local historical society also usually offers tours of Auburn's vintage neighborhoods.

The list of events changes so that there is something new to look forward to almost every year. In 1995 a hot-air balloon classic was added to the agenda, with colorful craft sent sailing into the early-morning and evening skies. In 1998 a Decorator Showcase home was the big attraction.

Since dining and accommodations in Auburn are limited, many festival-goers stay in Fort Wayne, Indiana's second-largest city. Most choose motels on the northern edge of the city, about 20 miles from the festival grounds. Fort Wayne offers a wider range of dining choices.

No matter where you decide to stay, it's worth taking the drive to Fort Wayne to discover one of America's finest museums devoted to Abraham Lincoln. There is a reason why this major new museum is located in a city of 200,000, one seldom associated with Lincoln. Fort Wayne is the home of the Lincoln National Corporation, a major insurance company. Over 90 years ago, founder Arthur Hall wrote to Robert Todd Lincoln for permission to use his father's name for the new company being formed. Robert agreed, and even sent along a famous photo—the one that graces $5 bills today. In gratitude, Hall later established a Lincoln Historical Research Foundation to honor the company's namesake.

The result is the largest privately owned Lincoln collection in the world, including an astounding 18,000 books; 5,000 original photographs; some 200 documents signed by Lincoln; 7,000 19th-century prints, engravings, newspapers, and sheets of music; 200,000 newspaper and magazine clippings; paintings and sculptures; and scores of artifacts. The collection became the nucleus of the museum, which opened in 1995.

Among the many treasures are rare signed copies of two of the most important American documents, the Emancipation Proclamation and the Thirteenth Amendment Resolution; Lincoln's legal-size wallet bearing his signature; an engraved penknife; original buttons, ribbons, and ballots from Lincoln's presidential campaigns; Lincoln's personal photos of his children; even the suit worn by the president on the night of his assassination.

The 11 galleries and four theaters of this striking new museum show off the best of this priceless collection, focusing on Lincoln's years in the White House. For those who may have visited Lincoln's boyhood home in Lincoln City, Indiana, or followed his footsteps to Springfield, Illinois, this museum completes the picture. It depicts the president's difficult role during the most critical years in American history, using both actual artifacts and the most modern techniques, including films and touch-screen monitors. Save plenty of time for this excellent museum.

If you've brought children along for this weekend, consider visiting Fort Wayne's first-class Children's Zoo, which has over 3,700 animals in a 40-acre park setting. A bright new museum in the city, Science Central, offers all the latest in participatory fun and learning.

One final option is to combine a day at the Auburn-Cord-Duesenberg Festival with an outdoorsy weekend at Pokagon State Park, about half an hour to the north, above Angola. Here you can stay in the handsomely renovated Potawatomi Inn, a lodge overlooking one of the scenic lakes that make this corner of Indiana a popular summer destination. The park offers hiking trails, horseback riding and hayrides, a swimming beach, fishing, and boat rentals.

Area Code: 219

DRIVING DIRECTIONS Auburn is reached via I-69. From Chicago, take I-80/90 to I-69 south, about 175 miles. It is about 15 miles north of Fort Wayne, about 140 miles from Indianapolis.

ACCOMMODATIONS Note that Auburn motels charge more during the festival. **Auburn Inn,** 225 Touring Drive, Auburn 46706, 925-6363 or (800) 255-2541, motel, pool, I–E • **Country Hearth Inn,** 1115 West Seventh Street, Auburn 46707, 925-1316, motel, pool, I, CP • **Holiday Inn Express,** 404 Touring Drive, Auburn 46706, 925-1900, M • ***Motels on the north side of Fort Wayne:*** **Fort Wayne Marriott,** 305 East Washington Center Road, I-69, Exit 112A, Fort Wayne 46825, 484-0411, M–E • **Don Hall's Guesthouse,** 1313 West Washington Center Road, I-69, Exit 111B, Fort Wayne 46825, 489-2524 or (800) 348-1999, upscale motel, indoor and outdoor pools, I, CP • **Fairfield Inn by Marriott,** 5710 Challenger Parkway, 489-0050, I-69, Exit 111B, Fort Wayne, I • **Residence Inn by Marriott,** 4919 Lima Road, I-69, Exit 111A, Fort Wayne 46808, 484-4700, all-suites motel, pool, breakfast buffet, I–M, CP • ***Pokagon State Park:*** **Potawatomi Inn,** I-69, Exit 154, 6 Lane 100, Lake James, Angola 46703, 833-1077 or (877) 768-2928, room, I–M; suites, M; cabins, I.

DINING **Joshua's,** 640 North Grandstaff, Auburn, 925-4407, M • **Auburn House Restaurant,** 129 West Eighth Street, Auburn, 925-1102, family dining, all three meals, I • ***Fort Wayne:*** **Cafe Johnell,** 2529 South Calhoun Street, 456-1939, the city's fine dining choice, M–EE • **Speedway Cafe,** 4429 Lima Road, 484-7013, no-frills place for steak, American fare, I–M • **Park Place Grill,** 200 East Main Street, 420-7275, varied menu, downtown location, M • **Casa D'Angelo,** 3402 Fairfield, 745-7200, Italian, I–M • **Mallory's,** Don Hall's Guesthouse hotel (see above), imaginative American menu, M–E • **Elegant Farmer,** 1820 Coliseum Boulevard North, 481-1976, prime rib is the specialty, generous portions, salad bar, I–M • **Old Country Buffet,** 5507 Coldwater Road, 483-1665, all-you-can-eat buffet, M • **Potawatomi Inn** (see above), I–M • **The Hatchery,** 118 South Elizabeth Street, Angola, 665-9957, excellent food and quaint ambience, M–E.

SIGHTSEEING **Auburn-Cord-Duesenberg Festival,** P.O. Box 271, Auburn 46706, 925-3600, five days including Labor Day Weekend. Festival includes: Kruse International Collector Car Auction, parade of vintage cars, Arts and Crafts Show, Quilt Show, Antique Show and Sale, and Decorator Showcase Home. Phone for current hours and fees • **Auburn-Cord-Duesenberg Museum,** 1600 South Wayne Street, Auburn, 925-1444. Hours: Daily 9 A.M. to 5 P.M. $$$ • **National Automotive and Truck Model Museum,** 1000 Gordon Buehrig Place (behind ACD Museum), 925-9100. Hours: Daily 8 A.M. to 6 P.M. Admission, $$ • ***Fort Wayne:*** **Lincoln Museum,** 200 East Berry Street, 455-3864. Hours: Tuesday to Saturday 10 A.M. to 5 P.M., Sunday 1 P.M. to 5 P.M. $$ • **Science Central,** 1950 North Clinton Street, Fort Wayne, 424-2400. Hours: Tuesday to Saturday 9 A.M. to

5 P.M., Sunday noon to 5 P.M. $$ • **Fort Wayne Children's Zoo,** 3411 Sherman Boulevard, 427-6800. Hours: late April to mid-October, daily 9 A.M. to 5 P.M. $$.

INFORMATION Fort Wayne/Allen County Convention and Visitors Bureau, 1021 South Calhoun Street, Fort Wayne, IN 46802, 424-3700 or (800) 767-7752; www.fwcvb.org; **Auburn Chamber of Commerce,** 136 West Seventh Street, P.O. Box 168, Auburn, IN 56706, 925-2100.

Fall

Overleaf: Mid-Continent Railway steam train. *Photo courtesy of the Wisconsin Dells Visitor Convention Bureau.*

Autumn Vistas in Brown County

The wooded hills of Brown County, Indiana, have a majesty beyond their measure. Stand at an overlook and gaze at the distant ridges, cresting like waves in a heaven-high ocean. You could easily imagine yourself in the mountains rather than the Midwest.

In fall, when mile after mile of forest bursts into brilliant hues, the region is a painting come to life. The views are most spectacular in Brown County State Park, Indiana's oldest and largest preserve, 16,000 pristine acres with many high points for savoring the scenery.

It isn't surprising that the beauty of these steep hills and hollows has long been a magnet for artists. T. C. Steele, Indiana's Impressionist painter, came in 1907, liked what he saw, and built his hilltop studio-home, The House of the Singing Winds, now a state historic site and a favorite with visitors. By the 1920s scores of painters had followed, and Brown County developed into an art colony that continues to this day. The first Brown County Art Gallery Association was founded in 1927.

Where artists gather, art lovers tend to follow, and so it is that Nashville, the quaint county seat, is now chockablock with shops—over 300, according to the local brochure, in a village with a population of just over 700. In the town's old homes (and a few newer quarters built to blend) are galleries showing paintings and crafts by regional artists and shops selling everything from corn wreaths to bird feeders to fine antiques. Working craftsmen and artists are found in many of the galleries.

But despite the influx of shops and shoppers, Nashville remains country at heart. It is surrounded by towns with names like Bean Blossom and Gnaw Bone, and log cabins are a common sight on the leafy back roads. You can find old-fashioned country cooking, and the evening entertainment includes a hearty helping of country music, mimicking that other Nashville farther south. High spots for country fans are the lively Bill Monroe Bluegrass festivals held in June, July, and early fall in a wooded amphitheater in nearby Bean Blossom.

Between the shops and entertainment and the lofty scenery, Nashville is understandably a prime fall destination. The rates and the crowds go up considerably in October, but many people feel the views are worth the crush.

If you don't want to drive the roads in slow motion during peak season, consider a weekday visit or a September trip. There's often a bit of early color, and you can enjoy it without the crowds. Mid-September also brings the Brown County Art Renaissance, a chance to see special exhibits of the town's early artists and a "paint out," which features many artists at work around the town gazebo and at the T. C. Steele State Historic Site.

Those who plan far ahead may be able to snag rooms at the Abe Martin Lodge in Brown County State Park, a rustic building of hand-hewn native stone and oak timbers cut in the park. The reasonably priced accommodations offer hotel conveniences, including TV and telephone. The lodge includes comfortable sitting areas with fireplaces and a rustic dining room. Family cabins tucked into the woods are a tremendous bargain; they're booked as much as two years in advance. The lodge's name, incidentally, stems from the early 1900s when the newcomers and the country folk in town didn't always appreciate each other's ways. A cartoon character named Abe Martin was created by an Indianapolis newspaperman to poke fun at the rural ways of Brown County. The locals could take a joke and eventually grew to be fond of Abe.

If the lodge is full, deciding where to stay becomes a pleasant dilemma. Inns in the center of Nashville are within easy walking distance of shops and dining options, while the tempting hideaways in the country offer peace and quiet and spectacular views of the foliage. In town, the nod goes to two newer properties designed to look as though they've been part of the town forever. The warm, homey Cornerstone Inn has different Victorian decor in every room, while the Artists Colony Inn is furnished in Shaker style, with four-poster beds and Windsor chairs made by local craftsmen.

Among the choices in the country, Russell's Roost, a hilltop retreat on 17 acres, is a standout. You may never want to leave once you see the views from the decks. As a bonus, hostess Mary Lou Russell is a silhouette artist—you can enjoy her work on the walls as well as her unique guest book with a cutout portrait of each former guest.

A variety of other individual log cabins in wooded settings are another option available to visitors, providing country ambience and modern comforts.

You need no guide to Nashville shops, since most are within a four-block area. The best work by many local artists is displayed at the Brown County Art Gallery, behind the courthouse at the corner of Main Street and Old School Way, and at the Brown County Art Guild, in a historic home on Van Buren Street. A wide array of crafts can be found at the Brown County Craft Gallery, a cooperative on the second floor on the corner of Van Buren and Main. The best place for quality antiques is Albert's, about a mile west of town on State Highway 46, where the handsome quarters also include suites for overnight guests.

Many individual craftsmen and artists have their own shops, and smaller galleries offer their own treasures; part of the fun of Nashville is browsing and making your own discoveries.

For scenery, there is nothing to match Brown County State Park and its many acres of forest. The park map available at the lodge clearly shows vista spots such as Hesitation Point, where the views stretch for miles. You can also rent a cassette tape at the lodge for a narrated auto tour of the scenic six-mile southern loop. Take along a picnic to enjoy beside one of the park's two lakes.

The original forest here was cut down by early settlers. The Depression-era Civilian Conservation Corps began the planting of the dense second-growth woodlands that now cover the region with black locust, black walnut, oak, hickory pine, and spruce trees. The gnarled sassafras supplies flavoring for the fragrant tea served at the Nashville House restaurant in town.

The CCC also constructed many of the existing buildings, the lodge, shelters, trails, and two log lookout towers. They cleared most of the vistas along the park roadway and built Ogle Lake, as well. If you want to learn more about the park's early days, you can rent a cassette at the lodge for a guided history walking tour.

You needn't be a serious hiker to enjoy the forest. There are two easy trails just over a mile in length and five moderate trails from three-quarters of a mile to three and a half miles. Watch for birds and wild-flowers as you walk—200 species of plants bloom between June and November, and over 150 species of birds have been recorded within the park boundaries. The roadless southwestern and eastern sectors of the park can be visited only on foot. You could also visit the saddle barn and enjoy the woods on a bridle trail.

The Nature Center has displays of live snakes, turtles, and other small inhabitants of the woods, as well as nature exhibits and talks and workshops with naturalists. For recreation, the park offers lighted tennis courts and, in the summer, a swimming pool. Hayrides leave every Friday and Saturday night in season at 6 P.M. from the Country Store parking lot.

When night comes, there's a wide choice of entertainment in town. The Brown County Playhouse, a summer theater past its 50th anniversary, extends its season into October. Country music can be heard at several places, including the Little Nashville Opry, the Red Barn, the Pine Box, and the Nashville Follies Theater.

More backroads beauty can be found by driving out of town in almost any direction. State Highway 135, a roller-coaster road of twists and turns, leads north to Bean Blossom, where country-music fans will want to stop for the Bill Monroe Bluegrass Hall of Fame and Country Star Museum. It is filled with Monroe memorabilia, tributes to other Bluegrass biggies like Lester Flatt and Earl Scruggs, and costumes and displays of country headliners like Johnny Cash, Dolly Parton, and Loretta Lynn. The Walkway of Stars in front of the entrance features 100 bronze stars.

The log cabin where Bill Monroe lived during some of his teen years remains. It was owned by Monroe's uncle Pendelton Vandiver, who is honored with Uncle Pen Day during the fall Bluegrass Hall of Fame Festival.

Drive south on Highway 135 about 14 miles to find Story, a dot on the map with the best restaurant in the area, housed in the old general store.

Nine miles to the east off Highway 46 is the T. C. Steele State Historic Site. In addition to the artist's beautiful home and art-filled studio, the 211-acre site includes hiking trails, a log cabin, a nature preserve, and gardens planted by Mrs. Steele.

Another highly recommended excursion takes you 18 miles west on Highway 46, past the big weekend flea market in Gnaw Bone, and into Columbus, a town of 32,000 with a cache of prize architecture many a big city might envy. I. M. Pei, Eero Saarinen, Cesar Pelli, Richard Meier, and Kevin Roche are among the luminaries who designed over 50 public and private buildings in Columbus. These are not monumental skyscrapers, but libraries, schools, fire stations, a county jail, a post office, and other public spaces—everyday living made more pleasant thanks to skillful design.

It all began with the Cummins Engine Company, whose corporate offices by Roche Dinkeloo and Associates are a fine example of architectural merit. In 1957 the Cummins Engine Foundation, hoping to build awareness of the importance of good architecture, offered to pay the architectural fees for a new public school-building if school officials would choose from an approved list of architects. The offer was later extended to all public buildings in Columbus, and many private firms got on the architectural bandwagon.

To see the happy results, stop by the local visitors center for a self-guiding architectural tour map, or take one of the daily bus tours. In addition to buildings, you'll see sculpture by Henry Moore (in front of the library) and an intriguing moving sculpture by Jean Tinguely in the shopping mall called The Commons. Even Columbus's Mill Race Park is exceptional, its picnic shelters, tower, amphitheater, boathouse, and river walk the very model of creative planning.

Columbus is a tribute to man-made environments, a perfect counterpoint to the natural beauty of Brown County.

Area Code: 812

DRIVING DIRECTIONS Nashville is on State Highway 135, just off State Highway 46, 60 miles south of Indianapolis. From Chicago, take I-80 east to I-65 south, connect with I-465 to skirt Indianapolis, and follow Highway 135 south, 235 miles.

ACCOMMODATIONS All rates go up about $10 in October; expect minimum stays on weekends. **Abe Martin Lodge,** Brown

County State Park, Box 547, Nashville 47448, 988-4418 or toll free (877) AMLODGE, lodge rooms, I–M, family cabins, M • **Cornerstone Inn,** 54 East Franklin Street, Nashville 47448, 988-0300 or (888) 383-0300, gracious Victorian decor, some fireplaces, whirlpools, M, CP • **Artists Colony Inn,** 105 Van Buren Street, P.O. Box 1099, Nashville 47448, 988-0600 or (800) 737-0255, tasteful Shaker decor, M–E, CP • **Russell's Roost,** 3736 Greasy Creek Road (off State Highway 135), Nashville 47448, 988-1600, extraordinary views, I–M, CP • **Allison House,** 90 South Jefferson Street, P.O. Box 1625, Nashville 47448, 988-0814, pleasant in-town home, M, CP • **Hotel Nashville Resort,** 245 North Jefferson Street, Nashville 47748, 988-8400 or (800) 848-6274, all-suite hotel within walking distance of town, kitchens, 2 baths, indoor pool, some Jacuzzis, M–E • **Albert's Mall Inn,** Highway 46 East, Nashville 47448, 988-2397, upscale antiques and suites with private entrances, M–E • **Lee's Retreats Log Cabins,** Helmsburg and Country Club Roads, Nashville 47448, 988-4117, one- and two-bedroom cabins with fireplaces, kitchens, M (check with Brown Country visitors bureau for complete list of other available cabins) • **Columbus Inn,** 445 Fifth Street, Columbus 47201, 378-4289, renovated 1895 city hall, M–E, CP.

DINING **Story Inn,** 6404 South State Highway 135, 9.5 miles southeast of Nashville, 988-2273, creative fare in an authentic country store setting, lunch, I; dinner, E–EE • **Nashville House,** Main and Van Buren Streets, 988-4554, attractive rustic setting, ham, fried chicken, biscuits, and other country treats, M • **Artists Colony Inn** (see above), pleasant ambience, varied menu, I–E • **Abe Martin Lodge** (see above), simple fare, good prices, I • **The Ordinary,** South Van Buren Street, 988-6166, tavern atmosphere, sandwiches to dinners, I–M • **That Sandwich Place,** Main and Van Buren Streets, 988-2355, good stop for lunch, filled with Indiana University memorabilia, I • **Peter's Bay Restaurant,** The Commons mall, Fourth and Jackson Streets, Columbus, 372-2270, good spot for lunch, I–M, or dinner, M–E, while you are in town.

SIGHTSEEING **Brown County State Park,** Highway 46, Box 608, Nashville, 988-6406. Hours: Daily 7 A.M. to 11 P.M. Office hours, Monday to Sunday 8:30 A.M. to 4:30 P.M. Nature Center, 988-7185, weekdays 8:30 A.M. to 4:30 P.M., Saturday, Sunday 9 A.M. to 5 P.M.; shorter hours in winter. Indiana cars, $; out-of-state, $$ • **T. C. Steele State Historic Site,** off Highway 46, 9 miles west of Nashville, 988-2785. Hours: Tuesday to Saturday 9 A.M. to 5 P.M., Sunday 1 P.M. to 5 P.M. Donation • **Columbus, Indiana, Visitors Center,** corner of Fifth and Franklin Streets, 378-2622 or (800) 468-6564. Hours: March through November, Monday to Saturday 9 A.M. to 5 P.M., Sunday 10 A.M. to

4 P.M.; rest of year, Monday to Saturday 9 A.M. to 5 P.M. Two-hour guided tours, Monday to Friday 10 A.M., Saturday 10 A.M. and 2 P.M., Sunday 11 A.M. $$$$; one-hour tours, $$$.

INFORMATION Brown County Convention and Visitors Bureau, P.O. Box 840, Nashville, IN 47448, 988-7303 or (800) 753-3255; www.browncounty.com

Berries, Bikes, and Buggies in Wisconsin

Of all the hues of autumn, none is more brilliant than the cranberry red of Warrens, Wisconsin.

Wisconsin is one of the nation's largest producers of cranberries, and the Warrens region is responsible for much of the crop. Over 4,000 cranberry acres produce an average of more than 28 million pounds of bright berries each year. Most of the businesses in town are cranberry-related, so it's no wonder that tiny Warrens celebrates the harvest season in grand style. The late-September Cranberry Festival, now in its third decade, attracts thousands for bog tours, parades, food, and fun.

While berries are the big draw, this is also prime territory for bikes and buggies, with the state's most famous bicycle trail and a thriving Amish community nearby.

Bogs line the roadways around Warrens. Watching the harvesting in action is fascinating, whether for the first or fortieth time. Many growers flood their bogs, then gently stir the water with contraptions that look like giant eggbeaters to bring the berries to the surface. They are then corralled into big pools of glowing red and loaded on trucks via conveyors, a sight that makes for memorable color photos.

Cranberry growing is a special art, and you'll have a new appreciation for what it takes after you visit the Cranberry Expo Ltd., a permanent indoor display developed near one of the larger bogs near Warrens by local growers, the Clinton Potters family. A guided tour through this minimuseum tells you all about the industry that began in Wisconsin about 1860, when early marshes were developed simply by digging ditches around stands of native vines. The first wooden tools, from hand rakes to harvest boats, were devised and built by resourceful growers, and the displays clearly show what improvements were made over the years in the design of the tools.

Cranberry buds form in late summer and lie dormant all winter. To protect the plants from the harsh Wisconsin weather, clever growers came up with the notion of flooding the bogs with water. The solid covering of ice that forms shields the plants from extreme temperatures and drying winds.

One of the most interesting little bits of information passed along is how cranberries are judged for quality. The main criterion? How high they bounce.

The Expo displays also include winning quilts from past Cranberry Festival competitions; each year there's a different theme. The gift shop is filled with glowing cranberry glassware as well as cranberry collectibles, from candles to mustards and sauces.

As for the festival, it fills the entire village with booths selling arts and crafts, a flea and antique market, good cooking, and lots of cranberry treats, including cranberry cream puffs. On display are winners of the scarecrow and photography contests, along with the winning entries from the "biggest cranberry" and "biggest vegetable" competitions. The best from the cranberry recipe contest and the prize entries in the annual quilt contest are also on hand. On Sunday at 1 P.M. the big parade kicks off, with the current cranberry queen presiding. Cranberries are for sale, of course, and the festival program incudes some tempting recipes for using them.

The roads around town are prime for bicyclers, especially circling north of town on County Road HH, the best bet for bog-watchers.

If biking is what you're after, you are also within a short drive of Wisconsin's best-known route, the Elroy-Sparta State Bike Trail. The first bike trail in the nation to be developed along an old railroad bed, the route follows the abandoned Chicago-Northwestern Railroad tracks and passes through three massive rock tunnels, one of them three-quarters of a mile long. The trail offers 32 miles of scenic views and an easy grade of no more than three percent.

Trail headquarters are in Kendall, about half an hour southeast of Warrens, where bicycle rentals are available. You can also arrange for a driver to take you in your car to the area where you want to begin your trip, and then return the car to headquarters so that it's waiting for you when you get back.

For longer trips, many of the inns along the route in Norwalk, Sparta, Wilton, Kendall, or Elroy will gladly assist bikers in planning an inn-to-inn tour; they'll also help transport your baggage along the way. Sparta, the northern end of the trail, is also the beginning of the La Crosse River State Trail, a 21-mile route heading west along the river to La Crosse, where it links with the Great River Trail north beside the Mississippi River. You can board a riverboat in La Crosse to admire the wooded riverbanks in their autumn glory.

Sparta offers two attractive Victorian inns, but if biking is not on your agenda, another good plan is to head for the closest lodging to Warrens, about 10 miles south in Tomah. Tomah's excellent Antique Mall at I-94 and State Highway 21 East will definitely interest antiquers: some 40 dealers under one spacious roof offer treasures of all kinds, from oak furniture to vintage clothing. Glassware seems to be a specialty. The mall also includes an art gallery, country collectibles, a Cranberry Corner, and a Christmas collection.

There are more small shops in town on Superior Avenue. Fans of the "Gasoline Alley" comic strip may find it interesting to know that the creator, Frank King, is a Tomah native, and that the alley in question is actually Superior Avenue. The characters and settings depict King's memories of his hometown.

Burnstad's European Village is a Tomah institution not to be missed for its shopping and dining. Brick and cobbled walkways meander through a collection of shops that include gifts, clothing, an Amish Shop, a Christmas Room, and a Children's Shop/Bookstore with a model railroad running through it. The pleasant European Cafe serves all three meals, with a creative continental menu in the evening. The house specialty is pie, so be sure to save room for dessert.

For less formal dining, Burnstad's offers the Village Buffet and neighboring Filippo's, with Mexican and Asian specialties, a salad bar, and what is billed as Wisconsin's largest hamburger.

One of the more unusual stops in town is the Harris G. Allen Telecommunication Historical Museum, named for a leader in the state's telephone industry. Located in the chamber of commerce office, it features over 100 telephones from around the world, dating back as far as 1894, and unique phones in the shape of a tree or the Eiffel Tower. You can use an old wall phone, "ring up central," talk through a tube phone, make a mechanical switch, connect one phone to another, and learn the basics of how a telephone works. There's also a re-creation of an old switchboard. Displays trace 100 years of communications progress.

There are several pleasant drives from Tomah, outlined in a handy self-guiding brochure available from the local chamber of commerce. A favorite excursion leads south through bucolic dairy-farm country on State Highway 131 to Ontario, then along State Highway 33 west toward Cashton, the center of Wisconsin's Amish population. You'll soon begin to notice Amish homes, modest white farmsteads marked by the lack of electrical wires overhead. Near 17th Drive is an Amish school, where children are taught English as well as math and geography. German remains the first language at home.

If you'd like a guided tour of the area, stop at Down a Country Road on Highway 33, two miles east of Cashton, where Kathy Kuderer not only runs a shop offering Amish crafts but also offers personalized tours along the back roads, from 15 minutes to one and a half hours, depending on your time and interest. Possible Amish-owned stops include a cheese factory, a bakery, and furniture and quilt shops.

On your own, watch on your left for County Road D and turn left to the top of a ridge that continues all the way to the Mississippi River.

You'll spy signs on many of the homes offering homemade baked goods, furniture, quilts, or maple syrup. You're welcome to drive up to the house to buy on any day except Sunday; the families rely on these products for extra income.

About four miles farther along, you'll come to the Hill and Valley Cheese Factory, one of the few factories left that handle raw milk fresh from the farm. It is a cooperative owned by Amish farmers who supply the milk. Tours are offered whenever cheese is being made, usually morning to early afternoon. Early afternoon is when you are most likely to find fresh cheese curds that are paid the highest compliment by connoisseurs—they are "the squeakiest," which means they are so fresh you hear a squeak while you take a bite.

If you come back into Cashton and head north again on State Highway 27, you'll be among beautiful rolling hills in the area known as the Coulee Region. Coulee is a French word meaning "low-lying area between hills." The placid farms nestled against the hillsides make a pretty picture; two of them offer bed-and-breakfast lodgings, wonderful options if you want to sit back and savor some of Wisconsin's finest scenery. Justin Trails is a perfect family choice, with a Disc Golf course (played with a Frisbee), farm animals to be petted, and trails for hiking in warm weather, cross-country skiing and snow-shoeing in winter.

Area Code: 608

DRIVING DIRECTIONS Warrens is off I-94 at Exit 135, County Road E. It is 234 miles from Chicago, 170 miles from Milwaukee, 162 miles from Minneapolis.

ACCOMMODATIONS **Holiday Inn,** State Highway 21 and I-94, Tomah 54660, 372-3211, pool, I • **Econo Lodge,** I-94 and U.S. 12, Tomah 54660, 372-9100, I, CP • **Tomah Comfort Inn,** 305 Wittig Road, Tomah 54660, 372-6600, indoor pool, I, CP • **Cranberry Suites,** U.S. 21 and I-94, Tomah 54660, 374-2801, motel, all suites, I, CP • **Justin Trails,** 7452 Kathryn Avenue and County Road J, off State Highway 27, Sparta 54656, 269-4522 or (800) 488-4521, attractive farm in sylvan setting, near Cashton, M–E, CP; king suite, E; cottages with fireplaces and whirlpools, EE • **Cannondalen Bed-and-Breakfast,** Route 1, Box 58, Cashton 54619, 269-2886 or (800) 947-6261, farmhouse tucked into a coulee, I, CP • **Ages Past Country House Bed-and-Breakfast,** 1223 Front Street, Cashton 54619, 654-5950, 1898 former rectory in Amish country, I–M, CP • ***Along the Elroy-Sparta State Bike Trail:*** **Strawberry Lace Inn,** 603 North Water Street, Sparta 54656, 269-7878, charming 1875 Italianate Victorian, antiques, fireplaces, M, CP • **Franklin Victorian,** 220 East Franklin Street, Sparta 54656, 269-3894 or (800) 845-8767, well-appointed 1890s home, paneling, stained glass, I–M, CP • **Whispering**

Pines Bed-and-Breakfast, R+E Z Box 225, Wilton 54670, 435-6531, farmhouse in the country, I, CP • **East View Bed-and-Breakfast,** 33620 County Road P, Elroy 53929, 463-7564, I, CP • **Stillestad,** N3260 Overgaard Road, Elroy 53929, 462-5633 or (800) 462-4980, I–M, CP.

DINING **Burnstad's European Cafe,** 701 East Clifton Street, Highway 12/16, Tomah, 372-3277, I–M • **Filippo's,** Highway 12/16 East, Tomah, 372-7190, I • **Carlton Restaurant,** 309 Superior Avenue, Tomah, 372-4136, railroad theme decor, steaks and varied menu, M • **Justin Trails** (see above), dinner by reservation, EE prix fixe.

SIGHTSEEING **Warrens Cranberry Festival,** P.O. Box 146, Warrens, 54666, 378-4200; two-day weekend festival in late September, parade on Sunday at 1 P.M.; phone for exact dates • **Cranberry Expo Ltd.,** County Road E, four miles east of Warrens, 378-4878. Hours: April through October, daily 10 A.M. to 4 P.M. $$ • **Telecommunication Historical Museum,** 306 Arthur Street, Tomah, 374-5000. Hours: Monday to Friday, 9 A.M. to 5 P.M., also open Saturday June through August. Donation • **Elroy-Sparta State Bike Trail Headquarters,** State Highway 71, P.O. Box 297, Kendall 54638, 463-7109, area maps, bicycle rentals, and drivers available to transport autos to stopping points. Hours: Daily May through October, 9 A.M. to 5 P.M., later during busiest summer months • **Down a Country Road,** State Highway 33, Cashton, 654-5318. Hours: Amish shop and personalized tours, May to October, Monday to Saturday 10 A.M. to 5 P.M. Cost depends on length of tour • **Hill and Valley Cheese Factory,** County Road D, Cashton, 654-5411. Hours: Monday to Saturday when cheese is being made, usually morning to early afternoon. Free.

INFORMATION **Tomah Area Chamber of Commerce,** 306 Arthur Street, P.O. Box 625, Tomah, WI 54660, 372-2166 or (800) 94-TOMAH; www.tomahwisconsin.com; **Sparta Area Chamber of Commerce,** 111 Milwaukee Street, Sparta, WI 54656, 269-4123 or (800) 658-BIKE; www.spartan.org

Leaf-Watching Along the Rock River

Autumn is the glory season in the Rock River Valley. Winding its way through Illinois toward the Mississippi beside steep wooded limestone bluffs, the Rock River makes a pretty picture any time of year, but when the maple, oak, and hickory leaves turn to glowing gold and russet, the 34-mile stretch between Rockford and Dixon is among the finest leaf-watching routes in this or any state.

The best of the scenery is between Byron and Grand Detour in Ogle County, and you needn't just admire it from afar. You can take your pick of three state parks within a 15-minute drive of one another and savor the color close-up on hiking trails and picnic areas. You can rent a canoe or board the *Pride of Oregon* for a placid cruise, admiring the bluffs from below. You can even lodge in a comfortable log cabin surrounded by the autumn woods.

For a change of pace, visit the former homes of two prominent onetime Illinois residents—the John Deere Historic Site in Grand Detour and the Ronald Reagan Boyhood Home in Dixon. The work of the state's most noted sculptor, Lorado Taft, can be seen in his former home of Oregon.

One of the attractions of traveling in this area is discovering the small, unspoiled towns along the way. Byron, the first stop on Illinois Scenic River Route 2 heading south after Rockford, has as its landmark a Civil War monument flanked by two cannons. At the south end of town, the 450-acre Byron Forest Prairie Preserve is an important restoration area containing more than 400 prairie plants once common in Illinois, including endangered species like Hill's thistle, prairie smoke, and shooting star. There are four self-guided trails for exploring, and two picnic areas. Adjoining the area is the 18-hole PrairieView Golf Course.

The Jarrett Prairie Center in the preserve offers a video presentation and museum displays about the early Native Americans who lived here and about once-common prairie animals. There are live fish, bee, and reptile exhibits and several hands-on exhibits for youngsters. A wetland habitat in in progress.

Oregon, the Ogle County seat, has a typical small-town courthouse square. While it is the center of the area, there's little in this town of under 4,000 that could be called touristy. Even Conover Square, a shopping complex in an old piano factory, is more country than commercial.

On the first weekend in October, however, things are lively in Oregon. The annual Autumn on Parade festival brings arts and crafts, a farmers market, a quilt show and heritage crafts, an auto show, events on the riverfront, and Blackhawk Rendezvous Living History Encampment at Oregon Park East, depicting life as it was in the 1800s. The Harvest Time Parade through town on Saturday at 1 P.M. features lots of floats and bands.

It was in Oregon that Lorado Taft established his Eagle's Nest art colony, on the bluffs opposite town. He presided here from 1898 until his death in 1936; the colony disbanded a few years later. Two of Taft's works can be seen in town: a fountain in Mix Park dedicated to the memory of early pioneers, and the Soldiers' and Sailors' Monument on the courthouse lawn.

Oregon's best-known landmark is Taft's best-known work, a 48-foot concrete statue of an American Indian towering over the Rock River. The statue stands in Lowden State Park, which encompasses 207 acres of the former art colony. The official name of the statue is *Eternal Indian,* but it is universally known as Black Hawk, for the legendary Sauk warrior who defended this land in the Black Hawk War. The figure weighs 100 tons and is said to be the second-largest concrete monolithic statue in the world.

The park also offers picnic areas, some splendid river views, and four miles of hiking trails.

Part of the land and many of the buildings of the old art colony are now part of the Lorado Taft Field Campus of Northern Illinois University, and are used for outdoor teacher education. Another Taft sculpture, *The Muses,* sits high atop the hill on the campus.

If you want to get out on the river, you can rent a canoe at T. J.'s Canoe at the Rock River Bridge in Oregon. You could also stop here just to browse the Native American Gift Center and Art Studio at the Eagle's Nest.

The paddle-wheeler *Pride of Oregon* leaves for lunch and dinner cruises from docks at the northern edge of town off Route 2 at Maxson Riverside Restaurant.

Castle Rock State Park, three miles south of Oregon, is one of the beauty spots of the area. Named for a sandstone butte that stands beside the river, the 2,200-acre park has deep ravines and unusual rock formations; its nature preserve is populated by white-tailed deer, foxes, wild turkeys, herons, and kingfishers. Climb the wooden steps leading to the top of Castle Rock for one of the best panoramic perspectives on the river.

White Pines Forest State Park, bounded by the towns of Mount Morris, Oregon, and Polo, is the valley's most popular attraction. It was established in 1927 to protect the state's last stand of virgin white pines. For many, part of the fun of a visit is being able to gently splash the car through shallow fords at the point where the road crosses Pine Creek.

Here you will find nicely appointed log cabins managed by the White Pines Inn. Both the rustic cabins and the inn itself were built in the 1930s by the Civilian Conservation Corps. The recently refurbished cabins are big enough to sleep four and come with TV, phone, and, in many cases, a fireplace. There's even a Sweetheart cabin with a queen-size bed, a romantic spot for lovers. Like most state-park properties, these are a bargain.

The White Pines Inn building is the center of activity; it has a dinner theater and the best gift shop in the area. The attractive beamed restaurant is famous for its generous breakfasts and the Sunday Cornhusker's Buffet. The reasonably priced dinner menu offers country specialties like chicken potpie, fresh baked breads, and Pine Creek Cobbler, along with more adventurous fare like venison, buffalo, rabbit, and walleye.

One of the better known bed-and-breakfast lodgings in the area is in Oregon. Pinehill is an 1874 Italianate home whose hostess, Sharon Burdick, keeps on display some 40-odd flavors of homemade fudge. The chocolates are for sale, and free samples are definitely part of the fun. Burdick has also devised a popular Blackhawk Chocolate Tour, which takes you to places where you can indulge your sweet tooth.

A few miles south is Grand Detour, a village of rambling Victorian homes and big shade trees. The Colonial Rose Inn, an Italianate home dating back to the 1850s, is both inn and highly regarded restaurant.

This is the town where an innovative young blacksmith named John Deere forged the first successful steel plow in 1837, a major step in the development of the Midwest. When Deere crossed the frontier from his Vermont home in 1836 to settle in Illinois, he found that the cast-iron plows that worked well in stony Eastern soil were impractical here because the rich Midwestern soil clung to the plow, requiring farmers to make frequent stops to clean off the blades.

Many were ready to leave Illinois before Deere came up with the idea of polishing steel from an old saw blade. Dirt fell away cleanly from the sleek plow that Deere devised in 1837. For 10 years Deere made his plows using imported steel, laboring hard to meet the demand. In 1847 he moved his business to Moline to take advantage of the waterpower and transportation offered by the Mississippi. The Deere company today is the world's largest manufacturer of farm equipment.

The home that John Deere built in Grand Detour still stands, as does a replica of his blacksmith shop. Guides provide an entertaining perspective on what life was like for pioneers on the prairie. A neighboring home is now a visitors center, with a formal sitting room adorned with paintings depicting the life of John Deere, the opening of the prairie, and the development of the plow. The site includes nearly two acres of natural prairie, a preserve that reminds visitors of the beauty and the challenge that pioneer farmers faced. A blacksmith often gives demonstrations on the site.

The river takes a sharp bend away from the road in Grand Detour before looping back toward Dixon. The drive here is not as scenic as the earlier part of this tour, but it leads to another interesting footnote in

American history, the boyhood home of Ronald Reagan. Here's a visit to reassure any who doubt that a small-town boy of modest means can, indeed, grow up to become president.

Known in those days as Dutch, Ronald was nine when his family moved to this small but comfortable six-room home. The future president shared a bedroom with his brother, Neil, whose nickname was Moon. The third bedroom of the house was a sewing room used by Mrs. Reagan, who supplemented the family's income by doing mending.

Guides fill you in on the early, quite ordinary life of the man who would become president. Dutch and Moon raised rabbits in the barn, helped with the garden, and spent many hours playing football in the yard with their friends.

Dixon will soon have another tribute to Ronald Reagan. The South Side School, which he attended from 1920 to 1923, is being renovated to become the Dixon Historical Center. Displays will cover Reagan's life.

Abraham Lincoln passed through Dixon as a 23-year-old soldier in the Black Hawk War of 1832. The Lincoln Monument State Memorial, in a small park downtown along the north side of the river, features a statue of a young Lincoln in military dress.

Having come to the end of this scenic drive, you now have the happy prospect of driving north again along the Rock River, an encore of some of the loveliest autumn scenery in the state.

Area Code: 815

DRIVING DIRECTIONS The suggested drive along the Rock River begins on Illinois Scenic River Route 2 southeast of Rockford, designated with signs as the Blackhawk Trail. From Chicago, take I-90 to U.S. 20 in Rockford, then Route 2 south. To approach from the south, take I-88 to Dixon and proceed north on Route 2. From Chicago follow State Highway 64 west to Oregon, 90 miles. Oregon is 23 miles south of Rockford via Route 2.

ACCOMMODATIONS **White Pines Inn,** 6712 White Pines Road, White Pines Forest State Park, Mount Morris 61054, 946-3817, log cabins, I • **Kable House,** Sunset Hill, Mount Morris 61054, 734-7297, 1930s home on spacious golf-course grounds, many suites, I–M, CP • **The Victorian Farmstead,** 7610 West Apple Road, Mount Morris 61054, 734-6388, country home, I, CP • **Pinehill B-&-B,** 400 Mix Street, Oregon 61061, 732-2061, M–E, CP • **Patchwork Inn,** 122 North Third Street, Oregon 61061, 732-4113, newly renovated 1840s inn, I–M, CP • **Paddle Wheel Inn,** 1457 Route 2 North, Oregon 61061, 732-4540 or (800) 468-4222, motel on the river, whirlpools and sauna, M–E, CP • **Colonial Rose Inn,** 8230 South Green Street, Grand Detour

61021, 652-4422, 1855 Victorian, M, CP • **Best Western Brandywine Hotel,** 443 Route 2, Dixon 61021, 284-1890, motel, pool, rooms, I, suites, E. See also Rockford, page 68.

DINING **Colonial Rose Inn,** Grand Detour (see above), M • **White Pines Inn** (see above), I–M • **Blackhawk Steak Pit,** Route 2 North, Oregon, 732-2500, I–M • **La Vigna,** 2190 Daysville Road, Oregon, 732-4413, Northern Italian, I–M • **Maxson Riverside Restaurant,** Paddle Wheel Inn, Oregon (see above), M–E • **The Pepper Mill,** State Highway 64, Mount Morris, 734-4141, steak, prime rib, seafood, I–M • **Leombruni's Italian Village,** 110 West Second Street, Byron, 234-2696, pasta and pizza, steaks, I–M • **Black Dog Cafe,** 105 North Franklin Avenue, Polo, 946-3591, special spot for breakfast and lunch, I.

SIGHTSEEING **White Pines Forest State Park,** 6712 West Pines Road, Mount Morris, 946-3717. Hours: Daily 8 A.M. to sunset. Free • **Lowden State Park,** River Road (east side of Rock River), Oregon, 732-6828. Hours: Daily sunrise to sunset. Free • **Castle Rock State Park,** 1365 West Castle Road, Oregon, 732-7329. Hours: Daily sunrise to sunset. Free • **Byron Forest Prairie Preserve,** 7993 River Road (east side of river), Byron, 234-8535. Hours: Monday to Saturday 8:30 A.M. to 4:30 P.M., Sunday 1:30 P.M. to 4:30 P.M. Free • **John Deere Historic Site,** 8393 South Main Street, Grand Detour, 652-4551. Hours: Daily April to October, 9 A.M. to 5 P.M. $$; under 11, free • **Ronald Reagan Boyhood Home,** 816 South Hennepin Avenue, Dixon, 288-3404. Hours: March to November, Monday to Saturday 10 A.M. to 4 P.M., Sunday 1 P.M. to 4 P.M.; rest of year, Saturday 10 A.M. to 4 P.M., Sunday 1 P.M. to 4 P.M. Free • ***Pride of Oregon* Riverboat Tours,** Route 2 North, Maxson Riverside Restaurant, Oregon, (800) 468-4222. Hours: April through October; lunch and dinner cruises, phone for current offerings • **T. J.'s Canoe Rentals,** west bank of Rock River Bridge at Highway 64, Oregon, 732-4516 • **Autumn on Parade Festival,** P.O. Box 234, Oregon 61061, 732-3465. Annual event on the first weekend in October; phone for current schedule.

INFORMATION **Blackhawk Waterways Convention and Visitors Bureau,** 201 North Franklin Avenue, Polo, IL 61064, 946-2108 or (800) 678-2108; www.promotion.com/bwcvb; **Oregon Chamber of Commerce,** P.O. Box 364, Oregon, IL 61061, 732-2100.

Finding Romance at Lake Geneva

Chief Big Foot knew a good thing when he saw it. A long time ago, the leader of the Potawatomi Indians decided to set his royal residence on the lovely shores of Lake Geneva in southern Wisconsin. The tribe's name for the lake meant "sparkling water."

Big Foot and his band were forced from their home in 1836 following the Black Hawk War. Chiefs of industry soon took their place, dotting the shorefront with lavish summer "cottages" that turned Lake Geneva into "the Newport of the Midwest."

You don't have to be a mogul to visit the lake today, as summer crowds will attest. But the tourists recede after Labor Day, and Lake Geneva is soon twice as nice, reflecting fiery fall color from its wooded shores. That's the time to plan a romantic lakeside escape—take a cruise to admire the color, pick apples at a nearby orchard, or drive the glowing rustic back roads. Or, if you want to give yourselves a lofty treat, you can survey the autumn scene from above in a hot-air balloon.

It was after the Civil War that the hilly, forested, very private land around the lake was discovered by Chicago's elite. A direct rail connection to Chicago in 1871 hastened the development, as did the great Chicago fire that same year, which caused many to look for shelter away from the city. The Swifts, Armours, Wrigleys, and Allertons were among the many prominent families who summered on the lake. Many of the original mansions still stand in their wooded settings, which one can admire from the decks of a sightseeing boat.

Land was set aside early for public beaches and parks, and everyone is made welcome in the pretty little town founded in 1836 and named for the lake. A visit is all the more appealing because the surrounding countryside remains wooded and unspoiled.

There are three villages around the 26-mile lake: Fontana, Williams Bay, and the largest center, Lake Geneva, where most of the shops are found and from where cruise boats leave for rides by the lovely homes.

You can go on a one-hour tour on the *Lady of the Lake,* a reproduction of a twin-stacked Mississippi paddle-wheeler, or you can opt for one of the special theme cruises aboard the *Belle of the Lake,* a replica of a turn-of-the-century lake steamer; two favorite choices are the 90-minute Ice Cream Social Tour (which includes rich sundaes) and the Sunday Champagne Brunch. Cruises emphasizing fall color take place through late October. The enclosed boats go out rain or shine.

The Mark Twain Dinner Cruise on the *Belle of the Lake* includes performances by a Twain impersonator who entertains with some of the humorist's insights on riverboat life, human nature, small towns, and bad habits.

For a longer look at the estates and more in-depth commentary on the area's history, select the two-hour afternoon tours on the *Walworth II,* the U.S. Postal Service boat that serves lakeside communities. These cruises continue daily through October, though the actual mail-boat tours (with a chance to watch the agile "postladies" as they leap on and off the docks at each stop) end on September 15.

Whichever cruise you choose, the narration will point out some of the high spots in the colorful history along the shore. Though many of the original estates have been subdivided and some homes razed in favor of modern mansions, many of the original Victorian properties remain. Maple Lawn, the first to be built, was begun in 1870 by a prominent businessman, Shelton Sturges, who lavishly entertained the guests who arrived via his elegant steam yacht, the *Arrow.* The house was purchased in 1890 by Henry H. Porter, chairman and director of many railroads, including the Chicago-Northwestern.

Other century-old homes with names like Alta Vista, Bonnie Brae, Gay Lynne, and Folly are highlighted, and the lifestyles of their owners are detailed. The Green Gables estate is still owned by the Wrigley family, though the original house was replaced in 1955 by a more contemporary brick home.

The Lake Geneva Yacht Club was and is an important part of life on the lake. Competitive sailing got a boost when Civil War hero Lieutenant General Philip Sheridan visited in the summer of 1874 and asked to see a sailing race firsthand. The race was named Sheridan in the general's honor, and a Sheridan Prize has been handed out ever since.

Gardening and golf, two other favorite pastimes of the lake's tony residents, gave rise to the Lake Geneva Garden Club and the Lake Geneva Country Club, which are still going strong.

For a more leisurely close-up of the homes, walk along the path that circles the outer rim of the lake, an old Potawatomi trail whose right of way is respected by the property owners around the lake. It is quite a remarkable walk: the lake and its yachts are on one side and the manicured grounds and mansions of Midwest tycoons past and present are on the other. You can pick up the path at the Big Foot Beach Park, Library Park, or any of the public beaches and parks along the shore.

Assuming you don't want to do the whole 26 miles, check out the autumn "hike-and-float" tours that pick up passengers at Williams Bay—a manageable eight-mile trek from Lake Geneva—and provide a comfortable boat ride back.

If you want to get out on the lake on your own, you can rent all kinds of craft locally, anything from ski boats, paddleboats, motorboats, and pontoon boats to Windsurfers, Jet Skis, and Wave Runners.

In town, you'll find a lakeside promenade and many nicely restored older buildings. Some special shopping stops include the minimall called Fancy Fare. Top-quality coats for the coming winter can be found at Overland Sheepskin, and Allison Wonderland has toys to delight the little ones. You can finish up with a traditional treat at Annie's Ice Cream Parlor on Main Street.

The statue of Andy Gump looking at the lake in Lake Geneva's Flatiron Park honors the comic-strip character created in 1917 by the late Sidney Smith, who was a familiar figure in town for many years.

If you take a drive around the lake, plan it for Saturday, the only day when you can tour the Yerkes Observatory in Williams Bay, the resident observation facility of the Department of Astronomy and Astrophysics of the University of Chicago. Some of the great scientists of the century have worked here, including Edwin Hubble and Carl Sagan. The classic building and its 90-foot dome were completed in 1897, a masterpiece of form and function and the most modern observatory of its day.

The observatory boasts the largest refracting telescope in the world, an enormous 40-inch lens, which is used to determine distances and motions of stars. It is moved from one position to another with electric motors, but it is so finely balanced that it can be moved by hand, in spite of its great weight of 20 tons. The mechanical operation of the telescope is demonstrated for visitors on Saturdays.

The most scenic driving in the region is along the "rustic roads." This statewide program was created by Wisconsin in 1973 to help preserve its lovely country lanes for bikers, hikers, and motorists. Each road is designated by a sign, and a number preceded by the letter *R*. Drive west of Lake Geneva on State Highway 50 and watch for the sign signaling Snake Road, a beautiful 2.7-mile loop through unspoiled country, canopied with color in the fall. This road actually parallels the lake in spots, and you can see split-rail fencing on estates and occasional glimpses of fine homes through the trees.

Several rustic roads are found east of Lake Geneva off Highway 50. A turn left on South Road leads to a gently winding 10-mile stretch through wooded areas of oak, maple, and hickory and attractive agricultural land. A shorter drive between State Highways 50 and 36 follows Back Road, Sheridan Springs Road, Spring Valley Road, and Church Road for 5.7 curvy miles with panoramic views of lush hills and valleys. This route crosses the White River and goes through the little community of Lyons, which has quaint architecture and churches. Cranberry Road leading into Berndt Road is a 3.6-mile drive through farmland, glacial marshes, and knobs adorned with a wide variety of trees and shrubs.

While you are out driving, you may want to stop for fresh apples at one of the area orchards. The closest to Lake Geneva is Schofields, about a mile and a half west on Highway 50.

If you want to get that balloon's-eye view of the countryside, Sunbird Balloons will oblige.

Having a lake view from your own window definitely enhances the romance of Lake Geneva. Several area resorts are on the water; they are discussed on page 109. When romance is on your mind, the best choice is the Geneva Inn, which combines hotel amenities with the mood and intimacy of a country inn. The 37 rooms—no two are alike—wind around hallways circling an atrium. All have stylish Waverly fabrics and English country decor. If you want to lounge in your four-poster bed, you can borrow a tape for the VCR hidden along with the television set in the armoire. Most rooms have peerless water views, as does the excellent dining room, aptly named the Grandview. This is the only lodging directly on the lake, though the more modest Elizabethan Inn across the street from the water has views from its own pier on the lake. The French Country Inn on Lake Como, a short drive from town, offers pleasant quarters and picturesque surroundings, even if the lake does not equal Lake Geneva.

Area Code: 414

DRIVING DIRECTIONS Lake Geneva is at the intersection of State Highways 120 and 50, just off U.S. Highway 12. From Chicago, follow I-90 west to U.S. 12 north, 72 miles. It is 47 miles from Milwaukee, 73 miles from Madison.

ACCOMMODATIONS All are less expensive on weekdays. **Geneva Inn,** N2099 State Highway 120, 53147, 248-5680 or (800) 558-3417, E–EE, CP • **French Country Inn,** W4190 West End Road, 53147, 245-5220, striking Danish-style main house, modern lodge on the lake, French country furnishings, M–EE, CP • **Elizabethan Inn,** 463 Wrigley Drive, 53147, 248-9131, antiques and pleasant furnishings in main house and converted stable, M–E, CP • **Roses,** 429 South Lake Drive, 53147, 248-4344, modest in-town inn, M–E CP • **Lazy Cloud Lodge,** N2025 North Lake Shore Drive, Fontana 53125, 275-3322, theme suites with whirlpools, fireplaces, canopy beds, E–EE, CP • For area resorts, see pages 109 and 111.

DINING **Grandview,** Geneva Inn (see above), 248-5690, elegant, lake view, E • **Kirsch's Restaurant,** French Country Inn (see above), 245-5756, continental, attractive setting and view, M–EE • **Red Geranium,** State Highway 50 East, Lake Geneva, 248-3637, one of the area's best, M–E • **D'Agostino's,** 300 Wrigley Drive, 248-6788, lake view from most tables, M • **Popeye's,** 811 Wrigley Drive, Lake Geneva, 248-4381, casual dining across from the beach, in the midst of in-town action, I–M • **Interlaken Resort,** 42450 State Highway 50,

248-9121, lake views, M–E; known for Sunday brunch buffet, M • **Scuttlebutt's,** 831 Wrigley Drive, 248-8855, gourmet burgers, ribs, etc., I–M • **Cactus Club,** 420 Broad Street, 248-1999, Southwestern cuisine, I–M • **Annie's Ice Cream Parlor and Restaurant,** 712 Main Street, 248-1933, come for lunch and rich Wisconsin ice cream in an old-fashioned setting, I.

SIGHTSEEING **Geneva Lake Cruise Line,** Riviera Docks, 812 Wrigley Drive, Lake Geneva, 248-6206 or (800) 558-5911. Hours: Fall hours vary, phone for schedules; one-hour tours, several times daily, two-hour tours once or twice daily in the afternoon, May through October, $$$$$; *Walworth II* Mail Boat Tours, June 15 to September 15, mornings daily. $$$$$; also Ice Cream Social and Dinner Tours, phone for dates and rates • **Yerkes Observatory,** State Highway 67, Williams Bay, 245-5555. Tours available on Saturday, usually in the morning; hours change with the season, so phone for current information. Free • **Schofields Orchard,** State Highway 50, 1½ miles west of Lake Geneva, 248-2307; phone for apple-picking hours • ***Boat rentals:*** **Marina Bay Boat Rental,** 300 Wrigley Drive, Lake Geneva, 248-4477 • **Gordy's Ski Boat Rental,** Lake Street, Fontana, 275-2163 • **Jerry's Marine,** Lake Street, Fontana, 275-2163 • ***Balloon rides:*** **Sunbird Balloons, 249-0660.** More Lake Geneva attractions, especially for families, are listed on page 112.

INFORMATION **Lake Geneva Area Chamber of Commerce,** 201 Wrigley Drive, Lake Geneva, WI 53147, 248-4416 or (800) 345-1020; www.lakegenevawi.com

Toasting the Season in Harbor Country

The popular region they call Harbor Country is the southernmost slice of Michigan's shoreline, just above the Indiana border. An easy 90-minute drive from Chicago, this area, from New Buffalo north, has long been a magnet for boaters and beachers. Warren Dunes State Park with its 240-foot towering hills of sand and two and a half miles of superb beach is one of the most visited spots in the state.

But autumn brings other charms to Harbor Country. Inland from the highway, the dunes give way to rolling hills filled with orchards and grapevines that thrive in the sandy, well-drained soil and temperate breezes from Lake Michigan. In fall the vineyards are lush with ruby grapes ripe for picking, a glorious sight. This is the only time of year when you can watch the whole process of winemaking, from vine to vats.

This is the season for romance, when you can settle into a cozy inn and walk the scenic sands or wooded trails hand-in-hand without crowds. You can still climb the dunes, of course, and watch the hang gliders taking off from the top. Fall is also apple-picking time, and provides the opportunity to browse the many area art galleries at your own pace.

Harbor Country began to prosper when the Michigan Central Railroad made New Buffalo its southern terminus in 1849 and visitors came by rail to transfer to steamships bound for Chicago. The harbor became a busy port for the lumber industry. Much of the lumber used to rebuild Chicago after the great fire of 1871 came from Harbor Country forests.

Some of the century-old giant maples and beeches, as thick as five feet across, have been preserved at Warren Woods Natural Area, a lovely spot for walks in the fall.

The first summer resorts opened in the late 1890s. Tourism began to boom when U.S. Highway 12 was paved about 80 years ago and visitors began coming by the carload. By the 1920s grand resorts had gone up and many prominent people had summer homes here, including poet Carl Sandburg. An art colony has flourished in the area ever since, inspired by the lake's many moods and flaming sunsets.

But resort fashions change. In the late 1940s, after World War II, the advent of superhighways, air travel, and air-conditioning lured vacationers elsewhere, and the cottages and hotels stood half-empty or abandoned. It wasn't until 1976, when a new bridge and breakwaters improved the harbor in New Buffalo, that development began again in earnest. Harborside condominiums and the first "dockominiums" lured boaters.

In recent years there's been a burst of new construction (too much to suit many old-timers). Many appealing shops and restaurants have opened, and some of the older hotels have been refurbished. And a few more celebrity names have appeared on the roster of summer residents.

Those who haven't been here for a while may be shocked by the development in New Buffalo: an ever-growing parade of condos, and a big luxury hotel, the aptly named Harbor Grand.

But continue north to Union Pier and the old small-town feel remains. Shops may be strung along the highway, but the homes and inns are safely tucked away on the lanes leading to the beach, and the small harbors are tranquil.

Two of the choicest inns are in private settings in Union Pier. If your romantic fantasy is a room with a lake view, the Pine Garth Inn will fulfill it. Six of the seven tastefully done rooms in this former estate look directly out on Lake Michigan, and some have private decks or terraces with water views. The light and airy decor features pretty florals and accents of twig furniture. If you opt for Emma's Room on the first floor, you'll have a log bed and a fireplace as well as a deck and a whirlpool tub. Many other rooms also have whirlpools for two.

The Inn at Union Pier, a short walk from the beach, is another stylish spot. Most of the rooms have high ceilings and are graced by ceiling-high ceramic Swedish stoves. This is actually one of the old-timers, the Hotel Karonsky, completely transformed. Rooms are in the main house or in new guest houses. The buildings are connected by walkways through a lovely wildflower garden and along a deck with a year-round outdoor hot tub.

The Pebble House in Lakeside, across the road from the lake, consists of three circa-1912 buildings connected by wooden walkways and pergolas. The inn has a comfortable enclosed porch and authentic Arts and Crafts decor. Amenities include a fireplace, a tennis court, and a lavish Scandinavian breakfast.

Two vintage hotels, Gordon Beach Inn in Union Pier and the Lakeside Inn in nearby Lakeside, have been restored. Though the rooms are a bit spartan, many original nice features have been retained in the lobbies, including stone fireplaces and antique furniture. The ambience at both inns is appealing.

Once you've settled in, head inland for wine tours and tastings. A good guide is "Travel Along Jewel-Colored Roads," a brochure available free from the Southwestern Michigan Tourist Council. It will show you the smaller roads to the vineyards and orchards.

If you can only do one winery, make it Tabor Hill, reached via I-94 east to Exit 16, Bridgman. A more meandering route follows U.S. 12 east past Galien, turning north on Red Bud Trail. On either route you'll see signs for Tabor Hill.

The winery is beautifully situated on a rise overlooking hundreds of acres of grapes. It was begun in 1970 by two Chicagoans who brought back hybrid vines from France. They thought the soil and the gentle breezes off the lake nearly matched the conditions of the French provinces. And they were right: their successful venture now produces some 40,000 gallons of wine each year, the second-largest operation in Michigan (St. Julian in Paw Paw is first). The winery has won over 500 awards.

A tour shows you the whole process of winemaking, and takes you into the cellar past rows of huge vats and small oaken casks where the wines are aging. The hand-carved oak casks show scenes telling the story of Tabor Hill's first seven years. Then comes the fun—the chance to taste. They will proudly tell you that Vidal Blanc Demi Sec, their most popular label, has been served in the White House.

After you sample a few vintages, you can picnic outdoors or enjoy a lunch or dinner in Tabor Hill's fine restaurant looking out at the vineyards.

Another attractive setting is almost next door at the Heart of the Vineyard Winery, a newer operation. The winery is in a restored 1881 post-and-beam barn. Cellar tours are offered and sampling is done at the hand-hewn barn or out on the veranda. An Amish-built round barn on the property is where luscious local fruits are distilled into brandies and cordials in a copper still. Tapas-style foods are available, as well.

Heart of the Vineyard is one of the wineries that also offers tasting rooms in and near Union Pier, including St. Julian. But it is far more fun to do your sampling at the vineyard.

Just east of Baroda, Lemon Creek, a winery and fruit farm, has double fun, wine tasting plus the chance to pick your own apples. The farm on 180 acres of rolling hills has been in the Lemon family for 148 years. They have devoted 110 of their acres to 15 varieties of grapes, most for the white wine that is bottled and labeled right on the farm. Once again, free tours and tastings are offered.

Take a detour four miles northeast of Eau Claire off State Highway 140 for the most famous orchards in southwest Michigan, Tree-Mendus Fruit Farm, where there are over 200 varieties of pick-your-own apple trees, plus the chance for an orchard tour with knowledgeable owner Herb Teichman, who loves his trees and will tell you more apple lore than you ever knew existed.

Teichman has a "museum orchard" with many heirloom fruits, some dating to the 1600s. He has done a rare demonstration of grafting, successfully growing 16 kinds of apples on one tree, including vintage varieties such as Ben Franklin's favorite, the Newton Pippin, and the Calville Blanca, favored by Louis XIII. It is definitely worth the fee to sign up for one of his orchard tours.

Another farm stop highly recommended for families is Zeiger Centennial Farm in Three Oaks, where visitors taking the Farm Hand Tour can help feed the animals and maybe even milk a cow. In fall, the farm creates a Maze in the Maize, a six-acre maze through the cornfields.

It's easy to find the shops and galleries in Harbor Country; they are clustered in New Buffalo and along the Red Arrow Highway, the main road.

Some furniture and home-furnishings stops are of note. Hearthwoods at Home on Whittaker Street in New Buffalo has log furniture made from local woods and lots of accessories to go with it; Liz Thomas offers fanciful hand-painted furniture at her studio on Union Pier Road; and Lovell & Whyte in Lakeside has just about everything for the home.

Lakeside has several other interesting stops, including the Lakeside Gallery on Red Arrow Highway and the Fenway Gallery on Lakeside Road. Lakeside Antiques is an antiquers' haven, as is Frog Forest Findings on York Road in Union Pier and the Harbert Antique Mall.

If you go to Harbert, don't miss the Harbert Swedish Bakery, where you can taste treats like kringlor, a coffee cake, Swedish limpa rye; and scorpor, a fried dessert.

Art galleries abound. Local Color in Union Pier shows the work of 90 artists, most of them local, and a number of galleries can be found on Whittaker Street in New Buffalo, showing everything from sculpture to model clipper ships. The Silver Crane Gallery is notable for its Southwestern art and a wonderful selection of handmade jewelry.

Train buffs will want to look into the New Buffalo Railroad Museum, an old caboose transformed to hold displays and a model train layout depicting the town at the turn of the century.

If you'd rather enjoy the colorful autumn woods than be indoors, the 480-acre virgin forest of Warren Woods Nature Area south of Bridgman is prime territory for walks. The Love Creek Nature Center in Berrien Center also has five miles of hiking trails. And at the shore, Tower Hill and the Great Warren Dune are waiting at Warren Dunes State Park.

Bicyclists should head east on U.S. Highway 12 to Three Oaks Spokes Bicycle Museum and Information Center. The small museum in the old train depot traces the evolution of the bicycle from the high wheeler to today's racers. You can also rent a bike here for countryside touring; ask for the map of bike routes.

If you are an avid cycler, you may want to join the annual Apple Cider Century bike ride held the last weekend of September, a tour through the back roads of Berrien County that draws several thousand participants each year.

Finally, if you would like to do your strolling amid flowers, take a drive to Fernwood, a botanic garden and nature center on 105 splendid acres. Winding woodland trails, eight acres of demonstration gardens, and a tall-grass prairie are among the features. There's also a visitors center with a fern conservatory, tearoom, and gallery.

When you get back to the inn, you can open your bottle of Michigan wine and toast to the many pleasures of Harbor Country.

Area Code: 616

DRIVING DIRECTIONS Harbor Country towns are along the Red Arrow Highway, reached via I-94 from the west, U.S. 12 from the east. From Chicago, follow I-94 to the U.S. 12 exit and proceed east to New Buffalo, about 75 miles. New Buffalo is 206 miles from Detroit. Union Pier is four miles north on Red Arrow Highway.

ACCOMMODATIONS **Pine Garth Inn,** 15790 Lakeshore Road, Union Pier 49129, 469-1642, on the lake, lovely decor and views, private beach, very special, E, CP • **The Inn at Union Pier,** 9708 Berrien Street, Union Pier 49129, 469-4700, E, CP; cottage rooms, M, CP • **The Pebble House,** 15093 Lakeshore Road, Lakeside 49116, 469-1416, Arts and Crafts decor, M–E, CP • **Tall Oaks Inn,** 19400 Ravine

Drive, New Buffalo, 49117, 469-0097, spacious, gracious suites in the dunes, Jacuzzis, elegant, M–E, CP • **River's Edge,** Community Hall Road, 9085 Union Pier 49129, 469-6860, rustic knotty-pine lodge, hand-hewn furniture, fireplaces, Jacuzzis, 30-acre grounds along the Galien River, M, CP • **Garden Grove Bed-and-Breakfast,** 9549 Union Pier Road, Union Pier 49129, 469-6346, 1925 cottage-style home, wooded garden, outdoor hot tub, M–E, CP • **Bauhaus on Barton,** 33 North Barton Street, New Buffalo 49117, 469-6419, in-town bed-and-breakfast painted flamingo pink and filled with 1950s ambience, M–E, CP • **Harbor Grand Hotel and Suites,** 111 West Water Street, New Buffalo 49117, 469-7700, luxury hotel, indoor pool, M–E • Two rustic restorations: **Gordon Beach Inn,** 16220 Lakeshore Road, Union Pier 49129, 469-0800, M, CP • **Lakeside Inn,** 15281 Lakeshore Road, Lakeside 49116, 469-0600, M–E, CP.

DINING **Tabor Hill Winery,** 185 Mount Tabor Road, Buchanan, (800) 283-3363, wonderful setting overlooking vineyards; lunch, I; dinner, M • **Jenny's,** 15460 Red Arrow Highway, Lakeside, 469-6545, Chicago chef gets good reviews in the country, American fare, M–E • **Solo Mio East,** 16038 Red Arrow Highway, Union Pier, 469-9636, another Chicagoan, popular Italian trattoria, M • **Miller's Country House,** 16409 Red Arrow Highway, Union Pier, 469-5950, longtime area favorite, charbroiled specialties, M • **Red Arrow Roadhouse,** 15710 Red Arrow Highway, Union Pier, 469-3939, local landmark, informal, good food, I–M • **Fanny's,** Gordon Beach Inn, Union Pier (see above), inspired by former Evanston eatery, "famous" spaghetti sauce, I–M • **Casual Chef Cafe,** 16090 Red Arrow Highway, Union Pier, 469-1200, sandwiches to dinners, I–M • **Cafe Gulistan,** 13581 Red Arrow Highway, Harbert, 469-6779, change-of-pace Middle Eastern menu, I–M • ***New Buffalo:*** **Skip's Other Place,** 16710 Red Star Highway, 469-3330, prime rib is the specialty, M–E • **Kent's,** 203 West Buffalo Street, 469-6255, eclectic menu, attractive setting, special desserts, M • **Hannah's,** 115 South Whittaker Street, 469-1440, wide-ranging menu, home cooking to Southwestern specialties, popular for Sunday brunch, I–M • **Redamak's,** 616 East Buffalo Street, 469-4522, legendary hamburgers, I • **Brewsters,** 11 West Merchant Street, 469-3005, small, casual, pizza and pasta, I.

SIGHTSEEING **Fernwood Botanic Garden,** 13988 Range Line Road, Niles (between Buchanan and Berrien Springs), 683-8653. Hours: early June to late October, Tuesday to Sunday 10 A.M. to 6 P.M.; rest of year to 5 P.M. $$ • **New Buffalo Railroad Museum,** 530 South Whittaker Street, New Buffalo, 469-2090. Hours: Memorial Day to Labor Day, Thursday to Sunday noon to 5 P.M. Free • **Three Oaks Spokes Bicycle Museum,** One Oak Street, Three Oaks, 756-3361. Hours: Daily 9 A.M. to 5 P.M., shorter hours in winter. Free • ***Wineries:***

Tabor Hill Winery, 185 Mount Tabor Road, Buchanan (I-94, Exit 16, follow signs), (800) 283-3363. Hours: Tours and tasting April to December, daily noon to 4:30 P.M. • **Lemon Creek,** 533 East Lemon Creek Road, Berrien Springs (I-94, Exit 16, north two miles to Lemon Creek Road, then east six miles), 471-1321. Hours: May through November, Monday to Saturday 9 A.M. to 6 P.M., Sunday noon to 6 P.M. Pick your own mid-June to mid-October • **Heart of the Vineyard,** 10891 Hills Road, Baroda (next to Tabor Hill, turn off Snow Road to Hills Road), 422-1617. Hours: May to November, daily 11 A.M. to 6 P.M. • **Tree-Mendus Fruit Farm,** 9351 East Eureka Road, Eau Claire (off State Highway 140), 782-7101. Hours: Late June to Labor Day, Wednesday to Monday 10 A.M. to 5 P.M.; Labor Day to mid-October, Friday to Monday 10 A.M. to 5 P.M. Days may vary; best to check. Varying fees for special tours • **Zeiger Centennial Farm,** 5692 West Warren Woods Road, Three Oaks, 756-9797. Hours: Usually open weekends through October 31, best to check current hours. Tours, $$ • ***Parks:*** **Warren Dunes State Park,** off Red Arrow Highway, Sawyer, 3 miles southeast of Bridgman, 426-4013. Hours: Daily 8 A.M. to 10 P.M. in season, hours may be shorter in winter. Admission per car, $$ • **Warren Woods Nature Center,** Elm Valley Road (off Warren Woods Road), south of Bridgman, phone c/o state park. Hours: Daily, dawn to dusk. Free • **Love Creek Nature Center,** 9228 Huckleberry Road, Berrien Springs, 471-2617. Hours: Tuesday to Sunday 11 A.M. to 5 P.M. Trails open dawn to dusk. Free.

INFORMATION **Harbor Country Chamber of Commerce,** 3 West Buffalo Street, New Buffalo, MI 49117, 469-5409; www.harborcountry.org • **Southwestern Michigan Tourist Council,** 2300 Pipestone Road, Benton Harbor, MI 49022, 925-6301; www.swmichigan.org

Autumn Splendor in Wisconsin Dells

Behind a wall of go-cart tracks, water slides, thrill shows, fudge shops, and miniature golf courses lies some of the most magnificent scenery in the Midwest: the Wisconsin Dells. These layered sandstone cliffs are a natural wonder, rising as much as 100 feet along a remarkable stretch of the Wisconsin River in the town also known as Wisconsin Dells.

A good proportion of the three million or so people who flock here each year—especially younger visitors—come expressly for the miles of amusements, which include Noah's Ark, America's largest water park, and an astonishing 400 holes of miniature golf.

But in the fall, when the water parks turn off their faucets, the tide of tourists recedes, and the oaks, maples, and birches turn to autumn hues, lovers of beauty don't have to look far to find the natural treasures that made the Dells a vacation mecca in the first place.

Another happy reason for the trip: though the beauty quotient goes up in the fall, rates go down considerably after Labor Day.

Indian legends say that a giant serpent created the sinuous river curves and stone cliffs the French-Canadian fur traders labeled *dalles,* but geologists have a more practical explanation. They say it was thousands of years of glacial waters eroding the ancient Cambrian sandstone that accounts for fascinating formations with names like Hawk's Bill, Chimney Rock, and Sugar Bowl, sights guaranteed to send photographers into frantic action.

One of America's first great photographers, H. H. Bennett, helped popularize the area with his 19th-century photos of logging on the river, many of which can be seen in the Bennett studio in town. The Dells have been drawing awed visitors ever since; enterprising residents were guiding individuals up and down the river in rowboats as early as the mid-1800s.

The riverbanks have been spared the commercialism that infects the rest of the town. As excursion boats multiplied and resorts, cottages, and billboards began springing up, local leaders tried without success to have the area declared a state park or a national monument. It was the owner of one of the excursion-boat lines, George Crandall, who foresaw the perils of development and began buying up riverside property.

On his death, Crandall's land and his enterprise, Dells Boat Company, was given to the Wisconsin Alumni Research Foundation (WARF), a semiprivate arm of the University of Wisconsin. With the cooperation of the local chamber of commerce, WARF began buying more property along the river, tearing down billboards and structures, and reforesting the recovered land. The result is a pristine shoreline that looks much as it did when the first visitors saw it over a century ago.

The first order of business is to see the river, and there are several ways to do that. The most dramatic scenery is on the Upper Dells cruise, a two-hour 15-mile trip that also allows you to get off the boat to walk through hidden canyons and scenic nature trails at Witches Gulch and Stand Rock, two of the more famous spots along the river. Stand Rock is the most prominent landmark, offering one of the best panoramas of the river. The Lower Dells tour takes just an hour, and it has its own share of scenery.

Jet boats are another option, the only way to circle all of Blackhawk's Island.

A much livelier way to see the area is on an action-packed hour-long amphibious tour on one of the "Wisconsin Ducks," land-and-sea vessels used for D-Day shore landings during World War II. These tours take in the river, Dell Creek, and Lake Delton (an artificial lake formed by damming a section of the river), as well as four miles of scenic wilderness trails through dramatic gorges and shaded dells filled with lush ferns. All of it is twice as beautiful in autumn Technicolor.

The tour comes with a good-natured narration complete with admittedly corny jokes, as well as some real history, such as the story of the lost town of Newport, whose last remains can be seen along the way.

If you bring the kids along (or you are still a kid at heart), sit in the rear of the duck, where you'll get the full benefit of the splash landing.

You can enjoy a more solitary look at the river via canoe, or see the countryside on horseback. Hikers can also take in the countryside on trails at Mirror Lake State Park, which is half surrounded by sandstone bluffs. Within the park, there is the rare opportunity to stay overnight in a home designed by Frank Lloyd Wright. The restored Seth Peterson Cottage, designed in 1958, was one of the last of Wright's projects. The restored cottage is open for tours the second Sunday afternoon of each month.

Two other recommended fall outings are the half-hour horse-drawn carriage tour through Lost Canyon, which leads through a fantasy of gorges so narrow you can reach out and touch the walls, and the autumn-foliage tours by steam train at the nearby Mid-Continent Railway Museum. Baraboo's Circus World Museum and International Crane Foundation are just 12 miles to the south; see pages 82–85 for more details. On the way south on U.S. Highway 12, you'll pass the Ho Chunk Casino, where you can while away some time—and cash—at the slot machines or blackjack table.

Dining in this area is heavy on supper clubs specializing in steak, ribs, and seafood. Jimmy's Del Bar, Fischer's, and Wally's House of Embers have been around for a long time and are reliable. The Cheese Factory's vegetarian specialties provide a good change of pace. Thunder Valley Inn serves Scandinavian home cooking and has family entertainers on Saturday. The prize for location goes to the rustic Ishnala, tucked away by itself above Mirror Lake.

You can't avoid the garish lineup along Wisconsin Dells' Broadway and on Highway 12 leading into town, since some of the best restaurants are here, but you can easily find lodgings that take you away from it all.

Cedar Lodge is a rustic log building right on the river. Rooms have vaulted ceilings and private decks, and kitchenettes are available. Romantics can choose rooms with whirlpools, or private log cabins with a fireplace as well as a whirlpool.

Just a few miles outside town, Chula Vista is a big resort and conference center on the river with an indoor pool and tennis. For resort amenities, the place is Christmas Mountain Village, with its own golf course, stables, indoor pool, tennis courts, and ski hill. This is basically a condominium community but accommodations are available to the public.

Among the bed-and-breakfast possibilities are the Historic Bennett House in town, the original 1863 home of the pioneer photographer, and Thunder Valley Inn, a 130-year-old log farmhouse just outside town.

Finally, if children are along and you want to get into the spirit of the world's capital of water amusements, give in and choose one of the gaudier resorts like the Wilderness Resort Hotel, Atlantic, Black Wolf Lodge, or Copa Cabana, where the indoor-pool complexes are nothing short of extravaganzas. The Wilderness's "Fort Exploratory" comes complete with underwater tunnels, water slide, and three rock waterfalls. Guaranteed, the kids won't be bored.

Area Code: 608

DRIVING DIRECTIONS Wisconsin Dells is off I-90/94, Exit 87. U.S. Highway 12 and State Highways 13 and 23 also lead into the town. It is 190 miles from Chicago, 53 miles from Madison, 116 miles from Milwaukee.

ACCOMMODATIONS Rates given are for peak season; all are less expensive after Labor Day. **Seth Peterson Cottage,** Mirror Lake State Park, information and reservations from Sand County Service Company, Box 409, Lake Delton 53940, 254-6551, Wright-designed cottage sleeps up to four, has full kitchen, EE, two-night minimum • **Cedar Lodge and Settlement,** E11232 Hillside Drive, P.O. Box 58, Lake Delton 53940, 254-8456, M–EE • ***Wisconsin Dells:*** **Meadowbrook Resort,** 1533 River Road, 53965, 253-3201, rooms, M; cabins, M–E • **Christmas Mountain Village,** Country Road H, S944 Christmas Mountain Road, 53965, 253-1000, condominiums, M–EE • **Chula Vista Resort,** 4031 River Road, 53940, 254-8366 or (800) 388-4782, M–EE • **The River Inn,** 1015 River Road, 53965, 253-1231 or (800) 659-5395, standard motel but many rooms have direct river views, M • **Wilderness Hotel and Golf Resort,** 511 East Adams Street, 53965, 253-9729 or (800) 867-WILD, next door to a golf course, M–EE • **Copa Cabana,** 611 Wisconsin Dells Parkway, 53965, 253-1511 or (800) 364-COPA, M–EE • **Historic Bennett House,** 825 Oak Street, 53965, 254-2500, I–M, CP • **Thunder Valley Inn,** W15344 Waubeek Road, 53965, 254-4145, I–M, CP.

DINING **Ishnala,** Ishnala Road, 253-1771, M–E • **Wally's House of Embers,** 935 Wisconsin Dells Parkway (U.S. 12), 253-6411, famous ribs, M–E • **Del-Bar Supper Club,** 800 Wisconsin Dells Parkway South, Lake Delton, 253-1861, popular, M–E • **Fischer's Restaurant,** Wisconsin Dells Parkway South, 253-7531, American menu, I–M •

The Cheese Factory, 521 Wisconsin Dells Parkway, 253-6065, open for all three meals, nice gardens, I–M • **Fields Steak & Stein,** Highway 13 north, 254-4841, prime-rib specials, M **Thunder Valley Inn** (see above), Saturday "Threshing Supper" and entertainment, M; great breakfasts until noon, including buffets Saturday and Sunday, I.

SIGHTSEEING **Original Wisconsin Ducks,** 1890 Wisconsin Dells Parkway, 254-8751. Hours: Mid-June to Labor Day, daily 8 A.M. to 7 P.M.; Labor Day to mid-October, daily 9 A.M. to 4 P.M.; mid-April to mid-June, daily 9 A.M. to 5 P.M. Tours leave every few minutes. $$$$$ • **Dells Boat Tours,** 11 Broadway, 254-8555. Hours: Daily 8:45 A.M. to 6 P.M. Early April through October; Upper Dells tour, two hours; Lower Dells tour, one hour. Check current tour times. $$$$; discount on 3½-hour combination tours, $$$$$ • **Lost Canyon,** Lost Canyon Road, Lake Delton, 254-8757. Hours: Mid-May to mid-September, daily 8:30 A.M. to dusk; rides leave frequently. $$$ • **Mid-Continent Railway Museum,** County Road PF off State Highway 136, North Freedom, 522-4261. Hours: Mid-May to Labor Day, daily 9:30 A.M. to 5 P.M.; September to late October, weekends only. Special fall color trains first two weekends in October; trains depart 10:30 A.M., 12:30 P.M., 2 P.M., and 3:30 P.M. $$$$ • **Mirror Lake State Park,** off U.S. 12, Lake Delton (just south of Wisconsin Dells), 254-2333, hiking, fishing, swimming, canoeing, cross-country ski trails. Hours: Information center, daily 8 A.M. to 11 P.M.; off-season, 8 A.M. to 4 P.M. Wisconsin residents, $$; out-of-state, $$$ • **Seth Peterson Cottage,** Mirror Lake State Park. Hours: Second Sunday each month 1 P.M. to 4 P.M. $ • ***Boat rentals:*** **Holiday Shores,** 254-2878; **Lake Delton Water Sports,** 254-8702; **Mirror Lake State Park,** 254-1233; **Point Bluff Canoes and Tubing Resort,** 253-6181 • ***Horseback riding:*** **Beaver Springs,** 254-2735; **Canyon Creek,** 253-6942; **Christmas Mountain Ranch,** 254-3935; **Dell View,** 253-7669; **OK Corral,** 254-2811.

INFORMATION **Wisconsin Dells Visitor and Convention Bureau,** 701 Superior Street, Wisconsin Dells, WI 53965, 254-8088 or (800) 22-DELLS; www.wisdells.com

Landmark Charm in Marshall

An unsuspecting traveler happening upon Marshall, Michigan, could hardly be blamed for thinking he had encountered a mirage. After all, who would expect to find a quaint 19th-century town just off a superhighway between Chicago and Detroit?

Sometimes referred to as the Williamsburg of the Midwest, Marshall has a story unique in the annals of Midwest history, not to mention a rich legacy of architecture—its own National Historic Landmark District with over 800 buildings. When some of the finest of these homes are opened to the public for two days each September, as many as 10,000 people descend on this town of 7,200. The House Tour has been a beloved tradition for over 35 years.

What made Marshall different from the beginning was the wealth of its settlers. While other pioneers may have come west to seek their fortunes, Marshall's pioneers brought fortunes with them. They were wealthy Easterners who expected to become even wealthier, getting a head start in the town thought sure to become the capital of the soon-to-be-state of Michigan.

The city's founder was Sidney Ketchum, an entrepreneur from upstate New York who envisioned a new business and political center for the Michigan Territory. A practical man, Ketchum chose the confluence of the Kalamazoo River and Rice Creek for his site in 1830: the river would provide shipping to Lake Michigan and the creek would provide power for mills. The town was named for John Marshall, the chief justice of the United State Supreme Court, whom Ketchum admired.

Early comers were so convinced of Marshall's rosy future that they set aside land as a "Capitol Hill" and built a columned Greek Revival "Governor's Mansion." By the time Marshall lost to Lansing in the legislature by one vote in 1847, its citizens had already built impressive residences for themselves in the styles they had known back east. Its streets are a catalog of American building styles.

Marshall also considers itself to be the place where public education got its start in the United States. Some of those early residents designed the public school system that was later adopted for the entire state, and one of the group, Reverend John D. Pierce, became the first superintendent of public instruction, not only for Michigan but also for the nation.

Today Marshall is a picturesque small town built around a center circle dominated by a Greek Revival fountain and is an architectural feast for strollers. The free printed walking tour by the Marshall Historical

Society includes some 136 buildings and 46 markers. The text continues the saga of the town's development.

Despite its setback in the legislature, Marshall prospered for a while. The coming of the railroad in 1844 provided a surge in the economy, as Marshall was selected for the railroad yards of the Michigan Central and became the switching station for the Detroit-Chicago run. Another tidbit of town history: America's first railroad union was formed in a small house on Hanover Street in 1863.

In 1872, however, the Michigan Central railroad maintenance shops were moved to nearby Jackson. For a brief time, the town found a new identity with the manufacture of patent medicines, but eventually Marshall almost literally went to sleep.

Half a century went by before a new mayor, Harold Brooks, took office in 1925 and saw the potential of restoring the town's architectural heritage. The town's wealthiest citizen, Brooks already owned a dozen key buildings in town, and he bought up many more, maintaining them until a proper buyer came along. He was the town's patron for more than 60 years, the catalyst for a preservation movement before preservation became fashionable. Among his legacies are the fountain in the center of town.

Many of the town's residents continue his work. Due to their efforts, 867 buildings were designated as part of a National Historic Landmark District in 1991, the largest such district in the nation in the "small urban" category.

One of the most unusual structures is Honolulu House, a fanciful curlicued curiosity with exquisitely painted ceilings in the highly decorative Victorian style. It was built around 1860 by Judge Abner Pratt, the first U.S. consul to the Sandwich (Hawaiian) Islands, to resemble the executive mansion he occupied while serving in the islands in the 1850s. The house is now headquarters for the Marshall Historical Society.

The rest of Marshall is far from a museum piece. Unlike historical showcases like Williamsburg, the well-preserved residences are occupied. The walking tour takes in dozens of period homes that reflect the town's three economic eras.

The handful of imposing columned Greek Revival buildings, including the ill-fated Governor's Mansion, are from the heady period when the town expected to become the state capital.

The second era of splendor came with the railroads. The 30-year building boom from the 1840s to 1870s accounts for many of the elaborate Italianate and Gothic Revival homes. One beauty is the stately 1869 Italianate Cook residence at 603 North Kalamazoo, set amid towering spruce trees and miniature gardens. Another is the J. Cronin Jr. home at 407 North Madison, a circa-1873 white-brick Italian villa with a 60-foot mansard roof tower and an observatory. The Clark-Sherman House, 123 West Prospect, an unassuming board-and-batten cottage in

Gothic Revival style, is typical of homes built by workers in the late 19th century.

More fine homes are found along North Kalamazoo and Michigan avenues, on the appropriately named Mansion Street, and on every block in the Historic District. The walking guide makes a tour more interesting, offering a bit of personal history of each house.

Eight or more prime homes are opened to the public once each year during the house tour, which is also the only time you can go inside the 1839 Governor's Mansion or visit the local Postal Museum without an appointment. The weekend also includes a Civil War encampment, crafts demonstrations, an antiques market and peddler show, a parade, and musical entertainment. It's an occasion that is worth braving the crowds. If you are too late to snag a room in town, Battle Creek has many options just 12 miles away.

A surprise attraction in Marshall is the American Museum of Magic, established by a lifetime collector of magic memorabilia. Magic fans also can look forward to the annual August gathering of magicians in Colon, about 40 minutes southwest of Marshall. Colon was the home of the famous Harry Blackstone and is headquarters for Abbot's Magic Company, the nation's largest producer of commercial magic supplies.

Another local collector is postmaster Michael Schragg, who has created a growing museum of postal memorabilia in the basement of the post office. Displays include a storefront post office from the 1890s and a horse-drawn mail buggy built in 1905. This is the second-largest postal collection in the country, surpassed only by the Smithsonian Postal Museum in Washington. It is open to the public during the annual house tour.

It's hardly a surprise to find that Marshall has become a center for antique shopping, with nearly a dozen shops in and around town. The choicest are the Marshall House Antique Centre at 100 Exchange Street, and the J. H. Cronin Antique Center on Michigan Avenue at Jefferson Street. McKee's Monument and Mercantile, 201 Exchange Street, offers vintage clothing and advertising memorabilia in a country-store setting.

On Michigan Avenue you'll also find some interesting little gift shops and the Espresso Yourself Coffee House.

Marshall boasts Michigan's oldest inn in continuous operation, the National House, an 1835 coach stop on the town's busy circle. It has been restored as a charming lodging filled with antiques.

An even nicer alternative in a country setting is McCarthy's Bear Creek Inn, a restored farm and barn on a knoll overlooking Bear Creek, about a mile from downtown. Rooms are furnished with period pieces and handmade chests, and many have bay windows overlooking the creek.

No trip to Marshall is complete without a visit to one of Michigan's best-known eating places, Schuler's, founded in 1909 and operated by the same family for four generations. A generous all-American menu is served in warm period surroundings that include lots of good advice painted on the beams, such as Ben Franklin's warning, "You may delay, but time will not."

Another longtime institution is Cornwell's Turkeyville, this one a three-generation family enterprise. The original turkey farm has grown into a restaurant/dinner theater and shopping complex, with a petting zoo and playground thrown in for the kids. The menu lists turkey everything from potpie to stir-fry, including an old-fashioned turkey-and-gravy dinner with cranberry sauce. Don't come expecting to see live gobblers—they have given way to the tourists and are now raised elsewhere.

Area Code: 616

DRIVING DIRECTIONS Marshall is near the intersection of two major highways, I-69 and I-94. From Chicago, take I-94 east to Exit 110, about 182 miles. Marshall is about 114 miles from Detroit, 64 miles from Ann Arbor.

ACCOMMODATIONS ***Marshall:*** **McCarthy's Bear Creek Inn,** 15230 C Drive North, 49068, 781-8383, I–M, CP • **The National House Inn,** 102 South Parkview, 49068, 781-7374, I–M, CP • **The Joy House,** 224 North Kalamazoo Avenue, 49068, 789-1323, 1844 home within walking distance of downtown, I–M, CP • **Amerihost Inn,** 204 Winston, Marshall 49068, 789-7890, motel, I • **Arbor Inn,** 15435 West Michigan Avenue, 49068, 781-7772 or (800) 424-0807, motel, I • ***Battle Creek:*** **Greencrest Manor,** 6174 Halbert Road, Battle Creek 49017, 962-8633, bed-and-breakfast home on expansive grounds, E, CP • ***Motels:*** **Appletree Inn,** 4786 Beckley Road, 49017, 979-3561, I • **Battle Creek Inn,** 5050 Beckley Road, 49015, 979-1100, I • **Holiday Inn Express,** 2590 Capital Avenue SW, 49015, 965-3201, I–M.

DINING **Schuler's,** 115 South Eagle Street, 781-0600, M–EE • **Cornwell's Turkeyville,** 18935 15½ Mile Road, 781-4293, I; dinner theater, EE.

SIGHTSEEING **Marshall Historic Home Tour,** sponsored by Marshall Historical Society, usually second Saturday and Sunday in September. Check with chamber of commerce for current dates and information • **Honolulu House,** 107 North Kalamazoo Street, phone chamber for information. Hours: May to October, daily noon to 5 P.M. $$.

INFORMATION **Marshall Area Chamber of Commerce,** 424 East Michigan Avenue, Marshall, MI 49068, 781-5163 or (800) 877-5163; www.marshallmi.org

Admiring the View in Alton

The Great River Road along the Mississippi River has its ups and downs where scenery is concerned. There are ho-hum places where the terrain is flat and the river narrow, even stretches where the road swerves away from the river entirely. But there are also spots where the beauty is great, and among the best of these is the magnificent drive from Grafton to Alton in southwestern Illinois.

This span of about 20 miles lies between the scenic spots where the Illinois and Missouri Rivers feed into the Mississippi. They call it the River Bend area because the river takes a sharp turn inward at Alton, one of the rare places where the current changes direction to run west to east.

Lovely anytime, this is a dazzling route in the fall, and an autumn outing is made even better because the lush orchard country of nearby Jersey and Calhoun counties is dotted with places where you can pick your own apples, sample fresh cider, or garner a perfect pumpkin to take home.

Near Grafton is Pere Marquette State Park, Illinois' largest state park; from its bluffs you'll find some of the most spectacular views of both the Illinois and the Mississippi. Three river towns are happy hunting grounds for antiquers. Elsah, a tiny charmer that still looks much as it did in the 1850s, has some prime bed-and-breakfast options among its period homes.

This area is also one of the world's richest in terms of archaeological interest. The valley where the Illinois joins the Mississippi has been called the Nile of North America because of the significant excavations and discoveries that have helped track nearly 10,000 years of human habitation on this continent.

Alton is the center of activity for the region, particularly for antiquers. The old warehouses on Alton's riverfront Broadway alone claim no less than 50 antiques shops.

With a population of 33,000, this isn't exactly a big city, but it does have a large share of historical high points, from early explorers to the Lincoln-Douglas debates to a Civil War Confederate prison, all of which you can follow by looking at the local monuments.

A symbol of Alton's earliest heritage is the giant figure of a bird mounted on the bluffs just north of town. It is a modern re-creation of the *piasa* (pie-a-saw), a pictograph of a giant birdlike monster created by resident Indians near the site where Alton now stands. The bird was described in the diary kept by Father Jacques Marquette, the French missionary who was among the first Europeans to reach this area, on his famed expedition down the Mississippi with Louis Jolliet in 1673. A plaque beneath tells the Indian legend of the piasa.

The next explorers to come this way were Meriwether Lewis and

William Clark, who encamped near the confluence of the Missouri and Mississippi Rivers just south of Alton on December 12, 1803, to train and outfit the men who would accompany them on their historic expedition to the Pacific. Lewis and Clark called their quarters Camp DuBois and their party of 45 men the Corps of Discovery. They remained until May 15, 1804, the longest time the party spent in any one place.

The grounds where the camp stood, at the mouth of Wood River Creek, is now the site of the Lewis and Clark Historic Site, 11 concrete pylons forming a rotunda. Each represents one of the 11 states traversed by the expedition and bears plaques recording the exploring party's activities in that state.

A striking modern structure named for Clark is the Clark Bridge spanning the Mississippi, which went up in 1990. This cable-stay bridge with its graceful fan-shaped design is unique in the United States.

The town of Alton was first plotted in 1818 by a land speculator, one Rufus Easton, who saw it as a prime location for a ferry site. It was named for Easton's oldest son; younger sons George, Langdon, and Henry and daughter Alby each got a street named for them, as well.

Alton was incorporated as a city in 1837, the same year it received national attention when a proslavery mob attacked and killed abolitionist newspaper editor Elijah P. Lovejoy. Lovejoy was revered as a martyr to freedom and to freedom of the press, and a memorial in his honor was erected at the corner of Monument and Fifth Streets.

Less than 300 yards from the place where Elijah Lovejoy was killed, Abraham Lincoln and Stephen A. Douglas held the seventh and last of their famous debates in 1858. The site where they spoke, in front of City Hall at the corner of Broadway and Market Street, is known as Lincoln/Douglas Square.

Alton was a key stop on the Underground Railroad and a main supply point for Union armies during the Civil War. Illinois' first state penitentiary became a prison and hospital for captured Confederate soldiers. A Confederate Monument in the Alton Confederate Cemetery on Rozier Street honors the 1,354 prisoners who died here of smallpox.

The town's cobblestone streets and stately 19th-century Victorian, Federal, and Greek Revival homes attest to Alton's days as a thriving port. The Eagle packet line of boats built here contributed to the local traffic on the Mississippi. Broadway on the riverfront now has a slightly funky look, and the old brick warehouses have become malls filled with antique and junktique shops, a mix that keeps visitors happily browsing in search of hidden treasures. Those who are used to big-city price tags will find many of these a refreshing change.

Some of the shops are more eclectic. The Mineral Springs Mall, a converted historic hotel, has a variety of wares and the Old Post Office on Alby Street is now a mall of shops with everything from toiletries to toy trains.

Upper Alton, northeast of downtown, is also a historic district.

According to legend, it became known as Pietown when women baked pies for Illinois troops stationed here during the Mexican War of 1846, a custom that continued during the Civil War.

On College Avenue, you'll find an unusual statue saluting one of Alton's more recent residents. It is a life-size bronze likeness of Robert Pershing Wadlow, the "gentle giant," who went into the *Guinness Book of Records* with the world's tallest recorded height, 8 feet, 11.1 inches. Shy and friendly, Wadlow was much loved by the community and was commemorated by the statue after he died in 1940 at the age of 22.

Alton's Museum of History and Art tells more about Wadlow and about the town's rich history.

There are fine views from Alton's riverfront park, and you can go out on the water aboard the *Alton Belle* Riverboat Casino. One of the more lavish riverboats, this floating Las Vegas has a grand staircase, classical statues, what seems like miles of polished mirrors, and a million sparkling lights. This is a free scenic cruise, but it can also be an expensive one if you heed the call of the casino.

You'll get quite a different kind of lookout over the Mississippi at the Melvin Price Locks and Dam at river mile 200.8. Known as Lock and Dam No. 26, it is the last of the navigational and flood-control dams that make up the Illinois waterway. This is one of the places where you can watch the fascinating procedure that raises and lowers the water level to allow giant barges through.

The lovely drive along State Highway 100 north to Grafton includes a special path for bicycles right along the river for some 20 miles between Alton and Pere Marquette State Park. The entire length of the road, 50 miles from Alton to Eldred, has been named the Great Rivers National Scenic Byway.

The first stop is quaint Elsah, the first entire community in America to be listed on the National Register of Historic Places. Once a major landing, Elsah was happily bypassed by progress once the steamboats were gone. It remains the picture of a 19th-century village, with narrow streets, a stone bridge, and many stone houses. The white Methodist Church would be at home in New England. A stay here is a delightful return to the peaceful past.

While you are in town, have a look at the handsome campus of Principia College on the bluffs overlooking the Mississippi.

Proceeding farther north, Grafton is the oldest town in the area. Founded in 1832, it is in the process of restoring its 19th-century rivertown ambience. The antiques district on Main Street is a lure for shoppers, but Grafton's real claim to fame is outside town.

Peerless Pere Marquette State Park is set on bluffs high above the Illinois River. It is named for Pere Marquette, one of the first explorers to visit the confluence of the Mississippi and the Illinois. A large white cross just east of the entrance commemorates his historic landing with Jolliet in 1673.

The park's 7,895 acres include picnic grounds that command wonderful vistas of the river and 15 miles of marked hiking trails that are among the most scenic in Illinois. There are also 12 miles of riding trails; horses can be hired at the park's riding stable. Watch for American bald eagles in the bluffs; this is one of their favorite haunts.

The classic rustic stone lodge was constructed by the Civilian Conservation Corps in the 1930s. It was expanded and modernized in 1990, but the original features were maintained, including the mammoth chandeliers, stone and timber beams, and a fireplace that soars 50 feet to the roofline. Besides the 50 guest rooms in the Pere Marquette Lodge, there are 22 cabins along the Illinois River shoreline. As at most state parks, these comfortable, modestly priced lodgings are a tremendous value.

Amenities for those who are lucky enough to snag a lodge reservation include an indoor swimming pool, whirlpool, saunas, a game room, and a tennis court. The lodge's restaurant is known for its lavish Sunday brunch, featuring fried chicken, pork, roast beef, and a mouthwatering dessert bar.

Grafton is near the heart of orchard country, which spreads out on both sides of the Illinois River. Take a ride into the countryside and you'll see lots of fruit stands, markets stocked with homemade jams and jellies, honey, melons, pumpkins, baked goods, and homespun crafts. One place to pick your own apples and pumpkins and sample cider is Eckert's Country Store and Farms, reached from the Great River Road by going east on State Highway 3 to Otterville Road. The visitors bureau in Alton will have more suggestions.

It's fun to take the free ferry across the Illinois River north of Grafton over to Brussels, a charming little town built on steep, low hills. Drive north and you're into countryside known for its watermelons, cantaloupes, and pumpkins. The road rejoins Highway 100 about 10 miles north at Hardin and proceeds another 10 miles or so to Kampsville, center of the region's rich archaeology and home of the Center of American Archaeology. The CAA's field school attracts hundreds of learners of all ages to work at active sites and gain a hands-on introduction to archaeology. The visitors center displays some of the artifacts that have been found, and explains how archaeologists work.

Another free ferry at Kampsville will bring you back across the Illinois River to Eldred, so you can wend your way south again to Grafton and get another look at the spectacular scenery along the Great Rivers National Scenic Byway.

Area Code: 618

DRIVING DIRECTIONS Alton is on State Highway 140 along the Mississippi River. From Chicago, take I-55 south and turn west on 140, about 281 miles.

ACCOMMODATIONS **Pere Marquette State Park Lodge,** State Highway 100, Grafton 62037, 786-2331, I • **Beall Mansion,** 407 East 12th Street, Alton 62002, 474-9090 or (800) 990-BEALL, elegant, champagne and chocolates, whirlpools, some fireplaces, M–E, CP • **Jackson House,** 1821 Seminary Street, Alton 62002, (800) 462-1426, white Victorian in Upper Alton historic district, antiques, I–M, CP • **Green Tree Inn,** 15 Mill Street, Elsah 62028, 374-2821, new inn built to look old, charming decor, balconies, I–M, CP • **Maple Leaf Cottage Inn,** 38-44 LaSalle Street, P.O. Box 156, Elsah 62028, 374-1684, quaint country decor, M, CP • **Corner Nest,** 3 Elm Street, Elsah, 62028, 374-1892, cozy, river views, I–M, CP • **Tara Point Inn and Cottages,** Box 1, Grafton 62037, 786-3555, intimate inn and two cottages with prime river views, M–E, CP.

DINING **Midtown Restaurant,** 1026 East Seventh Street, Alton, 465-1321, fried chicken, country ham, famous pork chops, I–M • **Castelli's Moonlight Restaurant,** 3400 Fosterburg Road, Alton, 462-4620, American, local landmark since 1937, I–M • **Tony's Restaurant and Third Street Cafe,** 312 Piasa Street, Alton, 462-8389, casual, steak to pizza, I–M • **Cane Bottom/My Just Desserts,** 31 East Broadway, Alton, 462-5881, top choice for lunch—and dessert, I • **Elsah Landing,** 18 LaSalle Street, Elsah, 374-1607, I • **Fin Inn,** Highway 100, Grafton, 786-2030, seafood amid aquariums, I–M • **Pere Marquette State Park Lodge,** Grafton (see above), attractive dining room, notable Sunday brunch, I–M.

SIGHTSEEING **Pere Marquette Highway Park,** Route 100, Grafton, 786-3323. Hours: Park is open daylight hours year-round; visitors center, daily 9 A.M. to 3:30 P.M. Free • ***Alton Belle* Riverboat Casino,** 1 Front Street, (800) 336-7568. Hours: Daily one-hour cruises on the Mississippi on the hour 8 A.M. to 2 A.M., weekends to 4 A.M. Free • **Museum of History and Art,** 2809 College Avenue, Alton, 462-2763. Hours: Monday to Friday 10 A.M. to 4 P.M., Saturday, Sunday 1 P.M. to 4 P.M. $ • **Center for American Archaeology,** Highway 100, Kampsville, 653-4316. Hours: May through November, Monday to Saturday 10 A.M. to 5 P.M., Sunday noon to 5 P.M. Donation.

INFORMATION **Greater Alton/Twin Rivers Convention and Visitors Bureau,** 200 Piasa Street, Alton, IL 62002, 465-6676 or (800) 258-6645, www.altoncvb.org

A Capital Trip to Madison

State capitals are often good places to visit, offering historic sites and museums, plus good restaurants catering to bigwigs who come to break bread with legislators.

College towns have their own charms—scenic campuses, sports, concerts, cosmopolitan culture, and a spirit of perpetual youth, evidenced in the shops, cafes, and clubs frequented by the students.

Seldom do the twain meet, but both capital and campus are found in Madison, Wisconsin. To make things even better, this is a town of great natural beauty, situated on a narrow isthmus between two lakes, Mendota and Monona, with water views everywhere.

Many publications have picked Madison as one of the country's best places to live, and University of Wisconsin alumni seem to agree. Many graduates are among the city's 195,000 residents, making for a tight job market and some of the best-educated waiters and salesclerks you'll ever meet.

Visitors are generally enthusiastic, as well, because there is much to see and do in Madison. Getting your bearings is easy, since much of what you'll want to see is between Capitol Square and the university, a distance of only eight blocks.

Visible for miles from its hilltop site, the capitol building dominates the center of town. By law, no building can rise higher than its 284-foot white granite dome. Atop the dome is a gilded bronze statue, *Wisconsin,* by Daniel Chester French.

The UW campus rises on a neighboring hill to the west, along the shores of Lake Mendota. Between the two is the State Street Mall, lined with shops, cafes, and the Madison Art Center.

The capitol makes a good starting point. Completed in 1917, it's the third building on this site. The columned exterior is an impressive example of Roman Renaissance architecture. The interior is exceptionally beautiful and merits a tour. Guides take visitors around on the hour, through the handsome rotunda, the governor's conference room, the skylit senate and assembly chambers, and the state supreme court, pointing out the many artworks along the way. The interior features 43 kinds of stone from around the world, decorative murals, glass mosaics, and hand-carved furniture. The 200-foot rotunda is topped by Edwin Blashfield's painting *Resources of Wisconsin.*

Two state museums are found across from the capitol. Concentrating on the history of Wisconsin and the upper Midwest, the State Historical Museum includes displays on Native American settlements, fur-trading days, and the exploration of the upper Mississippi River. The "People of the Woodlands" exhibit is one of the best—here you inspect a wigwam or go inside an Aztalan house and learn about the work of archaeologists.

The Wisconsin Veterans Museum is a must for military buffs. Dedicated to Wisconsinites who served their country in battle from the Civil War to the Persian Gulf War, it includes dramatic life-size dioramas of military equipment and soldiers in environments from steamy jungles to snow-covered forests.

Proceed from Capitol Square down State Street and you'll come to the Madison Children's Museum, which has a computer room, dairy exhibits, changing hands-on displays, and a Toddler's Nest specially designed for ages one to three. Farther on State is the Madison Art Center, with three attractive galleries of changing exhibits.

State is a street that blends small-town warmth with campus coffeehouse culture. Clothing runs the gamut from preppy to hippie, and you can buy anything from Badger souvenirs to beads or berets. Book and record shops abound. The Canterbury Booksellers Cafe serves up tasty fare with its books and has bed-and-breakfast rooms upstairs decorated with scenes from *The Canterbury Tales.*

If you are proceeding to the campus on a warm, sunny day, you'll come upon a student union building that resembles a resort, where students sip their coffee while basking on a big outdoor terrace overlooking the lake. Inside the Memorial Union are restaurants, delis, a theater, billiards, bowling, game rooms, and guest rooms for visitors with campus connections. The Union Galleries house more than 800 works by 500 artists with Wisconsin roots.

The UW—Madison Campus Assistance and Visitors Center on Langdon Street near the union will supply you with a self-guided tour map of the campus. Founded in 1849, the year after Wisconsin became a state, the university is highly respected for its academic programs and renowned for its lovely campus, which now encompasses nearly 1,000 acres.

Three buildings have been named National Historic Landmarks: North Hall, the first building on campus; Science Hall, completed in 1887; and the Armory-Gymnasium, which opened in 1894. Bascom Hall is the focus of the Bascom Hill Historic District; at the front is the Lincoln terrace with an imposing bronze statue of Abraham Lincoln and a superb view to the state capitol to the east.

The carillon tower, another campus landmark, often presents concerts on Sunday afternoon.

One of the most popular places for visitors in this dairy state is Babcock Hall, where a second-floor balcony is a vantage point for watching a modern dairy-processing plant in action. The best part of the tour is a stop at the Dairy Store to sample the 12-percent-butterfat ice cream made on the premises. You can also buy milk and cheese.

If you want to watch UW's herd of nearly a hundred contented cows being milked by machine, go to the Dairy Cattle Research Center in the late afternoon.

The campus museums are on the small side but have some worthwhile exhibits. The Elvehjem Museum of Art houses a collection of more than 15,000 paintings, sculptures, and decorative art dating from 2300 B.C. to the present. The trademark of the Geology Museum is its giant mastodon skeleton. Displays also include minerals, meteorites, fossils, plants, and animals.

The State Historical Society Research Collections, housed in a stately building on the lower campus, comprise the largest library in the nation devoted to North American history, with special emphasis on Wisconsin and the West. Its holdings cover all aspects of United States history, from genealogy to folklore, and the history of ethnic minorities of the region. You can while away many a fascinating hour looking through these materials. The newspaper collection is the nation's second largest; however small your hometown, you may well find the local paper on file.

When you want an outdoor break, Madison offers nearly 200 parks, including the 1,200-acre campus arboretum and Olbrich Botanical Gardens, with 14 acres of specialty gardens and a domed conservatory atwitter with tropical birds.

This city is nirvana for bicyclers, with miles of scenic paths. You can also rent canoes, kayaks, or fishing boats to take advantage of those beckoning lakes. Pick up a biking guide and rental information at the visitors bureau.

Sophisticated dining is one of Madison's special pleasures, offering anything from the latest in nouvelle cuisine to inexpensive ethnic eateries favored by students. In fact, according to one local tourist guide, Madison has more restaurants per person than any city in America.

An educated community and a great university with over 40,000 students also draws top entertainment. The Civic Center schedule each year may draw anyone from Itzhak Perlman to the Clancy Brothers, and you can count on a lineup of dance, film, music, and theater on campus.

Madison's most impressive lodging is the Mansion Hill Inn, originally known as the McDonnell Pierce house. Built in 1857 by Alexander McDonnell, the contractor for the second state capitol, the inn has many of the same design elements, such as ornate stonework, decorative ceilings, and five Italian-marble fireplaces. A four-story oval-shaped spiral staircase leads to a belvedere with panoramic views. The house has been restored into an opulent Victorian showplace.

The inn is on Big Bug Hill, the neighborhood north of the capitol building toward Lake Mendota that was home to Madison's most prominent early residents. This is one of many neighborhoods with fine old homes. The Madison Landmarks Commission has published several neighborhood walking tours that are available at the visitors bureau.

Also of note is the convention center on Monona Terrace, a 1938

Frank Lloyd Wright design with a stunning rooftop garden that was never executed during Wright's lifetime. Located on the lakeshore two blocks from the capitol building, the building was completed in 1997 and quickly became a major attraction for visitors. Exhibits include the Madison Sports Hall of Fame. Free concerts are held here regularly; in summer they take place in the rooftop garden.

Wright admirers can also visit his Unitarian Meeting House just a few minutes away from Monona Terrace.

Finally, some of Wisconsin's charming ethnic communities are within an easy drive from Madison, trips that are excellent reasons to extend your stay. See pages 194–197 for more on these unique towns.

Area Code: 608

DRIVING DIRECTIONS Madison can be reached via I-90 or I-94. From Chicago, follow I-90 west and turn north at Rockford, about 147 miles. It is 77 miles from Milwaukee via I-94 west to I-90 south.

ACCOMMODATIONS All listings have the same Madison zip code, 53703. **Edgewater Hotel,** 666 Wisconsin Avenue, 256-9071, on the lake, newly renovated, M–E; suites, E–EE • **Best Western Inn on the Park,** 22 South Carroll Street, 257-8811 or (800) 279-8811, near capitol building, M–E • **Madison Concourse Hotel,** 1 West Dayton Street, 257-6000 or (800) 356-8293, central location, M–E • ***Bed-and-breakfast homes:*** **Mansion Hill Inn,** 424 Pinckney Street, 255-3999 or (800) 798-9070, showplace, magnificently restored Victorian, M–EE, CP • **Canterbury Inn,** 315 West Gorham Street at State Street, 258-8899, gracious rooms above a bookstore, in the center of State Street action, M–EE, CP • **Annie's,** 2117 Sheridan Drive, 244-2224, two 2-bedroom suites, M–E, CP • **Collins House,** 704 East Gorham Street, 255-4230, Arts and Crafts–period furnishings, lake views, M–E, CP • **University Heights Bed-and-Breakfast,** 1812 Van Hise Avenue, 233-3340, 1923 Craftsman-style home in historic district, M–E, CP.

DINING **L'Etoile,** 25 North Pinckney Street, 251-0500, many consider it the city's best, M–EE • **Opera House Restaurant and Wine Bar,** 117 Martin Luther King Jr. Boulevard, 284-8466, elegant contemporary settings, regional/seasonal cuisine, M–E • **Blue Marlin,** 101 North Hamilton Street, 255-2255, seafood favorite across from the capitol, M–E • **Quivey's Grove,** 6261 Nesbitt Road, 273-4900, worth the drive for a wonderful country setting and elegant dining in a lovely 1855 stone house listed on the National Register, M • **Coyote Capers,** 1201 Williamson Street, 251-1313, "fusion" cuisine, imaginative chef, M–E • **Smoky's Club,** 3005 University Avenue, 233-2120, the place for steak, M • **Mariner's Inn,** 5339 Lighthouse Bay Drive, 246-3120, surf and turf in a great setting on Lake Mendota, M–E • **Essen Haus,**

514 East Wilson Street, 255-4674, traditional German, entertainment, I–M • **Deb & Lola's,** 227 State Street, 255-0820, Southwestern, I–M • **Wasabi Japanese Restaurant and Sushi Bar,** 449 State Street, 255-5020, "best sushi in the Midwest" says their ad; fans agree, I–M • **Himal Chuli,** 318 State Street, 251-9225, Nepalese, one of the more exotic of the ethnic choices on State Street, I • **Canterbury Booksellers Cafe,** 315 West Gorham at State, 258-8899, light fare for lunch or dinner, I • **Dotty Dumpling's Dowry,** 116 North Fairchild Street, 255-3175, known for their hamburgers and 40 kinds of brew on tap, I • **State Street Brats,** 603 State Street, 255-5544, Wisconsin's own brats and beer, I.

SIGHTSEEING **Wisconsin State Capitol,** capitol concourse, 266-0382. Hours: Tours depart hourly from the ground-floor information desk Monday through Saturday 9 A.M. to 11 A.M., 1 P.M. to 3 P.M., Sunday 1 P.M. to 4 P.M. Free • **State Historical Museum,** 30 North Carroll Street, Capitol Square, 264-6555. Hours: Tuesday to Saturday 10 A.M. to 5 P.M., Sunday noon to 5 P.M. Free • **Wisconsin Veterans Museum,** 30 West Mifflin Street, 267-1799. Hours: Monday to Saturday 9:30 A.M. to 4:30 P.M.; also Sunday noon to 4 P.M., April to September. Free • **Madison Art Center,** 211 State Street, 257-0158. Hours: Tuesday to Thursday 11 A.M. to 5 P.M., Friday 11 A.M. to 9 P.M., Saturday 10 A.M. to 9 P.M., Sunday 1 P.M. to 5 P.M. Free • **Monona Terrace Community and Convention Center,** Monona Terrace, 261-4000. Hours: Guided tours daily from the gift shop, 11 A.M. and 1 P.M. $; free on Monday and Tuesday • **Olbrich Botanical Gardens,** Olbrich Park, 3330 Atwood Avenue, 246-4718. Hours: Gardens daily 8 A.M. to 5 P.M., to 8 P.M. June to August; conservatory 10 A.M. to 4 P.M. Gardens free; conservatory, $ • **Madison Children's Museum,** 100 State Street, 256-6445. Tuesday to Sunday 10 A.M. to 5 P.M. $$ • **University of Wisconsin: Campus Assistance Center,** Armory building, 716 Langdon, across parking lot from the Memorial Union, 263-2400. Hours: Monday to Friday 8 A.M. to 5 P.M., Saturday 10 A.M. to 3:30 P.M., Sunday noon to 4 P.M. • **Babcock Hall Dairy Plant,** 1605 Linden Drive, 262-3045. Hours: Milk and ice-cream processing weekdays before noon; store, 1815 Linden Drive, Monday to Friday 9:30 A.M. to 5:30 P.M., Saturday 10 A.M. to 1:30 P.M. • **Elvehjem Museum of Art,** 800 University Avenue, 263-2246. Hours: Tuesday to Friday, 9 A.M. to 5 P.M., Saturday, Sunday 11 A.M. to 5 P.M. Free • **Geology Museum,** Weeks Hall, Charter and West Dayton Streets, 262-2399. Hours: Monday to Friday 8:30 A.M. to 4:30 P.M., Saturday 9 A.M. to 1 P.M. Free • **University of Wisconsin Arboretum,** 1207 Seminole Highway, 263-7888. Hours: Daily dawn to dusk. Guided tours on Sunday, May through October. Free • **State Historical Society of Wisconsin Library,** 816 State Street, 264-6534. Hours: Monday to Saturday 8 A.M. to 5 P.M., Monday to Thursday to 9 P.M. when classes are in session.

INFORMATION Greater Madison Convention and Visitors Bureau, 615 East Washington Avenue, Madison, WI 53703, 255-2537 or (800) 373-6376; www.visitmadison.com

Shops and Scenery in Geneva

Geneva, Illinois, is only 40 miles from Chicago, but it is another world. Though lots of lucky commuters call it home, Geneva is not just another suburb. This town of 18,500 along the Fox River is as delightful for visitors as for the folks who live there. It has charm and sophistication that belie its size.

Geneva boasts two business districts listed on the National Register of Historic Places. Their tree-lined blocks are filled with small-scale century-old storefronts and converted 19th-century homes that house over a hundred unique shops, the kind of personal, one-of-a-kind places you won't find at the mall.

The choice of restaurants is also exceptional for a small town, and when dinner is done, you can stay overnight in an elegant small four-star hotel beside the river, or in a mansion turned bed-and-breakfast just outside of town.

Autumn, when the wooded banks of the Fox are at their brilliant best, is an excellent time to get acquainted with Geneva. You can enjoy the fall color by car, along a prize 36-mile riverside bicycle path, or from the decks of mini-riverboats that sail out of St. Charles, an antiquer's mecca just five minutes down the road. On the first weekend of each month, St. Charles is home to the famous Kane County Flea Market, some 25 acres of tempting antiques and collectibles.

Add some nearby sightseeing attractions like Robert R. McCormick's 500-acre estate, Cantigny, with mansions, museums, formal gardens, and a superb public golf course, and it's hard to imagine a pleasanter escape. For Chicagoans, the short drive is an extra bonus.

Geneva was founded in 1835 by settlers who were exploring the Fox River. They originally called the outpost La Fox, but the name was changed when the growing town became the county seat the following year. The river provided power for mills serving agriculture and lumber, and Geneva prospered, becoming a supply point for pioneers continuing farther west. According to legend, the first retail establishment in town was a hardware and general store; the second sold satin and lace, beginning Geneva's tradition of specialized shops.

Checking out the stores is the first order of business for most visitors. Today's shoppers find quite a mix of temptations along State and Third Streets. On West State Street, the Sea Captain's Lady is arranged like a sea captain's home and filled with the exotic and unusual from the trade routes of the world. Just down the street, Karizma Clothiers offers artistic duds in natural-fiber fabrics plus a big selection of that 1960s perennial, Birkenstock footwear.

Keep walking and you'll come upon the Strawflower Shop with its unusual dried and silk floral arrangements; Cats 'N Dogs, with jewelry, sportswear, art, and collectibles featuring everyone's favorite pets; and Les Tissus Colbert, the only American outlet for 100-inch-wide bolts of fabric direct from mills in France and also a source for antique pine furniture.

Turn down Third Street for more pleasures—country-pine and oak furniture built by local craftsmen at the Wooden Nail; Illinois' largest Christmas store at the Kris Kringle House; everything for the garden at Betty's Garden Party; and dozens of varieties of coffee and tea at Coffee & Spice and Everything Nice. At the Berry House Shops, 227 South Third, an 1854 Greek Revival home has been transformed to hold fifteen shops with a potpourri of wares, plus a cafe and a shop serving a formal tea, a perfect afternoon break.

If the day is fine, you can take your pick of lunch spots with a river view. Atwater's at The Herrington is the most elegant, the venerable Mill Race Inn has country charm, and the Riverwalk offers a screened terrace with a prize view.

Or you might prefer to get a takeout lunch at the diner and picnic at Island Park in town, where you can feed your bread crumbs to the ducks. Or you could take a short drive to Wheeler Park, Geneva's lovely 57-acre preserve off State Highway 31 near the river, where there are picnic tables as well as flower and nature gardens, hiking trails, tennis courts, ball fields, and part of the Fox River Bike Trail. The park also offers miniature golf from late May to early September.

The bike trail is a beauty, and highly recommended, whether you want to cover one mile or all 36. It runs beside the river all the way from Aurora to Algonquin, then moves inland for a bit to Crystal Lake. You can pick up a free map at Mill Race Cyclery, 11 East State Street, beside the river bridge in Geneva. They'll also gladly rent you a bike if you haven't brought your own.

The bike trail heading south brings you to the Fabyan Forest Preserve, where you can still see the windmill that once ground flour and a lighthouse that guided river travelers. The Fabyan Villa is open for tours on weekend afternoons.

Die-hard shoppers can complete their Geneva tour or follow the river north a few miles into St. Charles, where the options include Antique Markets I, II, and III and the Market, located on Third Street in the section known as Old St. Charles. Inside are a dozen or so interesting small shops with anything from corn-husk pilgrim dolls to Western art, antiques to hand-painted perennial calendars.

Bargain hunters will want to investigate the Piano Factory Outlet Mall on First Street; Bass shoes, Corning and Revere cooking ware, Carter's children's wear, American Tourister luggage, L'eggs/Hanes/Bali, and many other familiar labels are all available at discount prices. Check out the third floor for a big selection of new and "gently used" books at the Book Rack, and a host of choices at the Cookbook Bazaar, featuring recipes from all 50 states.

If you've picked the right date, don't miss the giant Kane County Flea Market in St. Charles; it is one of the biggest in the Midwest.

For a scenery break, head for Pottawatomie Park and board one of the double-decker mini–paddle-wheelers that ply the Fox River.

While you are in St. Charles, check the current entertainment offerings at the Norris Theater, the area cultural center that sponsors frequent concerts and performances. The Norris Gallery in the same complex offers changing art exhibits.

Another evening option is to try your luck at the Hollywood Casino, a riverboat on the Fox River about eight miles south of Geneva in Aurora.

Be sure to save time one day for a visit to Cantigny, about 10 minutes east on State Street heading toward Wheaton. Watch for the turnoff sign at Winfield Road. This is the glorious former estate of Robert McCormick, the longtime publisher and editor of the *Chicago Tribune* and founder of radio and TV stations WGN.

Visitors begin at a museum building with a film about McCormick's life and an exhibit dedicated to Joseph Medill, McCormick's grandfather and the founder of the *Tribune.* They can then stroll through the formal gardens on the way to the mansion itself. The grounds are the scene of many special events, from craft fairs to vintage auto shows to a Revolutionary War reenactment.

The house remains as it was in the 1950s, a warm home filled with fine European and Far Eastern antiques. The grandest room in the house is the paneled 22-foot-high library, testimony to McCormick's love for the printed word. Guided tours give glimpses into the lifestyle of the family.

McCormick was proud of his army career and his rank as colonel, a title he used throughout his life. The newest addition to the estate is the First Division Museum, which salutes the military, with videos and exhibits portraying army life, from the World War I French village of Cantigny (for which the estate was named) to Omaha Beach to a Vietnam jungle.

Part of Cantigny's grounds are now a 27-hole golf course in a setting of oak and hickory trees, lakes, and streams. It was ranked among the nation's top 25 public courses by *Golf Digest.*

Admirers of Billy Graham will want to proceed farther east to the Wheaton College campus and the impressive columned Billy Graham Center, which offers a visual lesson on the history of evangelism in the United States from Colonial times to the present.

Deciding where to have dinner in Geneva is difficult, but 302 West, in the dramatic spaces of a former bank, gets top ratings from critics for its creative, handsomely presented American fare. However, Granada also has many admirers for its Spanish cuisine and wines and delectable tapas. If you prefer traditional Italian fare, Ristorante Chianti makes its own pasta fresh daily. And there are those appealing dining spots on the river to consider.

Want something less formal? Well, what about Mexican, Chinese, Pennsylvania Dutch, or the old-fashioned diner? You'll find all of these in this surprising small town.

Geneva has lodging for every taste, as well. The Herrington, a restored century-old limestone building that was once a creamery, offers elegant rooms with French country decor, a riverside gazebo, a spa, and nice amenities like high tea in the afternoon and milk and cookies at bedtime. Some of the 40 rooms come with fireplaces and whirlpool baths for two, and all have balconies, many overlooking the river. It is a posh hideaway with both intimacy and hotel conveniences.

Lovers of country inns should not overlook the Oscar Swan Country Inn, a gracious 1902 home that was once a private residence on eight peaceful treed acres. Furnishings are 1920s style, and the house still has a comfortable residential feel.

In St. Charles, the Hotel Baker, a 1920s landmark, has been restored as a luxury getaway, including suites with whirlpools. A final alternative, good if sports are important to you or you have children along, is the big, busy Pheasant Run Resort and Convention Center in St. Charles. You won't have the charm of Geneva, but you will have a host of activities, including indoor and outdoor tennis and pools, a spa, golf, and supervised programs for kids on weekends. The resort has both an adult dinner theater and a children's theater, and children stay free in parents' rooms.

Those who are into high tech will want to take time for another unusual tour, a detour heading back to I-88 on Kirk Road. Fermilab in neighboring Batavia boasts the world's biggest energy particle accelerator, or atom smasher, which allows scientists to study the basic structure of matter, including the nucleus of an atom. Pick up a self-guiding tour brochure in the atrium of Wilson Hall (you can't miss it; it's 15 stories high). The public observation area has an audiovisual program about the work of the laboratory, a model of the accelerator tunnel, and a scale model of the lab site.

All of this is on the cerebral side, definitely not for young kids. But everyone can enjoy a tour of the well-designed buildings and modern sculptures on the 6,800-acre grounds, and a look at the herd of grazing buffalo on the seven-acre prairie restoration area. The prairie also has seven miles of biking paths and an interpretive walking trail.

Neither atom smashers nor buffalo are what you might expect to find out here in the placid suburbs. It's just further proof that Geneva and its neighbors can be full of surprises.

Area Code: 630

DRIVING DIRECTIONS Geneva is on State Highway 38. From Chicago, take the Eisenhower Expressway (I-290) to I-88 west toward Aurora. Exit at Farnsworth/Kirk Road North and drive about six miles to Highway 38 and turn left. It becomes State Street in Geneva. About 45 miles.

ACCOMMODATIONS **The Herrington,** 15 South River Lane, Geneva 60134, 208-7433, E–EE, CP • **Oscar Swan Country Inn,** 1800 West State Street, Geneva 60134, 232-0173, M–EE, CP • **Hotel Baker,** 100 West Main Street, St. Charles 60174, 584-2100, E • **Pheasant Run Resort and Convention Center,** 54051 East Main Street, St. Charles 60174, 584-6300, dinner theater, supervised children's programs, many special packages available, M–E.

DINING **302 West,** 302 West State Street, Geneva, 232-9302, M–E • **Granada,** 14 South Third Street, Geneva, 262-1000, tapas and other Spanish dishes, M–E • **Mill Race Inn,** State Highways 38 and 25 at Fox River Bridge, Geneva, 232-2030, prime rib is the specialty, overlooking the river, outdoor gazebo, M–E • **Riverwalk,** 35 North River Lane, Geneva, 232-1330, informal, on the river, screened terrace, I–M • **Atwater's,** The Herrington (see above), elegant setting on the river, E–EE • **Ristorante Chianti,** 207 South Third Street, 232-0212, Italian, I–M • **Old Church Inn,** 18 North Fourth Street, St. Charles, 584-6300, restored church converted to restaurant, I–M • ***Informal dining options:*** **Tia Maria's,** 730 East State Street, Geneva, 232-9135, Mexican, I • **Gen-Hoe,** 537 East State Street, 232-8350, Chinese, I • **Geneva Diner,** 14 South Second Street, 232-1288, I • **Inglenook Pantry,** 11 North Fifth Street, Geneva, 377-0373, Pennsylvania Dutch, I.

SIGHTSEEING **Paddlewheel Riverboats,** Pottawatomie Park, St. Charles, 584-2334. Hours: 45-minute cruises along the wooded Fox River, June–August, weekdays 3:30 P.M., Saturday hourly 2 P.M. to 4 P.M., Sunday hourly 2 P.M. to 5 P.M.; May and September to mid-October, hourly 2 P.M. to 4 P.M. $$ • **Cantigny,** 1 South 151 Winfield Road, Wheaton, 668-5161. Hours: McCormick Museum and First Division Museum, Memorial Day to Labor Day, Tuesday to Sunday 10 A.M. to 5 P.M.; Labor Day to December 28 and March 1 to Memorial Day, Tuesday to Sunday 10 A.M. to 4 P.M.; February, Friday to Sunday

10 A.M. to 4 P.M. Last mansion tours start 45 minutes before closing. Closed January. Gardens and grounds, March 1 to December 28, Tuesday to Sunday 9 A.M. to sunset; February, Friday to Sunday 9 A.M. to sunset. $$ • **Fabyan Forest Preserve,** State Highways 31 and 25 south of Geneva, 232-4811. Hours: Villa and information center, Saturday, Sunday 1 P.M. to 4 P.M. • **Billy Graham Center,** 500 East College Avenue, Wheaton, 752-5909. Monday to Saturday 9:30 A.M. to 5:30 P.M., Sunday 1 P.M. to 5 P.M. Donation, $ • **Kane County Flea Market,** Kane County Fairgrounds, Main Street (State Highway 64) and Randall Road, 377-2252. Hours: First weekend each month, Saturday noon to 5 P.M., Sunday 7 A.M. to 4 P.M. Adults, $$; children under 12, free • **Fermilab National Accelerator Laboratory,** Kirk Road and Pine Street, Batavia, 840-3351. Hours: Self-guided tours daily 8:30 A.M. to 5 P.M. Free • **Hollywood Casino,** 1 New York Street Bridge, Aurora, (800) 888-7777.

INFORMATION **Geneva Chamber of Commerce,** 8 South Third Street, Geneva, IL 60134, 232-6060 • **St. Charles Convention and Visitors Bureau,** 311 North Second Street, St. Charles, IL 60174, 377-6161, out of state, (800) 777-4373.

A Taste of Europe in Wisconsin

A visit to New Glarus, Wisconsin, is about as close as you'll come to Switzerland without crossing an ocean. This tiny town terraced up a hillside has Tyrolean balconies, overflowing flower boxes, Swiss flags, canton shields, and painted facades like those you might see in the Alps. They still have Yodel Clubs here, and choral groups singing Swiss folk tunes.

To add a bit of Norway to the trip, you need only drive a few miles up the road to Mount Horeb, where the main street is lined with hand-carved wooden trolls.

The rich farmland of south-central Wisconsin attracted many European settlers in search of a better life, and in this particular pocket, they prospered in the New World without losing touch with the old.

New Glarus came into being because times were hard in the canton of Glarus in Switzerland in the 1840s. An economic crisis had closed many factories and left residents with no jobs and no choice but to look elsewhere for a living. The scouts who came to America seeking a promising spot stopped when they saw the fertile Sugar River Valley in

Wisconsin. They purchased 1,200 acres of land, and in 1845, 108 Glarus residents came to settle in the village they named for their hometown. By the 1880s, a successful cheese-making industry was under way. More immigrants followed and the community grew, all the while preserving the look and feel of the homeland.

The bigger cheese factories are now to the south in Monroe, but small factories in nearby Monticello still produce Swiss, Gruyère, butterkäse, and other favorites. You can buy their cheese in local stores.

The traditional cheese-making methods have been preserved at the Käserie, or Cheese Factory, at the Swiss Village Museum, where the antique copper vats and wooden forms are used for demonstrations several times throughout the year. A video display shows the process at other times.

At the historical village you can see what things were like in New Glarus at the start. The re-created pioneer settlement has 13 buildings representing life in the mid-19th century. These include an 1850s cabin, where a whole family lived in a space 14 by 16 feet; a one-room schoolhouse; the old print shop; a bee house; and a blacksmith shop. The replica of the first log church is furnished with the original 1849 benches and the original tin pitcher and chalice used for communion. The Kramerei (general store) is stocked with needlework, dishes, clothing, quilts, even an alphorn and Swiss cowbells that early farmers used for their herds. A modern Hall of History building has educational displays describing the Swiss immigration to the area.

Another interesting stop in town is the Chalet of the Golden Fleece, an authentic copy of a Swiss Bernese mountain chalet built by a wealthy villager, Edward Barlow, as a home for himself and his ever-expanding collections. Barlow donated the chalet to the village as a house museum showing off his Swiss furnishings, crafts, and assorted treasures, from 2,000-year-old Etruscan earrings to a jeweled watch once owned by King Louis XVI.

At either of these sites, or at the New Glarus Hotel, you can pick up a walking tour to the rest of the village, a nice way to while away an hour or two. The hotel dates to 1853, as do several of the town's homes. The Kulby home, 301 12th Avenue, has the sweeping rooflines and curves characteristic of the Swiss Emmental style.

The New Glarus Farm and Feed Company next to the river was built in 1851 to house the community sawmill. Puempel's Olde Tavern on Sixth Avenue, established in 1893, was the first home for many immigrants; inside are large murals depicting Swiss, Austrian, and American history. The Swiss Church, the third on this site, was built in 1900 at the then-exorbitant cost of $16,000.

The first cheese factory in New Glarus, built in 1873, is now the Whistle Stop Ice Cream Parlor, where you can have pizza and a sweet treat. The building at 101 First Avenue housed the last factory, which went out of business the same day in 1910 that the Helvetia Milk Company moved in. Helvetia later became Pet Milk; the homes at 75–87 and 35–55 Second Street were built by the Pet Company for their employees.

The original New Glarus Brewery on Fifth Street was built in 1867. Rumors say that the Capone gang took over during Prohibition. The only thing certain is that the brewery never reopened when Prohibition was repealed. A new New Glarus Brewing Company did open in 1993, and has gotten rave reviews for its handmade beers. You can tour the brewery and taste their highly rated European-style lagers and pilsners.

Shopping in New Glarus is a wonderful chance to pick up old-world items like Swiss lace, bells, clocks, handcrafted furniture and folk art, and Christmas ornaments, not to mention Swiss chocolates and bakery treats like stollen. The Kuchen Haus is a good example, offering linens and lace, candles and holders, and handmade wooden toys. Roberts European Imports has Swiss bells and chimes, Swiss Army knives, cuckoo clocks, and fondue supplies. The Swiss Miss Textile Mart offers traditional Swiss embroidery. You can't miss the shops—they're all clustered on three short blocks, mostly along First Street.

You can also buy delicious meats to take home at places like Ruef's Market on First Street, which has more than 15 varieties of Swiss sausage, including Kalberwurst, Kalberbrats, and Landjaeger.

Out in the rolling countryside, you can visit Swiss Valley Orchard, where the 2,000 dwarf apple trees include many European varieties, and sample the goods at the Apple Bakery. Beer and brats are also available. Farms like Zimmerview welcome visitors who want to buy fresh eggs or homegrown poultry.

Save plenty of appetite for schnitzel, *geschnetzeltes, roesti* potatoes, and fondue, the specialties at atmospheric local restaurants like the New Glarus Hotel or the Glarner Stube. The hotel features polka music on Friday and Saturday nights. A Swiss Polkafest held each spring is one of several festivals in New Glarus. For over 30 years, the Heidi Festival in June has featured a drama telling the timeless story of the little Swiss girl. Even older is the Labor Day tradition of the Wilhelm Tell Festival, with another drama depicting the story of Swiss independence. The annual Octoberfest brings a celebration of the season. All of the festivals include alphorn playing, yodeling, and folk dancing.

The nationality changes in the town of Mount Horeb, about 15 miles to the north via State Highway 92. Here you'll recognize the Norwegian heritage in the brick and frame gingerbread houses lining the streets, and in the figures that have given it the name of Troll Capital of the World. Favorite mischievous folk figures in Scandinavia, trolls are said to be friendly souls as long as you don't interfere with their favorite activities, such as stealing chickens. The statues lining Main Street, better known as Trollway, have names that describe their occupations, like the Gardener, or Sweet Swill, pictured with her pet pig.

There are several reasons besides a troll stroll to linger awhile in Mount Horeb. The Mount Horeb Mustard Museum boasts of the world's largest collection of mustards, some 400 varieties. Many are available for tasting, and there's a video to tell you all you ever wanted to know about mustard. Since this is also a shop, you can buy your favorites to take home.

Six antique malls keep shoppers happy (Main Street Antiques has the most wares, Hoff Mall has the most upscale selection), and Open House Imports will gladly supply your own trolls or any other Scandinavian craft you might fancy.

The small Mount Horeb Area Museum highlights the many groups that have contributed to the history of the area.

Schubert's, the old-timer on Main Street, is the place for tasting Scandinavian specialties and sandwiches on the rye bread called *limpa.*

For a less commercial look at Norwegian life, take a five-minute drive to neighboring Blue Mounds and Little Norway. There's an enchanted feel to this picturesque Norse farm settlement nestled in a secluded valley. It was built by a Norwegian family using authentic old-world log architecture, including some buildings with growing sod roofs. The many-gabled wooden church is modeled after a 12th-century Norwegian *stavkirke,* or stave church. Colorfully costumed guides take visitors through all the buildings, pointing out the many Norse antiques, arts, and crafts.

For a change of pace in Blue Mounds, you can go underground for a rarity in this part of the country, the eerily shaped formations at Cave of the Mounds, a National Natural Landmark. Nearby is Blue Mounds State Park, the highest point in southern Wisconsin. Two 40-foot observation towers offer superb views.

Both Mount Horeb and New Glarus lure bicyclers and hikers with special trails. Mount Horeb is a midway point on the Military Ridge State Trail, a 39-mile course from Governor Dodge State Park in Dodgeville to Verona along an abandoned Chicago-Northwestern Railroad line, winding through woods, wetlands, prairies, and farmland. From Mount Horeb, the easier part of the trail is west toward Blue Mounds, the more challenging trail to the east toward Verona.

The Sugar River State Trail beginning in New Glarus also travels a former railroad bed through 23.5 miles of beautiful countryside, across trestles and streams, and through the Albany Wildlife Area to the town of Brodhead. Bike rentals and shuttle service are available at trail headquarters in the old New Glarus railroad station. This gentle and smooth trail, no more than a one-percent grade, is easy for all ages, and a chance to admire the rich countryside that lured settlers to this part of Wisconsin long ago.

Area Code: 608

DRIVING DIRECTIONS New Glarus is on State Highway 69. From Chicago, take I-90 west to U.S. 20 west, turning north on State

Highway 26, which becomes State Highway 69 in Wisconsin, about 117 miles. It is 91 miles from Milwaukee, 208 miles from Minneapolis.

ACCOMMODATIONS **Spring Valley Creek Bed-and-Breakfast,** N9098 Old Madison Road, New Glarus 53574, 527-2314, Swiss farm in rural setting, I–M, CP • **Country House Inn,** 180 Highway 69, New Glarus 53574, 527-5399, 1892 farmhouse on 50 acres, M, CP • **Chalet Landhaus Inn,** 801 Highway 69, New Glarus 53574, 527-5234, motel, I–M • **Beat Road Farm Bed-and-Breakfast,** 2401 Beat Road, Verona, 53593 (off U.S. Highway 18/151, 6 miles east of Mount Horeb), 437-6500, comfortable home, pool, M, CP • **Best Western Karakahl Inn,** 1405 U.S. 18 Business, Mount Horeb 53572, 437-5545, attractive motel, indoor pool, I–E.

DINING **New Glarus Hotel,** 100 Sixth Avenue, New Glarus, 527-5244, I–M • **Chalet Landhaus,** New Glarus (see above), Swiss and Continental, M • **Glarner Stube,** 518 First Street, New Glarus, 527-2216, I–M • **New Glarus Bakery and Tea Room,** 534 First Street, New Glarus, 527-2916, light lunch and yummy desserts, I • **Schubert's,** 128 East Main Street, Mount Horeb, 437-3393, I.

SIGHTSEEING *New Glarus:* **Swiss Village Museum,** 712 Sixth Avenue, New Glarus, 527-2317. Hours: May through October, daily 9 A.M. to 4:30 P.M. $$ • **Chalet of the Golden Fleece,** 618 Second Street, New Glarus, 527-2614. Hours: May through October, daily 10 A.M. to 4:30 P.M. $$ • **Swiss Valley Orchards,** County Road O, 3.5 miles north of New Glarus, 527-5355. Hours: September to early November, daily; late June to August, weekends only • **Zimmerview Farm,** N8204 County Road J, New Glarus, 527-2018. Call ahead for visiting • **New Glarus Brewing Company,** Highway 69, New Glarus, 527-5850. Phone for tour information • ***Mount Horeb—Blue Mounds:*** **Mount Horeb Mustard Museum,** 109 East Main Street, Mount Horeb, 437-3986. Hours: Daily 10 A.M. to 5 P.M. Free • **Mount Horeb Area Museum,** 100 South Second Street, Mount Horeb, 437-6486. Hours: Friday and Saturday 10 A.M. to 5 P.M., Sunday 12:30 P.M. to 5 P.M. Donation • **Little Norway,** County Road JG off U.S. 18/151, Blue Mounds, 437-8211. Hours: 45-minute guided tours May to October, daily 9 A.M. to 5 P.M., to 7 P.M. in July and August. Last tour begins one hour before closing. $$$ • **Cave of the Mounds,** Cave of the Mounds Road off U.S. 18/151, Blue Mounds, 437-3038. Hours: Mid-March to mid-November, daily 9 A.M. to 5 P.M.; Memorial Day to Labor Day, to 7 P.M.; weekends only rest of the year. $$$$ • **Blue Mounds State Park,** County Road F, Mount Horeb, 437-5711. Hours: daily 6 A.M. to 11 P.M., office 8 A.M. to 4:30 P.M. Parking, $$$; Wisconsin residents, $$ • ***Bicycle trails:*** **Sugar River State Trail,** headquarters in old railroad depot, Railroad Street, New Glarus, 527-2334; bike rental and shuttle service available • **Military Ridge State Trail,** c/o Blue Mounds State Park, 437-7393. Trail passes available in Mount Horeb at A & W Restaurant, Kalseur's Fine Foods, and Mount Horeb Co-op.

INFORMATION **New Glarus Chamber of Commerce,** P.O. Box 713, New Glarus, WI 53574, 527-2095 or (800) 527-6838 • **Mount Horeb Chamber of Commerce,** P.O. Box 84, Mount Horeb, WI 53572, 437-5914 or toll free (88) TROLLWAY.

Old-Fashioned Fun in Amish Country

The spinning windmills, shiny horse-drawn buggies, and neat rows of sober-colored clothing flapping on the line tell the story. This is a corner of the Midwest where time stands still.

North-central Indiana boasts America's third-largest Amish settlement, some 15,000 to 17,000 strong. For those of us who live in a more complicated world, there's a fascination in seeing the old-fashioned lifestyle of these "plain people," who seem to manage just fine without such contrivances as clothes dryers, television sets, or cars.

A visit to Amish country is a chance to retreat to the slow lane and observe another way of life, to buy Amish handcrafts direct from the makers, enjoy hearty meals, and to revel in the beauty of the rolling countryside.

If you crave a handmade quilt, an excellent time to come is the last Saturday in September, when the annual Michiana Mennonite Relief Sale at the Elkhart County 4-H Fairgrounds in Goshen offers antiques and all kinds of crafts, and over 300 quilts go up for auction. Proceeds are used to help developing nations around the world.

Amish country has two main centers, Nappanee to the southwest, and Middlebury and Shipshewana, about 35 minutes to the northeast. Goshen is between the two. Both areas have many small bed-and-breakfast inns, and Goshen offers the tranquil, elegant Checkerberry Inn, one of the finest in the Midwest. It is also possible to stay on a Mennonite farm, a nice experience for families.

The Essenhaus Country Inn in Middlebury is also a winner. Though part of a big commercial complex, it is off by itself and has most attractive country furnishings. The restaurant is one of the most popular places to sample a typical heaping, family-style Amish meal.

An excellent way to see the area and learn a great deal more about it is to use the taped auto tours available from the Elkhart County Convention and Visitors Bureau, located just off I-80/90 at Exit 92. The tapes will guide you from Elkhart on a 100-mile Heritage Trail that takes in everything of importance. You may want to return to Elkhart on Sunday afternoon when most Amish attractions are closed to visit the Midwest Museum of American Art, which has many prominent American artists in its collections, or the National New York Central Railroad Museum.

Do heed the tape's advice to explore some of the back roads on your own. That's where you will find farms with signs out front inviting you into home craft workshops. These stops are likely to be the highlights of your stay. A special audio tape, the Furniture Crafters Tour, is available at the visitors center.

Since Nappanee has the only main attraction open on Sunday, on weekends it makes sense to start at Shipshewana and work back. To learn about the settlers who came to this region in the 1840s, make your first stop Menno-Hof, the Mennonite-Amish visitors center.

Created to provide curious visitors with accurate answers to their questions, the center is housed in a farmhouse and barn that was erected in the Amish tradition. It took six days and 200 volunteers to raise the barn and enclose the attached farmhouse.

You will learn here that both groups were part of the Anabaptist movement. They fled Europe in the 17th century to escape religious persecution, and though they have common origins and share many beliefs, members of the group broke into sects. The Amish are part of the conservative "old order," who retain conservative ways. The Mennonites for the most part have entered into their modern communities, driving cars and working in a variety of occupations. The restaurants and shops you see are owned by Mennonites, not Amish. Some Mennonites do choose to wear the old-order dress; others dress like their neighbors.

The old-order Amish still speak with an old-country dialect. It is their firm belief that duty to God means living simply and tilling the soil. They dress in dark, solid colors in the style of the 19th-century European ancestors. Cars and electricity, regarded as temptations to a more worldly life that lures people away from family and community, are forbidden. The Amish maintain their own schools and worship in each other's homes on Sundays.

Straw-hatted Amish farmers and their families often can be seen out working together in the fields. Even the youngest are given chores. The mule- and horse-drawn farm equipment is much the same as what their fathers and grandfathers used before them. Lack of technology does not seem to hinder them, however: their fields yield rich crops of corn, buckwheat, soybeans, sorghum, grains, and vegetables.

The farmhouses are always two-story wood-frame constructions, and painted white because it is the "plainest" color. Amish homesteads can be recognized not only by the lack of electric wires but also by distinctive additions on many homes known as *gross dawdis* ("grandfathers"). When a farmer reaches retirement age, an annex to the main house is built, allowing him to enjoy the fruits of his labor and be part of the family without getting in the way of the younger generation. A double addition marks a three-generation home.

Not all of the Amish are farmers. Many are skilled woodworkers and cabinetmakers, producing furniture with hand-rubbed finishes, dovetail drawers, and hand-carved detailing. Some make their living working in nearby factories. They will use power tools at work, even though they adhere to the old ways at home.

Nor do the Amish turn away from all modern ways. You'll notice places to tether a horse at the supermarket.

About 10 percent of Shipshewana's population of 600 are Amish, and 85 percent are Mennonites. The tiny town has become a major marketplace for area farmers, and a draw for visitors, as well. To see Shipshewana's chief attraction, you'll have to come on a Tuesday or Wednesday for the huge weekly flea market, an event that draws some 1,000 vendors and 30,000 to 40,000 shoppers to this dot of a town. The shoppers fill up 60 acres of parking. What's for sale at Shipshewana? Produce, furniture, toys, handcrafts, dolls, jewelry, antiques, T-shirts, baskets, clothing, and almost anything else you can name.

All of this began in 1922 as an event mainly for local farmers, with a sale of six pigs, seven cows, and several head of young cattle. Livestock auctions are still held on Wednesday mornings, and horse auctions on Friday; both are lively affairs, with a dozen auctioneers going at once, and with many Amish in attendance. One of the most colorful events is an auction of new and antique carriages held the first Friday and Saturday in June.

Shipshe, as the locals call it, also draws visitors because of the Riegsecker Marketplace. Mel Riegsecker began crafting miniature horse-and-carriages in 1968 as a hobby. His marvelously exact six-horse hitches, made to one-tenth scale, slowly began to sell, and when he made it into the Sears and Montgomery-Ward catalogs in the early 1980s, he soon had his own large manufacturing enterprise.

Shoppers liked to watch Riegsecker's crafters at work, so in 1985, he opened the Craft Barn in Shipshewana, featuring his own work as well as others'. From there, he went on to found a furniture factory, which makes the handsome desks and other pieces now for sale at the expanded Craft Barn, and to develop a whole block of varied shops bordering State Highway 5, along with a popular restaurant, the Blue Gate. One thing hasn't changed: you can still watch artisans making miniature rigs, each a work of art.

Riegsecker also offers buggy rides, an excellent way to see the town and learn tidbits of local life.

The constant activity means that little Shipshewana is filled with shops selling everything from quilts to popcorn. But you'll still see buggies parked and residents shopping at authentic local places like Yoder's Department Store and Hardware.

You'll find more shops wherever you go in Amish country, many of them selling handcrafted work. Amish Heritage Furniture on State Highway 13 in Middlebury is one of many places with pieces made by Amish craftsmen. You can watch them at work here through an observation window. Middlebury itself is a mix of Amish community and Midwestern small town.

Visitors are also welcome to watch cheese making and to taste delicious mild Colby cheese made by the Amish at the Deutsch Käse Haus on County Road 250 northeast of town.

For a break, you might buy some of that cheese plus other goodies for a picnic at Bonneyville Mill Park, north of Middlebury following County Road 8 to State Highway 120 to the turnoff on County Road 131. The 1832 mill, Indiana's oldest, is still operating; you can watch the grinding process and buy stone-ground flour from the millers. The mill is set in a lovely park with a pond, wooded walking paths, meadows, and gardens. Buggies parked in the lot and Amish families picnicking are common sights here. The mill, incidentally, is one of the few places in this area open on Sunday.

On County Road 8 on the way to the mill, not far out of Middlebury, you'll notice a sign for cider. Turn down the driveway and you'll find a modest house where the Millers, a conservative Mennonite family, everyone from young teens to grandparents, work together to make cider with a hand press. When we called in summer, all were sitting around the table peeling peaches, which a teen son then put into a hand grinder and turned into a big vat to make peach butter. This is the kind of happy experience that makes for lasting memories.

Two other recommended detours on side roads are the Otto House on County Road 200 South in Topeka, where the family makes beautiful hickory rockers and tables, and Ruth Otto Weaving on unpaved County Road 50 North, where a sweet young Amish girl minds the shop selling her mother's handwoven place mats and baskets. If you want to see where the Amish shop, look for the Honeyville General Store on County Road 400S, a quaint scene right out of the past. With an area map, it's easy to find your way.

When you head west, you'll find a most attractive, more cosmopolitan town of 24,000. The county seat, Goshen is known as the City of Maples because of its many trees. It is home to a classic Midwestern domed, columned courthouse and a handsome campus, Goshen College, a liberal-arts school associated with the Mennonite Church. Goshen also boasts some of Amish country's best dining at the Checkerberry Inn and the Brick House, and near the campus, a notable old-fashioned diner, the South Side Soda Shop, which has even been mentioned in *Gourmet* magazine.

This is where you will find the most upscale of the shopping complexes, the Old Bag Factory on Chicago Avenue off U.S. Highway 33. The former factory now houses 17 shops, including a collection of quality working artists and craftsmen. These include potter Dick Lehman, who creates wheel-thrown pottery before your eyes, artist Shirley Shenk, who offers original-design quilts, and Swarzendruber Hardwood Creations, where you can order custom furniture. Carriage Barn Antiques is particularly attractive as its wares are displayed in complete room settings.

On Sunday, head for Nappanee, a quaint town on the National Register, and its best-known attraction, Amish Acres. This is a nicely restored circa-1874 80-acre working Amish farm, complete with the original farmhouse and outbuildings such as the hog house, wagon shed, icehouse, brick oven, smokehouse, root cellar, and lye kiln. The 1876 bank barn was built with hand-hewn timbers cut from this farm. There are frequent demonstrations of the skills and crafts of old, such as quilt making, candle dipping, food drying, and sorghum-molasses making.

Many of the additions to the property, such as a 19th-century blacksmith shop and the Walnut Street house, which now accommodates a weaving loom, were moved from Nappanee and reconstructed. Even some of the shops are housed in authentic period buildings.

The rest of the complex is more commercial, with buggy rides, lots of shops, and a big, busy 400-seat restaurant. One nice touch: one of the classic round barns of the area, built in 1911, was moved to this site and converted into a theater featuring performances of Broadway musicals, including the show about the Amish, *Plain and Fancy.*

If you come on the third weekend in September, you'll find Nappanee abuzz with its annual Apple Festival, a three-day event that fills South Main Street with crafts, food booths, wood carvers, and country events like tractor pulls and crosscut saw competitions. There are pie-eating contests and prizes for those who bake best and peel fastest. Don't miss tasting the Dutch apple pie. You can also pick your own apples at Miller's Orchards, owned by an old-order Amish family.

The restaurant at Amish Acres specializes in bountiful, family-style, all-you-can-eat "Threshers Dinners," a feast of bean soup, hearth bread, beef and noodles, mashed potatoes, turkey with sage dressing and giblet gravy, country chicken, cider-baked ham, and roast beef. Amish favorites include locally made apple butter, spiced apple rings, sweet-and-sour cabbage salad, and gooey shoofly pie for dessert. There's a little more quantity than quality, but you'll surely go away satisfied, a nice ending to an Amish weekend.

<u>Area Code: 219</u>

DRIVING DIRECTIONS Amish country is south of I-80/90 below Elkhart. From Chicago, take Exit 92 for Nappanee, 101 for Goshen, and 107 for Middlebury and Shipshewana. Nappanee is about 100 miles from Chicago, 140 miles from Indianapolis, 175 miles from Milwaukee, and 190 miles from Detroit. Shipshewana, the farthest point east, is about 30 miles from Nappanee.

ACCOMMODATIONS **Checkerberry Inn,** 62644 County Road 37, Goshen 46526, 642-4445, exceptional in setting and decor, E, CP • **Indian Creek Bed-and-Breakfast,** 20300 County Road 18, Goshen 46526, 875-6606, newly built country Victorian, I–M, CP • **Spring View,** 63189 County Road 31, Goshen 46528, 642-3997, newer home on 48 acres, whirlpools, I, CP • **Das Essenhaus Country Inn,** 240 U.S. Highway 20, Middlebury 46540, (800) 455-9471, 825-9447, atrium lobby, handsome country furnishings, M • **The Country Victorian,** 435 South Main Street, Middlebury 46540, 825-2568, in-town small century-old Victorian, I–M, CP • **1898 Varns Family Inn,** 205 South Main Street, Middlebury 46540, 825-9666 or (800) 398-5424, in the same family for nearly 100 years, I–M, CP • **Patchwork Quilt Country Inn,** 1748 County Road 2, Middlebury, 46540, 825-2417, decorated with handmade quilts, I–M, CP • **Meadows Inn Bed-and-Breakfast,** 12013 U.S. 20, Middlebury, 46540, 825-3913 or (888) 868-3913, renovated 1920s Amish farmhouse, M, CP • **Market Street Guest House,** 253 East Market Street, Nappanee 46550, 773-2261 or (800) 497-3791, 1922 home, prize stained-glass windows, I, CP • **Victorian Guest House,** 302 East Market Street, Nappanee 46550, 773-4383, attractive 1893 Victorian in town, I–M, CP • **Olde Buffalo Inn,** 1061 Parkwood Drive, Nappanee 46550, 773-2223, unusual, 1840 farmhouse enclosed by new addition, basement turned into a tavern, basketball court in the barn, M, CP.

DINING **Checkerberry Inn** (see above), excellent Continental fare in lovely surroundings, EE, prix fixe • **Brick House Country Inn,** 16820 County Road 38, Goshen, 534-4949, restored 1870 home, good American fare, I–M • **Patchwork Quilt Country Inn** (see above) 825-2417, country fare in a charming century-old farmhouse, I–M • **Blue Gate Restaurant,** State Highway 5, Shipshewana, 768-4725, fried chicken and other tasty treats served by Mennonite ladies, very popular—expect long lines at lunch, I • **Buggy Wheel Restaurant,** Morton Street, Shipshewana, 768-4444, known for their Potluck Buffet, I • ***Family-style Amish meals:*** **Das Essenhaus Country Inn** (see above), I–M • **Amish Acres,** U.S. Highway 6, Nappanee, 773-4188, M, children, I.

SIGHTSEEING **Menno-Hof, Mennonite Amish Visitors Center,** State Highway 5, Shipshewana, 768-4117. Hours: Monday to Saturday 10 A.M. to 5 P.M. Donation, $$ • **Amish Acres,** 1600 Market Street (U.S. Highway 6), Nappanee, 773-4188 or (800) 800-4942. Hours:

March to December, daily 10 A.M. to 6 P.M. Guided tour and film, $$$. Combination tickets available with tour, buggy ride, and family-style Threshers Dinner. Musical performances, late April to November, Tuesday to Saturday at 8 P.M.; matinees Wednesday, Thursday, and Saturday 3 P.M. $$$$$ • **Bonneyville Mill Park,** County Road 131, Bristol, 535-6458. Hours: May to October, daily 10 A.M. to 5 P.M. Free • **Shipshewana Flea Market and Auction,** State Highway 5, Shipshewana, 768-4129. Hours: Flea market, May to October, Tuesday and Wednesday from early morning "till done." Auctions: antiques and miscellaneous, Wednesday 8 A.M.; livestock, Wednesday 11 A.M.; horses, Friday 9:30 A.M. Parking, $$ • **Michiana Mennonite Relief Sale,** Elkhart County 4-H Fairgrounds off U.S. Highway 33, Goshen, one Saturday in late September; phone visitors bureau for current information • **Nappanee Apple Festival,** 215 West Market Street, Nappanee, 773-2112, 3-day event, usually the last weekend in September • **Midwest Museum of American Art,** 429 South Main Street, Elkhart, 293-6660. Hours: Tuesday to Friday 11 A.M. to 5 P.M., Saturday and Sunday 1 P.M. to 4 P.M. $$, free on Sunday • **National New York Central Railroad Museum,** 721 South Main Street, Elkhart, 294-3001. Hours: Tuesday to Friday 10 A.M. to 2 P.M., Saturday, Sunday 10 A.M. to 3 P.M. $.

INFORMATION Elkhart County Convention and Visitors Bureau, 219 Caravan Drive, Elkhart, IN 46514, 262-8161 or (800) 262-8161; www.amishcountry.org

Winter

Overleaf: Amish settlements can be found in Illinois, Indiana, and Wisconsin.
Photo courtesy of Elkhart County Convention & Visitors Bureau.

Crafty Shopping in Mineral Point

The honey-colored limestone houses and steep, narrow streets of Mineral Point, Wisconsin, have the look of the Old World—and with good reason. In the 1830s, when Chicago was still a mudflat, the discovery of lead ore turned Mineral Point into a boomtown.

The news spread and skilled hard-rock miners from Cornwall saw an opportunity. They came to Wisconsin, bringing not only their mining know-how but also their skill at stone masonry, building cottages of native stone like those they had left behind in western England.

Mineral Point's hilly High Street is a mellow page from the past, especially when it is lavishly decked in fresh evergreen boughs for the Christmas season. Even the dog statue that has kept watch over the street for more than 100 years dons a big bow for the occasion.

There is no better place to look for unique Christmas gifts. When the ore ran out and the town faded, costs were low, and many artists and craftspeople were attracted to the picturesque old structures. Some three dozen painters, wood carvers, fiber artists, glassblowers, jewelers, potters, and other artisans now live and work in meticulously preserved stone buildings. Many of the artisans moved here from urban areas, giving this town of 2,500 a sophistication beyond its size. They have earned Mineral Point a spot in the book *The 100 Best Small Art Towns in America.*

A Christmas-shopping excursion to Mineral Point is all but guaranteed to yield one-of-a-kind gifts. The inns now occupying some of the fine older homes in town add the best of old-fashioned warmth. And for a change of pace, you're only a short drive away from the lavish Santa Claus displays at the House on the Rock.

The Christmas season begins in Mineral Point on Thanksgiving weekend, when over a mile of fresh evergreens are hung in the historic business district and businesses host an open-house weekend. Step back in time the first weekend in December, when you can shop by the glow of candlelight and take part in the Christmas Tour of Historic Homes.

From that point until Christmas, shops are candlelit for atmospheric shopping every Friday night. The Artisans Guild sponsors weekend Christmas Walks, open houses in studios where visitors are invited to drop in to visit with the artists and share cookies and cider. A white snowflake on a large red banner identifies the participating studios each week.

Special holiday entertainment is scheduled at the restored Mineral Point Opera House, built in 1914 as a grand arena for vaudeville.

Finding the shops in town is easy—they are clustered on High Street, on parallel Jail Alley and Fountain Street, and at the bottom of the hill on Commerce Street. Part of the fun is talking to the artisan-owners, watching them at work, and learning about the restoration of their buildings, many of which date from 1827 to 1854.

At the upper end of High Street are Christmas on High, with folk-art Santas, angels, and other holiday collectibles; the Johnston Gallery, offering porcelain and stoneware by owners Diana and Tom Johnston plus contemporary crafts by over 100 other artists; and Studio on High, a weaving studio and gallery featuring wearable art jewelry, pottery, and weavings. Down the hill, you'll find Against the Grain, the studio and gallery of talented Don Mahieu, who creates unique hardwood sculptures using burls, roots, and other highly figured pieces of wood. If you are looking for stocking stuffers, Mahieu's wood-inlaid earrings may fit the bill.

One of the most fascinating stops is the studio of ceramic sculptor Bruce Howdle on Commerce Street. The showroom displays his whimsical ceramic pigs and giraffes, four-foot vases, relief murals, and other intriguing pieces. If Howdle is not busy, he may take you into the studio to see some of his current major mural projects or photos of his work on display in places like Sportsman's Park near Chicago, the Omaha airport, and a wildlife center in Oklahoma.

Needlewood, in a fine 1847 home on Jail Alley, is a shop named for the retirement occupations of its owners, former executive Bert Bohlin, a woodworker, and his wife, needlework artist Jean. Together they produce unique boxes of wood decorated with needlepoint, hence the shop's name.

Nearby Jail Alley House claims to be the oldest gallery in town. It features work by local artist Tom Kelly, as well as pottery, jewelry, and antiques. Antiques are found in half a dozen other shops, most of them on High Street.

Streets like Jail Alley still bear names from the past. This one marks the time when the town jail was located in the rear of the old courthouse, backing on the street.

Another colorful example is Shake Rag Street, named for the wives who shook their dust rags to signal to their husbands working on the opposite ridge that it was time to come home for dinner.

When you've checked off all the items on your list, join the locals at the Red Rooster Cafe on High Street for a sampling of Cornish foods such as the flaky meat pies called pasties, and figgyhobbin, a dessert pastry rolled up with raisins. For a tasty snack, stop at Hook's Cheese, a factory on Commerce Street specializing in Colby cheese. Fresh cheese curds are available on Fridays.

Take time for a drive around town to see some of the important historic structures, including many fine homes built in the Victorian era, as well as the early stone structures. An architectural and historical guide with a map is available for a small fee at the Chamber/Main Street office on High Street.

You'll learn that on July 4, 1836, during the town's glory years, the Wisconsin Territory was created in Mineral Point, with Colonel Henry Dodge inaugurated as the first governor, giving rise to the local slogan, "the city where Wisconsin began." This is also the town where Wisconsin got its nickname, the Badger State, inspired by eager early prospectors who actually lived in the holes they dug while searching for ore, and became known as badgers.

Artists and preservationists have saved much of the town's special architectural heritage. Their efforts were responsible for the entire city, some 900 structures, becoming the first district in the state to be placed on the National Register of Historic Places.

Pendarvis, a collection of authentically furnished miners' homes, is the major historic site in town and was the spark of the preservation movement. The restoration was begun in 1935 by a pair of concerned citizens, Robert Moser Neal and Edgar Hellum, who did not want to see the old workers' cottages lost. After rehabilitating three stone houses on Shake Rag Street, the pair raised funds for further restoration by creating a restaurant named Pendarvis House, after an estate in the mining district of Cornwall. The menu was strictly Cornish fare and the small restaurant gained national renown, allowing Neal and Hellum to construct and plant terraced perennial gardens and restore another seven buildings, including early log houses and a cozy Cornish-style pub.

Now under the auspices of the State Historical Society of Wisconsin, Pendarvis is open to the public from May through October. You can get a good feel for the past just walking around the property.

When the lead had petered out, Mineral Point continued to prosper for a while from zinc, which had been discarded as a worthless by-product by the lead miners. From the Pendarvis parking lot, a walking trail open year-round takes you around the Merry Christmas Mine Prairie, where a large zinc mine operated from 1906 to 1913. It underlies the eastern part of Mineral Point Hill, where the original discovery of lead ore was made about 1825. Development of this site is under way to highlight early crevice mines and badger holes and to restore native prairie plants.

The 1868 Joseph Gundry House, one of the grand old Victorian homes once owned by the town's leading merchant, is now home to the Mineral Point Historical Society, open from May to October and for special events at Christmastime. The printed tours take you past many other handsome homes, such as the 16-room John Gray House on Maiden Street, owned by a miner who became prosperous as partner to Joseph Gundry; and the Moses M. Strong House on Fountain Street, the home of a onetime president of the state bar association and author of the authoritative early *History of Wisconsin.*

Near the top of High Street are two notable churches, the Gothic Revival Trinity Episcopal, completed in 1846, and the English Gothic First Methodist Church, dating to 1871. The latter is home to one of the oldest Protestant congregations in Wisconsin, organized in 1834.

Some of the graceful homes, such as the circa-1906 red brick William A. Jones House, are now bed-and-breakfast inns. For charm, it's hard to beat the 1853 stone and brick Mineral Point Inn, with its lovely private setting. One of the best-preserved examples of 19th-century Mineral Point is the recently restored, elegantly furnished Cothren House, a stone family estate built in 1853 (it's on the National Register). The log cabin on the grounds, built in 1835, is the perfect romantic hideaway.

Another interesting restoration is the Brewery Creek Inn, part of a three-story 1854 limestone former warehouse on Commerce Street that now houses a brewery and brewpub as well as the inn. Brewery tours are available year round.

For a cheery end to the weekend, proceed north about 20 minutes on U.S. Highway 151, merging into State Highway 23 North to reach the House on the Rock (see page 75), where each year proprietor Karen Donaldson's personal collection of over 6,000 Santas is added to the wonders on display. Life-size Santas representing Father Christmas images from around the world and holiday background music are part of the traditional holiday exhibit. It will surely send you home in the mood for a Merry Christmas.

Area Code: 608

DRIVING DIRECTIONS Mineral Point is on U.S. Highway 151, reached from Chicago by driving north on I-90 to Madison, then southwest on 18/151, about 180 miles. It is 45 miles from Madison, 120 miles from Milwaukee, and 250 miles from Minneapolis.

ACCOMMODATIONS The zip code for all listings is 53565. **Cothren House,** 320 Tower Street, 987-2612, M–E, CP • **William A. Jones House,** 215 Ridge Street, 987-2337, I, CP • **House of the Brau-Meister,** 254 Shake Rag Street, 987-2913, turn-of-the-century Queen Anne, I, CP • **Brewery Creek Inn,** 23 Commerce Street, 987-3298, some whirlpools and fireplaces, M–E • **Knudson's Guest House,** 415 Ridge Street, 987-2733, warm, homey, I, CP.

DINING **Chesterfield Inn,** 20 Commerce Street, 987-3682, fine dining in a mid-1800s stone building, I–M • **Royal Inn,** 43 High Street, 987-3051, town standby, steaks and basics, I–M • **Redwood Family Restaurant,** U.S. 151 North, 987-2242, pleasant dining room attached to motel, varied menu, pasties, I–M • **Brewery Creek Pub,** 23 Commerce Street, 987-3208, burgers and snacks, I • **Red Rooster Cafe,** 158 High Street, 987-9936, Cornish specialties, I.

SIGHTSEEING **Joseph Gundry House,** Museum of the Mineral Point Historical Society, 234 Madison Street, 987-2883. Hours: May through October, Thursday to Sunday 1 P.M. to 5 P.M. Donation. Phone for dates of Victorian Christmas open house. • **Pendarvis,** 114 Shake Rag Street, 987-2122. Hours: May through October, daily 9 A.M. to 5 P.M. $$$ • **The House on the Rock Holiday Tour,** State Highway 23, Spring Green, 935-3639. Hours: Mid-November to early January, daily from 10 A.M. to 6 P.M. $$$

INFORMATION **Mineral Point Chamber/Main Street,** 225 High Street, Mineral Point, WI 53565, 987-2580 or (888) POINT-WI; www.mineralpoint.com

Winter Glow in Galena

With its spired churches and brick mansions terraced up a steep hillside beside the Galena River, Galena, Illinois, still looks much the way it did when Ulysses S. Grant clerked in his father's leather shop here before the Civil War.

Galena is a page from the past—and a weekender's delight. For antiquing, architecture, inns, and year-round recreation, this Illinois oasis is hard to beat—which is why so many people throng the shops and fill the town's inns for most of the year.

Ah, but come winter, just as the town is at its most beautiful, aglow with a sugarcoating of snow, the crowds recede and Galena returns to the peaceful image that once earned it the label the Town That Time Forgot. There's no better time to feel the nostalgia of this old-fashioned village, where 85 percent of the buildings are on the National Register of Historic Places. If you make the trip before Christmas, you'll also find several tree farms in the area where you can choose and cut your own tree, and you can check off everyone on your gift list in a host of delightful shops.

Adding to the area's cold-weather attractions is a nearby four-star resort, Eagle Ridge, where a host of winter sports includes ice skating, sledding, an indoor pool, and 60 kilometers of groomed cross-country ski trails winding through the woods and around a lake.

There's even a small ski area just outside Galena, Chestnut Hill, overlooking the Mississippi. Galena's hilly location in the "driftless area" that the glaciers missed is one of its chief attractions.

Only a few of the historic sites are closed off-season. You can still visit the home of Ulysses S. Grant and a host of other interesting places, enjoy the ambience, browse the shops without being elbowed, and take your pick of lodgings in the town that has earned a new title as

Inn Capital of the Midwest. When the weather cooperates, one of the stables in town can provide a romantic sleighride.

If you want to try your luck, riverboat gambling beckons just across the Mississippi in Dubuque, Iowa, about 15 minutes from Galena. Though cruises stop in the winter, the casino action at the dock is nonstop.

The name Galena is the Latin word for lead sulfide. In the mid-1800s this was a boomtown producing 80 percent of the nation's lead. With a strategic location on a tributary of the Mississippi, it became the major steamboat stop between St. Paul and St. Louis. Until the end of the Civil War, Galena was the richest town in Illinois, a prosperous city of 16,000 when Chicago was getting started.

A series of fires prompted officials in the late 1850s to order that all new buildings be constructed of stone or brick. That's how the town-scape became a cohesive series of handsome red-brick structures, a remarkable collection of 19th-century architecture that remains almost unchanged. After the Civil War, the railroad bypassed Galena, trade waned, and—luckily for today's visitors—the town was too poor to modernize. Few buildings went up here after 1890.

Almost a century later, Galena was rediscovered by history buffs and Chicago artists, who bought cheap and began restoring the fine homes. Soon shops began to open, sprucing up the old Main Street.

Stop at the visitors center in the old town railroad station for a self-guided walking tour to help you identify the prize architecture found along Main and Bench Streets. Federal, Italianate, Queen Anne, Greek Revival, Second Empire, Gothic Revival, and Romanesque Revival are among the many styles represented, a virtual catalog of American architectural trends.

The Ulysses S. Grant Home was presented by the town to its most illustrious citizen on his return from the Civil War in 1865. The red-brick Italianate home is furnished with period pieces, including many original items belonging to the Grant family.

The Dowling House, the oldest in town, was built of native limestone in 1826. Beneath the low doorways are rough-hewn beams, stone hearths, primitive furnishings, and an extensive collection of Galena pottery.

Though it closes for the winter, you can still admire the elaborate lines and belvedere of the Belvedere Mansion, a 22-room Italianate beauty built in 1857 for J. Russel Jones, a steamboat magnate.

Houses are only part of the historic sightseeing scene. The restored 1845 Old Market House has an audiovisual show and an exhibit on local architecture. The Galena/Jo Davies County History Museum has its own presentation explaining the history of the town, lots of memorabilia, and Thomas Nast's famous painting, *Peace in Union,* showing Robert E. Lee's surrender to Grant at Appomattox.

You can also look into the second-oldest continuously operating post office in the United States and, in the Historic Collection at the Public Library, check Galena newspapers dating all the way back to 1834.

When you are ready for a break, have lunch above the winery at Grant's Place, where sandwiches and burgers are served by a waitstaff dressed as Civil War soldiers.

Most of Galena's many shopping temptations are right on long, curving Main Street. Some two dozen antiques shops beckon with everything from South American folk art to country quilts. Browsing door-to-door is part of the fun. The Toy Soldier Collection on Main Street is definitely worth a look for its dioramas tracing the history of military innovation. The hand-painted soldiers and military miniatures are created by owner W. Paul LeGreco, a Ulysses S. Grant look-alike, who sometimes greets visitors in uniform and often gives performances around town.

Galena has many resident artists whose work is included in the dozen galleries along Main Street. Rivertrace Gallery has one of the most interesting selections. Also among gallery offerings are fine art, jewelry, pottery, and art glass.

Some of the most creative dining in town is at the airy, arty Eldorado Grill. Among longtime favorite places in town are Silver Annie's, with its American menu; Cafe Italia, serving Italian specialties; and the Log Cabin, the town's oldest eatery, known for big, juicy steaks.

For lunch with a view, head for Chestnut Mountain Resort and a unique vista, the Mississippi River at the bottom of a ski slope. Skiers will find two triple and one quad chairlift and 16 runs, the longest at 3,500 feet. The mountain has a respectable Midwest elevation of 475 feet, and if the real white stuff does not fall, there's ample snowmaking. Festive times to come are during January's annual Klondike Kapers, or the February Winter Carnival when fireworks light up the slopes. Both events feature snow sculptures, and special events that include slalom races and freestyle skiing.

The choice of lodgings in Galena is all but overwhelming. For period atmosphere, try the DeSoto House Hotel, where the guest list has included Mark Twain, Susan B. Anthony, and Abraham Lincoln, who addressed citizens on Main Street in 1856 from the hotel's second-floor balcony. At the Eagle Ridge Inn and Resort outside town, there's a choice of inn rooms or villas with fireplaces and whirlpools. And if a log cabin is more your style, you can find that, too, at the Log Cabin Guest House, a collection of four authentic 1800s log cabins and a historic coach house on a quiet country lane west of town. A selection of the many fine homes turned to bed-and-breakfast inns is listed below.

Wherever you stay, it's a safe bet you'll warm up to the charming town of Galena.

Area Code: 815

DRIVING DIRECTIONS Galena is on U.S. Highway 20, about 160 miles west of Chicago.

ACCOMMODATIONS The zip code for all listings is 61036. **DeSoto House Hotel,** 230 South Main Street, 777-0090, restored historic hotel, circa 1855, I–E • **Farmer's Guest House,** 334 Spring Street, 777-3456 or (800) 373-3456, M • **Log Cabin Guest House,** 11661 West Chetlain Lane, 777-2845, five renovated 1830s cabins, whirlpools, fireplaces, E–EE • **Eagle Ridge Inn and Resort,** U.S. 20 East, 777-2444 or (800) 892-2269, M–EE • **Chestnut Mountain Resort,** 8700 West Chestnut Road, (800) 397-1320, recommended mainly for skiers who want to be right on the slopes, M • ***Bed-and-breakfast inns:*** **Aldrich Guest House,** 900 Third Street, 777-3323, 1845 Greek Revival home, M, CP • **Belle Aire Mansion,** 11410 U.S. 20, 777-0893, 1834 Federal style home on 11 acres, rooms, M, CP; suites, E, CP • **Captain Gear Guest House,** 1000 South Bench Street, 777-0222 or (800) 794-5656, 1855 Italianate mansion, many fireplaces, antiques, E, CP • **Hellman Guest House,** 318 Hill Street, 777-3638, stained glass, fine oak furnishings, and views, M, CP • **Park Avenue Guest House,** 208 Park Avenue, 1893 Queen Anne home, 777-1075, M, CP • **Queen Anne Guest House,** 200 Park Avenue, 777-3849, another fine Queen Anne Victorian, M, CP • **The Victorian Mansion,** 301 High Street, 777-0675, 1861 Italianate filled with fine antiques, M–E, CP.

DINING **Eldorado Grill,** 219 North Main Street, 777-1224, contemporary decor, gourmet fare, M–E • **Kingston Inn,** 300 North Main Street, 777-0451, homelike atmosphere, Continental specialties, M • **Cafe Italia,** 301 North Main Street, 777-0033, Italian favorite, I–M • **Silver Annie's,** 124 North Commerce Street, 777-3131, longtime local favorite, M • **The General's Restaurant,** DeSoto House Hotel (see above), varied menu, M • **The Log Cabin,** 201 North Main Street, 777-0393, I–M • **Grant's Place,** 515 South Main Street, 777-3331, informal dining, Grant memorabilia, I–M.

SIGHTSEEING **Ulysses S. Grant Home State Historic Site,** 500 Bouthillier Street, 777-0248. Hours: Daily 9 A.M. to 5 P.M.; may have shorter hours in winter. Donation, $ • **Galena/Jo Davies County History Museum,** 211 South Bench Street, 777-9129. Hours: Daily 9 A.M. to 4:30 P.M. $$; under age 10, free • **Old Market House State Historic Site,** 123 North Commerce Street, 777-2570. Hours: Thursday to Monday 9 A.M. to noon, and 1 P.M. to 5 P.M.; to 4 P.M. in winter. Donation, $ • **Dowling House,** 220 Diagonal Street, 777-1250. Hours: Memorial Day through October, Sunday to Friday 10 A.M. to 4 P.M.; Saturday

10 A.M. to 5 P.M.; April, November, December, open Friday to Sunday; January to March, open Saturday and Sunday. $$ • **Grant Hills Antique Auto Museum,** U.S. 20 East, 777-2115. Hours: Mid-May to October 31, daily except Thursday, 10 A.M. to 5 P.M.; January 1 to mid-May, open Tuesday, Wednesday, Saturday, Sunday. $ • **Dubuque Diamond Jo Casino,** Third Street Ice Harbor, Dubuque, IA, (800) 582-5956, cruises in warm weather, dockside gambling in winter, open daily, 24 hours on Friday and Saturday • ***Winter sports:*** **Eagle Ridge Nordic Ski Center,** 777-2444 or (800) 892-2269, November to March, weather permitting. Rentals available • **Chestnut Mountain Resort Downhill Skiing,** 8700 West Chestnut Road, (800) 397-1320, Thanksgiving to St. Patrick's Day, weather permitting, 9 A.M. to 10 P.M., midnight on Friday • ***Sleighrides:*** **Shenandoah Riding Center,** 200 North Brodrecht Road, 777-2373. Phone for current offerings and rates • ***Christmas-tree farms:*** **Ochs' Christmas Tree Farms,** Blackjack Road, Galena, 588-0897 • **Pine Hollow Christmas Tree Farm,** 4700 North Council Hill Road, Galena, 777-2975 • ***Warm-weather attractions:*** **Belvedere Mansion,** 1008 Park Avenue, 777-0747. Hours: Memorial Day to October 31, daily 11 A.M. to 5 P.M. $$; money-saving combination ticket available with Dowling House • **Vinegar Hill Historic Lead Mine and Museum,** 8885 North Three Pines Road (off State Highway 84), 777-0855. Hours: June to August, daily 9 A.M. to 5 P.M.; May, September, and October, Saturday and Sunday 9 A.M. to 5 P.M. $$ • ***Spirit of Dubuque*** **Sightseeing Cruises,** Third Street, Ice Harbor, Dubuque, IA (800) 747-8093. Various cruises May through October; check for current offerings.

INFORMATION **Galena/Jo Davies County Convention and Visitors Bureau,** 720 Park Avenue, Galena IL 61036, 777-3557 or (800) 777-4099; **Visitors Information Center,** 101 Bouthillier Street, Galena IL 61036, 777-4390; www.galena.org

Celebrating the Season at Pokagon

"EEEEeeeeeeeeee-Yi." The shrieks are loud and long from the toboggan slide at Indiana's Pokagon State Park—but then everyone seems to get back in line as soon as they get to the bottom. You move fast on this quarter-mile, double-lane refrigerated run—as fast as 40 miles per hour—which accounts for the screaming. But the speed is exactly why everybody loves it so much and wants to swoop down again and again.

There are few more exciting ways to make the most of winter—and few nicer places for a cold-weather getaway than this excellent 1,203-acre state park. It was named for a chief of the Potawatomi Indians, the first people to inhabit this delightful spot. The land was part of a million-acre tract, including the present site of Chicago, that Simon Pokagon was persuaded to transfer to the government for three cents an acre.

If you make the trip in early December, you can also enjoy a warm, small-town Christmas celebration in the pretty nearby town of Angola, and stock up on gifts at a major outlet center.

Whenever you come, you'll find that Pokagon's Potawatomi Inn is as comfortable as a resort hotel, at a fraction of the price. The attractive rustic look has been maintained along with the three beautiful stone fireplaces. Rooms are complete with phones, remote-control cable TV, clock radios, and coffeemakers.

In winter there's plenty to keep you busy, indoors and out, with or without snow on the ground. First of all, there's that slide. Because the raised platform is refrigerated, it remains ready for action day and night every weekend and school holidays from Thanksgiving through February. Toboggans, which can be rented by the hour, hold up to four people. The cost is moderate, and since the speedy descent takes only 35 seconds, it's easy to get in a lot of runs. In between you can enjoy coffee, soup, and sandwiches and a warm fire at the warming center near the top of the run.

The lake that is favored by swimmers and boaters in summer turns into an ice-skating rink when the temperature drops, providing another way to enjoy the great outdoors.

When Mother Nature obliges with snow, the park offers cross-country trails, with color-coded routes for every ability. Trail A, a one-mile track for beginners, is scattered with gentle slopes and curves on a wooded course that is easy-to-moderate in difficulty. Trail B stretches for four miles and challenges with steep and rugged areas and uneven terrain. A third trail, which serves as a bridle path in summer, is moderate, about three miles in length and without hills. Novices can take a few practice loops around the parking lot before setting out on the one-way trails.

You say you don't care to brave the cold? Then head for the indoor pool at the inn . . . or the whirlpool and sauna . . . or the fitness center. Check out the exhibits and programs at the Nature Center or have a seat in front of the Woodland Window to observe the winter birds. Find out what's going on at the inn activity room. Or go to the library or bring a book to a lounge at the inn, where you can curl up in front of a cozy fireplace. You won't lack for options.

If shopping is your favorite winter sport, you've also come to the right area. It is a short drive from the park to Prime Outlets at Fremont, at the intersection of State Highways 120 and 127, just off I-80/90.

Jones New York, Levi's, Florsheim, Carters, and Bass are among the familiar labels to be found among over 50 stores beckoning with bargains.

Antiquers should make haste five miles south to Angola, a handsome small town with a classic square (in this case actually a circle) rimmed with fine old red-brick structures and centered with an ornate 85-foot monument to the town's Civil War veterans. The memorable monument is topped with a statue of Columbia, a female figure holding a flag.

Angola was settled in the mid-1800s by pioneers from the Northeast, and named after a city in New York State. The 1868 brick Steuben County Courthouse on one side of the square is said to be a replica of Boston's Faneuil Hall. With a dusting of snow it becomes a picture-postcard setting.

A block to the south of the monument is the Steuben County Tourism Bureau, located in the Old County Jail, a brick-and-concrete structure completed in 1877 and now on the National Register of Historic Places. At one time, General Lewis B. Hershey lived in the old jail with his father, the sheriff. Hershey headed the U.S. Selective Service from 1941 to 1960; World War II veterans may remember seeing his signature on their draft cards.

If you follow Maumee Street (U.S. Highway 20) west, you'll arrive at the campus of Tri-State University, Hershey's alma mater, an attractive campus founded in 1884 and known for its engineering programs.

Angola's square was once a trading center for farmers and Indians. Now antiquers come in search of places like the Olde Towne Mall, 101 West Maumee, packed with every kind of collectible from china plates to Hoosier cabinets. Two other places to explore are the Then and Now Mini Mall at 200 West Maumee and the Angola Mini-Mall, off the square one block at 109 Gale Street.

Angola has a few pleasant bed-and-breakfast accommodations as well as a notable restaurant, the Hatchery, in a restored building that once actually served as a chicken hatchery. If you are tempted to stay in town, you can easily do so and still take advantage of the outdoor fun at Pokagon State Park.

There's Christmas activity to lure you to Angola on the first weekend of December, when the Sycamore Hill Bed and Breakfast holds a high-quality Christmas bazaar that has been a local tradition for more than 20 years. Jewelry, decorations, baskets, ornaments, and toys are among the items on sale. Many local crafters contribute handmade items and come in holiday garb to act as hostesses, even sharing their recipes for the homemade cookies offered. The two-story pillared home on 25 rolling acres is beautifully decorated for the holidays.

That same weekend, the Fairview Missionary Church sets up its Bethlehem Marketplace, an impressive and lively depiction of a scene as it might have been at Christ's birth, complete with costumed inhabitants and live animals. More than 250 parishioners work to set up and take part in the display, which varies slightly from year to year. Roman soldiers patrol and vendors hawk their wares to make things realistic. At the end, a crèche scene awaits.

When you've seen the sights and the shops, you can head back to Pokagon for a last go on the toboggan or a last lingering in front of the fireplace at the Potawatomi Inn.

Area Code: 219

DRIVING DIRECTIONS Pokagon State Park is five miles north of Angola on State Highway 127, off I-69 exit 154. It is two miles south of the Indiana Toll Road (I-80). Angola is at I-69 exit 148. From Chicago, take I-80/90 east to I-69 south, about 150 miles. The park is also approximately 150 miles from Indianapolis or Detroit.

ACCOMMODATIONS **Potawatomi Inn,** Pokagon State Park, 6 Lane 100A, Lake James, Angola 46703, 833-1077 or (877) 768-2928, inn rooms, I–M; suites, M, cabin units, I • **The Chef's Nest Bed-and-Breakfast,** 417 East Maumee Street, Angola 46703, 665-9080 or (800) 909-9080, caterer-owner will also prepare dinner for guests on request, I, CP • **Hartman House Bed-and-Breakfast,** 901 West Maumee Street, Angola 46703, same owner and phone as above, I–E, CP • **Sycamore Hill Bed-and-Breakfast,** 1245 South Golden Lake Road (just south of I-69 and U.S. 20 interchange), Angola 46703, 665-2690, I, CP • **Tulip Tree Bed-and-Breakfast,** 411 North Wayne Street, Angola, 46703, 668-7000 or (888) 401-0002, 1890s Queen Anne home, I, CP • **Holiday Inn of Angola,** 3855 North State Highway 127, Angola 46703, 655-9471, indoor pool, M.

DINING **Potawatomi Inn** (see above), I–M • **The Hatchery,** 118 South Elizabeth Street, Angola, 665-9957, highly rated, seafood, wild game among the specialties, M–E • **Hartman House** (see above), Cordon Bleu–trained chef, I–M • **Captain's Cabin,** 3070 West Shadyside Road, Angola, 665-5663, steaks and prime rib overlooking Crooked Lake, M • **Santa Fe Grill,** 1202 North Wayne Street, Angola, 650-5747, Southwestern specialties, I–M • **The Herb Garden,** 215 East State Highway 120 (½ mile east of Prime Outlets at Fremont), Fremont, 495-1658, log-cabin setting, lush garden atmosphere, I–M.

ACTIVITIES **Pokagon State Park,** 450 Lane 100, Lake James, off Highway 127, Angola, 833-2012. Hours: Daily 8 A.M. to 11 P.M. Admission per car, $$; Indiana cars, $. Activities include: **Toboggan Slide:** Hours: Thanksgiving through February, Friday 5 P.M. to 10 P.M., Saturday 10 A.M. to 10 P.M., Sunday and holidays 10 A.M. to 5 P.M.

Sleds hold up to four people, $$ per hour. **Cross-Country Skiing:** Daily, weather permitting, until 30 minutes before sunset. Skis may be borrowed free on Saturday and Sunday at the hut by North Beach parking lot • ***Christmas events:*** **Bethlehem Marketplace,** Fairview Missionary Church, Angola, 665-8402. Hours: Usually first weekend in December, 1 P.M. to 5 P.M. Donation • **Christmas Bazaar,** Sycamore Hill Bed-and-Breakfast (see accommodations, above), usually first weekend in December, 9 A.M. to 5 P.M. Free.

INFORMATION **Steuben County Tourism Bureau,** 207 South Wayne Street, Angola, IN 46703, 665-5386 or (800) LAKE 101; www.lakes101.org

Eagle Watching in the Quad Cities

One of the rewards of winter along the Mississippi River is the chance to spot the swoops and glides of the great American bald eagles, majestic visitors who like to spend the season nesting in the bluffs above the water. Once considered an endangered species, the eagle is again rising in population thanks to federal protection and conservation education. Some 2,500 of these magnificent birds now winter along the upper Mississippi. Eagle watching attracts tens of thousands of outdoor and birding enthusiasts each year, especially during Quad Cities Bald Eagle Days in late January or early February.

This quartet of towns spanning the Mississippi—Davenport and Bettendorf in Iowa, and Rock Island and Moline in Illinois—is a favorite territory for the birds because Lock and Dam No. 14 and No. 15, located along the river here, make fine fishing grounds and the bluffs provide old-growth forests for perching and roosting.

When many rivers are frozen solid, the flow of water between the dams and locks along the Mississippi prevents a complete freeze. This provides a haven for the eagles, who need open water in order to feed. To make things even better, fish are often momentarily stunned as they pass through the dams and come closer to the surface, where they make easy marks for sharp-eyed eagles, whose eyesight is seven times stronger than humans'. With an eagle's eyes, we would be able to read a newspaper a football field's length away.

Once it has spotted its catch from a perch on high, a wingspan of six to eight feet allows the eagle to dive quickly for its dinner and then soar upward again to the wooded bluffs. Clear, crisp mornings from mid-

December through February are prime times for viewing. Binoculars are recommended for close-ups, along with good winter clothing to protect from the cold.

The Quad Cities communities combine to provide a host of organized opportunities for eagle-minded visitors. While these are working towns rather than quaint tourist spots, they do also offer plenty of indoor attractions for winter visitors, from museums to antiquing to year-round riverboat gambling. The Quad City Botanical Center offers an indoor touch of green year-round, and for those who want to add skiing to the weekend agenda, the Snowstar Ski area east of Rock Island isn't far away.

The first organized eagle watch was sponsored by the Quad Cities Audubon Society in 1967. Now many organizations join in the Bald Eagle Days events, which feature indoor activities as well as outdoor eagle spotting. The Quad Cities Conservation Alliance (QCCA) Expo Center is the setting for the annual environmental fair featuring live demonstrations of birds of prey, wildlife art, and environmental exhibits as well as outdoor tours. More than 50 local conservation groups and companies take part.

Even if you can't make the special weekends, you'll still find ample opportunity for eagle watching. The Audubon Society continues to host field trips to view eagles, gulls, and wintering waterfowl. Bob Motz, a Quad Cities naturalist, offers private tours, two- to three-hour guided sessions ideal for families and small groups. Motz provides window-mounted spotting scopes and binoculars. If you prefer armchair viewing, try the riverfront Dock restaurant in Davenport, where binoculars are provided to entertain guests while they dine.

The Mississippi River Visitors Center on Arsenal Island, in the river between Rock Island and Davenport, is another great place for viewing—and for warming up when the winter weather begins to chill. The center is staffed by Army Corps of Engineers rangers who lead special weekends throughout January and February.

The Rock Island Arsenal is one of the chief historic attractions in the area. Rock Island was included in lands ceded by Sauk and Fox Indians to the federal government in a treaty signed in 1804. The army built Fort Armstrong here to keep peace in the region and keep the Mississippi open to traffic. It was abandoned in 1836, following the Black Hawk War, the last Indian uprising.

But with the outbreak of the Civil War, Congress needed a replacement for the Harper's Ferry Armory, which had fallen to Confederate forces. Rock Island was ideally situated to provide military supplies to troops stationed in the Mississippi River Valley and to soldiers guarding the frontier farther west.

A prisoner-of-war camp also went up near the north central shore of the island, 84 barracks designed to hold about 10,000 prisoners. The barracks are gone, but cemeteries on the island are the final resting place of nearly 2,000 Confederate soldiers and 125 Union guards.

In 1865 the arsenal was expanded in a master plan to create the "Grand Arsenal of the West." Brigadier General Thomas J. Rodman, the commander, is credited with the design of the handsome stone buildings that survive almost intact, forming one of the largest military projects of the late 19th century. The first storehouse, built in 1862, known as the Clock Tower Building, is the present home of the Army Corps of Engineers. The arsenal is still active manufacturing equipment for the armed forces.

At the Arsenal Island visitors center, you can pick up a map to guide you through the historic complex. Sights include the Confederate cemetery, the original 19th-century stone workshops, the officers' quarters along the river, and the site of the first bridge built across the Mississippi. In summer, the Colonel Davenport House, built in 1834, is also open for tours.

Year-round, visitors can stop into the Rock Island Arsenal Museum, established in 1905. The army's oldest museum after West Point, it depicts the history of the island and includes a collection of over 1,100 military firearms.

For a change of scenery (and season), visit the striking Quad City Botanical Center in Rock Island, where a 6,444-square-foot Sun Garden features over 100 tropical trees and plants, not to mention a 14-foot waterfall and bridge over reflecting ponds. The center holds quarterly flower shows, and the Window Box shop has many unique garden-related items and gifts to start you thinking spring.

Rock Island is the home of another major sightseeing stop, the Black Hawk State Historic Site. The stone lodge housing the Hauberg Indian Museum was built by the Civilian Conservation Corps in the 1930s on a steep, wooded tract bordering the Rock River. The museum interprets the culture of the Sauk and Mesquaki Indians who once lived on this land. The collection of Dr. John Hauberg, a Rock Island philanthropist, formed the core of the exhibits, which include full-size replicas of Sauk winter and summer houses and dioramas with life-size figures showing such activities as tilling cornfields, making maple syrup, and hunting buffalo.

One of the most visited sites on the Illinois side of the river is the administrative center of John Deere and Company in Moline, headquarters of the world's largest manufacturer of farm equipment. The award-winning modern complex designed by the late Eero Saarinen is magnificently landscaped with lakes, a Japanese garden, and sculptures, including a bronze by Henry Moore. The west office building offers a large, skylit indoor garden. Tours of the entire complex are offered on weekdays, and visitors are welcome every day to the showroom displaying Deere products, where you can find out how it feels to sit atop a giant tractor. The showroom features displays showing the changes in farm equipment over the years, and a unique three-dimensional mural by Alexander Girard, made up of more than 2,000 historical items tracing the development of American agriculture from 1837 to 1918.

The home and workshop where John Deere developed the first self-scouring steel plow in 1837 is in Grand Detour, about 70 miles away (see page 157). He moved his company to Moline in 1847 to take advantage of the waterpower and transportation provided by the Mississippi River.

The company has also helped to develop John Deere Commons, a $43-million project overlooking the river in Moline. It includes the John Deere Pavilion, an exhibition hall celebrating the story of John Deere, and serves as a welcome center for those touring other Deere facilities. The commons also includes the Radisson Hotel, restaurants, and a ground transportation center.

Across the river in Iowa, Davenport has the best of the sightseeing. The Putnam Museum of History and Natural Science features the heritage of the region and also has a wing devoted to the archaeology of the Far East and Egypt. Children enjoy the hands-on Discovery Room, and everyone will admire the mounted exhibits in the newest addition to the museum, the Hall of Mammals.

The Davenport Museum of Art, right next door, has some fine pieces for a small museum, including Mexican, Haitian, and Asian collections, a wide range of American paintings, and a regional collection featuring Grant Wood, Thomas Hart Benton, and other Midwestern artists.

Families can visit the Family Museum of Arts and Science in Bettendorf, offering hands-on science fun, the chance to hop down a rabbit hole or explore the marvels of the human heart, as well as a specially designed TotSpot for youngest visitors.

Antiquers will find plenty of opportunity to hunt for treasure in all of the towns. Davenport has two of the biggest shops, Riverbend Antiques, 425 Brady in "Old Town," covering a full half block, and the Antique America Mall, 702 West 76th Street, with over 150 dealers.

In Rock Island, the lively area near the river, known as the District, has antiques and other shops as well as restaurants, nighttime entertainment, and Jumer's Rock Island Casino. If you need to change your luck, cross the river for two more riverboat casinos, in Davenport and Bettendorf.

Area Codes: Illinois, 309; Iowa, 319

DRIVING DIRECTIONS The Quad Cities are rimmed by a circle made by I-80 and I-280 and connected also by I-74 running across the Mississippi. From Chicago, take I-55 west to I-80 west, about 165 miles.

ACCOMMODATIONS **The Abbey Hotel,** 1401 Central Avenue, Bettendorf, IA 52722, 355-0921 or (800) 438-7535, former abbey, best in the area, M–E, CP • **Plaza One Hotel,** Third Avenue and 17th Street, Rock Island, IL 61201, 794-1212 or (800) 447-1297, walking distance to the District entertainment, M • **Radisson on John Deere Commons,** 1415 River Drive, Moline, IL 61265, 764-1000, I–M, CP • **President's Casino Blackhawk Hotel,** 200 East Third Street, Davenport, IA 52801, 328-6000 or (800) 553-1173, restored vintage hotel, indoor pool, I–M; suites, M–E • **Jumer's Castle Lodge,** 900 Spruce Hills Drive, Bettendorf, IA 52722, 359-7141 or (800) 285-863, elaborate German Old World decor, M • ***Bed-and-breakfast homes:*** **The Potter House,** 1906 Seventh Avenue, Rock Island, IL 61201, 788-1906 or (800) 747-0339, elegantly restored Colonial, I–M, CP • **Victorian Inn,** 702 20th Street, Rock Island, IL 61201, 788-7068 or (800) 788-7068, antique furnishings, M, CP • **Top o' the Morning,** 1505 19th Avenue, Rock Island, IL 61201, 786-3513, river views, I–M, CP • **Fulton's Landing,** 1206 East River Drive, Davenport, IA 52803, 322-4069, 1871 stone mansion, river views, I–M, CP.

DINING **Captain's Table,** 4801 River Drive, Moline, IL, 797-9222, on the Mississippi, M–E • **Bender's Restaurant,** 5400 27th Street, Moline, IL, 797-5375, all-you-can-eat prime rib Friday and Saturday, ribs Sunday–Thursday, I–M • **Spaghetti's,** 703 15th Avenue, East Moline, IL, 755-5025, old-fashioned Italian, I–M • **Rexie's Gourmet House,** 430 14th Street, Rock Island, IL, 794-0244, steaks and basics, I–M • **Blue Cat Brew Pub,** 113 18th Street, Rock Island, IL, 788-8247, fresh-brewed beer and light fare, I • **The Dock,** 125 South Perry Street, Davenport IA, 322-5331, river views, M • **Christie's,** 2207 East 12th Street, East Davenport, IA, 323-2822, restored early 1900s home, fine dining, E • **Iowa Machine Shed Restaurant,** 7250 Northwest Boulevard, Davenport, IA, 391-2427, farm decor, family-style meals, I–M • **Jumer's Restaurant,** Jumer's Castle Lodge (see above), Bettendorf, IA, Old World decor, German cuisine, I–M.

SIGHTSEEING **Quad Cities Bald Eagle Days,** QCCA Expo Center, 2621 Fourth Avenue, Rock Island, 788-5912. Annual weekend event in late January; contact the center for this year's plans. For additional eagle-watching opportunities, contact the visitors bureau • **John Deere & Company Administrative Center,** John Deere Road, Moline, IL, 765-4847. Hours: Showroom, daily 9 A.M. to 5:30 P.M. Free • **Mississippi River Visitors Center,** U.S. Army Corps of Engineers, Clock Tower Building, Rock Island, IL, 794-5338. Hours: Daily 9 A.M. to 5 P.M., to 9 P.M. mid-May to mid-September • **Quad City Botanical Center,** 2525 Fourth Avenue, Rock Island, IL, 794-0991. Hours: Monday to Saturday 10 A.M. to 5 P.M., Sunday 1 P.M. to 5 P.M. $$ • **Black Hawk State Historic Site,** 1510 46th Avenue (State Highway 5), Rock

Island, IL, 788-0177. Hours: Daily sunrise to 10 P.M. Free; includes **Hauberg Indian Museum,** 788-9536. Hours: Daily 9 A.M. to noon, 1 P.M. to 4 P.M. $ • **Rock Island Arsenal Museum,** Rock Island Arsenal, Rock Island, IL, 782-5021. Hours: Daily 10 A.M. to 4 P.M. Free • **Davenport Museum of Art,** 1737 West 12th Street, Davenport, IA, 326-7804. Hours: Tuesday to Saturday 10 A.M. to 4:30 P.M., to 8 P.M. on Thursday, Sunday 1 P.M. to 4:30 P.M. Donation • **Putnam Museum of History and Natural Science,** 1717 West 12th Street, Davenport, IA, 324-1933. Hours: Tuesday to Friday 9 A.M. to 5 P.M., Saturday 10 A.M. to 5 P.M., Sunday noon to 5 P.M. $$ • **Family Museum of Arts and Science,** 2900 Learning Campus Drive, Bettendorf, IA, 344-4106. Hours: Monday noon to 8 P.M., Tuesday to Thursday 9 A.M. to 8 P.M., Friday, Saturday 9 A.M. to 5 P.M., Sunday noon to 5 P.M. $$ • ***Riverboat casinos:*** **Jumer's Rock Island Casino,** 18th Street at Riverfront, Rock Island, IL, (800) 793-4200 or (800) 477-UWIN • **Lady Luck Casino,** Bettendorf Riverfront, east of I-74, Bettendorf, IA, 759-7280 or (800) 724-5825 • **President Riverboat Casino,** 130 West River Drive, Davenport, IA, 322-8000 or (800) BOAT-711 • ***Skiing:*** **Snowstar Ski area,** 9500 126th Street West, Taylor Ridge, IL (via State Highway 92 from Rock Island), 798-2666 or (800) 383-4002. Thirteen trails, two quad chairlifts, night skiing, snowtubing.

INFORMATION **Quad Cities Convention and Visitors Bureau,** 2021 River Drive, Moline, IL 61265 (309) 788-7800 or (800) 747-7800; http://quadcities.com/cvb

Getting a Lift at Boyne

Where can you find big-time skiing in the Midwest? There's an easy one-word answer: Boyne. Whether you're talking about Boyne Mountain or Boyne Highlands, these two northern Michigan resorts are as good as it gets in this region, rating tops in almost every ski magazine poll and drawing half a million skiers each year.

Vertical drops over 500 feet and an annual snowfall over 120 inches are part of the reason. Equally important, skiers find state-of-the-art high-speed chairlifts, and, in seasons when Mother Nature is stingy with snow, some of the best snowmaking in the business. A smaller neighbor, Nub's Nob, also offers skiing challenges, and there's plenty of terrain for cross-country ski enthusiasts, as well.

In summer, the Boyne region around Little Traverse Bay is known as Michigan's Riviera. Towns like Harbor Springs and Petoskey have been drawing well-heeled visitors for more than a century. Many of the lodgings, shops, and fine dining establishments now remain open in winter. They are part of the area's appeal for skiers, compensation for the lengthy drive to get here.

The area began to change into a year-round destination in 1947 with the development of Boyne Mountain, outside the town of Boyne Falls. The guiding spirit was avid skier Everett Kircher, a University of Michigan graduate and Detroit businessman. Boyne Highlands followed in the 1960s, located in the steep hills outside Harbor Springs. Kircher is now head of one of the largest individually owned ski empires in the country, including the two Boynes, Big Sky in Montana, and Brighton Ski Bowl near Salt Lake City. He is also the co-inventor of the Boyne Snowmaker, which set the industry standard, and he pioneered the design of much of the snow-grooming equipment in use today.

To attract skiers to Boyne Mountain in its early years, former Olympian Stein Ericksen was hired to teach Austrian skiing techniques. Ericksen moved west, but an Austrian-American ski school is still a mainstay at both Boyne resorts.

Kircher kept his resorts in the news with the world's first triple chair at Boyne Highlands in 1964, the first four-person chair at Boyne Mountain in 1969, and more recently, the first six-seat high-speed chairlift in America, also at Boyne Mountain.

In order to keep his employees occupied year-round, Kircher began developing golf courses at each resort; these have become one of the area's biggest summer draws.

Accommodations at Boyne Highlands are comfortable and attractive, ranked by *Ski* magazine among the nation's top 40 ski resorts. Among its 44 runs are cruising trails up to a mile in length. The Zoo Bar is tops for après-ski conviviality.

But while the amenities are less polished, accomplished skiers will definitely appreciate the challenge of Boyne Mountain with its many black-diamond trails, including the legendary "Hemlock." Boyne's Nordican cross-country center is also highly rated.

Nub's Nob, while smaller in size, also has its share of challenges, with runs like the steep "Chute."

Both Boyne mountains attract top competitions that draw many spectators. In recent years the U.S. Men's Pro Tour has brought the fastest male skiers from around the world to the Highlands' South Challenger slope, and the American Pro Snowboard series attracted the best in the sport for a thrilling half-pipe competition at Boyne Mountain.

For fun off the slopes, both mountains have ice-skating rinks, heated outdoor pools, and giant hot tubs. Many other facilities for sledding, skating, and ski touring are found around the area.

If you don't choose to stay at one of the Boyne slopes, there are many options. The tasteful and elegant Kimberly Country Estate is one of the loveliest inns in the Midwest, and several hotels offer Victorian ambience. Budget watchers will find many motels with indoor pools, and the region has a number of small, welcoming bed-and-breakfast inns.

The towns in this region make for interesting exploring. The first development was the Bay View Association, founded in 1875 just outside Petoskey as a Methodist religious retreat. Bay View was patterned after the chautauquas popular in the East, with camp meetings, music, and educational programs featuring well-known speakers. The first attendees lived in tents, but Bay View quickly grew into a colony of gingerbread Victorian cottages and more elaborate public buildings, attracting speakers like William Jennings Bryan, Helen Keller, and Booker T. Washington.

More than 400 of the charming original dwellings remain. They are part of a National Historic District that is one of the largest single collections of historic homes in the country. An active summer program of lectures, concerts, and Sunday-evening vespers still goes on, and some of the residences are occupied by new generations of the original founding families.

Two of the classic old hotels also remain, the 1911 Terrace Inn and a landmark, Stafford's Bay View Inn, built in 1886. The Bay View has been nicely restored by Stafford Smith, who also owns the more recently renovated Perry Hotel in neighboring Petoskey and a number of the area's most popular restaurants. Stafford's Perry Hotel, a historic landmark, is the only turn-of-the-century hotel surviving in Petoskey. One of its most famous guests was a young Ernest Hemingway, who lived and wrote at nearby Walloon Lake, and stayed here in 1916.

The success of Bay View led to the development of two resort associations in Harbor Springs, across the water on the north side of Little Traverse Bay. Harbor Point and Wequetonsing lacked the religious affiliation of Bay View but had the same idea; the association owns the land and must approve the cottage owners.

Harbor Springs grew into one of the most exclusive resort towns in America, the choice of families like the Fords, Upjohns, Wrigleys, and Gambles (of Procter and Gamble). Take a drive past the stately homes of Wequetonsing to see how carefully the lovely, sedate residences have been maintained. As in Bay View, many of these homes have been in the same family for generations.

A drive along East Bluff Drive leads past another parade of Victorian showcase homes and yields fine views of the town and the bay. In summer the harbor is filled with luxurious sailboats and yachts.

The quaint downtown of Harbor Springs has several upscale galleries and shops, many of which stay open for ski season. One special stop on North State Street is Pooter Olooms, offering charming antiques and folk art from Scandinavia, Austria, and France. Adjacent is Primitive Images, with lots of log, birch-bark, and twig furniture. You can often see demonstrations of glassblowing at Boyer Glassworks across from the post office on State Street, just off Main. L'Esprit Antiques on Main Street has many armoires and Art Deco pieces from France and the United States.

In the old days, vacationers from Harbor Springs used to come across Little Traverse Bay by steamer to shop in the exclusive stores in Petoskey's "Gaslight District." The shops aren't as posh as they used to be, but there's still plenty of browsing to be done here, among some 80 stores on and around Lake Street.

One of the best-known shops is American Spoon Foods, started by Detroit native Justin Rashid as a one-man shop specializing in local Michigan fruits, vegetables, and wild morel mushrooms, which are particularly plentiful in this area. Now a partnership between Rashid and noted chef Larry Forgione, American Spoon products are sold in over 400 stores and served in some of America's best restaurants.

Two galleries to watch for on Lake Street are Arktos, with art featuring animals, and the Ward & Eis Gallery, with Southwestern art and crafts.

Several shops specialize in jewelry made with "Petoskey stones," fossilized coral that can be found along the shores of Little Traverse Bay. The coral has been designated as the official state stone of Michigan.

Andante in Petoskey is the area choice for gourmet dining, but you may well want to take a drive south to tiny Ellsworth and two of Michigan's most notable restaurants, the Rowe Inn and Tapawingo.

Area Code: 616

DRIVING DIRECTIONS Harbor Springs is on State Highway 119, accessible from I-75 and U.S. 131. From Chicago, take I-94 east to I-196 north to U.S. 131, about 360 miles. It is 260 miles from Detroit via I-75 north to State Highway 32 to U.S. 131. Commercial air service is available from Detroit and Chicago to Pellston Regional Airport, 10 miles north of Harbor Springs.

ACCOMMODATIONS Ask at all lodgings about money-saving weekend and midweek ski packages that include lift tickets and some meals. **Boyne Highlands Resort,** 600 Highlands Drive, Harbor Springs 49740, 526-3000 or (800) GO BOYNE, includes Boyne Highlands Lodge, M–E, and Heather Highlands Inn, with condo hotel, suites, and apartments, fireplaces, E–EE • **Boyne Mountain Lodge,** Boyne Falls, 49713, 549-6000 or (800) GO BOYNE, M • **Stafford's Bay View Inn,** 2011 Woodland Avenue, Petoskey 49770, 347-2771 or (800)258-1886, old-fashioned century-old charmer, nicely updated facilities, M–E, CP; fireplace and whirlpool rooms, E–EE, CP • **Terrace Inn,** P.O. Box 266, Bay View, Petoskey, 49770, 347-2410 or (800) 530-9898, Victorian-era hotel, I–M • **Stafford's Perry Hotel,** Bay and Lewis Streets, Petoskey 49770, 347-4000 or (800) 456-1917, renovated 1899 hotel, hot tub, M–E • **Water Street Inn,** 200 Front Street, Boyne City 49712, 582-3000 or (800) 456-4313, all-suite motel, E • ***Motels with indoor pools:*** **Best Western of Harbor Springs,** 8514 State Highway 119, Harbor Springs 49740, 347-9050, M • **Birchwood Inn,** 7077 Lakeshore Drive, Harbor Springs 49740, 526-2151 or (800) 530-9955, M • **Apple Tree Inn,** 915 Spring Street (U.S. 131), Petoskey 49770, 348-2900 or (800) 348-2901, M • **Bay Winds Inn,** 909 Spring Street (U.S. 131), Petoskey 49770, 347-4193 or (800) 204-1748, M • ***Bed-and-breakfast homes:*** **Kimberly Country Estate,** 2287 Bester Road, Harbor Springs 49740, 526-7646, very special, tasteful and elegant, E–EE, CP • **Highland Hideaway,** 6767 Pleasantview Road, Harbor Springs 49740, 526-8100, I–M, CP • **Deer Lake Bed-and-Breakfast,** 00631, East Deer Lake Road, Boyne City 49712, 582-9039, M, CP.

DINING **Stafford's Pier,** 102 Bay Street, Harbor Springs, 526-6201, on the waterfront, varied menu, M–E • **Andante,** 321 Bay Street, Petoskey, 348-3321, charming intimate cafe, gourmet food, E–EE • **H.O. Rose Room,** Stafford's Perry Hotel, Petoskey (see above), Continental menu, M–EE • **Stafford's One Water Street,** at that address, Boyne City, 582-3434, varied menu, M–EE • ***Worth a drive for gourmet fare:*** **Tapawingo,** 9502 Lake Street, Ellsworth, 588-7071, EE • **Rowe Inn,** County Road 48, Ellsworth, 588-7351, EE • ***Summer addition:*** **Legs Inn,** end of State Highway 119, Cross Village, 526-2281, authentic Polish and American cuisine, lake views, a local favorite, I–M.

SIGHTSEEING **McCune Arts Center,** 461 East Mitchell, Petoskey, 347-4337, art gallery, theater, films; check current schedules.

ACTIVITIES ***Downhill skiing:*** **Boyne Highlands,** Highlands Drive, Harbor Springs, (800) GO BOYNE, vertical drop 541 feet, 44 runs, 8 chairlifts, 360 acres of skiable terrain • **Boyne Mountain,** U.S. 131, Boyne Falls, (800) GO BOYNE, vertical drop 500 feet, 41 runs, 9 chairlifts, 260 acres of skiable terrain • **Nub's Nob,** Nubs Nob Road, Harbor Springs, 526-2131 or (800) SKI-NUBS, vertical drop 427 feet, 40 runs, 8 chairlifts, 300 acres of skiable terrain • ***Cross-country skiing:*** **Boyne Nordican Center,** Boyne Mountain (see above), 50 kilometers of trails (half are groomed), five kilometers lighted for night skiing. Fee • **Boyne Highlands,** 28 kilometers of groomed trails, loops for all abilities. Fee • **Nub's Nob,** 20 kilometers of groomed, tracked trails, including one very challenging six-kilometer loop. Fee • **Petoskey State Park,** Highway 119, Petoskey, 4.4-kilometer groomed course, hilly. Parking fee • **Avalanche Trail,** Ann and Lake Streets,

Boyne City, 582-3641, nine kilometers of ungroomed trails. Free • **Birchwood Country Club,** Middle Road, north of Harbor Springs, three groomed loops from 3.2 to 4.8 kilometers. Free • ***Ice skating:*** **Avalanche Preserve,** 1129 Wilson Street, Boyne City, 582-3641, outdoor ice rink, sledding hill, open days and evenings. Free • **Harbor Springs Skating Rink,** 740 East Main Street, Harbor Springs, 526-5810. Hours: Outdoor arena open Tuesday to Friday 3 P.M. to 9 P.M., Saturday and Sunday 1 P.M. to 7 P.M. Limited rentals • **Petoskey Winter Sports Park,** Winter Park Lane, Petoskey, 347-1252, ice skating, hockey rink, sledding, ski hill with rope tow. Hours: Weekdays 4 P.M. to 9 P.M., weekends noon to 9 P.M. • ***Snowmobile rentals:*** **County Wide Services,** 853, State Highway 119, Harbor Springs, 347-8822 • ***Roller skating:*** **The Sports Center,** 1588 River Road, Petoskey, 347-1032. Indoor arena open Thursday to Sunday year-round.

INFORMATION Boyne Country Convention and Visitors Bureau, P.O. Box 401, East Mitchell Street, Petoskey, MI 49770, 348-2755 or (800) 845-2828; www.boynecountry.com

Happy Landings in Wisconsin

They fly through the air with the greatest of ease, those graceful ski jumpers in Westby, Wisconsin. For more than 30 years, the best of these amazing athletes have shown off their style during the annual Ski Jump Competition, held the second weekend in February in the scenic Timber Coulee outside Westby. (*Coulee* is the French word for a "valley tucked between high bluffs.")

Members of the U.S. and Canadian Olympic teams and Olympic-caliber athletes from Canada and as far away as Finland and Norway gather in this small western Wisconsin town to compete in one of America's top ski-jumping events. Some 11 countries have been represented in recent years. Even the most sedentary spectators will appreciate the extraordinary coordination and skill required to soar 300 feet through the air above Timber Coulee, one of only four Olympic large-size hills in North America, the size used to conduct jumping events in the winter Olympics.

Visitors will also appreciate the strong Norwegian heritage that is still evident in Westby. Other winter recreational opportunities nearby beckon those who want to strap on their own skis for a less hazardous outing. If the wintry outdoors does not appeal, Amish communities close by offer colorful touring, and a stay in La Crosse, half an hour from Westby, can add city pleasures to the weekend.

The members of the Snowflake Ski Club, sponsors of the annual contest, were showing their Norwegian roots when they built the first ski-jumping hills in the 1920s. Competition now takes place on five hills, including the big 112-meter Timber Coulee constructed in 1960. Major competition began the next year, and the excitement continues to build. The event is usually one of the trials for the U.S. Olympic ski team. A new record was set in 1995 with a gravity-defying 125-meter jump—by a 16-year-old.

Spectators buy a two-day pass, then stand or park in a big field at the base of the hills, where they can see all the action. Stands selling hot lunches and coffee help to warm the proceedings, and an announcer keeps you apprised of who's winning. You can also get reports on your car radio.

Westby is only a dot of a town, but it has special Scandinavian charm, starting with the Norwegian-style log *Stabbur* that serves as a visitors center. Step into Our Saviors Lutheran Church on Main Street to see the unique windows, some 200 feet of them, patterned after *rosemaling,* a beloved form of Norwegian folk art that incorporates lovely floral designs.

You can see and buy examples of rosemaling at Dregne's Scandinavian Gifts, along with everything Norse, from crystal to carvings to clogs. Trolls stand in the shop windows and the bakery window, and even the pharmacy has a sign painted in rosemaling flower designs. The window next to Borgen's Cafe on Main Street features mannequins dressed in colorful Norwegian folk costumes.

The Westby House, a classic Victorian home just a stroll from Main Street, is the best place to stay—provided you can snag one of the four guest rooms. A handful of country inns are available in nearby small towns. You can opt for a farmhouse inn that is also a Nordic skiing center, or proceed half an hour to La Crosse, where the Martindale House is a sophisticated showplace inn.

When you're not admiring the ski jumpers, you'll find a variety of pleasures awaiting near Westby. Beyond Coon Valley is Norskedalen, a 350-acre Norwegian cultural and nature center owned by the University of Wisconsin—La Crosse Foundation. The visitors center offers a video and exhibits on the region's Scandinavian heritage and on local nature. The gift shop stocks interesting Norwegian handicrafts as well as nature-related items. On the grounds are Bekkum, a restored pioneer farmstead (open for tours in warmer weather), an arboretum, and six miles of hiking trails available to cross-country skiers or snowshoers in winter.

If you come back in summer, you can visit the Skumsrud Heritage Farm operated by Norskedalen. This separate open-air museum a half mile west of Coon Valley features 11 19th-century buildings and Scandinavian artisans demonstrating and selling their crafts.

If downhill skiing is your sport, Mount La Crosse, two miles south of La Crosse on Highway 35, offers 17 trails, three lifts, a quite respectable 516-foot vertical drop, and the longest downhill run in Wisconsin. Even experts will find the Damnation run a challenge, spilling off a rugged ridge overlooking the Mississippi River Valley and into a tree-lined bowl. It is billed as the steepest run between Stowe and Jackson Hole. The slopes are lit for night skiing, and the convivial St. Bernard Room was named the best skier's bar in the Midwest by *Skiing* magazine. Cross-country skiers will find a wooded five kilometers set aside for them.

A drive eight miles north of Westby on Highway 27 leads to Cashton, the heart of Wisconsin's Amish country. Turn right on Highway 33, and right again on County Road D for a back-roads tour and a visit to the Hill and Valley Cheese Factory. For more about this area, see page 152.

Farther north off Highway 27 toward Sparta is Justin Trails, a delightful country farmhouse turned bed-and-breakfast inn that is a perfect winter hideaway. The inn's Nordic Ski Center provides 15 kilometers of groomed trails right outside the door and a trailhead warming lodge with heated bathrooms, a snack shop, and picnic tables. Snowtubing on two giant hills, and snowshoes for exploring miles of marked trails on the expansive grounds, are also possibilities. Suites have a fireplace and whirlpool to warm you when you come home.

If you choose to head toward the Mississippi River and La Crosse, the Martindale House is the recommended lodging. Restoration of the 1850s Italianate mansion earned Wisconsin's Historic Preservation Achievement Award in 1992. The house is filled with antiques and has a lovely Scandinavian Room that reflects the background of the Swedish hostess. Once again private quarters are available—the Carriage House Suite, offering a heart-shaped Jacuzzi.

A busy city of 51,000, La Crosse was founded in 1841 by an Indian trader, and got its name when French settlers saw Indians playing a game similar to lacrosse. Look for the sculpture called *La Crosse Players* in town near Riverside Park.

Situated directly on the Mississippi, La Crosse prospered first as a trading center and later as a lumber town—the mills took advantage of easy river transportation. A drive along Cass Street takes you past many fine homes once owned by 19th-century lumber barons. You can learn more about the city's past at the Swarthout Museum in the main library.

If weather allows, another drive not to be missed is up Grandad Bluff for one of the most picturesque points in the area, a 600-foot bluff with a full overview of the city and the Mississippi Valley.

The city's Riverside Park was created by dredging the Mississippi. It contains two local landmarks. A 25-foot wooden statue of Hiawatha presides over the sacred meetingplace of three rivers, the Mississippi, Black, and La Crosse. *The La Crosse Eagle,* an impressive 35-foot-tall sculpture standing guard over the Mississippi, was intentionally crafted of corten, a material that rusts, in order to create its varied colors.

Not far from the river is one of La Crosse's best-known landmarks, the world's largest six-pack, standing tall near the Heileman Brewery, where free tours are offered year-round. Visitors are greeted by an image of King Gambrinus, the legendary Flemish king and patron saint of the brewing industry.

One of the city's handsomest sights is the Romanesque Mary of the Angels Chapel, built to serve the Franciscan Sisters of Perpetual Adoration. Since August 1, 1878, day and night without interruption, at least two members of the community have knelt before the Altar of Exposition of the Blessed Sacrament, keeping vigil and praying for the community, the church, the city, and the world. Their vigilance was once given national attention in a feature on CBS-TV. The ornate brick and terra-cotta facades, beautiful stained-glass windows, and chapels with altars of Italian marble and inlaid mosaics of green and gold Venetian glass and mother-of-pearl are well worth a tour.

The attractive campus of the University of Wisconsin—La Crosse is nicely situated between the Mississippi and the bluffs. Take a drive around the buildings, or, on weekdays, join a guided tour. The university has a full schedule of concerts, plays, art shows, and lectures open to the public.

While not a shopping mecca, La Crosse has its share of interesting stops, especially in Old Towne North between the 1000 and 1500 blocks of Caledonia Street. Your sweet tooth will appreciate a visit to Mississippi Brittle Pecan Candies at 1232 Caledonia, where you can watch the yummy candy being made. Antiquers will find wares from many dealers at the big Antique Center of La Crosse Ltd. in a century-old building at 110 South Third Street.

The Pump House, a Romanesque Revival building that actually served as a pump house, has been converted to a cultural center with three galleries displaying work by local and regional artists. Handsome wildlife paintings and other types of art, including Susan Sampson's unique designs for beer mugs, can be seen at the Sampson Art Gallery, 600 North Third Street. The gallery includes Sampson's state heritage collection, 12 life-size paintings of famous Wisconsin residents, including Russian-born Golda Meier and native son Frank Lloyd Wright.

When it comes to dining, La Crosse has two notable choices: the restored Freight House, a national historic site specializing in steaks and prime rib, and Piggy's—always included on "Best of Wisconsin" lists—where the pork dishes are nothing short of fabulous.

If you are looking for outdoor activity, bring along your ice skates and take advantage of winter rinks with warming houses in Copeland, Hickory, Pettibone, and Trane city parks. You can take a spin indoors at the rink at Green Island Park, Seventh and Cook Streets.

A less strenuous sport is eagle watching, best practiced along Highway 35, which skirts the Mississippi River. Hundreds of American bald eagles winter in this area, sunning themselves on the branches along the river bluffs and feeding in the open pools. Lock and Dam No. 7, five miles north of La Crosse, has an observation deck, and Lock and Dam No. 8, 12 miles south of the city on Highway 35 in Genoa, is another favorite viewpoint. The eagles swooping down for their dinners will add another set of graceful descents to your ski-jumping weekend.

Area Code: 608

DRIVING DIRECTIONS Westby is south of I-90 at the intersection of Highway 27 and U.S. 14/61. La Crosse is 24 miles northwest, about half an hour's drive, reached via U.S. 14/61 west to Highway 35 north. From Chicago, take I-90 northwest, turning south on Highway 27 for Westby, or driving directly into La Crosse, about 273 miles. La Crosse is 204 miles from Milwaukee.

ACCOMMODATIONS **Westby House,** 200 West State Street, Westby 54667, 634-4112 or (800) 434-7439, I–M, CP; suite E, CP • **Justin Trails,** 7452 Kathryn Avenue and County Road J, off Highway 27, Sparta 54656, 269-4522 or (800) 488-4521, attractive farm in sylvan setting, cross-country skiing on property, M–E, CP; king suite, E; cottages with fireplaces and whirlpools, EE • **Viroqua Heritage Inn,** 220 East Jefferson, Viroqua 54665, 637-3306, I–EE, CP • ***La Crosse:*** **Martindale House,** 237 South 10th Street, La Crosse 54601, 782-4224, M, CP, suite, E, CP • **Radisson Hotel,** 200 Harborview Plaza, La Crosse 54601, 784-6680, overlooking the river, M • **Days Inn,** 101 Sky Harbor Drive, La Crosse 54603, 783-1000, I–M • **Best Western Midway Hotel,** 1835 Rose Street, La Crosse 54603, exceptionally nice motor inn, indoor pool, 781-7000, M.

DINING **Old Towne Inn,** Main Street (U.S. 14), Westby, 634-3991, fine country dining, I–M • **Westby House** (see above), serving tasty lunches, I • **DiSciascio's Coon Creek Inn,** U.S. 14/61, Coon Valley, 452-3182, highly rated Italian, I–M • **Piggy's,** 328 South Front Street, La Crosse, 784-4877, not to be missed, I–E • **Freight House,** 107 Vine Street, La Crosse, 784-6211, M–EE • **Moxie's,** Best Western Midway Hotel (see above), American menu, I–E • **Mr. D's Donut Shop and Restaurant,** West Avenue and State Street, La Crosse, 784-6737, come for breakfast or lunch and don't miss the donuts, I.

SIGHTSEEING **Snowflake Ski Jumping Tournament,** Snowflake Ski and Golf Club, Timber Coulee, County Road P, between Westby and Coon Valley, 634-3787. Annual ski-jumping event, usually second weekend in February; phone for current dates, admission • **Norskedalen,** off U.S. 14/61, Coon Valley (between Westby and La Crosse), 452-3424. Hours: Visitors center open Monday to Friday 9 A.M. to 4 P.M., Sunday noon to 4:30 P.M. April 15 to October 31 also open Saturday. Trails open year-round for hiking, cross-country skiing, snowshoeing. Tours of Bekkum Pioneer Homestead, April 15 to October 31. Tours of Skumsrud Heritage Farm, Memorial Day to Labor Day, Saturday 10 A.M. to 4 P.M., Sunday noon to 4 P.M. $$ • **Heileman Brewery Visitors Center,** 1111 South Third Street, La Crosse, 782-BEER. Hours: Brewery tours on the hour, September through May, Tuesday to Saturday 11 A.M. to 3 P.M.; June to August, Monday to Saturday 10 A.M. to 4 P.M., Sunday 10 A.M. to 3 P.M. Free • **Pump House Regional Center for the Arts,** 119 King Street, La Crosse, 785-1434. Hours: Tuesday to Saturday 9 A.M. to 5 P.M. Donation • **Mary of the Angels Chapel,** St. Rose Convent, 715 South Ninth Street, La Crosse, 784-2288. Hours: Monday to Saturday 9 A.M. to 11 A.M. and 1 P.M. to 3:30 P.M., Sunday 1 P.M. to 3:30 P.M. Donation • **Swarthout Museum,** 112 Ninth Street South, La Crosse, 782-1980. Hours: Tuesday to Friday 10 A.M. to 5 P.M., Saturday and Sunday 1 P.M. to 5 P.M. Donation • **University of Wisconsin—La Crosse,** 1725 State Street, La Crosse, 785-8000. Hours: Guided tours leave from the admissions office, 115 Main Hall, Monday to Friday at 11 A.M. and 2 P.M. when school is in session. Free. For a recorded listing of music, theater, art shows, lectures, and planetarium shows, phone 785-8900 • ***Skiing:*** **Mount La Crosse Ski Area,** Highway 35, La Crosse, 788-0044 or (800) 426-3665, downhill and cross-country.

INFORMATION **Westby Tourism Council,** c/o Country Collectibles, 105 South Main Street, Westby, WI 54667, 634-4000 • **La Crosse Area Convention and Visitors Bureau,** 410 East Veterans Memorial Drive, La Crosse, WI 54601, 782-2366 or (800) 658-9424.

Spas and Sports in French Lick

What should it be? A soak in the mineral baths, a swim in the glass-domed indoor pool, a set of tennis, or a turn in the bowling alley? At the French Lick Springs Resort, you won't have to worry about winter weather—you can stay busy all day inside the big resort hotel. When you do want to get into the great outdoors, the 2,600-acre grounds are great terrain for cross-country skiers, and a downhill ski area, Paoli Peaks, is just 15 minutes away.

Fresh from a major renovation, French Lick makes for a great winter getaway, as well as the chance to discover the most historic resort in the Midwest.

The first pioneers to report on this valley of bubbling mineral springs were French explorers of the late 1660s, who discovered that their livestock benefited from licking the salt deposits, or salt licks, formed by the springs. This was the inspiration for the name given by settlers who followed in the late 1700s, when this part of the Indiana Territory was still considered the "Far West." In 1812 a government fort stood on the site of today's resort hotel.

The area's fate was determined when a local physician, Dr. William Bowles, saw the commercial potential in the soothing waters of the mineral baths and purchased the site and three mineral springs from the state of Indiana. The first hotel went up in 1842, a time when the fashionable were crowding Eastern mineral-water spas like Saratoga Springs, New York, and the hotel soon became a favorite of Eastern as well as Midwestern society.

The most potent spring was named Pluto's Well after the Greek god of the underground, and the water was bottled and widely sold as "Pluto Water." Copper statues of Pluto, created at the turn of the century and now restored, stand in the dining room and in the lobby garden.

Even headier days were ahead. The original hotel burned in 1897, and the site was purchased by Thomas Taggart, a leader in the Democratic Party. The enormous hotel he opened in the early 1900s was soon patronized by both the famous and the infamous. In the Roaring Twenties, it attracted movers and shakers of the Democratic Party as well as the not-so-democratic world of organized crime, in the person of one Al Capone and his associates.

The list of prominent guests also included show-business luminaries like Lana Turner, George Jessel, and Bing Crosby, and composer Irving Berlin. During its heyday the resort was served by 12 trains daily from

Chicago, Indianapolis, St. Louis, Cincinnati, and Louisville. A railroad spur went right to the front door.

For many years French Lick was the unofficial summer retreat of the Democratic Party. It was here, during the 1931 National Governors' Conference, that Franklin Roosevelt gained support for the presidential nomination.

Like so many other resorts, French Lick lost its allure after World War II, when air travel became cheap and easy and people looked farther afield for their vacation spots. The hotel had gone way downhill under a series of owners, but in 1991, a Louisville real-estate developer bought the property at auction and began a complete renovation.

The lobby once again is elegantly furnished, its multicolored tile floor, chandeliers, and priceless millwork and moldings restored. The rooms have been modernized and redecorated. The spa still offers therapeutic Pluto mineral baths, as well as massages, body treatments, and exercise classes; there's also a well-equipped gym. Winter facilities include the indoor pool beneath a retractable glass dome, six bowling lanes, and eight indoor tennis courts, as well as 10 lighted outdoor courts. The stables provide horseback riding when weather permits.

Skiers will find nearby Paoli Peaks to be a friendly, relaxed area served by four chairlifts. A good place for learning for all ages, it offers a special first-time skier package. The vertical drop is 300 feet; the longest run is 3,300 feet. The slopes not only offer night skiing but also midnight skiing on Friday and Saturday, and on New Year's Eve, quite a unique way to welcome the New Year. The French Lick resort's special packages include skiing.

Families will find supervised activities for children at the hotel during holiday periods and spring break, as well as Saturday programs throughout the winter. In summer the Pluto Club for children is open daily. Summer also brings family entertainment many evenings.

Golfers who return in warmer weather will find two fine courses, the gentle Valley Course and the Hill Course, whose rolling fairways and undulating greens were designed by the dean of golf-course architecture, Donald Ross.

The rates at French Lick are surprisingly moderate for the many amenities available.

If you relax and enjoy all of the resort activities, you'll need few other diversions. If you do want to do some sightseeing, the best bet is Marengo Cave, some 30 miles southeast. A National Historic Landmark, the cave is open year-round and the constant temperature of 52 degrees can seem positively balmy on a cold winter day. It is rightfully famous for its fanciful underground formations, such as the Crystal Palace. There's more about the cave on page 99.

The town of French Lick is tiny, with only a smattering of shops. In summer the main attraction is the Indiana Railway Museum, offering rides through the Hoosier National Forest and the 2,200-foot Burton

Tunnel. You can't help but know that this is the birthplace of sports legend and Indiana Pacers coach Larry Bird, since Larry Bird Boulevard is marked with an enormous sign in the shape of a basketball.

If you admire fine church architecture, take a drive south to Ferdinand to see the Church of the Immaculate Conception, considered one of the best examples of Romanesque architecture in the country. You can't miss the majestic domed church—it rises like a castle on the hill above the town. It boasts brilliant stained-glass windows, handsome wood panels, handcarved pews from Germany, and an interior dome that rises 87 feet above the marble floor. The ornately decorated church features many angels, created to serve as protectors. The outside is adorned with Italian pagodas with terra-cotta ornamentation; the winding stairs inside are a favorite challenge for visitors.

The church is part of the buildings and 190-acre grounds of the Sisters of St. Benedict, a religious community that includes the Marian Heights Academy, a boarding school for girls. The sisters offer guided tours that include the academy and, in summer, the outdoor stations of the cross and Lourdes grotto.

Traces of the German origins of this region can also be seen in neighboring Jasper, a few miles closer to French Lick. St. Joseph Church, an 1880 Romanesque-style structure, boasts priceless German stained-glass windows, Austrian-designed mosaics with 50 million stones, a marble altar, and pewter statues. Fourteen poplar trees from local forests form beams to support the 90-foot vaulted ceiling.

If you are interested in modern architecture, look for the Holy Family Church on the southeast side of Jasper, a modern marvel featuring the nation's second-largest stained-glass window, 67 feet long and 45 feet high. The building is said to include the longest unsupported wood beam ever used.

Jasper also shows its Bavarian heritage in a popular restaurant, the Schnitzelbank. Owned by the same family for three generations, the restaurant is known for the glockenspiel on its Bavarian-style tower. The gift shop has German souvenirs such as beer steins and whimsical nutcrackers.

This is also the home of the noted Kimball Piano Company. The corporate showroom, open weekdays, displays pianos, as well as other fine furniture made by the company.

Back in French Lick, you can once again admire the huge turn-of-the-century American resort, a revitalized symbol of a grander resort age. While it isn't quite what it used to be in its glory days, French Lick remains a very special place, one of a kind in the Midwest.

<u>Area Code: 812</u>

DRIVING DIRECTIONS French Lick is on State Highway 56 in southern Indiana. From Chicago take I-90 east to I-65 south, then I-465 skirting Indianapolis to State Highway 37 south to Paoli. At Paoli, take U.S. 150 9 miles west, then State Highway 56 South to French Lick, 275 miles. It is 108 miles south of Indianapolis.

ACCOMMODATIONS **French Lick Springs Resort,** 8670 West State Highway 56, French Lick, IN 47432, 936-9300 or (800) 457-4042, M, or E, MAP. Special packages are available for golf, tennis, and spa programs and in conjunction with the Paoli Peaks Ski Area.

DINING **French Lick Springs Resort** choices: **Le Bistro,** informal dining and late-night dancing, overlooking grounds and Dome Pool, M • **Jack's Steak House,** casual dress, fine dining and wines, M–E • **Recreation Center and Uno's Pizzeria,** pub near bowling and games, I • **Country Club,** overlooking the Donald Ross golf course, open for dinner in golf season, M • **Schnitzelbank,** 393 Third Avenue, State Highway 162, Jasper, 481-1466, German menu and ambience, I–M.

SIGHTSEEING **Paoli Peaks Ski Area,** off U.S. 150, Paoli, 723-4696 • **Marengo Cave National Landmark,** State Highway 64, 10 miles north of I-64, Exit 92, via State Highway 66, Marengo, 365-2705. Hours: Memorial Day to Labor Day, daily 9 A.M. to 6 P.M.; rest of year 9 A.M. to 5 P.M. Crystal Palace 40-minute tour, $$$$ or 70-minute Dripstone Trail tour, $$$$. Combination tickets available • ***Area churches:*** **Church of the Immaculate Conception,** 802 East 10th Street, Ferdinand, 367-1411. Hours: Tours Monday to Friday on the hour, 10 A.M., 11 A.M., 1 P.M., 2 P.M., 3 P.M.; Saturday, Sunday 1 P.M. to 3 P.M. Donation • **St. Joseph Church,** 13th and Newton streets, Jasper, 482-1805. Hours: Daily 8 A.M. to 9 P.M. in warm weather, shorter hours in winter. Free • **Holy Family Church,** 950 Church Avenue, off Highway 162, Jasper, 482-3076. Hours: Daily 8 A.M. to 8 P.M. Free.

INFORMATION For French Lick area, contact **French Lick Springs Hotel,** (800) 457-4042. For Ferdinand and Jasper, **Dubois County Tourism Commission,** P.O. Box 404, Jasper, IN 47547, 482-9115.

Winter Wonder at Starved Rock

Winter is the magic season at Starved Rock State Park. Waterfalls are frozen in motion, sculpted in shimmering crystal, and woodlands turn into a snowy wonderland crowned in whipped cream white.

Boots and warm gear for hiking are all that is needed to take in these glorious sights. Cross-country skiing, snowshoeing, sledding, and ice skating are more ways to enjoy the great outdoors in this great state park.

When you want to be indoors, a big indoor swimming pool, kiddie pool, whirlpool, and sauna make for weatherproof fun for all ages. Meanwhile, the fire crackles invitingly in the massive stone fireplace in the lodge.

Nor do you have to go out into the cold to find pleasant dining. The attractive lodge dining room serves all three meals, including a special children's menu. The dinner choices range from pasta to prime rib, and the lavish Sunday brunch is a treat. The Starved Rock Cafe offers lighter fare and the Back Door lounge with big-screen TV is a lively gathering spot for sports fans.

There are few better places to make the most of a winter weekend, especially during the annual mid-January Winter Wilderness Weekend, when guided hikes take visitors to see the spectacular ice falls, and free cross-country ski instruction takes place at Matthiessen State Park, just two miles away.

Starved Rock is a crown jewel in the Illinois park system any time of year, 2,603 acres of thick forest running for five miles along the Illinois River, with 18 scenic canyons laced with waterfalls slicing through the bluffs. The river views are fantastic.

The park is best known for its rugged sandstone rock formations, especially the Starved Rock, standing 125 feet high above the river. The history of the rock goes way back. Explorer Robert La Salle built a French fort on "Le Rocher" ("the rock") in 1682. According to legend, it was nearly a century later, in 1769, that the name was changed to Starved Rock, inspired by a group of Illini Indians who took refuge atop the rock from an attacking war party. They were surrounded by their enemies and eventually starved to death.

The park lodge of native stone and logs was built by the Civilian Conservation Corps in the 1930s and retains its rustic charm, especially in the aptly named Great Room with giant log beams and an enormous double-faced stone fireplace said to weigh some 700 tons. The room is furnished with fine Native American rugs and artwork. Chairs grouped around coffee tables make for sociable settings, and you'll often find families here playing Scrabble or Monopoly. Kids also gravitate to the video games on the second floor.

An addition to the lodge provides attractive modern pine-paneled guest rooms, some with bluff views, all with private baths and conveniences such as TV and telephones. There are several deluxe bay-window rooms and a few junior suites. Eighteen cabin rooms are cozy, many with wood-burning fireplaces. Given the moderate price of these comfortable accommodations, it's no surprise that rooms in season are booked as much as a year in advance. They are much easier to come by in winter.

Cross-country skiing and snowshoeing are available in the park picnic area, but there's even more opportunity just a short drive away at Matthiessen State Park, where several miles of trails and ski rentals are available on weekends. The park often holds its own Cross-Country Ski Weekend in early February, with basic instruction and guided ski hikes.

Though it is smaller, 1600-acre Matthiessen does have its own bluffs and a beautiful mile-long canyon where impressive Cascade Falls tumbles down 45 feet over the rocks. Access to this waterfall is easier than those in many of the canyons at Starved Rock.

There's more to see and do in the surrounding area. Utica is on the Michigan and Illinois Canal National Corridor, America's first National Heritage Corridor, following the route of the historic canal that connected the Great Lakes with the Mississippi River. The construction of the canal in 1848 gave birth to many towns along the way, including the lakeside settlement now known as Chicago. In the first five years after the canal was completed, Chicago's population quadrupled.

The Illinois Waterway Visitors Center, two miles east of Utica at the Starved Rock Lock and Dam, is maintained by the U.S. Army Corps of Engineers. It provides upper- and lower-level observation areas for close-up views of the locks in operation, the big barges that ply the river with cargoes of coal and grain, and the small towboats that propel these heavy loads through the locks. Exhibits and a slide presentation tell of early Midwestern river travel, from fur traders to steamboats.

Some of the towboats have retractable pilot houses that allow them to pass under low bridges in the Chicago area. One of these, the *John M. Warner,* is part of the center and can be explored. Built in 1943, it ran until 1982; much of the original equipment remains intact.

Continuing east another four miles toward Ottawa, you'll come to Buffalo Rock State Park, a small park overlooking the river with a scenic road circling a bluff as it climbs to the top, where there are lovely river views. The western edge of this park has five huge earthen sculptures molded from Illinois clay. Called *Effigy Tumuli,* this unique earth art, created by artist Michael Heizer, is in the shape of a snake, turtle, fish, frog, and insect, a tribute to the Native American burial grounds that inspired it.

If shopping is your favorite winter sport, Utica's Victorian-style village business district is definitely worth a look. "Downtown" is actually Highway 178, which is called Mill Street until it reaches Canal Street, where it becomes Clark Street. The wares offered run the gamut from Amish-crafted oak furniture at the Village Oak Haus to motorcycle leather and Grateful Dead memorabilia at Stonehead. Four Feathers features Native American jewelry, art, and crafts; Clark Street Studio and Village Pottery sells wheel-thrown pottery by the resident potter; the Carver and the Artist has hand-carved wooden wildlife figures; and there are several antique and gift shops with a wide assortment of collectibles. Utica has a few informal dining choices as well.

When you're done, that big fireplace is waiting to welcome you back to Starved Rock Lodge, the perfect warm ending to a winter's day.

Area Code: 815

DRIVING DIRECTIONS From Chicago, take I-55 south to I-80 west; Starved Rock State Park is on State Highway 178 in Utica, off I-80, 94 miles from Chicago.

ACCOMMODATIONS **Starved Rock Lodge,** Starved Rock State Park, Highway 178 and 71, P.O. Box 570, Utica 61373, 667-4211 or (800) 868-ROCK, lodge rooms, I; executive rooms and junior suites, M; cabins I–M • **Landers House Country Lodging,** 115 East Church Street, Utica, 61373, 667-5170, bed-and-breakfast home one mile from the park, I–M, CP • **Holiday Inn Express,** 120 West Stevenson Road, Ottawa 62350, 433-0029, indoor pool, some whirlpools in rooms, I.

DINING **Starved Rock Lodge** (see above), 667-4227, I–M • **Cajun Connection,** 2954 North Highway 178, Utica, 667-9855, gumbo, jambalaya, and all that jazz, I • **Canal Port Bar and Grill,** 148 Mill Street, Utica, 667-3010, relaxed, fried chicken is the specialty, I • **Duffy's Tavern and Eatery,** Mill and Canal Streets, Utica, 667-4324, casual dining in an old Victorian building, I • **Country Cupboard Ice Cream Sandwich and Pizza Shoppe,** 402 North Clark Street, Utica, 667-5155, pizza, sandwiches, salads, and homemade ice cream, open March to November, I.

SIGHTSEEING **Starved Rock State Park,** State Highway 178, Utica, 667-4906. Hours: Park open daily 5 A.M. to 10 P.M. Office hours, 8:30 A.M. to 4 P.M. Visitors center, Monday to Friday 1 P.M. to 4 P.M.; Saturday, Sunday 9 A.M. to 4 P.M.; guided hikes offered on Saturdays, weather permitting. Free • **Matthiessen State Park,** Highway 178, Utica, 667-4868. Hours: Daily 8 A.M. to 10 P.M. Cross-country ski rentals available on weekends, December through March when snow permits. Free • **Illinois Waterway Visitors Center,** Dee Bennett Road off Highway 178, Utica, 667-4054. Hours: Daily 9 A.M. to 5 P.M., to 8 P.M. Memorial Day to Labor Day. Free • **Buffalo Rock State Park,** Dee Bennett Road, Ottawa, 433-2220. Hours: Daily 8 A.M. to sunset. Free.

INFORMATION **Heritage Corridor Visitors Bureau,** 623 South Clark, P.O. Box 378, Utica, IL 61373, 667-4356.

Following Indiana's Antique Alley

Centerville, Indiana, is only a tiny dot on the map, but it is well known to antiquers. It is the home of Webb's, the world's largest antique mall, spanning two entire city blocks.

China and crystal, Hoosier cabinets, lamps, quilts, toys and trunks, paintings, pewter and pottery, silver, old records, kitchen tools, clocks and watches, political memorabilia, mantels, and other architectural antiques—name it and you'll find it here among the thousands of wares offered by over 300 dealers, all under one enormous roof. Some of the items are only trinkets, others treasures, but the mix is irresistible. Since there's a restaurant on the premises, die-hard antiquers can easily spend a day, completely oblivious to winter weather.

Nor is Webb's the only collectors' lure. Centerville is located on Indiana's "Antique Alley," U.S. Highway 40, the old "National Road," which was the first federally funded highway in the nation and is a National Historic Civil Engineering Landmark. Perhaps with this historic past as inspiration, dozens of malls and individual dealers have sprung up within a 33-mile stretch between the towns of Richmond, a few miles east of Centerville, and Knightstown to the west. The Wayne County visitors bureau in Richmond can supply a complete list.

Centerville itself is a delightful village. The original historic Main Street (U.S. 40) was too narrow to allow adding to the fronts of buildings, so homeowners in the 1820s and 1830s left narrow alleys crowned with arches between their row houses to allow access to the rear, where many maintained shops. The quaint brick buildings and their distinctive archways are similar to the row houses of the mid-Atlantic, which is where many of these early settlers came from. Nicely preserved, they comprise a historic district of over 100 buildings. You can see the best of it on a three-block tour of Main Street, roughly between First and Ash Streets.

One of the earliest homes, the 1823 Lantz House, is now a charmingly furnished bed-and-breakfast inn with a unique history. The first owner of this Federal-style home was Daniel Lantz, a well-known wagon maker. An estimated 49,000 wagons passed through Centerville during the Gold Rush, with many stopping at the Lantz shop for repairs. A walking-tour brochure available at the inn gives the history of this and other interesting homes, many owned by citizens who were important in early Indiana history.

Main Street also offers several small antiques shops, one of the most charming being the Tin Pig, where country antiques and accessories are shown within room settings. Jag's Cafe, with a massive bar dating to 1893, is a fine stop for lunch or dinner, served in a period setting of Tiffany lamps and memorabilia. Webb's Antique Mall is found just two short blocks off Main.

Another recommended stop is Scott Shafer Stoneware, where you can watch Shafer at work making pitchers, pie plates, teapots, platters, and other attractive and useful items.

More shopping and sightseeing await in nearby Richmond. Settled in 1806 by German immigrants and Quakers from North Carolina, Richmond has grown into the largest city in the area, a trade and distribution center for the rich agricultural lands of Wayne County.

The city's two historic districts include many lovely early homes. Self-guided tour maps are available at the tourism bureau. One of the finest Victorian homes, the 1876 Gaar Mansion, is open for tours on the first and third Sundays of each month.

Many facets of the town's early history are displayed at the Wayne County Historical Museum, housed in a former Quaker meetinghouse. Exhibits range from an 1823 log cabin and a working 1880s blacksmith shop to a turn-of-the-century pioneer general store to vintage cars manufactured locally.

The Joseph Moore Museum offers a change of pace with natural-science exhibits that include an Egyptian mummy, skeletons of prehistoric mastodons, and birds and mammals in their natural habitats. It is on the attractive campus of Earlham, a small college known for its progressive educational program.

Sports fans may want to look into the Indiana Football Hall of Fame, which honors the state's many athletes, from Knute Rockne and the famous "Four Horsemen of Notre Dame" to the Indianapolis Colts. Seeing the changes in football uniforms from the early days of the sport to the present is fun even for nonfans.

The largest of the local antique shops is the Top Drawer Antique Mall, 801 East Main Street, with some 35 dealers. Your sweet tooth will be pleased with a stop at Olympian Candies at 625 East Main, a family-owned store that has been selling homemade candies since 1909. More sweet treats are waiting at The Three Sisters, a gift shop at 725 East Main, selling Abbots Candy, which is made in nearby Hagerstown.

Come back in summer to see Richmond's Hill Memorial Rose Garden in Glen Miller Park abloom with 2,000 plants representing more than 73 varieties. Two other attractions at their best in warmer weather are Hayes Regional Arboretum, with a bird sanctuary, hiking trails, and a three-mile auto nature tour, and Whitewater Gorge Park, where three branches of the Whitewater River converge, producing a gorge with fossil-laden vertical cliffs and miles of hiking trails.

Heading west of Centerville on U.S. 40, two sightseeing stops await in Cambridge City. The Huddleston Farmhouse Inn Museum was built by John Huddleston in 1841 to house his large family and welcome a stream of wagon parties traveling west on the National Road. Here they could have a meal; stable, feed, and rest their horses; buy provisions; and find overnight shelter. Sometimes there were as many as 40 guests in one night.

The farmhouse, authentically restored by Historic Landmarks Foundation of Indiana, tells the story of the life of one early Hoosier farming family and of travelers along the National Road during the busiest decades of westward emigration, the 1840s and 1850s. Many special events are scheduled, from Civil War living history encampments to harvest suppers on Saturdays in October and November; the latter re-create the hearty meals that the Huddlestons cooked on the open hearth for their weary guests.

Cambridge City was also home to the six Overbeck sisters, artists recognized for the whimsical art pottery they created in the first half of this century. The largest collection of their work, including many delightful animal figures, can be seen in a downstairs gallery at the Cambridge City Library. Just ask at the desk, and you'll be taken down to the exhibit.

A detour north for a few miles will bring you to Hagerstown, where you can tour the Abbot Candy Factory on weekdays and visit the Collectible Classics Car Museum, a cache of over 30 vintage cars.

The shops we visited proceeding west along Antique Alley were sometimes disappointing, though the Knightstown Antique Mall had some interesting wares from 75 dealers.

But it didn't matter. We had already found enough treasures and pleasures to make for a memorable weekend.

Area Code: 765

DRIVING DIRECTIONS From Chicago, take I-80/90 east to I-65 south. At Indianapolis, take I-465 circling the city and head east on I-70 to the Richmond exit, about 253 miles. Richmond is 70 miles from Indianapolis. Centerville is 6 miles from Richmond via U.S. 40 west.

ACCOMMODATIONS **Historic Lantz House Inn,** 214 West Main Street (U.S. 40), Centerville 47330, 855-2936 or (800) 495-2689, I–M, CP • **Clarion Leland Hotel,** 900 South A Street, Richmond 47374,

966-5000 or (800) 535-2630, I–M • **Philip W. Smith Bed-and-Breakfast,** 2039 East Main Street (U.S. 40), Richmond 47374, (800) 966-8972, I • **Holiday Inn Holidome,** 5501 National Road East (U.S. 40), Richmond 47374, 966-7571, indoor pool, I–M

DINING **Jag's Cafe,** 129 East Main Street (U.S. 40), Centerville, 855-2282, 1893 bar, steaks, seafood, sandwiches, I–M • **Olde Richmond Inn,** 138 South Fifth Street, Richmond, 962-2247, I–M • **Taste of the Town,** 1616 East Main Street (U.S. 40), Richmond, 935-5464, casual, recommended locally, I–M • **Little Sheba's,** 175 Ft. Wayne Avenue, Richmond, 962-2999, quaint ambience in former grocery, sandwiches and light fare, I.

SIGHTSEEING **Webb's Antique Mall,** 200 West Union Street, Centerville, 855-5542. Hours: Daily 9 A.M. to 5 P.M., to 6 P.M. March through November. Free admission • **Wayne County Historical Museum,** 1150 North "A" Street, Richmond, 962-5756. Hours: February to mid-December, Tuesday to Friday 9 A.M. to 4 P.M., Saturday and Sunday 1 P.M. to 4 P.M. $$ • **Gaar Mansion,** 2593 Pleasant View Road, Richmond, 966-7184. Hours: March through December, first and third Sundays each month, 1 P.M. to 4 P.M. $$ • **Indiana Football Hall of Fame,** 815 North "A" Street, Richmond, 966-2235. Hours: May through September, Monday to Friday 10 A.M. to 4 P.M., Saturday noon to 4 P.M.; rest of year, Monday to Friday 10 A.M. to 2 P.M., weekends by appointment. $ • **Joseph Moore Museum,** Earlham College, U.S. 40 West, Richmond, 983-1303. Hours: year-round on Sunday 1 P.M. to 5 P.M.; also September to mid-December and January 15 to April, Monday, Wednesday, and Friday 1 P.M. to 4 P.M. Free • **Huddleston Farmhouse Inn Museum,** P.O. Box 284, Cambridge City, 748-3172. Hours: February through December, Tuesday to Saturday 10 A.M. to 4 P.M., also Sunday 1 P.M. to 4 P.M. from May through August. $$ • **Museum of Overbeck Art Pottery,** Cambridge City Public Library, 33 West Main Street, Cambridge City, 478-3335. Hours: Monday to Saturday 10 A.M. to noon and 2 P.M. to 5 P.M. Free • **Collectible Classics Car Museum,** 403 East Main Street, Hagerstown, 489-5598. Hours: June through August, Monday to Saturday 11 A.M. to 5 P.M.; rest of year, Thursday, Friday 5 P.M. to 8 P.M., Saturday, Sunday noon to 4 P.M. $$.

INFORMATION **Richmond-Wayne County Convention and Tourism Bureau,** 5701 National Road East (U.S. 40), Richmond, IN 47374, 935-8687 or (800) 828-8414; www.visitrichmond.org

A Tasty Brew in Milwaukee

In Milwaukee, they don't believe in hibernating in winter. Instead, the city celebrates.

Every year the United States International Snow-Sculpting Championship takes place on the grounds of the downtown Marcus Center for the Performing Arts. Participants representing some 15 nations, some from as far away as Brazil and Bulgaria, compete for prizes for the most spectacular entry. Each country's three-man team is given a block of snow six feet long, six feet high, and 10 feet wide to perform their magic, and the intricate creations are nothing less than amazing. Watching them take form is part of the fun. One year a block of ice was carved into a full-size car.

Professional judges decide on the Champions Award, but on Saturday spectators are also invited to cast their vote for the "People's Choice."

On a warmer note, February brings the International Arts Festival, each year celebrating a different national heritage. All of the city's theaters and museums take part with special performances and exhibits showcasing the composers, musicians, playwrights, and artists of the country being honored. Recent years have featured Germany and Ireland.

Festival or not, there's always special warmth to Milwaukee, where they've retained a rich German heritage—and the title of beer capital of the Midwest. Tours and tastings are available both at big breweries like Miller and at new microbreweries that are changing America's beer tastes. What better way to spend a wintry day than to go on a brewery tour followed by a delicious sauerbraten dinner and perhaps a visit to a traditional tavern?

Though downtown has its full share of new skyscrapers and an attractive walkway has added a festive note to the Milwaukee River, it is still European charm that sets this city apart. The first sight that greets many visitors driving into town is the Allen-Bradley Clock, which made it into the *Guinness Book of Records* as the world's largest four-faced clock tower. (The story goes that Allen-Bradley gave in to a British plea to forget about chimes so that Big Ben could keep its distinction of being the largest four-faced *chiming* clock.)

Another 19 pointed clock towers are found around town, 12 of them downtown, a strong reminder of the German influence that permeates the city. The town the Indians called Gathering Place by the Waters was founded in 1846 and prospered as a center for brickmaking, flour milling, meatpacking, and brewing. In the 1850s and 1860s, it dominated the Great Lakes wheat trade and was the early home of the Grain

Exchange. The elaborate gold leaf and murals of the three-story 1879 Grain Exchange Room in the Mackie Building, 225 East Michigan Street, have been beautifully restored.

Steel making arrived, manufacturing continued to grow, and many ethnic groups, including a large number of Poles, came to the thriving city to find work. But the largest and most influential group by far were the Germans, many of whom were fleeing from the unsuccessful revolutionary movements of 1848. By the end of the last century, Milwaukee had six German-language newspapers and numerous German theaters, music societies, and intellectual groups. It became known as the *Deutsch-Athen am Michigan See*—the "German Athens on Lake Michigan." The German spirit of *gemütlichkeit* ("friendly conviviality") still permeates the city.

Old World Third Street is the last portion of the original German retail district, a block that has intentionally preserved its cobblestone paths and half-timber buildings of the past. Here's where you will find Mader's, one of the most famous of the city's traditional German restaurants, established in 1902, and the old-fashioned sausage- and wurst-making company begun by Fred Usinger in 1880.

Beer has been a way of life in Milwaukee since the 1840s, when brewer and winemaker Jacob Best and his sons emigrated from Mettenheim, Germany, and introduced lager beer, a lighter alternative to the heavier ales then popular. When German immigrant and Lake Michigan steamboat captain Frederick Pabst married the daughter of brewery owner Best, he gave his name to the family business. By the start of this century Milwaukee was home to over 300 breweries, and the Pabst, Blatz, and Schlitz brewing empires were in full swing. Though Prohibition took a heavy toll, and recent consolidation has brought the number down to fewer than 10, Wisconsin remains the country's largest per-capita producer of beer. The average resident quaffs some 30.5 gallons a year.

The tour of the Miller brewery, the largest in Wisconsin, is a fascinating look at a giant automated plant of today. The Milwaukee plant alone produces 29,000 cases of beer every day. Here, visitors see a video explaining the brewing process, then look down from the balcony on the fast-moving automated bottle-and-can line. Next comes a shipping center bigger than five football fields, able to hold more than half a million cases—which is just one and a half days' supply of the total amount of Miller beer that is sold. Workers get around this vast room on bicycles.

Next stop is the brewhouse, where beer is produced in shiny custom-made kettles with computerized instrument panels. Afterward comes the historic Caves Museum, a restored section of the original Plank-Road brewery where beer was stored before the age of mechanical refrigeration. It houses a collection of brewing implements from the last century.

The tour ends in a Bavarian-style tasting room, where bountiful samples of Miller brews are served up in a setting of stained glass, wood carving, and displays of antique beer steins.

A visit to Milwaukee's microbreweries introduces the current generation of brews, many of which can only be tasted locally. Randal Sprecher was superintendent of brewing operations at Pabst until 1985, when he started what is now the oldest and largest microbrewery in Milwaukee. By 1994, the company had expanded into new space in a former elevator car factory. Tours of the brewhouse show how Sprecher is reviving old-world brewing traditions. The lager cellar is decorated with Bavarian murals and historical artifacts. After the tour, an indoor beer tent offers oompah music and samples from a dozen different beers and sodas on draught.

The Lakefront Brewery, founded by two brothers, Russell and James Klisch, in a former bakery, is another example of a locally owned microbrewery specializing in handmade beers in the old tradition. Friendly guides and an intimate setting here have earned *Milwaukee* magazine's citation for "Best Brewery Tour."

You can taste these and other local brews and varieties from around the world in Milwaukee's many taverns, a congenial way to pass the evening. In recent years brewpubs have been added to the possibilities, each making and serving its own beer. Some suggestions are noted at the end of this chapter.

Fans of early architecture will find plenty to admire in Milwaukee, starting with the 1895 city hall at 200 East Wells Street, a Flemish Renaissance masterpiece filled with ornately carved woodwork, leaded glass, stenciled ceilings, and stained-glass windows. The eight-floor atrium is rimmed with fine ironwork balconies. The building is open to the public on weekdays.

The Pabst home is the only remaining mansion of the beer barons, and it is now unfortunately squeezed between nondescript modern structures, but the Flemish Renaissance–style residence, completed in 1893, remains a showplace. The opulent 37-room home with 12 baths and 14 fireplaces is graced with handsome carved wood, stained glass, and ornamental ironwork. The intricately carved wooden panels in the study, imported from a 17th-century Bavarian castle, contain more than a dozen secret compartments.

Pabst lived here until 1904, when the house was given to the Roman Catholic archdiocese; it served as the archbishop's residence until the mid-1970s. Wisconsin Heritage, a nonprofit organization, now owns the home and has undertaken an extensive restoration program.

Another example of Mr. Pabst's largesse is the lavish 1895 Pabst Theater, which has been beautifully restored and again offers theater and dance programs. Free tours are given on Saturdays at 11:30 A.M.

The Marcus Center for the Performing Arts, the city's major showcase for music and theater, is also a beauty, recently renovated to the tune of $25 million.

Another place to look for interesting events is the Broadway Theatre Center, which includes a Baroque opera theater styled after a European opera house, as well as a smaller experimental theater. It is located in the Third Ward District, a onetime warehouse area along Water, Broadway, and Milwaukee Streets that is rapidly turning into Milwaukee's hip neighborhood for art galleries, boutiques, coffeehouses, and antiques shops. The Milwaukee Antique Center, at 341 North Milwaukee Street, is the city's largest.

The Charles Allis Art Museum is named for the first president of the Allis Chalmers Company; he built the English Tudor mansion in which the museum is housed in 1910. The furnishings and art are much as Allis left them. They include eclectic sculptures, a Tiffany window and lamp, portraits by the German master Lucas Cranach the Elder, and a fine collection of paintings and objets d'art.

The Villa Terrace Decorative Arts Museum is a lovely Italian-style villa with stepped gardens cascading toward Lake Michigan. Constructed as a private home in 1923, it now holds a collection spanning five centuries, including one room dedicated to the delicate wrought-iron creations of Cyril Colnik, an Austrian-born craftsman whose tables, candelabras, railings, and doorknobs are found all over town, including in the library and in the kitchen of the Pabst mansion.

Churches are among this city's great architectural treasures. The old St. Mary's Church was born the same year as Milwaukee, in 1846. It is built of the special locally made light-colored brick seen so often in Milwaukee (the town was once known as the Cream City because of it). The painting of the annunciation above the main altar was a gift from King Ludwig I of Bavaria in 1865.

St. Josaphat's Basilica, the first Polish basilica in North America, was built by poor immigrant parishioners and local craftsmen with materials salvaged from the demolished Chicago Federal Building. Its majestic dome is modeled after St. Peter's in Rome, and the interior is adorned with a remarkable collection of relics, portraits of Polish saints, glowing stained glass, and beautiful wood carving.

The St. Joan of Arc Chapel is a marvel among the modern buildings of Marquette University. Built during the 15th century in Lyon, it was brought to America from France in 1926 and exactingly reconstructed.

A final church not to be missed is the Annunciation Greek Orthodox Church. This Byzantine-style church with a bright blue dome was the last major building from the drawing board of Frank Lloyd Wright.

Modern Milwaukee has many treasures to share as well, sights that are as appealing in winter as they are in summer. The Milwaukee Art Museum, designed by Eero Saarinen, was the beneficiary of many gifts from wealthy brewing families. Among its special treasures are modern works by Picasso, Miró, Chagall, O'Keeffe, Lichtenstein, and Warhol, a rich collection of Haitian art and American folk art, and the Frank Lloyd Wright School Collection of decorative art and design. Among the best-known paintings are Francisco de Zurbarán's *St. Francis,* Monet's *Waterloo Bridge,* and *Hark! The Lark* by Winslow Homer. A major expansion now under way will add a dramatic wing-like roof rising high above the lakefront, described as looking "like a bird taking flight."

The Milwaukee Public Museum is a treasure trove that takes you from the famous "Streets of Old Milwaukee" exhibit to South and Middle America, through 33 European cultures and into a Costa Rican rain forest complete with 19-foot cascading waterfall. Allow plenty of time to wander. It is part of the Museum Center, a three-part complex that also includes the Discovery World museum and an IMAX theater. Discovery World, officially known as the James Lovell Museum of Science, Economics and Technology, offers over 140 hands-on exhibits and regularly scheduled live science demonstrations.

Even though a visit to the zoo may seem unseasonal, you can see the Oceans of Fun Sea Lion Show at the superb Milwaukee County Zoo year-round. Other indoor attractions include the feline exhibit, with its lions, tigers, jaguars, and cheetahs free to prowl in open outdoor yards; the popular primate complex is home to the Apes of Africa area, which replicates the West African rain forest, and the primates exhibit, with little show-offs like orangutans and spider monkeys. Hundreds of colorful birds move freely in the naturalistic tropical surroundings of the aviary, and the aquarium building has a splendid 25,000-gallon Pacific Coast display as well as reptiles.

You can also enjoy garden strolls anytime at the Mitchell Park Horticultural Conservatory, usually referred to locally as the Domes. One of these seven-story domes is a tropical wonderland, another re-creates the desert, and the third has changing exhibits, including legendary Easter and Christmas extravaganzas.

Shoppers can stay warm making their way through the Grand Avenue Retail Center, a skylit downtown mall of some 130 shops and boutiques, which blends the historic 1915 Plankinton Arcade with harmonious new construction.

The lower rotunda of the Plankinton Arcade is home to the International Clown Hall of Fame, filled with clown memorabilia including costumes from famous clowns from all over the world. The Wall of Fame includes paintings of beloved clowns including Red Skelton, Lou Jacobs, and Emmett Kelly Sr. Clown performances are part of the fun.

If you are in town on a weekday, you can tour the facilities of a Milwaukee company with a devoted clientele, the Harley-Davidson motorcycle factory. If you are a Harley admirer and want to see the latest finished products, Milwaukee also boasts the highest-performance dealership in the world, House of Harley-Davidson, and another enormous showroom called Milwaukee Harley-Davidson, each with a huge display of motorcycles and accessories.

The season is always right for a visit to the Pettit National Ice Center, the training ground for the U.S. Olympic speed-skating team. Gold-medal winners are familiar faces at this arena, which houses one of the fastest 400-meter speed-skating ovals in the world. The public is welcome to tour the center, and public skating sessions run at least twice each day.

If you want to know what kind of weather is ahead, just look up at the tear-shaped light on top of the Wisconsin Gas Company. Yellow means cold, red is warm, blue means no change, and flashing in any color is a prediction of rain or snow—time to head for a tavern and lift a stein to Milwaukee, a city that knows how to brew a wonderful winter weekend.

Area Code: 414

DRIVING DIRECTIONS Milwaukee is on the western shore of Lake Michigan, at the intersection of I-94, I-43, and U.S. 41. From Chicago, follow I-94 north, 95 miles.

ACCOMMODATIONS Ask about weekend package rates. **Pfister Hotel,** 424 East Wisconsin Avenue, 53202, 273-8222 or (800) 558-8222, landmark, old-world charm, indoor pool, EE • **Wyndham Milwaukee Center Hotel,** 139 East Kilbourn Avenue, 53202, 276-8686, E • **Hyatt Regency Milwaukee,** 333 West Kilbourn, 53203, 276-1234, M • **Milwaukee Hilton,** 509 West Wisconsin Avenue, 53203, 271-7250, M • **Holiday Inn Milwaukee City Centre,** 611 North Wisconsin Avenue, 53203, 273-2950, M–E • **Astor Hotel,** 924 East Juneau Avenue, 53202, 271-4220, small and gracious, best budget choice, I–M.

DINING *Fine Dining:* **Sanford Restaurant,** 1547 North Jackson Street, 276-9608, French, award-winning chef, EE • **Grenadier's,** 747 North Broadway, 276-1724, Continental, M–E • **Boulevard Inn,** 925 East Wells Street, 765-1166, American, M–E • **The English Room,** Pfister Hotel (see above), grand setting, Continental menu, M–EE • **Bartolotta's Lake Park Bistro,** 3133 East Newberry Boulevard, 962-6300, French bistro fare on a bluff overlooking Lake Michigan, M–E • *German:* (All with old-world ambience) **Karl Ratzsch's Old World Restaurant,** 320 East Mason Street, 276-2720, city's best-known German restaurant, circa 1904, M–E • **John Ernst's Restaurant,** 600 East Ogden Avenue, 273-1878, established 1878, M–E • **Mader's,** 1037 North Old World Third Street, 271-3377, since 1902, M–E • *Italian:* **Mimma's Cafe,** 1307 East Brady Street, 271-7337, I–E • **Buca di Beppo,** 123 North Van Buren Street, 224-8672, I–M • **Louise's Tratto-**

ria, 801 North Jefferson Street, 273-4224, M • **Osteria del Mondo,** 1028 East Juneau Street, 291-3770, M • ***More local favorites:*** **Pieces of Eight,** 550 North Harbor Drive, 271-0597, seafood with a panoramic lake view, M–E • **Saz's,** 5539 West State Street, 453-2410, known for ribs, I–M • **Cafe Knickerbocker,** 1028 East Juneau Avenue, 272-0011, chic surroundings, Continental menu, M • **Elsa's on the Park,** 833 North Jefferson Street, 765-0615, informal, varied menu, very popular, I–M • **Historic Turner's,** 1034 North Fourth Street, 273-5590, old-timer, the place to try Milwaukee's famous Friday-night tradition, the fish fry, I–M • **Safe House,** 779 North Front Street, 271-2007, spy decor, say the password to get in, I–M • **Old Town,** 522 West Lincoln Avenue, 672-0206, Serbian, very popular, M • **Wells Street Station,** 117 East Wells, 276-7575, pastas and pizzas on the river, I • ***Taverns and Brewpubs:*** (Just a sampling) **Brown Bottle,** Schlitz Park, 221 West Galena Street, 271-4444, atmospheric former tap room for the Schlitz brewery • **Slim McGinn's,** 388 South First Street, 271-7546, 1890s Pabst-built pub • **Gasthaus Zur Krone,** 839 South Second Street, 647-1910, German ambience, board games, zither music, 225 kinds of beer • **Hooligan's,** 2017 East North Street, 273-5230, neighborhood favorite since 1936, big selection of micro beers • **Von Trier,** 2235 North Farwell Avenue, 272-1775, German-style lounge, 20 imported draft beers • **Water Street Brewery,** 1101 North Water Street, 272-1195, modern brewpub, brewery tours offered • **Milwaukee Ale House,** 233 North Water Street, 226-2337, featuring ales brewed on premises, tours. ***Breakfast:*** **LePeep,** 250 East Wisconsin Avenue, 273-7337, BIG portions, I.

SIGHTSEEING **Betty Brinn Children's Museum,** Miller Pavilion, O'Donnell Park, 929 East Wisconsin Avenue, second floor, opposite the lakefront, 291-0888. Hours: Tuesday to Saturday 9 A.M. to 5 P.M., Sunday noon to 5 P.M. $$ • **Charles Allis Art Museum,** 1801 North Prospect Avenue, 278-8295. Hours: Wednesday to Sunday 1 P.M. to 5 P.M., Wednesday also 7 P.M. to 9 P.M. $; under age 12, free • **Harley-Davidson,** 11700 West Capital Drive, 535-3666. Hours: Tours available weekdays, usually Monday, Wednesday, Friday 9:30 A.M., 11 A.M., and 1 P.M., but tours may be more frequent in warmer weather and days and hours may change; call to confirm. Free • **Discovery World, the James Lovell Museum of Science, Economics and Technology,** 712 Wells Street, 765-0777. Hours: Daily 9 A.M. to 5 P.M. $$ • **International Clown Hall of Fame,** 161 West Wisconsin Avenue, Grand Avenue Mall, 319-0848. Hours: Monday to Saturday 10 A.M. to 4 P.M. $; additional fees for clown shows • **Milwaukee Art Museum,** 750 North Lincoln Memorial Drive, 224-3200. Hours: Tuesday, Wednesday, Friday, and Saturday 10 A.M. to 5 P.M., Thursday noon to 9 P.M., Sunday noon to 5 P.M. $$; under 12 free with an adult • **Milwaukee County Zoo,** 10001 West Bluemound Road, 771-3040. Hours: Memorial Day through September, Monday to Saturday 9 A.M. to 5 P.M., Sunday and holidays to 6 P.M.; rest of year, daily 9 A.M. to 4:30 P.M. $$$; fees often reduced November to March. Parking, $$ • **Milwaukee Public Museum,** 800 West Wells Street, 278-2700. Hours: Daily 9 A.M. to 5 P.M. $$$ • **Mitchell Park Horticultural Conservatory,** 524 South Layton Boulevard, 649-9800. Hours: Daily 9 A.M. to 5 P.M. $$ • **Pabst Mansion,** 2000 West Wisconsin Avenue, 931-0808. Hours: Monday to Saturday 10 A.M. to 3:30 P.M., Sunday noon to 3:30 P.M. $$$ • **Pettit National Ice Center,** 500 South 84th Street off I-94, a few minutes west of Milwaukee, across from the state fairgrounds, 266-0100. Hours: Daily 8 A.M. to 9 P.M. Spectators free, except for special events. Guided tours, $$; skating, $$; skate rentals, $. Check for current public skating hours • **Villa Terrace Decorative Arts Museum,** 2220 North Terrace Avenue, 271-3656. Hours: Wednesday to Sunday noon to 5 P.M. $; under age 12, free • ***Churches:*** Churches' hours vary; best to call to confirm public hours. **Annunciation Greek Orthodox Church,** 9400 West Congress Street, 461-9400 • **St. Mary's Church,** 836 North Broadway, 271-6180 • **Joan of Arc Chapel,** 601 North 14th Street at Wisconsin Avenue, Marquette University, 288-7039 • **St. Josaphat Basilica,** 573 West Lincoln Avenue, 645-5623 • **St. Stephen Catholic Church,** 5880 South Howell Avenue, 483-2685 • ***Brewery tours:*** Winter hours may vary, so phone ahead. **Miller Brewing Company,** 4251 West State Street, 931-2467 or (800) 944-LITE. Hours: Monday to Saturday 10 A.M. to 3:30 P.M.; tours on the half hour May through September, on the hour rest of the year. Free • **Sprecher Brewing Company, Inc.,** 701 West Glendale Avenue, Glendale (a short drive north of downtown), 964-BREW. Hours: Saturdays on the half hour, 1 P.M. to 3 P.M. Weekday tours offered in summer and holiday weeks. Reservations are recommended. $ • **Lakefront Brewery,** 818 East Chambers Street, 372-8800. Hours: Friday 5:30 P.M., Saturday 1:30 P.M., 2:30 P.M., and 3:30 P.M. $.

INFORMATION Greater Milwaukee Convention and Visitors Bureau, 510 West Kilbourn Avenue, Milwaukee, WI 53203, 273-7222 or (800) 554-1448.

Crossing Bridges in Parke County

Forget all that hype about Madison County. If you want to see covered bridges, there's just one place to go: Parke County, Indiana, the self-proclaimed Covered Bridge Capital of the World.

This west-central section of the state is the kind of country photographers dream about—curving country roads, meandering streams, one-room schools, small towns with handsome courthouse squares, maple-sugar shacks, old gristmills, and a state park with the wildest, most dramatic scenery in the state.

And then there are the bridges, 32 of them, wooden spans dating from 1856 to 1920. Some are still drivable, while others are walking bridges, too fragile to hold cars. Connoisseurs look for those designed by Parke County's master bridge builders, a pair of Joes: Joseph A. Britton, who was responsible for 13 bridges, and Joseph J. Daniels, who contributed nine of the spans.

Whoever the designer, the wooden bridges are a bit of nostalgia so appealing that some two million people arrive each year for the 10-day fall Covered Bridge Festival. But it seems a shame to share the back roads with hundreds of flea market booths and hordes of tourists. Instead, why not shake off the winter doldrums by attending a less crowded event, the annual Parke County Maple Fair, held for two weekends in late February and early March at the fairgrounds in Rockville, the county seat.

Along with bridge watching, this is a chance to visit the old-fashioned maple camps out in the country and to enjoy hearty pancake-and-sausage feasts.

Handcrafts and home-baked goodies are for sale, but this time they are indoors at the fairgrounds, so the well-tended roads remain pristine and the countryside is all the more beautiful dusted with snow. Buses take you to the sugar shacks from the fairgrounds, or you can follow the routes on your own.

Rockville is the quintessential country town, with a central square dominated by a classic 1879 courthouse with a tall dome. There are enough small shops on the square to please browsers; most of the antiques are on the east side of the square. The best dining in town is at the imaginatively decorated Herb Garden on the west side; don't miss the desserts. And take time for a look into the attractive Country Grapevine shop next door.

On the north side of the square is the Covered Bridge Art Association Gallery, where you'll find more paintings of covered bridges than you ever knew existed. When you see the real thing, you may be inspired to whip out a palette yourself.

A trip to the sugar shacks will give you a firsthand look at a longtime tradition marking the end of winter. When the last hard freeze is past, syrup makers head for the woods to tap into the maples and drive spiles into the holes. A spile is a small, slightly tapered metal cylinder with a hook to hold a pail. There is a hole in either end so the sap can run through to drop into the container or, in some cases, into plastic tubing leading to a holding tank.

If you've never seen the process, you may be surprised to learn that the sweet sap running into the buckets is as thin and clear as water. When the buckets are full, they are taken to the sugar house, where the sap is emptied into an evaporator to simmer slowly over the fire until it thickens into a golden, gooey, delicious syrup. You may understand better why maple syrup is so costly when you learn that it takes 50 gallons of sap to produce one gallon of syrup.

Clouds of smoke day and night mark a sugar house in action. The first day of boiling is a great occasion for the whole crew, enough to make them forget the trials of frozen buckets or tangled lines that slowed the process.

To get a closer look at some of the county's covered bridges, pick up one of the free maps provided at the visitors center in the old train station in Rockville. Five routes have been mapped out and plainly marked for drivers. Each has its own attractions, but if time is limited, two routes are prime.

The Black Route will take you south across Raccoon Lake through J. J. Daniels's Neet Bridge and J. A. Britton's McAlister's Bridge to Bridgeton, a tiny jewel of a town, whose old mill, 1868 double-span bridge, and two-block village center are all on the National Register of Historic Places. Most of the town's brick and wooden homes and handful of businesses are more than a century old, a precious snapshot of the past. If you want to know about the town's surprisingly rowdy early history, pick up a copy of the brochure "A Tour of Bridgeton" at the Mitchell House or at Bridgeton 1878 shops in town or at Buy-the-Book in Rockville.

Continue following the Black Route signs, and when you get to State Highway 59, make a left turn toward Mansfield, another very special spot. The double-span bridge built here by Daniels in 1867 near a waterfall looks across the creek to the picturesque Mansfield Roller Mill, Indiana's newest official historic site (it was given that status in 1995). Powered by the original 1884 water turbine and using most of its 1880s milling machinery, the mill still grinds grain. You can buy stone-ground cornmeal to take home. The mill will most likely be in operation during the Maple Fair weekends.

Keep heading north on Highway 59 to rejoin the Black tour route, making a left on County Road 160 South and again on U.S. Highway 36 toward Billie Creek Village, Parke County's main tourist site. Thirty historic buildings have been assembled here to form a turn-of-the-century village where craftsmen demonstrate old-time skills like quilting and cider pressing. During the Maple Fair, the village sets up its own old-fashioned maple-syrup camp, run without benefit of gas or electric power. The sap is boiled over a wood fire.

This being Parke County, no self-respecting village is complete without a covered bridge, and Billie Creek offers three of them. The oldest is the Billie Creek Bridge, built by J. J. Daniels in 1895 and still open to traffic. The other two bridges were moved to this site. All are nicely situated for photographs.

Billie Creek's general store is one of the best places in the county for a wide variety of crafts and homemade jellies and jams.

For wilder scenery, the Blue Route will take you north to the most beautiful spot of all, the 1882 Narrows Bridge spanning Sugar Creek in Turkey Run State Park. Allow plenty of time to explore this park, for it is a marvel, boasting giant stands of virgin forest and dramatic, nearly vertical bedrock cliffs along Sugar Creek. A footbridge across the creek leads to 14 miles of trails that weave through tall sycamores, poplars, and black-walnut trees, in and out of canyons, beside the cliffs, and along bluffs overlooking the waterway. There are few more spectacular settings in the Midwest, and it is easy to see why Sugar Creek is considered a prize route by canoers.

The comfortable Turkey Run Inn is the best place to stay in the county and offers a pleasant dining room, as well. The park nature center, active year-round, provides a wildlife observation window for watching birds and small animals outdoors from a cozy indoor seat.

If you can't get lodgings in the park, Parke County's options are limited, so consider the half-hour drive to Crawfordsville in Montgomery County for a stay at Yount's Mill Inn, part of a historic 1851 mill complex on 10 acres bordering Sugar Creek. The old stone millkeeper's home is filled with fine antiques and lovely quilts, and the breakfasts are sumptuous.

Crawfordsville offers a wider choice of restaurants, including an excellent Mexican cafe. It is also close to Shades State Park, which lacks the amenities of Turkey Run but offers even more rugged, less populated terrain along Sugar Creek. Crawfordsville has its own canoe-rental facilities, and attracts many who like the solitude of Shades State Park.

Should you come back in warmer weather, you'll also find some worthwhile sightseeing in Crawfordsville. The most unusual site is the Old Jail Museum and its rotary cellblock, one of only six known rotating jails ever built and the only one in operating condition. The cells turn so that there is maximum security with a minimum amount of contact with prisoners; guards can give out food from one spot.

The Ben Hur Museum, a rather eccentric space, was designed as a study by the town's most famous resident, General Lew Wallace. Best known as the author of *Ben-Hur,* Wallace was quite a Renaissance man—military hero, diplomat, artist, violinist, and inventor.

Crawfordsville also boasts an antebellum treasure, the Lane Place, a lovely columned home from the 1840s. The scenic grounds are the setting for the town's major event, the Strawberry Festival, held the second weekend in June, a nice occasion for a return visit.

Area Code: 765

DRIVING DIRECTIONS Rockville, the center of Parke County, is at the intersection of U.S. Highways 41 and 36. From Chicago, take I-94 south to I-80 east to U.S. 41 south, 150 miles. It is 55 miles from Indianapolis.

ACCOMMODATIONS **Turkey Run Inn,** Turkey Run State Park, State Highway 47, Marshall 47859, 597-2211, comfortable, handsome park lodge, indoor pool, I • **Billie Creek Inn,** U.S. 36 East adjacent to Billie Creek Village, 569-3430, attractive contemporary motel, I–M, CP • **Parke Bridge Motel,** 304 East Ohio Street, Rockville 47872, 569-3525, modest in-town motel with rooms decorated on local themes, I • **Knoll Inn Distinctive Suites,** 317 West High Street, Rockville 47872, 569-6345 or (888) 569-6345, all suites, whirlpools, M, CP • **Suits Us Bed-and-Breakfast,** 514 North College Street, Rockville 47872, 569-5660, I, CP • **Yount's Mill Inn,** 3729 Old State Road 32 West, Crawfordsville 47933, 362-5864, lovely historic home, I–M, CP • **The Maples,** 4814 Highway 47 South, Crawfordsville 47933, 866-8095, Colonial-style home, some fireplaces, Jacuzzi room, I–M, CP.

DINING **Herb Garden,** Town Square West, Rockville, 569-6055, delightful decor, innovative menu, I • **Weber's Family Restaurant,** 105 South Jefferson, east side of the square, Rockville, 569-6153, home cooking, all three meals, I • **White Horse Cafe,** U.S. 41, south edge of Rockville, 569-9450, home cooking, Western memorabilia, I • **Turkey Run Inn** (see above), pleasant dining room in state park, I • **Long Horn,** Rosedale Road, 8 miles south of Rockville, 548-9282, rustic setting, country foods, fried biscuits and apple butter, I–M • **Little Mexico,** 211 East Main Street, Crawfordsville, 361-1042, delicious authentic Mexican dishes, I • **The Bungalow,** 210 East Pike Street, Crawfordsville, 362-2596, Italian/American, home setting, I–M • **Philly's Pub & Prime,** 1570 U.S. 231 South, Crawfordsville, 361-9281, I–M.

SIGHTSEEING **Parke County Maple Fair,** P.O. Box 165, Rockville 47872, 569-5226, held at 4-H Fairgrounds, U.S. 41, one mile north of Rockville, last weekend in February and first weekend in March; phone for current information. (Same sponsors for fall Covered Bridge Festival) • **Billie Creek Village,** U.S. 36, one mile east of Rockville, 569-3430. Hours: Daily 9 A.M. to 4 P.M., extended hours during festivals. $$ • ***Crawfordsville:*** **Ben-Hur Museum,** Pike Street and Wallace Avenue, 362-5769. Hours: June through August, Wednesday to Saturday 10 A.M. to 4:30 P.M., Tuesday and Sunday 1 P.M. to 4:30 P.M.; April, May, September, October, Tuesday to Sunday 1 P.M. to 4:30 P.M. $ • **The Lane Place,** 212 South Water Street, 362-3416. Hours: June to August, Wednesday to Saturday 10 A.M. to 4:30 P.M., Tuesday and Sunday 1 P.M. to 4:30 P.M.; April–May, September–October, Tuesday to Sunday 1 P.M. to 4:30 P.M. $$ • **Old Jail Museum,** 225 North Washington Street, 362-5222. Hours: Same as Lane Place, above. Free • ***State parks:*** **Turkey Run State Park,** Highway 47, Marshall, 597-2635. Hours: 8 A.M. to 11 P.M., may be shorter in winter. Fee per car, $$; Indiana cars, $ • **Shades State Park,** Highway 234, Waveland, 435-2810. Hours: 8 A.M. to 11 P.M. Fee per car, $$; Indiana cars, $ • ***Canoe rentals:*** **Turkey Run Canoe Trips,** Rockville, 597-2456; **Clements Canoes, Inc.,** Crawfordsville, 362-2781.

INFORMATION **Parke County Tourist Information Center,** 401 East Ohio Street (U.S. Highway 36), P.O. Box 165, Rockville, IN 47872, 569-5226 • **Montgomery County Visitors and Convention Bureau,** 412 East Main Street, Crawfordsville, IN 47933, 362-5200 or (800) 866-3973; www.crawfordsville.org

Chicago for All Seasons

It was Mark Twain who called it "that astonishing Chicago"—and the description still fits. No matter how many times you visit (and even if you live here), there is always something new to see and do in this vibrant, beautiful, and ever-changing city. From Christmas festivities to the world's largest food festival each summer, this is a city for all seasons.

That old "Second City" label is a misnomer, for ever since the first steel-frame skyscraper went up here in 1885, followed by the first elevated railway in 1892, Chicago has been a city of "firsts," "mosts," and "biggests." Chicago boasts the world's tallest building (and three of the top 10) and the world's leading financial futures exchange, first planetarium in the Western Hemisphere, biggest indoor aquarium, and largest public library.

Like many great cities, Chicago is full of contradictions, which adds to the rich flavor and fun of a visit. It is a town renowned for both architecture and pizza, acclaimed for its symphony and its blues and jazz clubs, and known for both windy, old-style politicians and pioneering drama companies like Steppenwolf. Sophisticated audiences applaud the great Lyric Opera while raucous fans cheer on the Cubs and the Bulls. Chicago's potpourri of ethnic neighborhoods (77 at last count) could keep explorers happily occupied for months. It boasts the largest population of Poles outside of Warsaw.

In the past decade, Chicago has blossomed with even more attractions. Navy Pier, once an almost dormant outpost on the lake, has come to vigorous life as an entertainment center. A dying warehouse district has been reborn as River North, filled with a growing number of galleries, boîtes, and bistros. The "Magnificent Mile" of shopping along Michigan Avenue keeps adding new tenants and more vertical malls; it now packs nearly every major retailer in America into a 20-minute stroll. Museums that were already among the nation's greatest continue to grow with exciting contemporary additions and attractions.

Some things needed no improvement. Chicago boasts a remarkable park system, much of it along a 29-mile lakefront of almost unsullied green lawns and golden beaches, providing recreation for residents and visitors alike. The parks create an incomparable setting for the city's museums, as well as for one of the rare major city zoos that remains free to all. Seventeen miles of bike paths make for some of the most scenic city cycling in the world. The parks are packed with festivals and free concerts all summer.

Indeed, whole books are written trying to detail the myriad pleasures of this great urban center of middle America. But this is a book about weekends, so I am going to assume that you are on a first visit (or first in a long time) and recommend what I think are the most important sights. Be forewarned: you'll still have to pick and choose, because you can't possibly taste all of Chicago's best in one weekend.

The hotels recommended below mostly are those on or near the Magnificent Mile, North Michigan Avenue; staying at any of these allows you to walk to many of the city's top attractions, hop convenient buses to the rest, and browse the shops in between. This is the city's most elegant neighborhood, but it also holds some surprisingly reasonable lodgings, even a high-rise Motel 6 in the space of the former Richmont Hotel.

You can get an exciting overview of this city by the lake at Navy Pier, one of the Chicago's jewels. The view from the top of the 15-story Ferris wheel here yields an unforgettable panorama of two of the city's glories, its skyline and its shoreline. Redeveloped in 1995, Navy Pier is a city playground encompassing 50 acres of parks, gardens, shops, and restaurants. Besides the Ferris wheel, there is a musical carousel in summer, an ice-skating rink in winter, year-round entertainment in a soaring crystal palace, a six-story IMAX theater, and a big, wonderfully creative Children's Museum.

An even more dazzling look down at the city and its lake is seen from the observatories on the 103rd floor of the Sears Tower or the 94th floor of the John Hancock Building. The skyscraper was born in Chicago, and many of America's greatest architects worked here, including Louis Sullivan, whose best-known disciple was Frank Lloyd Wright, and Mies van der Rohe. Because great architecture is so much a part of Chicago's identity, an excellent way to get acquainted with the city is to take on one of the tours sponsored by the Chicago Architecture Foundation (CAF). From May to October, the CAF Architecture River Cruise glides by some 50 of the city's most important sites, with informed narration to tell you about the city's great architectural heritage. Walking tours are held almost daily, and when the weather isn't conducive to walking, you can opt for a bus tour. Some city tours include Frank Lloyd Wright's Robie House; others go to Oak Park, where Wright's home and studio and some of his great early Prairie Houses are found.

There are many gems among the city's 34 museums, but two that should not be missed, even in a short stay, are the Art Institute and the Museum of Science and Industry.

In spite of its South Side location requiring a half-hour express bus ride from Magnificent Mile hotels, the Museum of Science and Industry is the city's most visited attraction, and for good reason: this first of all interactive museums is still one of the most innovative. The vast building covers over 15 acres and has more than 2,000 exhibits arranged in six thematic "learning zones."

The museum opened in 1933 with a pioneering exhibit that remains one of its most popular, a reproduction of a southern Illinois coal mine with walls made of real coal. Visitors descend in an actual hoist to the bottom of the mine shaft and board a work train for demonstrations and explanations of how mining is done. Other equally realistic exhibits include a self-guided tour of an actual U-505 submarine, a simulated space shuttle flight, and "Take Flight," a simulated trip aboard a real United Airlines 727 plane.

Other popular displays include a 16-foot-tall walk-through pulsating human heart, the cornerstone of an exhibit that gives visitors a peek inside their own bodies. A most amazing wall of displays, many using actual embryos, traces the growth of a human being from fertilized egg to newborn infant.

Up-to-the-minute additions to the museum let you experience the future: you can play a game of virtual catch with a friend using an imaginary ball generated by a computer, or you can pretend you're a brain surgeon diagnosing a patient's tumor and eradicating it using computer-aided radio surgery.

The Art Institute of Chicago, one of America's best art museums, is famed for its Monet collection (the largest outside France) and its specially commissioned Chagall windows. Even on a limited visit, you can search out such masterpieces as El Greco's *Assumption of the Virgin,* Seurat's Pointillist masterpiece *A Sunday on La Grande Jatte–1884,* Grant Wood's *American Gothic,* Vincent van Gogh's *Self-Portrait,* Edward Hopper's *Nighthawks,* and Georgia O'Keeffe's *Black Cross, New Mexico.*

A notable architecture collection includes the 13-story-high Trading Room designed by Louis Sullivan for the 1893–94 Chicago Stock Exchange, a magnificent blend of stenciled decorations, molded plaster capitals, and art glass.

With more time, you can explore the vast holdings covering every period of ancient, Asian, European, and American art, as well as works from Africa, Oceania, and the Americas, decorative arts, prints and drawings, textiles, and photography. The Thorne Miniature Rooms, exacting replicas of European and American interiors, are among the museum's unique treasures. The Kraft General Foods Education Center provides young visitors with a wonderful interactive introduction to art.

Outside the museum building, Henry Moore's *Large Interior Form* and Edward Kemeys's lovable *Lions* are the start of a veritable museum of outdoor sculpture in and around Chicago's downtown Loop. (The Loop is the name given to the commercial hub of the city, a rectangle of roughly six blocks by eight blocks surrounded by elevated train tracks.)

Using a self-guiding brochure from the tourist office, walk west from the Art Institute on Adams Street to Alexander Calder's *Flamingo* in the Federal Center Plaza. Turn north on Dearborn for a block and just past Monroe to take in Marc Chagall's *Four Seasons* in the First National Plaza, on to Madison for an untitled work by Pablo Picasso in the Daley Civic Center Plaza, and a Miró sculpture standing 39 feet tall across Washington Street from the Picasso.

Turn east for one block on Washington Street to State Street to view an architectural treasure, the interior of the original Marshall Field store, the center of retailing in the city for over a hundred years, restored to its original magnificence with an inner court 13 stories high and a six-story rotunda topped by a Tiffany dome made of over a million pieces of glass. Two blocks south on State is another early masterpiece, the Carson Pirie Scott department store, designed by Louis Sullivan in 1899.

The map also points out some 35 significant buildings around the Loop, from early Sullivan structures to Mies van der Rohe's Federal Center, to the world's tallest building, the 1972 Sears Tower by Skidmore, Owings and Merrill.

Worth a detour is Louis Sullivan's 1886 Rookery building at South LaSalle and Adams; it has magnificent wrought-iron work, soaring spaces, and a ground-story court remodeled in 1905 by Frank Lloyd

Wright. Don't miss taking a look at the Grand Army of the Republic room in the landmark Chicago Cultural Center at Washington and Michigan; this impressive space is adorned with rare pink marble, sparkling mosaic tiles, Tiffany windows, and a magnificent luminous stained-glass dome. The center hosts many free exhibits and programs and is also home to the Museum of Broadcast Communications.

What next? What about a shopping break? Few boulevards can match the variety and the vibrancy of North Michigan Avenue, unique among shopping districts because it combines deluxe stores like Tiffany, Cartier, Chanel, Burberry's, and Neiman Marcus with a more democratic mix of lower-end stores from the Gap to Filene's Basement, all in one compact, walkable area.

Water Tower Place, the first and still the most glittery of the major vertical malls, is anchored by two major department stores, Marshall Field and Lord & Taylor. The shops at 900 North Michigan include the first out-of-town branch of New York's exclusive Henri Bendel's, as well as Bloomingdale's. Saks Fifth Avenue is the anchor store for Chicago Place, where you can also find Louis Vuitton, Talbots, Ann Taylor, Williams-Sonoma, and a host of smaller boutiques. Turn the corner at the north end of the street to Oak Street for high-end boutiques like Giorgio Armani and Gianni Versace.

You'll also find superstores like Nike Town, Virgin Atlantic records, and Viacom. Soon to open is the North Bridge project bringing some of the few stores not here already, a Nordstrom's department store and a big Disney store.

Though the artists who originally occupied the lofts of River North have been priced out, the area is loaded with upscale art galleries, furniture stores, and specialty shops. Most of the shops are along Superior, Huron, and Erie Streets between Orleans and Wells Streets. This is also where you'll find the many theme restaurants that young visitors love.

Try to take in at least some of the recently landscaped Museum Campus and its three important occupants, the Shedd Aquarium, the Field Museum of Natural History, and the Adler Planetarium. Bring a camera; the campus is worth a visit just for the city views, and each museum has its own prize perspectives.

The Shedd Aquarium, Chicago's "ocean by the lake," is home to some 6,000 aquatic animals from around the globe in the original building, plus the showstopper Oceanarium, a dazzling glass-enclosed pavilion on the lake that re-creates a Pacific Northwest coastal environment. Here you can walk a realistic coastal nature trail and watch sea otters, harbor whales, and dolphins from viewing areas above and below the water. The whales and dolphins are put through their paces daily.

A stroll away is the Field Museum, featuring excellent natural history and cultural exhibits, including a walk-through Egyptian tomb. Here you can watch professionals at work at the Fossil Preparation

Laboratory, cleaning and reassembling the frame of "Sue," the biggest and most complete T. rex skeleton ever found. The museum paid a cool $8.3 million for Sue at auction in 1997, expecting her to become the most famous dinosaur in the world. She is due for a grand unveiling in the year 2000. Meanwhile the preparations are a fascinating sight rarely shared with the public.

The third component of the Museum Campus, the Adler Planetarium and Astronomy Museum, has a major addition, the dramatic Sky Pavilion, unveiled in 1999, with state-of the-art computer-animated exhibits on the solar system and the Milky Way galaxy, plus the StarRider Theater, where viewers participate in explorations of the heavens by using controls built into their armrests.

Not to be outdone, the Chicago Symphony has opened its own exciting learning center for music, known as ECHO, a first in music education. Interactive technology allows visitors to explore what it takes to put together a symphony orchestra. The music labs are for groups only, but the interactive A-Musing Room is open to all, an entertaining experience that gives insight into how different instruments work, with experiments in timing, pitch, rhythm, tone, and vibration. Participants can actually create and record music on their various "instrument boxes," and hear what they have done by plugging their box into ECHO's Orchestra Wall. One young visitor summed up the center well in one word: "cool."

Chicago offers more museums for every taste, from contemporary art to architecture to Jewish culture. Sampling all of them will require many a weekend.

For a change of pace and a final look at what makes Chicago a special place, take a 10-minute bus ride north to Lincoln Park. Along with the newly opened Nature Museum of the Chicago Academy of Sciences and the Conservatory, with its exotic plants and changing seasonal gardens under glass, you'll find Lincoln Park Zoo, home to more than 2,000 animals. The zoo's popular Great Ape House has the largest collection of lowland gorillas in North America, and the McCormick Bird House provides a lush tropical setting for toucans, red-legged honeycreepers, and the rare Bali mynah. Other residents of the zoo include endangered big cats, polar bears, penguins and puffins, antelopes, elephants, zebras, rhinos, giraffes, and Australian koalas. If you've brought the kids along, take in the Children's Zoo, where they can make hands-on acquaintance with small animals. Then walk over to the Farm-in-the-Zoo, a working model of a traditional Midwestern farm, where they can watch milking and butter-churning demonstrations.

The conservatory, zoo, and farm are absolutely free, and almost every city museum has a day when visitors are admitted free—more good reasons why so many people leave Chicago singing the old refrain, "This Is My Kind of Town."

Area Code: 312

DRIVING DIRECTIONS Chicago can be reached by car via I-90, I-94, I-55, or I-88 into I-290. It is 91 miles from Milwaukee, 177 miles from Indianapolis, 287 miles from Detroit.

PUBLIC TRANSPORTATION You can easily get around Chicago via public transportation, els, subways, and buses that cover all the main sights, $1.50 per ride. Save by buying visitor passes, good for unlimited rides for one, two, three, or five days. Bus rides provide sightseeing as they transport you; buses to main attractions include: **Museum of Science and Industry:** #6 Express (extra fare), board at Michigan Avenue and South Water Street or along the State Street Mall; #10 on weekends, North Michigan Avenue and State Street to museum • **Art Institute,** #151, board along Michigan Avenue going southbound • **Lincoln Park Zoo,** #151, board along Michigan Avenue going northbound • **Museum Campus: Shedd Aquarium, Field Museum, Adler Planetarium:** #146, board on North Michigan Avenue or State Street • **Navy Pier:** #29, State Street; #56, Milwaukee Avenue; #65, Grand Street; or #66, Chicago Avenue. The quickest and cheapest way to travel to downtown Chicago from both O'Hare and Midway airports is by train, $1.50; just look for the signs.

ACCOMMODATIONS Ask at all hotels for weekend-package rates; those marked * were offering good packages at press time. ***Top of the line:*** **Four Seasons,** 120 East Delaware Place, 60611, 280-8800 or (800) 332-3442, indoor pool, EE • **Ritz Carlton,** 160 East Pearson Street, 60611, 266-1000 or (800) 621-6906, indoor pool, EE • **The Drake,** 140 East Walton Street, 60611, 787-2200 or (800) 553-7253, grand old-timer overlooking the lake, EE • ***Small and chic:*** **The Whitehall,** 105 East Delaware Place, 60611, 944-6300 or (800) 948-4255, EE • ***Tremont,** 100 East Tremont Street, 60611, 751-1900 or (800) 621-8133, EE • **The Talbott,** 20 East Delaware Place, 60611, 994-4970 or (800) 621-8506, EE, CP • **Hotel Monaco,** 225 West Wabash, 960-8500 or (800) 397-7661, E–EE • **Hotel Allegro,** 171 West Randolph Street (in the theater district), 236-0123, E • ***Indoor pools:*** **Chicago Marriott,** 540 North Michigan Avenue, 60611, 836-0100 or (800) 228-9296, top-notch service, E–EE • ***Inter-Continental, Chicago,** 505 North Michigan Avenue, 60611, 944-4100 or (800) 33-AGAIN, interesting decor, E–EE • **Omni Chicago,** 676 North Michigan Avenue, 60611, 944-6664, EE • ***All-suite accommodations:*** **Residence Inn by Marriott,** 201 East Walton Street, 60611, 943-9800 or (800) 331-3131, E–EE • **Doubletree Guest Suites,** 198 East Delaware Place, 60611, 664-1100 or (800) 222-TREE, indoor pool, EE • **Summerfield Suites,** 166 East Superior Street, 60611, 787-6000 or (800) 833-4353, E–EE • ***Lenox Suites,** 616 North Rush Street, 60611,

337-1000, M–E, CP • *Moderately priced choices:* ***The Raphael,** 201 East Delaware Place, 60611, 943-5000 or (800) 821-5343, excellent value, M–E • **Courtyard by Marriott,** 30 East Hubbard Street, 60611, 329-2500 or (800) 228-9290, M–EE • ***Best Western Inn of Chicago,** 162 East Ohio Street, 60611, 787-3100, E • **Best Western River North,** 125 West Ohio Street, 60610, 467-0800 or (800) 528-1234, indoor pool, M–E • **Motel 6,** 162 East Ontario Street, 60611, 787-3580, no frills but great rates, M • **Ramada Congress,** 520 South Michigan Avenue, 60605, 427-3800, M–E • **Hampton Inn and Suites,** 33 West Illinois Street, 60610, 832-0330, M–E, ***Days Inn Lake Shore Drive,** 644 North Lake Shore Drive, 60611, 943-9200, M–E • ***Discount hotel reservation services:*** **Chicago Hotel Reservations,** (800) 96-HOTEL; **Hot Rooms,** (800) HOTEL-OO. ***Bed-and-Breakfast accommodations:*** **Bed-and-Breakfast Chicago, Inc.,** (773) 248-0005.

DINING *Top-of-the-line:* **Charlie Trotter's,** 816 West Armitage Avenue, Lincoln Park, 248-6228, sleek townhouse, superb American food with a French accent, EE • **Everest,** 440 LaSalle Street, One Financial Plaza, downtown, 663-8920, fabulous French on the 40th floor, EE • **Ritz Carlton dining room,** Ritz Carlton Hotel (see above), New French cuisine, elegant decor, EE • **Seasons,** Four Seasons hotel (see above), creative American with slight Oriental flavor, notable Sunday brunch, EE • **Spiaggia,** 980 North Michigan Avenue, second floor, 280-2750, fine Italian, elegant decor, M–EE • **Gordon,** 500 North Clark Street, River North, 467-9780, sophisticated American fare, attractive room, dance music on weekends, M–EE • **Frontera Grill,** 445 North Clark Street, 661-1434, extraordinary Mexican food, no reservations, expect long waits, I–M; within is **Topolobampo,** more intimate, possibly even better, and they take reservations, M–E • *Magnificent Mile:* **Park Avenue Cafe,** Doubletree Guest Suites (see above), outpost of a New York favorite, creative New American dishes, M–EE • **Bistro 110,** 110 East Pearson Street, 266-3110, good bistro fare, Sunday jazz brunch, M–E • **Ritz Carlton Cafe,** Ritz Carlton hotel (see above), eclectic menu, snacks to full dinners, I–M • **Shaw's Crab House,** 21 East Hubbard Street, 527-2722, favorite spot for seafood, M–E • **Cafe Spiaggia,** 980 North Michigan Avenue, 280-2764, pretty and less pricey than the big restaurant, pizza, pastas, M • **Cafe Gordon,** Tremont hotel (see above), less formal sibling of the well-established restaurant, M • **Blackhawk Lodge,** 41 East Superior Street, 280-4080, ambience of a north-woods lodge, regional American menu, M • *River North Area:* **Coco Pazzo,** 300 West Hubbard Street, 836-0900, soaring loft setting, innovative Tuscan cuisine, M–E • **Brasserie Jo,** 59 West Hubbard Street, 595-0800, less expensive way to sample the fine fare of chef Jean Joho of Everest, M • **Kiki's Bistro,** 900 North Franklin Street, 335-5454, cozy, popular, bistro fare, M • **Zinfandel,** 59 West Grand Avenue, 527-1818, updated comfort food,

M • **Maggiano's,** 526 North Clark Street, 644-8100, old-fashioned Italian, known for huge portions, M–E; pastas, I • **Papagus Greek Taverna,** 620 North State Street, 642-8450, colorful dining room, Greek food, I–E • **Mambo Grill,** 412 North Clark Street, 467-9797, Latino treats, I–M • **Mango,** 712 North Clark Street, 337-5440, American-eclectic, I–M • ***Downtown theater and Loop area:*** **Rhapsody,** Chicago Symphony Center, 65 East Adams Street, 786-9911, talented chef, attractive surroundings, best bet even if you aren't going to the symphony, M–E • **312 Chicago,** 136 North LaSalle Street, adjacent to Hotel Allegro, 696-2420, creative seasonal menus, M • **Trattoria No. 10,** 10 North Dearborn Street, 984-1718, chic cellar, favorite for business lunches, M–E • **Berghoff,** 17 West Adams Street, 427-3170, longtime local tradition for old-fashioned German food, I–M • ***West Randolph*** (the growing trendy dining area): **Marche,** 833 West Randolph, 225-8399, bistro fare, funky decor, M–EE • **Bluepoint Oyster Bar,** 741 West Randolph, 944-5990, good choice for seafood lovers, M–EE • **Toque,** 816 West Randolph, 666-1100, contemporary French/American, M–EE • ***Family favorites:*** **Rainforest Cafe,** 605 North Clark Street, 787-1501, jungle setting with robotic animals, flapping butterflies, faux rainstorms, M • **Michael Jordan's,** 500 North LaSalle Street, 644-DUNK, the giant basketball on top is almost a landmark, I–M • **Ed Debevic's,** 640 North Wells Street, 664-1707, '50s-style diner, I • **Hard Rock Cafe,** 63 West Ontario Street, 943-2252, the idea is old but kids still love it, I–M • **Rock and Roll McDonald's,** 600 North Clark Street, 664-7940, full of memorabilia, second-busiest McDonald's in the world, I • **Planet Hollywood,** 633 North Wells Street, 266-STAR, all that Hollywood stuff, I–M • ***Pizza:*** Deep-dish "stuffed" pizza is Chicago's specialty. The best-known emporiums have many locations; these are convenient to the Magnificent Mile: **Pizzeria Uno,** 20 East Ohio Street, 321-1000 • **Pizzeria Due,** 619 North Wabash Street, 943-2400 • **Original Gino's East,** 160 East Superior Street, 943-1124 • **Giordano's,** 747 North Rush Street, 951-0747.

SIGHTSEEING ***Museums:*** **Art Institute of Chicago,** 111 South Michigan Avenue, 443-3600. Hours: Monday to Friday 10:30 A.M. to 4:30 P.M., Tuesday to 8 P.M., Saturday 10 A.M. to 5 P.M., Sunday noon to 5 P.M. $$$$; free on Tuesday • **Museum of Science and Industry,** 57th Street at Lake Shore Drive, 684-1414. Hours: Monday to Friday 9 A.M. to 4 P.M., Saturday and Sunday 9:30 A.M. to 5:30 P.M., extended hours in summer. $$$; Crown Space Center and Omnimax Theater $$$; combination tickets $$$$ • **Museum Campus,** Lake Shore Drive, includes: **Field Museum of Natural History,** Roosevelt Road at Lake Shore Drive, 922-9410. Hours: Daily 9 A.M. to 5 P.M. $$$; free on Wednesday • **John G. Shedd Aquarium,** 1200 South Lake Shore Drive, 939-2438. Hours: Monday to Friday 9 A.M. to 5 P.M., Saturday, Sunday 9 A.M. to

6 P.M., Memorial Day to Labor Day daily to 6 P.M. $$$$; aquarium only free on Thursday; oceanarium still charges admission • **Adler Planetarium and Astronomy Museum,** 1300 Lake Shore Drive, 922-7827. Hours: Monday to Friday 9 A.M. to 5 P.M., Friday to 9 P.M., Saturday, Sunday 9 A.M. to 6 P.M. $$; free to all on Tuesday • **Terra Museum of American Art,** 666 North Michigan Avenue, 664-3939. Hours: Tuesday to Saturday 10 A.M. to 5 P.M., Tuesday evening to 8 P.M.; Sunday noon to 5 P.M. $$; under age 14, free; free to all on Tuesday and first Sunday of each month • **Museum of Contemporary Art,** 220 East Chicago Avenue, 280-2660. Hours: Tuesday and Thursday to Sunday 10 A.M. to 5 P.M., Wednesday 10 A.M. to 8 P.M. $$$; under age 12, free; free to all first Tuesday of each month • **Spertus Institute of Jewish Studies Museum,** 618 South Michigan Avenue, 322-1747. Hours: Sunday to Thursday 10 A.M. to 5 P.M., Thursday evening to 8 P.M., Friday 10 A.M. to 3 P.M. $$ • **Chicago Athenaeum,** Museum of Architecture and Design, 6 North Michigan Avenue, 251-0175. Hours: Tuesday to Saturday 11 A.M. to 6 P.M., Sunday noon to 5 P.M. $$ • **Chicago Children's Museum,** Navy Pier, 600 East Grand Avenue, 527-1000. Hours: Daily 10 A.M. to 5 P.M., to 8 P.M. on Thursday, $$; free on Thursday 5 P.M. to 8 P.M. • **Nature Museum of the Chicago Academy of Sciences,** Fullerton Avenue and Cannon Drive, Lincoln Park, (773) 549-0606. Hours: opening in 1999, after press time. Phone for hours and admission • ***Other attractions:*** **Chicago Cultural Center,** 78 East Washington Street, 346-3278. Hours: Monday to Friday 10 A.M. to 6 P.M., Saturday 10 A.M. to 5 P.M., Sunday noon to 5 P.M. Free • **ECHO** (Eloise W. Martin Center of the Chicago Symphony Orchestra), 67 East Adams Street, 294-3000. Hours: Tuesday, Wednesday 10 A.M. to 7 P.M.; Thursday to Saturday 10 A.M. to 7:30 P.M., Sunday 11 A.M. to 5 P.M. Music labs available for groups, reservations required. A-Musing Room open to ages 8 to adult. $$$ • **Sears Tower Skydeck,** 233 South Wacker Drive, 875-9696. Hours: March to September, daily 9 A.M. to 11 P.M.; rest of year to 10 P.M. Adults, $$$ • **John Hancock Center,** 875 North Michigan Avenue, 751-3681. Observatory hours: Daily 9 A.M. to midnight. $$$$ • **Lincoln Park Zoo,** 2200 North Stockton Drive, 294-4660. Hours: Daily 9 A.M. to 5 P.M. Free • **Navy Pier,** 600 East Grand Avenue, 595-PIER. Hours: Open daily. Includes Cineplex Odeon Theater, Ferris wheel, carousel, Skyline Stage, Children's Museum, shops, restaurants, sightseeing cruises in summer, ice skating in winter. Check for individual hours and fee • ***City tours:*** **Chicago Architecture Foundation,** 224 South Michigan Avenue, 922-3432, ext. 127. Exhibitions and wide variety of year-round walking and bus tours, architectural cruises; phone for current offerings • **Chicago Neighborhood Tours,** c/o Chicago Cultural Center, 742-1190. Saturday tours of ethnic neighborhoods, late February through early December. Phone for current offerings.

INFORMATION **Chicago Office of Tourism,** Chicago Cultural Center, 78 East Washington Street, Chicago, IL 60602, 744-2400 or (800) 2-CONNECT for free visitors packet. **Information Centers:** Chicago Waterworks, North Michigan Avenue and Pearson Street; Chicago Cultural Center; and Illinois Market Place, 700 Grand Avenue at Navy Pier.

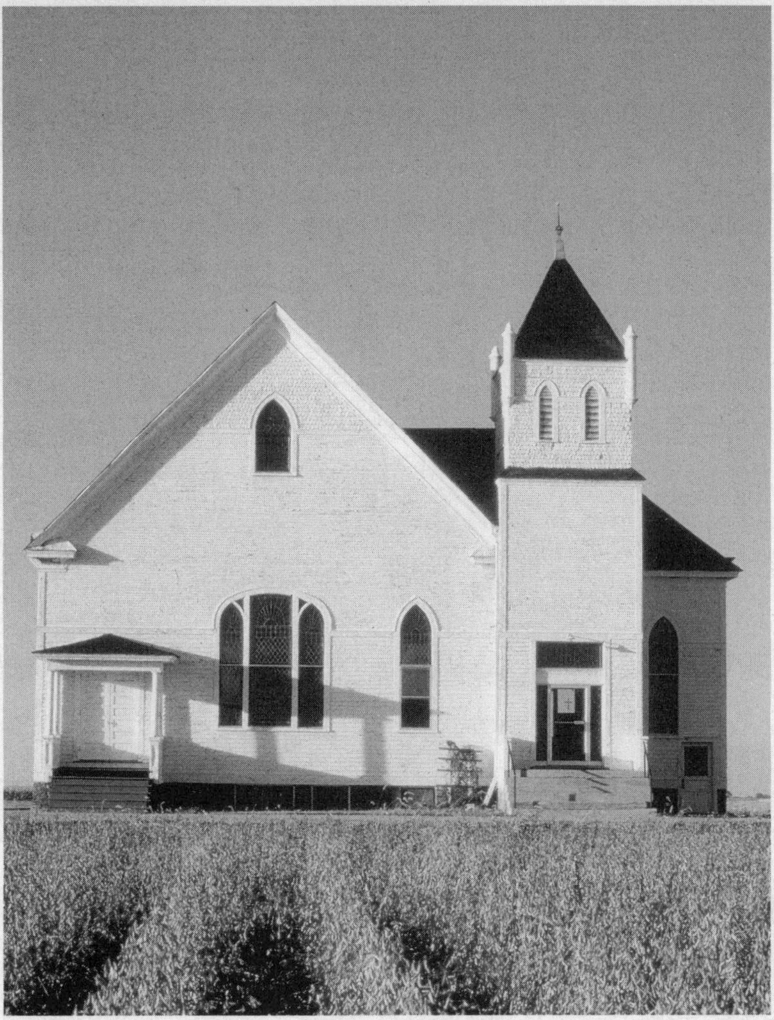

Maps

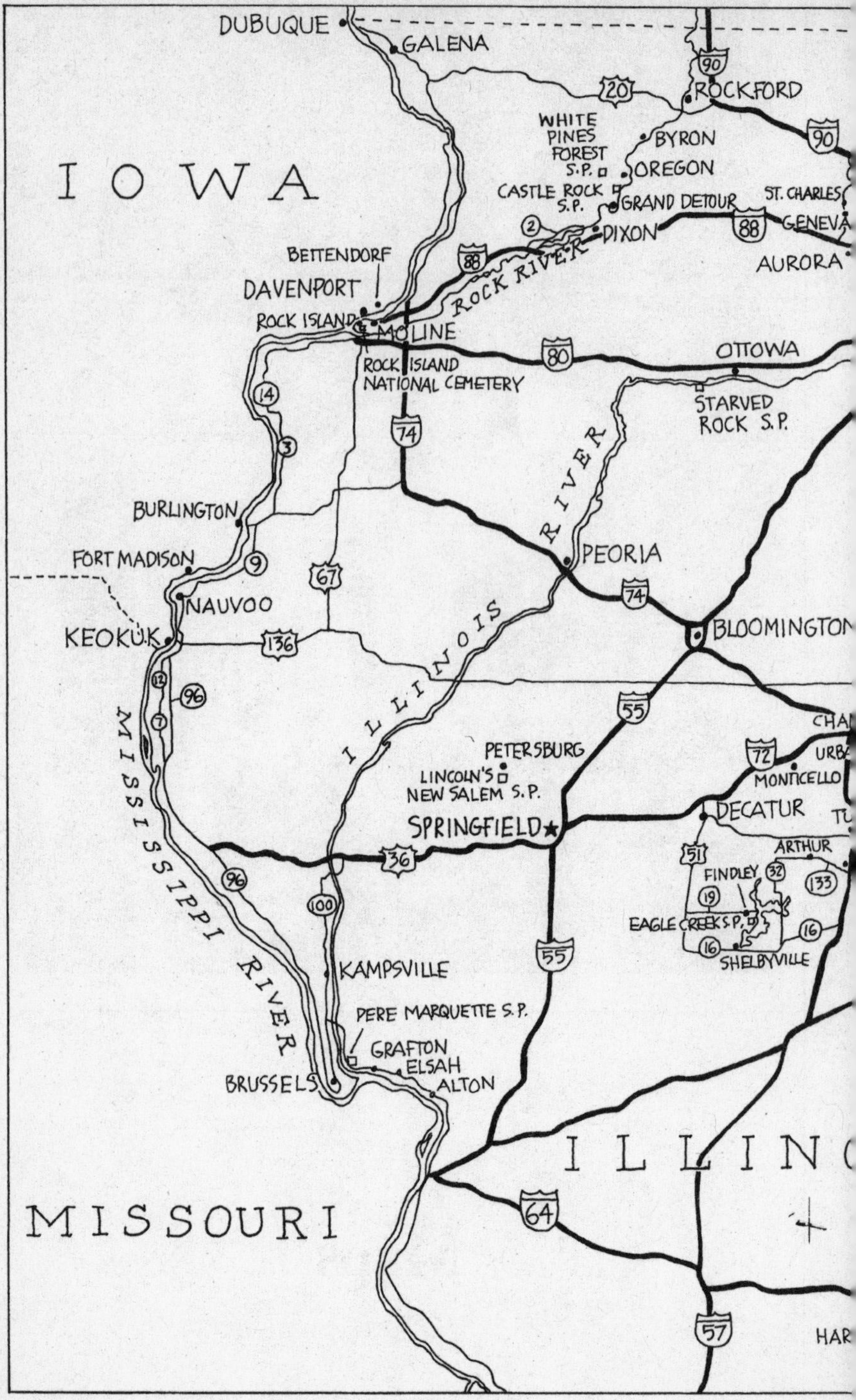
DUBUQUE
GALENA
ROCKFORD
WHITE PINES FOREST S.P.
BYRON
OREGON
CASTLE ROCK S.P.
GRAND DETOUR
ST. CHARLES
GENEVA
AURORA
DIXON
IOWA
BETTENDORF
DAVENPORT
ROCK ISLAND
MOLINE
ROCK RIVER
ROCK ISLAND NATIONAL CEMETERY
OTTOWA
STARVED ROCK S.P.
BURLINGTON
FORT MADISON
NAUVOO
KEOKUK
PEORIA
ILLINOIS RIVER
BLOOMINGTON
MISSISSIPPI RIVER
PETERSBURG
LINCOLN'S NEW SALEM S.P.
SPRINGFIELD
DECATUR
MONTICELLO
ARTHUR
FINDLEY
EAGLE CREEK S.P.
SHELBYVILLE
KAMPSVILLE
PERE MARQUETTE S.P.
GRAFTON
ELSAH
ALTON
BRUSSELS
ILLIN
MISSOURI
90
20
88
2
80
74
14
3
9
67
136
12
7
96
55
72
36
100
51
32
19
133
16
64
57

LAKE
MICHIGAN
MICHIGAN
FOREST
EVANSTON
CHICAGO
MICHIGAN CITY
12
INDIANA DUNES NAT'L LAKESHORE & S.P.
94
80
90
CHESTERTON
PORTER
SOUTH BEND
ELKHART
MIDDLEBURY
SHIPSHEWANA
POKAGON S.P.
20
ANGOLA
GOSHEN
19
119
15
33
6
NAPPANEE
AUBURN
INDIANA
FT. WAYNE
65
69
OHIO
41
31
LAFAYETTE
231
74
NOBLESVILLE
CONNER PRAIRIE
SHADES S.P.
CRAWFORDSVILLE
TURKEY RUN S.P.
47
INDIANAPOLIS
70
CENTERVILLE
RICHMOND
ROCKVILLE
36
40
KNIGHTSTOWN
CAMBRIDGE CITY
70
465
TERRE HAUT
74
McCORMICK'S CREEK S.P.
BEANBLOSSOM
NASHVILLE
46
CINCINNATI
COLUMBUS
BLOOMINGTON
BROWN COUNTY S.P.
421
37
65
7
BEDFORD
CLIFTY FALLS S.P.
MADISON
SPRING MILL S.P.
56
VINCENNES
KENTUCKY
41
56
FRENCH LICK
MARENGO
JASPER
64
231
FERDINAND
64
LOUISVILLE
DALE
CORYDON
164
SANTA CLAUS
WYANDOTTE CAVES
62
LINCOLN CITY
EVANSVILLE

WISCONSIN
MINNESOTA
IOWA
ILLINOIS
MISSISSIPPI RIVER
WISCONSIN RIVER
STOCKHOLM
NELSON
TREMPEALEAU
WARRENS
SPARTA
TOMAH
LA CROSSE
CASHTON
COON VALLEY
WESTBY
VIROQUA
WISCONSIN DELLS
LAKE DELTON
BARABOO
DEVILS LAKE S.P.
SPRING GREEN
LAKE MENDOTA
MADISON
LAKE MONONA
MARQUETTE
PRAIRIE DU CHIEN
McGREGOR
GOVERNOR DODGE S.P.
BLUE MOUND S.P.
BLUE MOUNDS
MOUNT HOREB
WYALUSING S.P.
DODGEVILLE
MINERAL POINT
NEW GLARUS
NELSON DEWEY S.P.
CASSVILLE
PLATTEVILLE
HAZEL GREEN
MONROE
GREEN BAY
APPLETON
OSHKOSH
LAKE WINNEBAGO
GREEN LAKE
RIPON
FOND DU LAC
ELKHART LAKE
GREENBUSH
PLYMOUTH
KETTLE MORAINE STATE FOREST
MANITO
SHEB
EAGLE
MILWAUK
DELAVAN
LAKE GENEVA
FONTANA
KEN
CHICAGO
PENINS
FISH
EGG
CEDAR
94
90
41
43
35
131
33
27
14
61
12
18
151
78
133
81
23
39
69
80
11
82
44
67

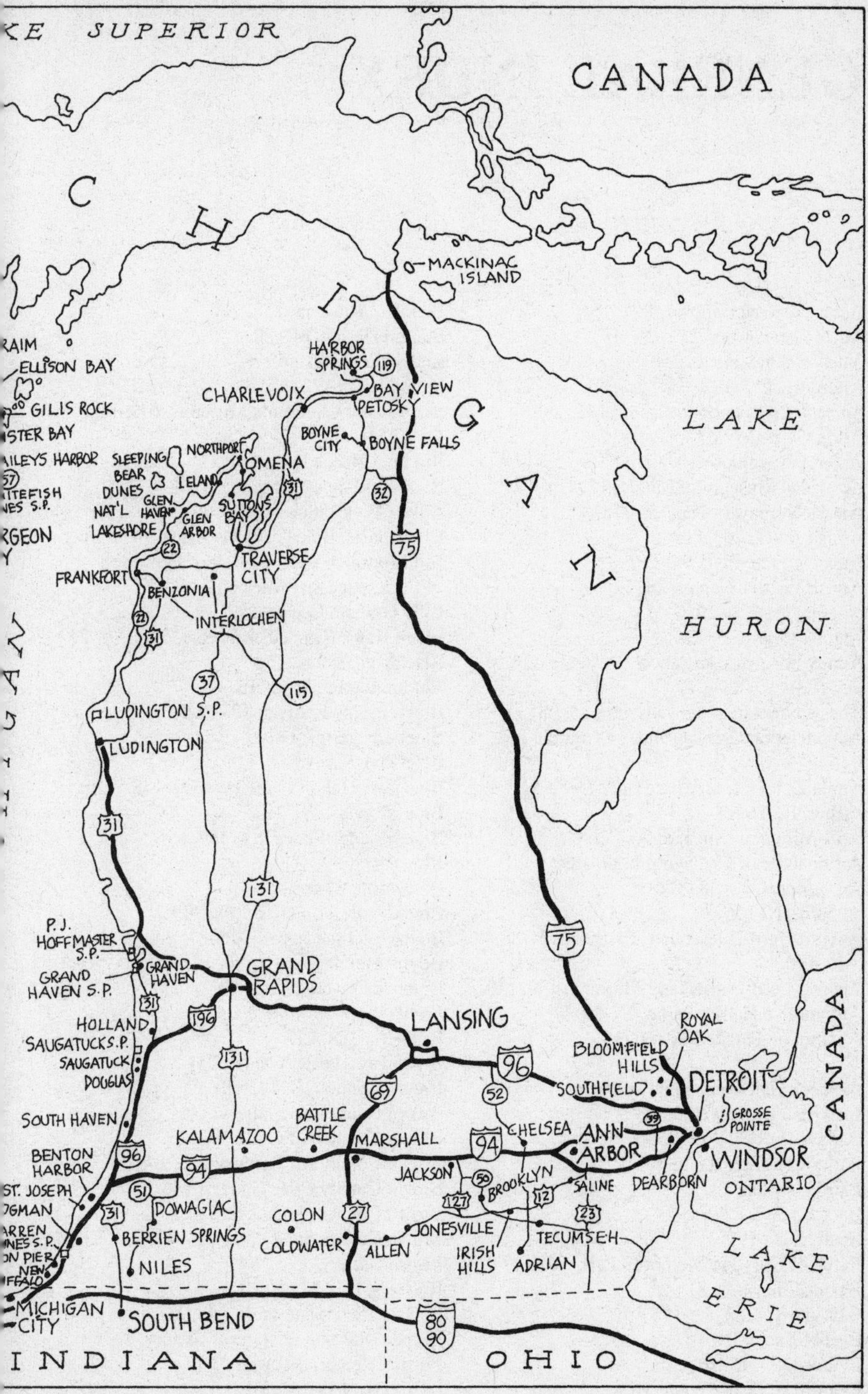
SUPERIOR
CANADA
MACKINAC ISLAND
ELLISON BAY
GILLS ROCK
HARBOR SPRINGS
119
BAY VIEW
PETOSKY
CHARLEVOIX
BOYNE CITY
BOYNE FALLS
LAKE
NORTHPORT
OMENA
SLEEPING BEAR DUNES NAT'L LAKESHORE
LELAND
GLEN HAVEN
GLEN ARBOR
SUTTONS BAY
31
32
75
22
TRAVERSE CITY
FRANKFORT
BENZONIA
INTERLOCHEN
HURON
37
115
LUDINGTON S.P.
LUDINGTON
31
131
75
P.J. HOFFMASTER S.P.
GRAND HAVEN
GRAND HAVEN S.P.
GRAND RAPIDS
196
31
HOLLAND
SAUGATUCK S.P.
SAUGATUCK
DOUGLAS
131
LANSING
ROYAL OAK
BLOOMFIELD HILLS
96
SOUTHFIELD
DETROIT
69
52
CANADA
GROSSE POINTE
39
SOUTH HAVEN
BATTLE CREEK
CHELSEA
ANN ARBOR
KALAMAZOO
MARSHALL
94
BENTON HARBOR
96
WINDSOR
94
JACKSON
50
BROOKLYN
SALINE
DEARBORN
ONTARIO
ST. JOSEPH
51
127
12
DOWAGIAC
31
COLON
27
23
JONESVILLE
BERRIEN SPRINGS
COLDWATER
TECUMSEH
ALLEN
IRISH HILLS
ADRIAN
LAKE ERIE
NILES
MICHIGAN CITY
SOUTH BEND
80 90
INDIANA
OHIO

GENERAL INDEX

CATEGORY INDEX

Churches

Cultural Activities

Festivals and Crafts

Nature and Science